Cat *and* Mouse

by Brian Alan Lane

with original writings
by Bill Suff

DOVE
BOOKS

ISBN: 0-7871-0860-X

Printed in the United States of America

DOVE BOOKS
8955 Beverly Boulevard
Los Angeles, CA 90048
(310) 786-1600

Distributed by Penguin USA

Text design by Jacaru

First Printing: February 1997

10 9 8 7 6 5 4 3 2 1

*With thanks for the support of
my friends, family, everyone at Dove Books,
and that great editor and gifted writer,
Lee Montgomery, who did the unthinkable
and went out on a limb for me.*
—B.A.L.

Contents

Preface

As you go from left to right, there are three signposts on the road of the "true crime" story.

You begin with the "objective", journalistic report and re-telling. Newspaper clippings collected into chapters. The author a craftsman but a nonentity—his or her voice intentionally stilled in exchange for "truth".

At the halfway mark along our highway, you run across *In Cold Blood*. You get Capote's invention of "faction", the nonfiction novel. A true story, investigated by the author after the fact, and then reborn as a character drama about what "certainly was" and "must have been". A tapestry, not a report; threads spun from ver-ifiable facts, but the fabric woven by the writer's mind. The kind of story that jurors themselves create during deliberations in order to make sense of and judge the madness.

At the far end of the true crime panorama is Dominick Dunne, and all those stories that you know are true but the names have been changed and the author's "improved" the drama for the sake of drama. Truth always has more power than fiction, but truth doesn't always make for the best story because a beginning, middle, and end, and a nice, comfortable three-act structure, don't always exist in nature. Dunne memorializes cocktail party conversations for five hundred pages.

Cat and Mouse falls somewhere between the nonfiction novel and the cocktail party conversation, although I do not presume for a moment that my work is on par with Capote and Dunne.

In dealing with Bill Suff, the convicted Riverside Prostitute Killer, I had unique access to people and material that the journalists couldn't touch. More than anything, I had access to Bill himself.

My goal was not to improve the public record, not to be limited to facts that could be proved and verified, but rather to understand the interpersonal dynamics of these crimes. I was at all times more interested in people's impressions, in feelings, rumors, and hearsay. I wanted to know what people really thought, I wanted to hear everything they would only say off-the-record.

What sparked me was the fact that Bill is a writer, and I wanted to create a book that would guide all of us in reading between the lines of Bill's work, a dream that could only be realized if the book were freed from all constraints.

The only way to accomplish this was to inject myself into the proceedings, not because I'm so important but because you have to know my biases in order to judge my report. And, I think I rightly felt that I was living out a fantasy that everyone would like to indulge in if you could do so safely: I was going to walk into the den of a living, breathing serial killer, and I was going to see if I could get back out alive.

You will now get to see what I saw, and you will get to decide what you see.

Guilt or innocence is not the issue.

This then is neither fiction nor nonfiction. It's "true crime" because the crimes are real, and it's a "true" story because everything in it is what I believe, everything in it is what is "real" for me. Everything contained in this book is emotionally honest and tremendously candid, but its meaning is left to you.

As a moral and legal matter, I have to make a final point: I have written about Bill as a *de facto* serial killer because a jury has in fact convicted him. He is no longer entitled to a presumption of innocence.

However, Bill has at all times professed his innocence, and he is entitled to his appeals. There is no doubt in my mind that, aside from the question of true culpability, Bill's arrest was unconstitutional, his trial prejudiced, and his death sentencing improperly argued.

Once arrested, Bill Suff never had a chance, and, as a lawyer, I'm not happy about that. The system can and must do better. We need to look long and hard at how we investigate and prosecute serial killers, because, in the rush to convict and close cases, we are leaving too many active serial killers out there, out of the reach of law enforcement.

But that's another book.

In light of Bill's appeals, please know that none of the "facts" presented herein can or should be used to prove the case either against him or for him.

There are no "facts" in this book.

Everything is impression, everything a personal conclusion and construct of my own, no matter the record or testimony or memory on which it is based.

When interviewing people, I took no contemporaneous notes, made no recordings, and shredded my outlines. All that exists of this book is what you now have before you.

Bill's writings are presented unedited and uncorrected.

BRIAN ALAN LANE
LOS ANGELES, CALIFORNIA

PEOPLE v. WILLIAM SUFF CR 44010

VICTIMS

#	Name	Found	RIC
1	LYTTLE, KIMBERLY E.	FOUND 6/28/89	RIC 0231-89
2	LEAL, TINA C.	FOUND 12/13/89	RIC 0503-89
3	FERGUSON, DARLA J.	FOUND 1/18/90	RIC 0027-90
4	MILLER, CAROL L.	FOUND 2/8/90	RIC 0056-90
5	COKER, CHERYL	FOUND 11/6/90	RIC 0525-90
6	STERNFELD, SUSAN M.	FOUND 12/21/90	RIC 0588-90
7	PUCKETT (MILNE), KATHLEEN L.	FOUND 1/19/91	RIC 0030-91
8	PAYSEUR, CHERIE	FOUND 4/26/91	RIC 0186-91
9	LATHAM, SHERRY A.	FOUND 7/4/91	RIC 0339-91
10	HAMMOND, KELLY M.	FOUND 8/16/91	RIC 0433-91
11	McDONALD, CATHERINE	FOUND 9/13/91	RIC 0488-91
12	ZAMORA (WALLACE), DELLIAH H.	FOUND 10/30/91	RIC 0585-91
13	CASARES, ELEANOR	FOUND 12/23/91	RIC 0681-91

Characteristics / Evidence categories (chart rows):

- DRUG USER
- PROSTITUTE
- PERSONAL ITEMS MISSING
- VICTIMS' PERSONAL ITEMS FOUND
- TYPE OF SITES: DUMPING AREAS
- BODIES NUDE
- BODIES POSED
- CAUSE OF DEATH: ASPHYXIATION
- SIMILAR STABBING TO CHEST AREA
- RIGHT BREAST CUT OFF
- SUFF'S CAT'S HAIR
- SUFF'S PUBIC HAIR
- SUFF'S HEAD HAIR
- FIBERS: SISAL ROPE
- FIBERS: BAG RED ACETATE
- FIBERS: BAG WHITE NYLON
- FIBERS: BAG BLUE NYLON
- FIBERS: GOLD PILLOW
- FIBERS: GREEN BLANKET
- FIBERS: GRAY CARPET/VAN
- FIBERS: UPHOLSTERY SIDE PANELS/VAN
- FIBERS: SEAT FABRIC/VAN
- MISC. HAIRS & FIBERS ASSOC. TO DEFENDANT
- TIRES: ARMSTRONG CORONET ULTRA TRAC
- TIRES: DUNLOP
- TIRES: UNIROYAL XTM
- TIRES: YOKOHAMA Y382
- TIRES: YOKOHAMA 371
- SHOES: PROWINGS COLTON
- SHOES: PROWINGS PASO ROBLES
- SHOES: CONVERSE
- PAINT CHIPS

Letter codes appearing in the tire rows (tire position notations):
RF (right front), RR (right rear), LR (left rear), LF (left front), and combinations such as RF/RR, LR/LF, RF/LF.

Introduction
DEAD AND COUNTING

Charlotte Palmer, Lisa Lacik, Kimberly Lyttle, Tina Leal, Darla Ferguson, Carol Miller, Cheryl Coker, Susan Sternfeld, Kathleen Puckett, Cherie Payseur, Sherry Latham, Kelly Hammond, Catherine McDonald, Delliah Zamora, Eleanor Casares.

While the world was consumed with the trial of O.J. Simpson and the murders of Nicole Brown Simpson and Ron Goldman, there was another trial—a more important trial—going on just a few miles away.

That is, if you define "more important" by a higher body count.

Higher, much higher.

And, in the gradations of murder, if "important" means torture, mutilation, and cannibalism, then O.J.'s alleged crimes in L.A. were mere misdemeanors compared to what had been going on down the road in Riverside.

Yeah, there's murder, and then there's murder.

Charlotte Palmer, Lisa Lacik, Kimberly Lyttle, Tina Leal, Darla Ferguson, Carol Miller, Cheryl Coker, Susan Sternfeld, Kathleen Puckett, Cherie Payseur, Sherry Latham, Kelly Hammond, Catherine McDonald, Delliah Zamora, Eleanor Casares.

If you grew up in Los Angeles, you lived through "The Manson Horrors," "The Nightstalker," "The Hillside Strangler," "The Freeway Killer," and a host of other madmen and bloodletters, all of whom made you worry that it wasn't safe to go out but maybe it was even more dangerous to stay home.

When these lunatics were running around, the cops got mobilized, the mayor begged for calm, schools closed, people set themselves curfews, security companies flourished, Dobermans were in, and earthquakes, fires, and floods were welcome relief.

At least you knew who to blame for the earthquakes.

So, after the murders of Nicole and Ron, when the cops *didn't* set up a task force, and the mayor *didn't* tell you to stay home and lock your doors, and property values in Brentwood *didn't* go down (they went *up*), it was a pretty telling sign that everyone who knew anything knew that the killings were personal—committed either by that maniac husband who then hopped an alibi plane to Chicago to play golf, or by those maniac Colombian drug dealers who presumably hopped their own getaway plane back to Colombia to play what? Soccer, maybe.

The Nicole/Ron killings were done before anyone knew that anyone cared enough to bother to commit them. And then the killings were done and there would be no more, no threat to the public at large—you could eat at Mezzaluna without fear that you were being stalked by "The Mezzaluna Mauler" and you could enjoy Ben & Jerry's ice cream without concern that it would be found melting later by your back door as your corpse lay melting in the muggy night.

These killings had nothing to do with dinner, and everything to do with celebrity.

Which is why the O.J. trial consumed us, and the Bill Suff trial got lost.

Lost to everyone except all the victims, the victims' families, the hundreds of cops who pursued the case for half a decade, and the population of an entire county that had long lived with the gnawing realization that the Devil himself was loose in their midst.

Charlotte Palmer, Lisa Lacik, Kimberly Lyttle, Tina Leal, Darla Ferguson, Carol Miller, Cheryl Coker, Susan Sternfeld, Kathleen Puckett, Cherie Payseur, Sherry Latham, Kelly Hammond, Catherine McDonald, Delliah Zamora, Eleanor Casares.

These are believed to be only half the victims of the Riverside Prostitute Killer, but, across three counties, more than two dozen unsolved murder cases were "closed" with Bill Suff's arrest. And, while the murder spree was going on, there was no reason not to believe that any woman could fall victim, any woman who crossed the killer's path.

Bodies "officially" began piling up in 1986, when Charlotte Palmer's half-nude corpse was found carefully posed along a roadside near the desert oasis of Sun City in Riverside County, California. Charlotte hadn't been tossed there like some rag doll, she'd been carefully, painstakingly posed to convey some sort of meaning, and she'd been left in a place where she was certain to be found at first light. The killer might as well have pinned a note to her—he was telling the world a story, he was announcing himself and explaining just what sort of demon he was. Charlotte Palmer was his prop—he was the debuting debutant, he was the one that mattered, the one who had something to say, something to prove.

But who could read the "story" of this murder scene, who could interpret this "art", what was the killer conveying beyond the fact that he could strike with impunity, he could mock both his victim and the authorities, and he was absolutely going to strike again and again and again, until caught?

How many open-air, roadside galleries would be filled with these murderous pastiches before these killings would come to an end?

Charlotte Palmer was a pretty woman and she was in good shape. She was not using drugs, and she had undigested fast-food chicken in her stomach at the time she died.

She seemed to have been strangled.

Traces of that gray/brown glue/goo from duct tape were found around her ankles, wrists, and thigh. She was pretty well bruised from head to toe.

Charlotte had last been seen in Sun City. She had no known job there, so she was officially classified as "transient", and maybe she did a little hooking to earn enough to move on from place to place until she found the place she was looking for, certain that she'd know it when she got there.

She hoped.

And maybe the night of her death Charlotte was hooking, or maybe she just accepted a ride from a kindly stranger on his way up the freeway to that place that might be the place that she was looking and hoping for.

Either way, the two of them—Charlotte and her benefactor—picked up a little KFC and shared a laugh as they headed out onto the blacktop that whispers forever through the desert dark.

And then, when she was soft and warm and contented with food, running her tongue along her teeth to rub off the last taste of grease even though you can still smell the stuff for hours after, Charlotte suddenly got whacked across the face, took an elbow to the throat, and found herself tied up with tape, raped and beaten and murdered, posed later at the side of the road.

If she could have looked back down at herself lying there, Charlotte Palmer must have wondered one simple thing: how in the hell did this happen?

But the police didn't wonder at all—they knew: a serial killer had just crossed the county line.

And, even though this guy signed his crime with a flourish, with the pose, he did not leave one hard evidentiary clue that could lead to his capture or conviction.

This guy planned his crime. He planned it, committed it, and then cleaned up afterward. No bloody glove here. A guy like this, a guy worried enough to make sure he wouldn't get caught, couldn't get caught; he wasn't some trucker just passing through, and this killing was in no way personal. No, this guy was careful, he was organized, he was impassioned but focused, and, scariest of all, he had to be living right here in Riverside, living with his victims and his pursuers, living right under their noses, living as their friend and neighbor.

Hey, neighbor!

He could be anybody.

But he had to be a nobody.

Somebody who was so indistinctive he could move freely, and yet so sociable you wouldn't suspect him as weird or out of place.

He probably even had a wife or girlfriend. And surely a dog or a cat or some fish.

And, over the course of the many years of his murders, it's fair to say that, without realizing it, damn near everybody who lived in Riverside stood next to or drove past or tipped a hat to or saw their man somewhere going about his business.

His business of murder.

A business he would get even better at as time went on, as he got even better organized, more brazen and yet more careful.

Charlotte Palmer, Lisa Lacik, Kimberly Lyttle, Tina Leal, Darla Ferguson, Carol Miller, Cheryl Coker, Susan Sternfeld, Kathleen Puckett, Cherie Payseur, Sherry Latham, Kelly Hammond, Catherine McDonald, Delliah Zamora, Eleanor Casares.

When they found Lisa Lacik's body next door to Riverside County in 1988, the authorities got really worried. She'd been strangled and posed—a familiar tune at this point, with other murders in other counties—and there were no good clues, but, unlike previous victims, she'd been horribly mutilated with a knife. She'd been explored, exposed, ransacked, and debased, and her right breast had been cut off.

Typically, it was hard to get the authorities from different counties to trade information and evidence, to even know for certain that they were all dealing with the same serial killer, but, finally, after several more murders in Riverside, it became more politically expedient to subsidize a task force rather than ignore a bunch of dead, chopped-up hookers, and so all the counties were brought together, along with FBI advisors and profilers and DNA experts and computer jockeys.

Thank God for election years, right?

However, now, in the autumn of 1990, the murders began to happen fast and furious. In Riverside there had been a lag—nine months had passed between Carol Miller and Cheryl Coker—but the renewed attacks were even more vicious than before. Where there had been an almost twisted whimsy, a taunt and a leer in the previous murders, Cheryl Coker's death was very angry and almost desperate and even a little bit rushed. There was the palpable sense that now, here we go, there might finally be a chance to catch this guy because he was upping the ante, operating right on the edge of control versus risk.

There was therefore a real urgency—catch this guy, or else watch the body count go through the roof. It's not that the killer wants to be caught, it's that he can't stop himself from killing, even when he might get caught, even when he might fuck up.

Charlotte Palmer, Lisa Lacik, Kimberly Lyttle, Tina Leal, Darla Ferguson, Carol Miller, Cheryl Coker, Susan Sternfeld, Kathleen Puckett, Cherie Payseur, Sherry Latham, Kelly Hammond, Catherine McDonald, Delliah Zamora, Eleanor Casares.

Despite the task force, bodies. In Riverside alone, a body a month in the latter half of 1991.

And still, no clues, not enough to do anything but tantalize the investigators. Some fibers, some hair, some shoe prints, some tire tracks. Duct tape had given way to surgical tubing that left no trace evidence at all. No fingerprints anywhere ever. Could've been any-body. Had to be somebody. Might as well have been a ghost. No matter the warnings, hookers still kept getting killed, mutilated, and posed. A head stuck in the ground. More shorn right breasts. Cigarette burns on the skin. Bite marks. A lightbulb in a uterus. A sock down a throat. Odd clothes put on the bodies after death.

And then, in January 1992, a break.

A cop with a hunch. A cop willing to make an unlawful search on a guy in a van who'd been trying to solicit a hooker.

An arrest.

Bill Suff.

Average look, average build, average guy. Forty years old or thereabouts. Personalized license plates with his name on 'em.

Bill Suff was a Riverside County employee and, unbeknownst to the county, an ex-con. He'd lied on his employment application. You know where they ask "Have you ever been convicted of a felony?"—he'd checked the "no" box, and then no one had checked him. If you answer "yes", then they check, like you'd lie by saying "yes" but not by saying "no".

Somewhere there's a theory—social psychology—that people who admit to some guilt are probably hiding something worse, and, if you admit to any guilt, then you can't be trusted. The "truth" is that even the most guilty people think they're innocent and you just can't run background checks on everybody. Besides, if they're really that bad and that guilty, they've probably covered their tracks anyway.

So, personnel departments by and large ignore what applicants put on the personnel departments' forms. The honor system. Innocent until proven guilty, and then let some other department handle it.

In Riverside, once arrested, the presumed innocent Bill Suff proved to be married, with a cat and some fish—didn't you just know it!—and an infant daughter who'd just been taken away by the authorities because she'd been abused. Two decades earlier, he'd crushed his first baby daughter to death and consequently served ten years in the Texas State Penitentiary at Huntsville.

A mistake, he said. It was all a mistake. He was innocent of everything they accused him of before, everything they were accusing him of now, and everything else they didn't even yet know they were going to accuse him of but would surely get around to.

It was a mistake and it was a frame-up.

They had the wrong man.

The cops had him all wrong, Bill said. People who knew him liked him, Bill said. He had lots of friends, Bill said.

And, indeed, he did. He went out of his way to make friends. He was a grown-up Cub Scout. He was a responsible person. He curried favor and made affability his trademark. He liked positive attention. He liked to be liked, and he loved to be needed. His friends got up at trial and swore that the Bill "they knew" couldn't have committed these crimes.

This of course begged the question.

The question was, Who was the Bill that the dead hookers knew?

After getting out of jail in Texas in 1984, Bill had returned to his home county of Riverside. The prostitute murders started soon thereafter. Interestingly, the little lag time of nine months in 1990 when there were fewer killings happened to coincide with the "honeymoon" first months of his life with child-bride Cheryl Lewis. The fresh spate of killings began late that year just after Bill found out that Cheryl was pregnant. Coincidentally or not, the woman he killed after his "honeymoon" was also named Cheryl—Cheryl Coker. Nonetheless, there had always been killings "in and around" during all of Bill's time in Riverside County—he'd been homicidally active from day one, no matter that he'd also always had female friends and heavy romances, and even regular trysts with hookers who walked away twenty bucks richer but none the wiser.

Charlotte Palmer, Lisa Lacik, Kimberly Lyttle, Tina Leal, Darla Ferguson, Carol Miller, Cheryl Coker, Susan Sternfeld, Kathleen Puckett, Cherie Payseur, Sherry Latham, Kelly Hammond, Catherine McDonald, Delliah Zamora, Eleanor Casares.

The pieces came together easily, and the authorities were certain they had their man—if Bill Suff wasn't the Riverside Prostitute Killer, then no one was.

Unfortunately, the evidence was still tough to come by. It would take years before this case would be ready to come to trial—both the prosecution and the defense needed all the time they could get.

It wasn't until early in 1995 that the gavel rapped and the trial began. O.J. was then on center stage, and Bill Suff got lost.

Of course, Bill was "convicted" from the moment of his arrest. The county sighed relief and got on with their lives . . . back in 1992. Three years later, the trial was not even a formality; it was just an exercise, something that had to be done before Bill could be shipped off to Death Row.

Yawn.

The first Riverside case—Charlotte Palmer—was dropped late in the game because there was really no evidence there at all. The Lisa Lacik case—in San Bernardino County—was put on semi-permanent hold, waiting in the wings if and only if Bill should somehow overturn his Riverside convictions on appeal.

And so the Riverside prosecutor put up a wall full of photos of dead girls, looking pretty in life and gruesome in death, and Bill Suff was pronounced formally and officially guilty. In fact, there has never been a serial killer trial in the United States where the defendant was not found guilty. A wall full of dead girls gets you a guilty verdict every time, no matter the evidence. See, Americans are not really so sporting as they pretend—we may appreciate the drama of the perfect crime, but in the end we want the crimes stopped and we want someone blamed and we want closure, and, whether you committed the perfect crime or not, you go to jail. No jury acquits, someone always gets convicted—that's how we sleep at night.

The O.J. jury didn't acquit O.J.; they convicted the Los Angeles Police Department. They convicted white America. They convicted history.

In Bill Suff's case, the jury convicted him of serial murder, despite the fact that most of his individual murders were "perfect". His only "solace" comes from the additional murders for which he will never even be tried. He's on Death Row, but he's gotten away with murder. He's on Death Row, but he can profess his innocence because no one asked why he did what he did. No one even dared ask how. Why the lightbulb? How did you convince her to come with you? Tell us about the breasts, Bill, and what did you mean by that cookbook you wrote in jail? And your computer and your audiocassette recorder—what was it that got erased?

Bill Suff's on Death Row, and we could all just forget about him and note his execution ten or fifteen years from now, except for one thing: the man is a writer, and, although his writer's voice is sweet and romantic and innocent, full of fun and fantasy, there is an undercurrent of pain, loss, retribution, and maybe just plain malevolence crucial for us to hear before it's too late, before the next Bill Suff crosses our path.

And, in his writings, whether he meant to or not, Bill answers all our questions. Everything. General and specific. He didn't testify at trial, but now he spills his guts without knowing it. For even in Bill's lies you can hear the truth, the sizzle of his passion burning not from flame but ice.

This book contains the stories about Bill Suff that never came out at trial, the tricks and the horrors that no one knew or wanted to know since he was going to get convicted anyway.

Courtroom observers were repulsed by what they heard on the record, but that was nothing compared to what's in this book.

Conviction should not end our fear.

Right now there are forty to fifty serial killers still active in the United States, and what's terrifying is just how close so many other people are to following in those ghastly, grisly footsteps.

How close is any one of us to killing someone?

Closer than you think. Closer than you want to be. Too close.

This then is a story of one writer connecting with another writer, dueling with words and printed pages, and yet knowing that the stakes are truly life and death. The innocent wanted to know if he could be guilty, and the guilty wanted to know how to regain his innocence—who would corrupt whom? This is the one chance you will ever get to cross over into the mind of a serial killer and see the world through his eyes, to taste the blood he still spills there.

For you will find that the killing is done but not over.

And the trial is over but not done.

Let the games begin.

CHAPTER 1

The Scene of the Crime

If someone took you to the edge of the world and threw you off, the place you'd land in would be the town of Lake Elsinore, Riverside County, California.

Lake Elsinore is not a place where people go when they get lost, it's the place where people wind up who are lost.

It's a place where, once you're there, you stay lost.

And then you die.

Actually, you were already dead or dying when you got there.

Not that anyone noticed.

Crank cookers, crooked crankers, bikers, people who've been abducted by aliens, everyone who wants to forget the past and anyone who wants to avoid the future—they make up the loose-knit population of Lake Elsinore, a place where if you say, "Morning, and what's your name?" you're more likely than not to get a tire iron rammed in one eye and out the back of your head.

A bar there was called Out of Luck, and what would be Main Street anywhere else in the world is called Lost Chance Road.

And the Lake is a boiling mudhole in the middle of endless, shifting desert.

"Ramshackle" is too kind a word to describe the housing there. Like the desert, people's homes shift around in the darkness of night. Trailers, lean-to's, corrugated tin shelters—you swear you saw 'em one day, but they're sure as hell gone the next. Or maybe you've just lost your bearings in the heat. Maybe the sweat got in your eyes and the heat waves got you dizzy and your nose led you astray because the place has no smell. Just a vague "ozone high" from the heat.

Even the dead bodies there don't seem to smell. Desperately starving animals become corpses fast, and the sun dries out what's left and bleaches the bones even faster. Within just a few short hours, you're past the point where a coroner can run definitive tissue samples, by nightfall you're mummified, and by the next morning you're dust.

That's why Lake Elsinore is a favored dumping ground for serial killers. Toss a body there, and there won't be much left for the district attorney to identify, let alone make a case against the perpetrator.

Even better, because of the wide vistas and infinite horizon, you can dump a body so it's never ever found, just another speck of sand in the desert, or, if you're like Bill Suff, you can pose and position the body so everyone for fifteen miles around can see it at daybreak. For the serial killer with an artistic bent, the sweeping dunes of Lake Elsinore comprise a canvas where you can show off your deathstrokes without fear of compromise or comparison.

But I'm getting ahead of our story. The relevance of Lake Elsinore is not so much that Bill Suff dumped most of his many murdered prostitutes here; it's that he grew up in this place, lived and loved and learned fear in this place.

And then he transposed Lake Elsinore into his mind so he could carry it with him everywhere—to Texas where he slaughtered his infant daughter, then back to California where he annihilated grown women for years—envisioning them all in elaborate masquerades and scenarios staged in the various secret places throughout and around Elsinore that had become for him a rich, robust, romantic adventure/fantasy/reality where life and death were not opposing points on a continuum but rather equal and simultaneous states of existence.

In Elsinore, Bill charged around on his flying steed, slew dragons, saved damsels in distress, made off with the golden fleece, and confronted, defeated, or at worst stalemated evil. Here, Bill found meaning in emptiness, saw visions in the night, and listened for the voice of a God which would batter him by silence. (God, like Bill's own father, was to be feared not for what He did, but rather for what He failed to do.) But here, in Elsinore, Bill found his own voice. From music, to story and poetry writing, to cartooning, Elsinore was the place where this young man's groin first tightened, where he became possessed of the temerity to feel he had the right to leave his mark on the world.

In 1967, when Bill was sixteen years old, his father, William Sr., dropped Bill's mother off at work, at the coffee shop they owned, told her he was running down to the store and would be right back, and then drove to Michigan, where he remains to this day.

When I asked Bill how he felt about his father abandoning the family that way—a wife and five kids, Bill the eldest, leaving his mother to scrape and claw for a living before she met and married an order-barking, one-legged military man called Shorty, whom the other kids all think of as their "real" father—Bill told me he was angry at William Sr.

It is one of the few times that Bill has admitted to any anger or hostility toward anyone—most of the time, Bill preaches love and compassion more than Jesus Christ himself. But then, it's natural that Bill would be angry at his deadbeat dad, isn't it?

"I wasn't mad 'cause Dad left," said Bill, "I was mad 'cause he didn't take me with him."

Bill was mad because now there was no escaping Lake Elsinore. Now, like all his future victims, there was no way to escape himself. In his mind, he himself had begun to die, and, once he was dead, he was free to kill. It was only a matter of time.

The Game Begins

My phone rang. My office is in my home, and the phone rings day and night because I do a lot of film projects overseas where their daytime is my nighttime and my nighttime is my best work time. Now it was late morning—Pacific daylight time—L.A. time. I was just recovering from brain death and getting refocused after a long night of writing and no sleep—it's like having a hangover, but without the guilt. In fact, the more beat-up you feel, the prouder you are—marathoners have their walls, and couch potatoes their couches, but whatever architecture, furniture, or graven image you define yourself by, you push yourself to your physical limits and that justifies the limit on your creative work which you always wish was better and more courageous. See, writing comes from one place and one place only: from fear. You fear the world, you fear your marriage, you fear for your children and you fear them too, you fear yourself, and more than anything you fear what you write, but writing is the way you whistle in the dark and hold the fear in momentary check. And then, when you wake up in the morning and read what you've written, you simultaneously and contradictorily fear that you have no idea where these words came from or who could have put them there even though you want to make sure that the entire world sees and comprehends them and offers you thanks.

At all costs you want to be judged, but only if it's a favorable judgment.

On the phone was my book agent, Peter Miller, calling from New York. He was, per usual, unconcerned about writers' angst.

"There's this guy Bill Suff the serial killer—his brother wants to sell the story. Talk to the brother and see if you're interested. I don't know if there's anything here or not—let me know what you think. But don't waste a lot of time on it."

Don Suff is the brother. He'd apparently been in touch with the tabloid television show *Hard Copy* during Bill's trial, and the executive producer over there referred Don to Peter. Now Peter figured I might find an angle on a story that was seemingly seamless.

The problem was that the Bill Suff story was old news. The killings had gone on for years; Bill had finally been caught and charged with the crimes; he'd been in jail awaiting trial for the better part of three years; his trial had happened concurrently with the O.J. trial; and he'd been convicted, now awaiting sentencing.

Everyone had heard about the Riverside Prostitute Killer, and everyone was certain that Bill was guilty even though he denied it, and that was the name of that tune.

The worst part, from a modern-day journalistic marketing perspective, was that Bill was an old-before-his-time, John Wayne Gacy "pudgeball" kind of guy. In other words, forget the TV movie. Mark Harmon wasn't about to play Bill Suff, and none of those *Melrose Place* babes was going to play a junkie street hooker whose neck got in the way of Bill's ham hands and noose-knotted surgical tubing.

Sure, Bill had killed a lot of women, but he was just one in an endless stream of serial killers who had killed a lot of women.

However, I didn't know any of those other serial killers—Bill was the first serial killer I would ever meet. Dead hookers and a live murderer—this was my chance to take a walk on the wild side, my chance to rise above the surmise of mystery fiction writing and enter the real world of the criminal mind.

Who are these guys, these serial killers? Why do they do what they do? And just how much like them are we?

"I was maybe five years old, and maybe a little less. I was the oldest child, and I played by myself a lot. We had this planter alongside the house—my father had planted bamboo and some kind of low fern—caterpillars loved to congregate there and I loved to collect the caterpillars. Worms were slimy, but caterpillars were fuzzy and friendly and colorful, and I dug a little hole in the planter, lined it with leaves, and gently placed my caterpillars in it. I cut some of the bamboo shoots and planted them in the hole so the caterpillars could climb or dine. I had an orange caterpillar, and several black ones—no, I didn't name them, but I could tell one from the other, and I noted and memorized their individual markings. Every night I'd lay a big fern leaf across the hole so the caterpillars would sleep for the night, and then in the morning I'd take out the caterpillars and hold them in my hand, stroke their manes, show them off to the neighborhood kids. Then one day I came out and found the caterpillars were all dead. They were mush. The fuzz of the orange caterpillar was everywhere in the hole. My first thought was that one of the other kids had come over and jealously killed the cater-pillars. Maybe the kid was trying to play with them or grab them or steal them and got too rough. Or maybe he was just trying to kill them. Either way, I was heartbroken. I looked at that orange fuzz blowing around the hole and I just knew that this devastation was all my fault—if I hadn't tried to covet and contain the beautiful caterpillars, they'd still be alive. If you find beauty in this world, people come in and take it from you, not because they want it for themselves but just because they don't want you to have it.

"It never occurred to me that maybe my caterpillars were still alive and well, that they'd just molted, shed their fur, and crawled out of the hole to build their cocoons so they could turn into butterflies. I don't know why I didn't think of that then, why I might have been confusing a natural process for a sinister plot; I just know that I felt a tremendous loss and I needed some-one—including myself—to blame.

"Anyway, several years later, my mother was driving me and my brother to the market. In the street was a tortoise. It was dead. A tire track had torn through the back of its shell, leaving the poor animal frozen in midstep, its head stretched all the way up and out, eyes wide and alert. The tortoise was in the center of the road—the killer had intentionally veered out of his lane in order to run it over. My brother and I had several tortoises as pets—I knew this wasn't one of ours, but the instant I saw the animal, looking so posed and alive and yet so clearly and needlessly dead, I burst into hysterics. In my entire life, I have never cried so uncontrollably. To this day I remember how completely out of control and horrific the world suddenly seemed to me at the sight of that dead tortoise. I'd led a protected and happy life until then, and somehow I now knew it was all a lie."

The words of Bill Suff, convicted infant slayer and serial killer?

No, the words of a nice, shy, Jewish boy from the San Fernando Valley. Me. Born to nice parents and raised in a nice middle-class existence where I never wanted for anything but never asked for what I couldn't get.

Yet, if I suddenly went up in a tower and blazed away with an AK-47, everyone would point to my turtle and caterpillar stories as proof that I'd lost my bearings a very long time ago. And my years of writing murder mysteries, inventing ways for people to die on paper, would be a prosecutor's wet dream. *Hunter, Matlock, Remington Steele,* and all my other television scripts would testify against me. In fact, when I was consulting for the series *M.A.N.T.I.S.*, didn't I have a heated argument with one of the producers about why serial killers kill, like I knew best? I was writing a script where a killer would kidnap and then impersonate his victims, jealously trying to live their lives before finding each insufficient. I maintained that my villain had no sense of acceptable self, and so he needed to control and become the people he most envied, only to find that each was just as weak and vulnerable and human as he. See, murder is the great equalizer. Paupers and presidents don't die any differently from one another. And serial killers get only momentary relief, a momentary high from each killing. But then they are alone with themselves once more. All the secondary motives for serial killing—media attention, control over the victim—dissipate once the victim is dead. Now all the killer can do is kill again. The act of killing is both the sustenance and the famine. The successive killings are really just one act stretched out over time. There is no final exorcism; there is finally only the killer's own death or capture to stop his act. The world of emotion that each of us lives in cannot be changed by anything we do—however and whenever that die is cast, we spend the rest of our lives in fight and flight that only conserves and justifies our reality, no matter how false or inconsistent it may be with everyone else's.

However, the M.A.N.T.I.S. producer insisted that I was full of crap. "Of course a killer has a motive—everyone has a motive for every act, but people are either good or evil, and they're to be judged by their acts—their intentions don't matter." Accordingly, as rewritten by the producer, the serial killer in my story became a guy who was simply out to avenge his partners' attempts to steal from him and kill him.

To my mind, this was now not a serial killer.

In a given moment of anger, fear, pain, or jealousy, we each of us can find ourselves shot through with the urge to kill. For most of us the urge is juxtaposed, countered by either self-recrimination or simple relief—you feel better having gotten the emotion out while recognizing it for what it is, or your conscience simply clamps down on the impulse and that is that.

And, no matter how perfect our upbringing, we each suffer enough cumulative hurt and confusion that, in a moment of weakness, could lead to murder.

But that is still not serial killing.

Serial killing is an entirely different animal.

Serial killers are born waiting for the slings and arrows that will unleash the torment they already feel. While the rest of us pile up pain throughout our lives, able to endure more because of what we've already endured, serial killers are bursting with pain from the git-go, and life experience then shows them that there is indeed an outlet, that in this mobile world one person can cruise around wasting people by the dozens and never get caught.

And I couldn't wait to meet with Bill Suff to ask him all about it.

"I'll tell you one thing, I know I can get him to confess for this book of ours," Don Suff told me over the phone in July of 1995. "Even though he's my older brother, it's like he looks up to me and confides in me—always has. Yeah, I'll get him to confess."

"Well, that would certainly be newsworthy," I said, "but, with all due respect, if Bill hasn't confessed up 'til now, then I don't think he's ever going to. Maybe he doesn't really know he's done it—on a conscious level."

"Hey, Bill is not crazy."

I almost laughed. Don Suff was righteously and angrily defending his brother's sanity, as if it was better to be a serial killer than to be insane. Or, better put, Don was telling me that on the one hand, his brother was a serial killer, while on the other hand, no way could Bill be such a thing.

It was my first conversation with Don. It began with a lot of business talk and even more false bravado. Don wanted to clear the family's name; he didn't want anyone blaming his mother for what Bill had become. By the same token, Don wanted to air the family's secrets for a price. "There are things I can tell you that no one knows. Stuff about Billy. Stuff about the family. We refused to cooperate with the prosecutors. We just tried to hold this family together, but this town has put us out of business just because we're related to Billy, because we have the name Suff. I haven't worked in months— I had a nonalcoholic youth nightclub, shut down by rezoning after Bill was arrested—they wanted me out. And my mom and my sister both lost their child-care and foster-care licenses. Anything the police and the politicians and the media could dig up on us, they did. Now I need to make some money so my mom and I can move out of town. How much you think we can get for this book?"

"Maybe I can get you on *Leeza* or one of the tabloid shows for an appearance fee, for some quick cash."

"That'd be great. You really think so? We need like a thousand, maybe a little more, so we can move to Nevada."

"I'll make some calls. But in the meantime, let's talk about Bill—when did you know that he was a serial killer?"

"Not until he was convicted. I wouldn't believe it until then. I tried not to follow the trial, but every time I heard any of the testimony it seemed pretty convincing. I just didn't want to believe it. I still can't accept that my brother's a serial killer. I mean, how do you accept something like that?"

"And you had no idea while it was going on all those years?"

"No." A long pause, and then: "I used to see Bill all the time after he came back from Texas around 1984. He used to come visit me and my wife at home—sometimes he'd stop by and see her when I wasn't there. Gives me the chills now to think about it— him alone there with her." Another pause. "He used to bring her presents. Clothes and jewelry. Said he got 'em at swap meets."

"But they were from his victims?"

Don didn't answer. Through the phone I could see him shaking. At Bill's trial, the evidence had been circumstantial at best— this guy didn't evade the authorities for all those years by leaving a lot of clues around; he was a very tidy and careful killer, no matter how brazen. But, the most damning items were the clothing, jewelry, and personal effects from the dead women—Bill had gathered these things up and taken them home, given them to his own wife or to friends and coworkers. His wife never seemed to ask why he would get her used clothes that weren't her size.

"I was just thinking," said Don, "I really hadn't seen Bill for a few months and then he heard I was building the nightclub and he started hanging around. He was arrested just before we opened. I bet he was planning on using the place to pick out his victims. Can you imagine?"

"But he just killed hookers, right?"

Incredibly, the Riverside Prostitute Killer operated for years in the same place, enticing his victims into his van from their promenade along a short stretch of University Avenue. Of course, there were other victims in neighboring cities and counties, trials which still await Bill should his present convictions ever be overturned, but the amazing thing is that, despite tremendous public awareness and a massive multijurisdictional police task force, Bill kept driving along University Avenue in Riverside and the hookers kept hopping in with him. And everyone guessed that the killer had to be masquerading as a cop in order to get the hookers to trust him, but not until his arrest did the authorities discover that Bill worked for the county of Riverside at the materials procurement ware-house—he minded the store of cop uniforms.

"Well, Bill told me he used to go with hookers, even when he was married or had a girlfriend."

"You're saying he 'dated' hookers?" This had not come out at the trial, as far as I knew. Bill's life and routine had remained a mystery. His hours and his days went largely unaccounted for. From old motorcycle accident injuries to hideous allergies and some curious phobias, Bill took off a lot of time for sick leave; and when he was working he regularly volunteered to ferry female work-release inmates for the city, or do earthquake preparedness demonstrations "in the field" at other city and county facilities, or otherwise find some semilegitimate excuse to be out and about in his van with its BILSUF license plates.

All this posed a particular problem for prosecutors. It quite liter-ally made District Attorney Paul Zellerbach knowingly lie to the jury. In the case of the last victim, who had been killed at night and whose body Bill admitted discovering (not killing, merely discovering) in the dead of night, Zellerbach felt compelled to present false evidence that she was killed the next morning, just before noon. This "proof problem" was twofold: first, Bill's admission was not admissible, com-ing after he had asked for an attorney and the cops had pretended not to hear, even though they were audiotaping the interrogation and had to have known that Bill's defense lawyers were hardly going to be as deaf as they. (Or maybe not—maybe the cops really didn't think anyone in their small, frontier town would dare defend Bill, let alone plead him innocent. After a repeatedly botched investigation over so many years, the cops swaggered around, arrogantly parading them-selves and Bill before the media once they finally collared him and declared the case to be closed, trial or no.) The second aspect of the proof problem was that the dead woman's sister was sure that she had talked with her sister by phone on the morning after she was in fact already dead. See, Bill's movements were hard enough to trace, but his victims' were nigh on impossible. Not only don't the friends and relatives of junkie hookers know where the junkie hookers are or were at any given moment, but the junkie hookers themselves would be hard-pressed to log in with the right or any answer.

So Zellerbach was stuck with the sister's mistaken testimony, because she was the only person who could identify certain items found at Bill's as the personal possessions of the dead woman.

Hence, Zellerbach lied to the jury and Bill couldn't cry "foul" without taking the stand to admit to something that supposedly the Bill of Rights protects him from having to admit to. And the wheels of justice ground on. Grind on, big wheels.

Don answered my question: "Yeah, Billy said he often used the services of prostitutes."

This I found fascinating. It made some sane sense that Bill could kill hookers and then go home and not harm his wife, but what sense did it make that Bill killed some prostitutes but not others? Was there something about a particular girl—some way that she looked, some way that she acted—something that triggered Bill's violence, or was it just that some nights he wanted to get laid and other nights he wanted to commit murder?

"My brother Bobby testified for the prosecution that Billy said he hated prostitutes and wanted to kill them, but that's not true."

"I thought the family didn't cooperate with the prosecution?"

"The D.A.'s investigators got to my mom and tricked her into helping them at first, but she didn't know anything, none of us did. And Bobby just wanted the attention, to be in the headlines, so he made up the story about Billy saying he hated prostitutes. Bobby's not real truthful."

So much for this close-knit family.

"All right, Don, then tell me—I don't want to make you or your family look bad, but level with me—was there anything in your background, in Bill's background, that you now think might have led him to become a serial killer?"

"His first wife. I think she became a prostitute. When she and

Billy were in Texas, when he was in the Air Force. I think that's what made him kill. That and Dijianet dying." (*Dijianet pronounced Day-sha-nay*)

"Dijianet?"

"Billy's daughter. She was a baby—eight weeks old. Billy and Teryl—that's his first wife; the second wife is Cheryl—Billy and Teryl, they were convicted of murdering Dijianet. But we—the family—we don't really know what happened. Billy says Teryl did it, that she shook her too hard or something."

I was reeling and I was pissed and I felt like my time was being wasted, and Don knew it. He knew that I was suddenly finding it a little hard to accept the family's naiveté about Bill's guilt for the prostitute killings, in light of the fact that they all knew that Bill was a child killer. Don also knew that I was no longer going to buy into the whitewashed family history he'd originally planned to spoon-feed me. I got the impression that this sudden awareness on Don's part had less to do with me or my silent reaction to his words than the simple fact that, once he had said the words aloud, Don himself listened to them for the first time. His brother was a baby killer. Anyone who could kill a baby was capable of any and every horror ever conceived. Prostitute murders were *de rigueur* for someone experienced in infanticide.

"Go on," I said icily. I knew that if I told my wife, my agent, or anyone else about that dead baby, then this book would never happen. It's funny where lines get drawn in the sand. When you write about someone, that person is glorified by the simple act of focusing attention on him or her, and, while we all may be willing to allow such glorification for a prostitute killer, we don't countenance biographies of men who kill babies. On the other hand, we are fascinated by women who kill babies or children, and those stories turn into both books and miniseries. We just cannot believe it when women kill their children—we have to stop and examine the situation in minute detail just to accept that it happened, and even then it defies reality, more unreal than real, a true perversion of the natural order of things. But men who kill their children are simply repugnant—we accept that evil men commit such crimes, and we simply want these men out of our sight and off our planet as quickly as possible. In jail, these men are immediately marked for death by the other inmates, yet Bill Suff had survived, hadn't he? How was this possible? It had to be that even though he wasn't sexy Ted Bundy, he nonetheless had a disarming personality that belied his crimes. Pleasant but respectful. Charming but reticent. Eddie Haskell on Valium.

"Look," said Don Suff, "Billy was in Texas, and Dijianet died, and Billy and Teryl were both convicted for it, and the family didn't know what to make of it. We didn't want to see the case files or the autopsy report or the evidence or the pictures of the dead baby. We really didn't want to know. If we knew the details, then we could never forgive Billy. You can't forgive someone for killing a baby; you can't say 'I know he did a terrible thing, but he's still my brother'; you just can't live with it—you can't be related to some-one who would do something like that."

"So you pretend it never happened?"

I could tell that Don was close to tears. Dijianet Suff died in 1973. More than twenty years had passed, and Don had never once had the chance to talk about it, to cry about it, to scream about it. This was a public event but still a family secret. Dijianet Suff was gone before the family ever knew her, but she haunts them to this day.

As for Billy, I correctly guessed that this crime was the one that embarrassed him. He didn't want to tell his family about it, and they didn't want to hear it. He told them pretty much after the fact that Dijianet had died and he'd been tried and convicted and that was all. He didn't want his family at the trial and he seems to have needed time to get his stories straight and build a wall over his emotions about it. As many times as I have looked into his eyes and asked him about Dijianet's death, no real reaction comes out. He gets glib about how he was asleep, had nothing to do with it, and has no idea what happened, although he can guess that Teryl did it and then went to work that day, leaving him to wake up later and find the baby dead. However, at the time, according to notes in his own handwriting that he slipped to his lawyers, he surmised that if Teryl didn't do it, then the CIA did. Other outrageous and conspiratorial outsiders and interlopers were also possibilities. When I told Bill about these notes, he denied making them. Period. As voluble and forthcoming as Bill can be about so many things, Dijianet's death is locked away in a place so inaccessible that no one, including Bill, will ever have at it again.

In fact, it was Ted Bundy who explained that even serial killers have certain crimes or certain acts tied to certain crimes that make them anxious. I won't go so far as to call it a matter of conscience, but it is what passes for self-rebuke in a serial killer. Bundy regretted that, on one occasion, he'd taken the heads of two of his victims and brought them home, to the place he shared with his girlfriend and her child. Bundy hid the heads from his girlfriend, and he ultimately toyed with them and then burned them in the fireplace, but he was ashamed and worried that somehow his girlfriend would find out. It wasn't that he was afraid she'd find out he was a mass murderer; it was that she'd learn that he'd betrayed her in her own home. Since Bundy was always reticent to discuss the sexual aspects of his crimes, it would seem that he felt that by masturbating into those skulls at home, he was cheating on his girlfriend, and that bothered him.

"You think that Dijianet's death somehow helped to provoke the prostitute killings?" I asked Don.

"Billy and Teryl were both convicted and given sentences of seventy years. But a female prison guard helped Teryl file her appeal, her conviction got overturned, and she got out right away, while Billy served ten years."

"So you think Bill is angry at Teryl, and that's who he sees in his mind's eye when he's killing hookers?"

"When Teryl got out of jail, she moved in with that prison guard, and they've been together in a lesbian relationship ever since. I think that Billy loved Teryl, but she cheated on him, worked as a prostitute to get more money, and then became a lesbian. I think it turned him upside down and inside out. Billy didn't have a lot of girlfriends growing up—Teryl was it. And there's one other thing—"

"Yeah?"

"She was pregnant when they got married. But not by him."

Bill Suff had two children by Teryl Cardella. There was Bill Jr., and then there was Dijianet. I was momentarily confused. "Are you telling me that Bill's son, a son named after him, is not his flesh and blood? Did he know it at the time?" Suddenly I was thinking maybe all this was a motive for mass murder—this was certainly a plot we'd buy if we saw it on a TV soap opera. Little did I know that I had it all wrong, and truth would once again prove stranger than fiction. In fact, truth would prove unbelievable were it not for the fact that it was, after all, true.

"No one outside the family knows this. Teryl was pregnant. First she said she'd been raped by several black men. Then she said the father was someone who was in prison. Then she admitted that the father was her stepfather, and they'd been having relations for years. She'd been put in a church-sponsored home for juvenile delinquents to keep her away from her stepfather. Her family says she seduced him."

"How old was she?"

"She was just sixteen when she married Billy."

"So she was barely a teenager when she was supposedly seducing her stepfather. That's not seduction—it's rape."

"Either way, Billy married her knowing that it wasn't his child, but he didn't want them to keep the child, he didn't want to raise her, so they told everyone it had died, and then my mother and my stepfather took the baby and we pretended she was our baby sister."

"Pardon me?"

"Teryl's child became my sister, and Teryl and Billy moved to Texas so he could be in the Air Force medical corps. Then they had Bill Jr. and Dijianet."

"Did Teryl's child—your ersatz sister—know the truth?"

"No, not until recently when a friend of the family told her. As soon as she found out, she ran away and hasn't come back. The person who told her is Terry, an older married guy who was having an affair with her. He and his wife were friends with my mother and father—I call my stepfather 'father'; that's Earl, 'Shorty'—anyway, my father got drunk one night and told Terry about my sister, that's how come he knew." There was a long pause; and then: "Actually, Terry was Teryl's stepfather."

"Wait a minute—Teryl's stepfather slept both with her and with the daughter he probably had by her? And then he told the daughter that her parents weren't her parents?"

"I don't know, I don't really know. All I know is now my sister—Teryl's daughter—is with a guy who drinks and abuses her. And I think she's thinking about joining the army."

Feeling like you ought to put this book down and go take a shower? I wouldn't blame you—that's how I felt in talking to "Donny". But I also started to feel just the wee littlest bit excited. I began to sense that if I dug deep enough, then everything about Bill would make perfect, tied-up-in-a-bow, sensible, inevitable sense. Maybe no one did notice what a ticking time bomb this guy was all the time he was growing up, but someone should have and everyone could have, had they bothered to look. The expression "smoking gun" came to my mind. I suddenly felt certain that I would someday be able to explain why Bill cut off the right breasts of some of his victims, and why he stabbed others through the heart in addition to strangling them, why he posed their corpses in exotic, erotic positions, mutilated their genitalia, left some nude while dressing others in clothes that were not their own, and the *pièce de résistance*: why on Earth did Bill Suff stick an energy-efficient General Electric 95-watt Miser lightbulb, intact, up the vagina and into the womb of one woman?

"There's one other thing you might find interesting," said Don Suff quite dramatically, "my brother Billy is a great writer. Let me mail you his short story, 'Tranquility Garden'—he wrote it while he was in prison in Texas."

Subsequently, all my wife could say was: "What, are you crazy? You gave these people our home address??"

CHAPTER 3

"That Forever Tear"
(a poem)

and

"Tranquility Garden"
(a short story)

written by
Bill Suff

That Forever Tear

I'm kissing you, our lips don't part;
  And loving you, with all my heart.
I'm holding you so close to me,
  And marvel at the sight I see.

You're beautiful, beyond compare;
  I reach for you, but you're not there!
It's just a dream, I realize;
  And once again tears fill my eyes.

I have this dream 'most every night;
  I reach for you, and hold you tight.
But come the dawn, you'll disappear;
  And again I shed, that forever tear.

Tranquility Garden

The day had been warm and at 4:00 that afternoon, it was just beginning to cool off. A warm breeze blowing in from the ocean, coming over the mountains and through the open living room window.

Jeannie was sitting in a chair, facing the window to catch the breeze. She was totally absorbed in the magazine she was reading and didn't hear the knock the first time. The knock came again and she set the magazine aside. The knock came again as she reached the open door.

The young man at the front door smiled and stood up straighter as the door opened.

"Hello, Jeannie. How are you?"

"Why, Lee! Hello. I didn't know you were home. When did you arrive?"

"Oh, a little while ago." He shrugged and looked down at the welcome mat. "Are your parents home?"

"Uh, n-no, Lee. They went to Riverside. They'll be home soon. Why don't you come in and wait."

"No, thank you. I came to see you. Mom wrote me you're getting married soon."

"Yes, I am. Next Thursday. You remember Ricky. We went to high school together."

"Yes, I remember." He hesitated, then uncertainly asked, "Jeannie, can you come with me? Just for a walk. We'll be back before dark."

"Well, I don't know. I was expecting Ricky to call and . . ."

"It's important, Jeannie." He blurted out.

Jeannie thought it over and chewed on the inside of a lip. Lee stood on the porch with a pleading look in his eyes. Finally, Jeannie said, "OK Lee, but not too far. I promised to cook dinner tonight."

She grabbed a light sweater and walked out of the house with a young man in a rumpled, army uniform.

They were crossing a small, grassy field. They had been talking about the wedding preparations and what had been going on in Lake Elsinore since Lee left two years ago, to join the Army.

"Lee, what did you really want to talk about? You didn't come all the way here just to hear me talk about Ricky, the wedding and the goings-on around here. What do you really want?"

"I came back from . . . my assignment, to find out if you were really going to marry Ricky. To find out if you would change your mind."

She stopped, hands on her hips and glared at him. "That's an awfully foolish question! Of course I'm going to marry Ricky and I will not change my mind. What makes you think I would change my mind?"

"I was just hoping you wouldn't marry him. That you'd . . . uh . . . marry me . . . instead."

"Lee, you've been gone from here over two years. Things have happened. I like you Lee, but not as much as I did in school. I found out I was in love with Ricky. Why should I forget him and marry you?"

"Please, don't get mad at me, Jeannie. Let's continue our walk and talk a little longer."

"No, Lee. I don't think we should go any further. Take me back home."

"*Please*, Jeannie. Let's walk just a little further. I want you to see something. I know you'll like it. It's only a little bit further."

She looked around to see where they were and was surprised they had walked so far. "Well, only a *little* bit further. It'll be getting dark soon." They started walking again. Slowly, yet they covered the ground so fast, it was unbelievable.

Soon they were in a small, grassy meadow with trees and a small stream in it. Jeannie looked around, astonished at the sight. "Why, it-it's beautiful here. I didn't know there was anyplace as pretty as this around here."

"I used to come here all the time when I was younger. I would sit here, under this very tree and read books, write poetry, or dream of lovely things. I'm sure other people have been here, but I've never seen any signs of anyone else around. I've never told or shown this place to anyone. Not even my mother. She's heard me talk of a place I call 'Tranquility Garden', but she never found out where it was. You're the only person I've ever brought here, the only one I've ever told about it. I'd like to be buried here, right under this tree. I only wish that I told my mother of this place. You can see why I want to be buried here, can't you?"

Jeannie looked at him and saw the tears forming in his eyes. "Yes, Lee. I can see why. But you can tell your mother now. Tonight, after you take me home."

"No. I don't have time. I only have a little while left before I have to go back. I shouldn't be here now, but I had to see you and talk to you before . . . it was too late. I wanted you to see the 'Tranquility Garden' first. You see, Jeannie, you're the only girl I've ever really fallen in love with. Sure, there have been other girls I thought I was in love with, but I found out there was only you. None of them gave me the feeling I have when I'm near you."

"Lee, that's very flattering. But I'm in love with Ricky. And what do you mean you've only got a little while before you have to go back?"

He looked around the small meadow as if he hadn't heard her question and then sat down beneath the tree. He leaned back against the tree and closed his eyes. "It's so nice here. So . . . tranquil. That's how I picked its name. I wish I could just . . . live here . . . forever." He finished the sentence and opened his eyes. Tears started rolling down his cheeks. "I love this place. Almost as much as you, Jeannie." He looked up at her and smiled weakly.

Jeannie came over to his side and knelt down beside him. She pulled a handkerchief from a pocket and gave it to him.

"Lee, what's wrong? Are you in some kind of trouble? You aren't AWOL are you?"

He shut his eyes again, as if thinking about the questions. Opening his eyes, he glanced at Jeannie, then at the meadow around them. Looking down at his scuffed boots, he answered, "Yes, I guess in a way, I am kinda AWOL."

"Lee! You can get in deep trouble for being AWOL. Won't they arrest you or something?"

He looked around again. "No. No, I won't be in trouble. They won't arrest me for it." He looked at the stream, reached out for Jeannie's hand and smiled at her. "Come with me, I want you to see something else."

She was reluctant at first, but then got up and let him lead her to the stream.

"Look there. See how clear it is? And it's fresh water, too." He knelt down and cupped some of the cool water in his hand. "Actually, it's kind of sweet."

He drank the water. "Try some, Jeannie. It tastes real good."

"No. I'm not thirsty right now. Lee, why did you go AWOL?"

"I told you, Jeannie. I had to see you. To talk to you. To ask you to marry me. Jeannie, marry me now. Before I have to go. Before it's too late."

She looked into his eyes. The tears were still there, ready to fall. She looked away, a lump forming in her throat. "No, Lee. I'm marrying Ricky. I'm sorry, but that's the way it has to be." There were tears starting to form in her eyes, too.

Lee stooped down and cupped another handful of water. He drank it and then stood up. "I love this place. Jeannie, promise me something. Please, just do one thing for me."

She looked back at him again. There was an odd feeling she had when looking into his eyes. Something odd about his eyes. They were blue, a bright, shining blue. She looked away from his eyes, almost afraid to look into them. Afraid of the feeling that was coming over her. "What is it Lee? What do you want me to do?"

He reached for her shoulders and turned her to face him. She kept her eyes averted from his. He lifted her chin, "Look at me, Jeannie."

Slowly she raised her eyes to meet his.

"Jeannie, will you promise me that, sometime soon, you'll come back here and plant some flowers? And then, whenever you get a chance, you'll come back here and watch over things?"

"But, Lee." She turned and waved an arm around the small meadow. "I wouldn't be able to take care of this place by myself."

He shook his head. "No, Jeannie. It won't be hard. You don't even have to do anything really. What I'm asking is that after the flowers start growing, you'll come down here and watch them. Make sure nothing goes wrong while they are growing. And don't tell anyone of this place. Except my mother, of course. Visit this place, keep it . . . alive. Most of all, when you come here, remember how beautiful this place is."

She now looked back to his eyes. She felt a cold chill travel down her spine. His eyes were glowing brighter than before. She thought, if it were dark, they would probably light up whatever he looked at, like a flashlight. Then she thought about the dark. Surely it must be getting dark soon. They'd walked so far, it must be late. She raised her arm to look at the time, but Lee stopped her arm.

"Jeannie? Will you do that for me?" he pleaded.

She thought back to his question. "OK, Lee. I'll do it. I don't know why, though. You'll be able to do that when you come home. For good, I mean."

He smiled and looked over the meadow again. He walked back to the tree and stood there, head down, almost reverently. He looked up again and back to Jeannie. "Make sure that no one bothers with this spot. I want this spot to be where I'm buried."

She saw the tears in his eyes start falling again. And once

again she felt the tightness in her throat. But she *couldn't* marry Lee. Plans had already been made and set. Besides, she was in love with Ricky. She couldn't just drop him. No, there wasn't any use in questioning the matter anymore. It had been already settled.

But he asked again.

"Jeannie, please marry me. Tonight, before I leave."

"No, Lee. I can't. Why do you keep asking me? I've already explained to you why I can't."

"I keep hoping you will change your mind."

"Lee, I know we've been gone for a long time. It must be getting dark soon. Will you please take me home now. I don't know which way to go."

He smiled. "All right. I'll point out certain landmarks on the way home, so you can find your way back next time."

They started back and as they topped the first small hill, Lee stopped and turned around. He looked back over the small meadow. It was only half the size of a football field. A small oasis in the middle of a vast countryside of dried grass and uncultivated fields. He stared for a few more seconds. And then, to the meadow, he said, "Goodbye old tree. I'll be back one day and then never leave. Goodbye . . . 'Tranquility Garden.'"

Jeannie shuddered a little and looked at him, trying to read his meaning of those words. She gave up as he grasped her hand and started walking again.

"This is the only hill that offers this good a view. And you can't even see the meadow from any of the surrounding mountains." He pointed to one of the peaks to the left of them, "That's Mount San Jacinto and across from it is Tahquitz Peak. I've been on both, with a telescope. You can see those two peaks from the meadow but from the peaks, no matter how hard you look, you can't see 'Tranquility Garden.'"

They continued walking, with him pointing out various landmarks. She was just beginning to realize how far they had walked. It seemed impossible. They couldn't have walked *that far*!

She lost her train of thought when he brought her attention to something else.

" . . . 'Dan's Feed and Seed' will have any kind of seed you're hunting for. I worked there before I joined the service. I've checked with the county tax assessor and found out the land is not owned in that area. All around it is owned by the state forestry department. But the meadow is sitting in the middle of a half-acre of land that has never been claimed. So you won't be trespassing on anyone's property. And by now, that little matter will be taken care of."

To Jeannie, it seemed as if they had only left the meadow a few minutes before. But already they were turning onto the road that Jeannie's parents lived on. She knew how to get back to the meadow, but she didn't know how they had traveled that distance as fast as they did.

At the gate he stopped and held her hand a little tighter. She turned in the direction he was looking. The sun was just dipping behind the mountains in the distance.

"That's where I have to go, over the mountains and across the sea. But I'll be coming back soon. Maybe too soon." He turned back to her. "Jeannie, once again, I'm asking you to marry me. We can still catch the Justice at his chambers, before he goes home."

Jeannie was near tears when she answered him. "Lee you've made it very hard for me. But I still have to say no. You're very sweet and I almost wish things were different. But I'm still going to marry Ricky. I'm sorry, Lee." There was definite pain in her heart now.

He smiled weakly and then kissed her. She didn't resist him. "Goodbye Jeannie. Please remember your promise. I leave 'Tranquility Garden' to you. Remember me and my love for you. Don't forget me."

With that, he turned on his heel and swiftly walked up the street, towards a group of trees. At the edge of the trees he stopped and turned back to Jeannie. She was still standing at the gate and he raised his hand. She heard his words softly in her ears, "I love you, Jeannie."

She glanced up, beyond him and the trees and saw the mountains, remembering his words " . . . over the mountains and across the sea." Then she remembered a letter from him, not too long ago. A letter she never answered.

When she looked back down, he was gone, disappeared through the trees. She looked harder, through the trees, but still couldn't see him. It was swiftly getting darker. She glanced at her watch for the first time since they had left. She was astonished when she saw it was only 5:30. She raised her arm to listen. The watch was still ticking. The walk couldn't have taken only an hour and a half! Yet, when she walked into the house, she saw the time *was only* 5:30.

She went to the kitchen and started preparing dinner. Several times she had started to tell her parents about Lee's visit that day, but she couldn't keep the thought long enough to say anything.

For the next two days she found her thoughts returning to Lee and his visit. When she went to the seed store, she found there was already an order for seeds waiting for her, in her name. On the second day after Lee's visit, she went back to 'Tranquility Garden' and started planting seeds.

She felt oddly at peace when there. And she came to find out, that while she was there, the time seemed to stand still. She felt she had been there hours but when leaving she would glance at her watch and see only a short time had passed. Three times that day she had gathered her things together and started leaving. She never had the desire to look at her watch while in the meadow itself.

On that second day, after visiting 'Tranquility Garden', Jeannie had received a letter from the county tax assessor's office. Inside she found the deed to a section of land. Roughly locating it on a map, she found that it was in the vicinity of 'Tranquility Garden'.

The deed was in her name and was free of all costs for the next ten years. It was paid for and made out in her name. Lee paid for it and had the paperwork completed Thursday, August 20th. That was Lee's birthday. Then she started as she realized that was the day he came for the visit. Today was the 22nd, Saturday. She felt that cold chill come over her again. The same way she felt when she was talking to Lee. What was going on? she thought.

Thursday, Lee had visited her; also that was the day the seed order was placed and that's when the tax assessor was paid. Well, he could have done all of that before he came to visit her. But why did he do it? He didn't know what my answer was going to be. And why didn't he cancel them when his proposal was refused? She couldn't understand his reasoning.

Before she could think any more on the matter, she heard the phone start ringing. Then her mother was calling to her, "Jeannie, will you answer that? My hands are greasy."

"All right, mother," she answered and moved to the phone. "Hello?"

"Hello, Jeannie? This is Rob. Mom would like you to come over here, just as soon as you can. It's very important."

She noticed a slight trembling in his voice.

"What's the matter, Rob?"

"I'm not sure. But it's something to do with you."

"All right, I'm on my way." She hung up and told her mother she was going over to Rob's house and would be back soon.

Walking the three blocks to Rob's house she wondered what was wrong. How could she have something to do with anything there? Rob was Lee's younger brother. Could Lee have written something to their mother? About 'Tranquility Garden'? Yes! That must be it. She should have gone over there sooner to tell his mother where it was and what he had said about it.

Jeannie found her steps quickening as she thought of Lee.

Finally reaching the house, she knocked on the door and was startled when it was immediately opened. Lynn was standing there, tears streaking her face. "Momma's in the kitchen, Jeannie."

Jeannie was really getting worried now. Lynn was Lee's only sister and they were closer than most sisters and brothers.

When she walked into the kitchen, Lee's mother rose from a chair, crying and handing two letters to her, left the room.

Jeannie sat down at the table and started reading the letters. The first was from Lee, dated Wednesday, the day before his visit. The letter was to his mother.

Wed. 19 Aug. 1970

Dear Mom,

How are you and the family? I'm ok. This has to be short because I'm assigned to go out on a patrol in a little while. The fighting has been pretty thick lately. The Viet Cong have been hitting real hard and we've been notified to be ready to move out at a moment's notice.

It got pretty bad this morning. The Cong hit us at daybreak and hit us hard. You remember Johnny Jackson? I wrote you about him before. Well, he got in the way of one bullet, nothing serious. He laughed about it, after he finished cussing. It went through his right forearm and caused him to be airlifted out this afternoon. Anyway we lost about 15 men. We got some rein-forcements when they took out Johnny.

Mom, this part concerns Jeannie. I know, she's getting mar-ried to Rick. But I want you to tell her to wait before she gets mar-ried. Tell her that I have something very important to tell her and something that she *has* to see. I'm coming home Saturday. My tour of duty over here ends Friday and I leave Saturday. I should be home by Monday sometime. But I need you to tell Jeannie that I *am* coming home and need to see her *before* the wedding.

Well, it's almost time for me to leave for patrol. We're sup-posed to be patrolling around the province of Quangtri. That's pronounced Kwäng-Trãy. There was some action reported near there yesterday.

There's the first call. I'll write more tomorrow morning when I get back.

Love from your Son,
Lee

That was all to his letter. Jeannie started wondering about it. Lee visited her on Thursday, and he wasn't supposed to be home before Monday. Could he have really been AWOL?

She put aside his letter and started reading the second one. Her heart started with a lurch when she saw who sent the letter.

20 August, 1970
Quangtri, V.N.

Dear Mrs. Burress,

My name is Captain Warren Fox, and the commanding officer of "Company B" of the Army's 7th Division, stationed in the
Quangtri Province. Last night, 19 August, a patrol was sent out
to observe movements of Viet Cong forces.

On the way back to the base this morning, approximately
7:30 A.M. (Viet Nam time) the patrol was ambushed. I regret to
be the person that has to inform you of your son's death.

Jeannie almost fainted when she read that part of the letter.
Slowly she read further.

Your son, Pfc Lee Burress, was in the process of trying to pull
the lieutenant, in charge of the patrol, back under cover when
he was shot.

I assure you, his death was immediate, and he did not suffer any.

The rest of the letter was about transporting him home. "But,
that's crazy," she started. "I saw him at 4:00 that afternoon." And
then she remembered the time difference. She started figuring out
the times, wanting to prove that the letter had to be wrong.

She knew there was nine hours difference between Viet Nam
and California.

"But that means he died around 3:30 that afternoon." She
shook her head not wanting to believe it. And then remembering
some of the things he said brought it to her.

He had only a little time before he had to be back. And he said
he was AWOL "kinda." And the time almost standing still.

It shocked her now. She didn't believe in ghosts, but surely . . .
He couldn't . . .

The only sound then was Jeannie falling to the floor, in faint.

Bill Suff's Stuff

D ay in and day out I read a lot of material by aspiring authors. Whenever I am producing a television show, I continuously read work samples from writers looking to be hired, and many of my friends are writers who ask me to review their "works-in-progress" and then give them notes. It has been my experience that every gas station attendant and his uncle thinks he has a novel or TV episode inside him bursting to get out, and who can blame them? What with the quality of popular writing nowadays—the poor storytelling and the even more pathetic, repetitive stories themselves—today's gas station attendant could well be tomorrow's or even today's John Grisham.

When I first read Bill Suff's stuff, I was surprised. I think perhaps I was expecting Jack Abbott, that murderer/prisoner/writer whom Norman Mailer championed (to his everlasting embarrassment) some years ago. Abbott wrote *In the Belly of the Beast*, a raw, searing, violent look at his violent life, crime, and the prison system. As you may recall, Mailer helped get Abbott out of jail and into posh parties, after which Abbott committed more violent crimes and wound up back in stir. Where he belonged. I think he died a violent death there, or maybe it was in a shoot-out on his way there. Either way, Abbott's gone and I don't care enough about him to look him up in my encyclopedia. Frankly, I'd hate to find that he's listed there. I don't even want to know that Mailer's got an entry.

But, unlike Abbott, what's interesting about Suff's creative stuff is that it's sweet and sad and innocent. Truly innocent. Reality impinges as lost love and death, so it's all about tragedy, but it's not about pain or violence; it's actually about hope and what could have and should have been. It also insists on an afterlife and spirituality that is good and true and immortal, mitigating today's pain with the certainty that, whatever mistakes we make here, eternity will set it right.

From a "writing standpoint", there are three indicia to apply: Has the writer exhibited the craft and talent to communicate that which he intended? Has the writer created an original story or merely mimicked something he's read? Has the writer challenged himself to be special and insightful in a way that justifies all writing as a lasting legacy?

Bill's material hints at being professional on all scales. Trust me, this puts him up in rarefied air—it takes a hundred writers or more before you find one who "gets it". Bill clearly has command of the language and his craft, although he's also still working at improving word choice and sentence structure. While his plot is at once familiar, it's also personal in a way that makes it original. Is this material so moving and important that it deserves to be saved in a time capsule? In context, yes, because it answers questions about him and, like it or not, he has had a tremendous impact on a tremendous number of people's lives—he matters, now and forever. Bill's crimes orphaned three dozen children, including his own (Bill Jr. by Teryl; and Bridgette by second wife, Cheryl, to whom Bill was married during the final years of his rampage—both children taken away by their respective States and placed in permanent foster care). Numerous other people—from cops to lawyers to journalists—lived and breathed Bill Suff for the "best" years of their professional lives. Yes, Bill matters. He also has something to say, and we really ought to listen.

For a moment then, let's play psychiatrist-detective, as I did when Bill's handwritten draft of "Tranquility Garden" arrived in my mail.

As I read the story, the hero tries to convince the heroine to break off her engagement to another man and commit to the hero instead. She declines. She then learns that the hero is dead, and that she'd been communing with his spirit.

Accordingly, I couldn't wait to ask Bill what would have happened had the heroine agreed to commit to the deceased hero. I thought I'd found a murderous hole in his logic. I just couldn't wait for him to tell me that, if the heroine fell in with the ghost, then the heroine would have to be murdered in order to join him.

However, when I posed the question to Bill, he acted like I was the idiot for missing the only obvious and correct answer: "If the heroine chose to commit to the hero, *then he wouldn't have died.* They would have lived happily ever after."

At first this seems a terribly charming solution, but it quickly degenerates into sheer terror. *The heroine killed the hero. She still loved him, but she chose to deny him the living reality of that love.*

"Tranquility Garden" was written while Bill was in jail in Texas, taking writing classes and ultimately earning himself a college degree in sociological services. At the same time, he was writing letters to Teryl's parents and others. Bill's fiction and poetry may have been sweetly tragic, but his letters were clear paeans to his pain: "With Teryl gone, I feel like I have died," he wrote, "I am dead now. I am alive, but I am dead."

This theme plays itself out in Bill's later writings, as you shall see. And, I finally found I had to agree with Donny: after the final betrayals by Teryl, whatever shining vestige of humanity Bill had hung on to throughout his pained childhood and adolescence abruptly flickered out and died. His soul ceased to be. Of course, Teryl was not the cause, merely the final straw, and, had it not been her, it likely would have been someone or something else that proved the definitive betrayal. But the thing is, once he was now soulless, once he was now dead, Bill was immortal. He was dead, but he discovered that nonetheless he went on. "I am alive, but I am dead." Get it? I do. These are the same words I said to myself after the deaths of my mother, brother, and best friend in an auto accident in which I was the driver and sole survivor. My mother had finally worked up the nerve to divorce my father after years of unhappiness, and we were on our way to Vegas for a couple of days to "toast" the occasion. But all had gone awry when a defective radial tire shredded on the interstate. For me, I had to think: Wasn't it some sort of mistake that I'd survived? Was I now living on borrowed time, or was I left here for some higher purpose?

My mother and best friend died the day of the crash, but my brother lingered in a coma for several days. I recall vividly the moment of his death, the doctors shooing me from the room as the monitors flatlined and the charger on the heart paddles whined, readying to fire off a last, futile jolt. Head in hands, the world spinning a web of darkness, I was sitting in a chair in the private nurses' lounge when the doctor came in to tell me what he knew I already knew. He was a young man and he'd sworn days earlier that my brother would make it. Now he said nothing; he just reached out and touched his hand to my shoulder and then withdrew, leaving me alone, and, in that next instant, I wanted to be dead so badly, I actually died. It was an instant that, like time itself, was there and gone and yet lasts for all time. Past, present, and future, all co-existing. I wanted to die, and I think what happened is that my heart skipped a beat, and in that skip I was dead, and I knew it. But then, against all my conscious will, despite the unendurable psychic pain I would have to face, Darwin went ahead and did his thing—my genes, my molecules, my enzymes, all those physical, physiological, biochemical, totally incomprehensible processes that make humans the fittest to survive, all surged through my system and snapped me back to life. I was bungeed back out of a pure black abyss and suddenly found myself alive again. Alive, but dead, angry that I was back; alive, but dead, emotionally blunted; alive, but finding that the chemistry which made me breathe did so by blocking out the pain which had made me want to die, while the price for that freedom from pain proved to be the evisceration of my soul. It would take me many years to track down and barter for the return of that soul, and I cursed Darwin every step of the way. Like Bill Suff, I was a ghost, an amoeba, an ant—I'd been nuked and survived, and I'd had no say in it coming or going.

Of course, I didn't start serial killing. I treaded water for a long time, but I finally found the shore again, rocky though it was. I was alive but dead, and then I came all the way back to life. Unfortunately for Bill (and his victims), once he was dead, he stayed dead—the cumulative total of his past left him no choice, the same as my own past sent me in the opposite direction. And so when Bill kills, it's a reality he's come to accept because life and death are one and the same to him, and his victims are always still alive, always with him. He hasn't killed them, he's simply drawn them into his world. For all eternity. And that's why Bill won't confess—confess to what? *It's not that he's not guilty, it's that there were no crimes.* That's why serial killers routinely whip polygraphs.

Now take a peek at the reproduction of the actual handwritten page from "Tranquility Garden" (see photo insert). The scripting is tiny and orderly—you almost need a magnifying glass to read it. (Bill's later work does require a magnifier—examine his handwriting in his prison logs—see photo insert.) Partly this is a reflection of Bill's orderly, precise mind and obsessiveness and need to manipulate you into working at connecting with him, investing time and effort into making him a part of your life, into making each of you codependent on the other even as he maintains ultimate control; and partly this tiny handwriting is due to the lack of paper given inmates—you've got to learn to cram as much as you can onto each page. But bear in mind that as an inmate you are writing in pencil (you can't have a pen because the metal and plastic parts could be used to pick locks or stab guards or worse), and, to write so small you have to sharpen the pencil point after every couple of words . . . but of course you have no pencil sharpener, so you improvise by notching your fingernail or filing the pencil against the edge of your metal cot-frame.

And then, finally, you have to get inventive to make a thorough presentation: Bill actually changes his handwriting for the "letter" portions of the story. This is not just words on paper, this is graphic art, fully pictorial, telling you so much about the man who created and crafted it even while it manipulates the reader to respond as he wants. "Tranquility Garden" is Bill Suff's story—a story about Bill

Suff and yet not about Bill Suff—note how he first used his own name as the hero, but then erased it and changed it to "Lee," pressing so hard on the lead that it crunched and spread, darker than the other words. And Lee's birthday—August 20—is Bill's birthday, and the last name of Lee's mother is the maiden name of Bill's own mom.

Clearly, in the "fictional" story, Bill wants to be Bill Suff, but yet he cannot be, and he wants you to know all of that, to let him play it both ways. "Hey, I'm not who I say I am!" he screams silently, but is he warning us or flaunting himself? Are we to be terrified or intrigued, or both? Of course, practical necessity dictates that he cannot allow himself to reveal too much of himself without it coming back to haunt him—prosecutors might see this, the parole board might see it, people who sit in judgment might see it, he himself will certainly see it, and, like every writer, he knows he will find something surprising, something he doesn't want to see, so better to distance even himself. At heart, Bill wants to take the witness stand, but he must also preserve his deniability. No matter what, he must survive. No matter what, he will survive. Is that cowardice or cleverness or manifest destiny? Is he playing games or just giving in to evolution? Or is there somehow still some sick hope in this simple soulless hulk that some way, some day, he can find life again, forgive and be forgiven, if only he has enough time?

Alive, but dead. Dead, but alive, and marking time.

And prison is all about marking time—that's what makes prison and death indistinguishable—that's why Bill is so comfortable in prison. He proclaims his innocence as to all counts at all times, but yet he never bangs on the bars of his cell, never cries, always acts the "model" prisoner. Texas let him out for "good behavior" after ten years of a seventy-year sentence. He'd earned his degree, showed—through his writing and drawing—that he could express his emotions in "acceptable" ways, and so he was declared "rehabilitated". He "deserved" another chance. He'd made a "mistake", but he'd "learned" a lesson. He was entitled to "a life". But, of course, Texas didn't understand that Bill Suff was long dead. Death had caged him when he was roaming in our midst, and he'd felt no differently, no worse, when he'd been ware-housed out of our sight. Texas prison time was no punishment, and neither had jail resuscitated him. Freed from the Texas jail, he wasn't about to make himself "a life", he was about to take some.

So, the hero of "Tranquility Garden" is not Bill, but rather his alter ego. Him, but not him. Dead, but alive. And, you, the reader, are now part of Bill's story, part of his reality. Bill Suff knows that you and others like you have gotten a hold of this book. He knows you're interested, maybe you're titillated, maybe you're repulsed, but, however you position it, *you care about him now. For an hour or two tonight while you read these words, Bill Suff matters to you.* To him it's like he waved and smiled and got your attention, offered you something you wanted—you hopped in the van with him and now he's in control of you, and, dead or alive, you're not getting away. Justify it any way you will, you've allowed yourself to become yet another of Bill Suff's victims. I know I am.

Thumbnails

Here are a few words on some of the players in this drama:

Elizabeth Ann Suff Mead is Bill's mom. You call her "Ann". She looks you in the eye, always returns your phone calls, and if some joint says it's "No Smoking", it means "No Ann". In a world without movies, Ann'd be Barbara Stanwyck. Another time, another place, another family, and she'd've been a star. Here, she's hardscrabble. Her favorite expression is: "You'll get over it."

Other than Bill, the Suff Kids are Bob, Don, Ken, Roberta, and stepsisters Deena and Bernice. They're mostly redheads and wiry, and none of 'em ever stops talking. They're like a flock of chicks cheeping and jumping all over themselves when they see you coming with the feed. All the boys have had problems with the law, but: "They'll get over it".

Paul Zellerbach is the Riverside district attorney who prosecuted the case against Bill. Considering all the media attention, he thought it would be his stepping-stone to the big time. What he didn't realize was that when you get handed a case you "can't lose", it's also a case you "can't win". Marcia Clark and Chris Darden made millions by screwing up; Paul Zellerbach got forgotten because he made his job look too easy. Next time he'll remember to heighten the drama. Zellerbach now says that the Suff case opened his eyes—after years of prosecuting hookers, of looking at them as "lost" or "bad" or just plain "criminal", he discovered that they were real people, good people, from good families, and their choice to sell their bodies was born of desperate circumstance. Nonetheless, his office still prosecutes hookers.

Floyd Zagorsky was Bill's first lawyer. Floyd's a public defender, and he was willing to go to any length to defend Bill, who he knew could not get a fair trial in Riverside. Zellerbach got Zagorsky thrown off the case by pointing out the conflict of the public defender representing Bill when that same office had previously represented the now-dead hookers who had previously been tried by Zellerbach for hooking. Got that?

Frank Peasley, Esq., and Randy Driggs, Esq., were the private-sector attorneys appointed by the County to take over Bill's case. Neither man wanted the appointment, but you can't turn down one appointment if you ever expect to get another.

Both men knew that, more than anything else, this case would be about surviving this case. To their credit, as of this writing, both men are still around.

Peasley is a quiet man who always managed to make sure he was gone whenever I came by. The only times I ever saw him were in court. He gives the impression that he believes that if he lowers his eyes and bows his shoulders, then you can't see him looking at you. He keeps his hands jammed in his pockets so they won't get picked. I am told he is actually a very nice man but shy. He's also a damn fine defense lawyer, and maybe that's precisely because he gives nothing away.

Driggs couldn't be more opposite. He's voluble, funny, erudite, got that Florida drawl goin', and he's flamboyant without being showy. Randy knows how to work a room, but he comes across as genuine when he's doing it. In fact, he is genuine; and, like me, he likes Bill. Randy likes a lot of people. When we sat down to talk about this case, he was free with facts and opinions, and he steered me in all the right directions except one. The one thing he told me that was wrong was when he said: "You know, Brian, I'm just sorry that Bill Suff isn't more interesting." I look forward to having lunch, fine wine, and going through this book with Randy once it's published.

Tricia Barnaby was Bill's lead defense investigator. She is not merely the stereotype of the "private dick", she is the caricature. Craggy-faced, with nails in her eyes. Squat, solid, stolid. She can take it, and she can dole it out. One can only imagine what it must have been like being a female private investigator in macho shit-kickin' frontier-town Riverside, but Tricia avoided that problem by being a man. I was shocked to learn that she was once married and had a kid. My sense is that if you were her kid and came to her with "Mom, I gotta tell you something—" she'd cut you off with her own "I already know, and I've got pictures to prove it." You're not her kid, you're a dossier. But I could be wrong. In any event, she was Bill's most stalwart supporter, not so much because she thought he was innocent but because she knew he was getting a raw deal. She may even have had a certain affection for him, and she still writes to him—I know that right now as he sits on Death Row, he is certain that he is in love with her and only recently realized it. Since Bill tends to fall in love only with women who he believes are already in his thrall, this tells you something about the Bill-Tricia dynamic. For that reason, Tricia would never give me the time of day—she was sure I was out to betray Bill.

Bonnie Ashley was, off and on for years, Bill's girlfriend in Riverside. She's blonde and pretty and successful in business and what the hell was she doing with this guy? Bonnie does "personal-ity color charts" that tell her who her friends should be. Bill must've come up the right color. I wonder, was it blood red?

Teryl was Bill's first wife, Cheryl his second, and both were minors when he first dated them. Teryl was on the cutting edge of high style for her time and financial status, Cheryl was a Plain Jane. They both stood by while Bill beat their babies. No doubt he chose these women because he believed they would not know how to fight him. I am the last person to judge people who stay in rela-tionships that have become destructive, because I know firsthand how easy it is to be the supreme apologist for a partner who's gone wrong. Somehow you internalize your partner's guilt and make it all your fault. Unfortunately for themselves and their babies, Teryl and Cheryl never escaped from Bill. They were like prisoners of war—when the Allies showed and threw open the doors to the concentration camps, the survivors were reluctant to walk out. When horror has become your life, you lose all perspective and all hope. You are dead, but alive. Where do you go when there is no place to go?

On our list of players, last precisely because she is not least is Karen Williams, the model-beautiful, African-American paralegal who coordinated the Suff case for Peasley and Driggs. Karen knows more about this case than anybody, and she has it in perspective better than anybody. Somehow she was able to memorize every detail of this case, scan every picture, absorb every horror, and not let it bother her. Home to her husband and child every night, and leave the case behind, yet she was and is the "go to" person for anyone who has any question about anything that happened during all those years before, during, and after the trial. She's amazing, and she saved my bacon many a time not just by answering my questions but by interjecting an "Oh, please!" and then volunteering her opinion as to what was really going on in people's minds and behind the scenes. Karen is simply the most trusted person involved in this whole sordid affair. She's the rock. Her personal network extends to the district attorney, the police department, the witnesses, the victims' families, everyone. And if she vouches for you, you're okay. You need something done? Consider it done. You want to spin out sick theories as to the significance of the mutilations? She's got theories of her own, and they're none too complex. No point in fighting against reality by trying to explain it. Just accept what is. See the whole picture, but live the day one hour at a time. I once asked Karen if she wanted to write a few words for this book, to explain her role or express her feelings about having been a part of this important piece of criminal-justice history. Her response? "Get a life."

CHAPTER 6

Cat and Mouse

My first wife was a schizophrenic. For a long time her doctors tried to define her condition without labeling it—she "exhibited agitated depression", she "expressed bipolar behavior", she "evidenced separation anxiety"—like somehow she wasn't as bad off as she was because what she had didn't have such a fearful name or a certain diagnosis. She just "wasn't acting right", as if her actions did not have a direct, high-speed conduit to a brain that needed some serious rewiring.

Her "condition" stayed secret because I was always home writing and the doctors could palm her off on me for continuous caretaking. Work made me reclusive, and she could hide while I worked. And the doctors could delusionally presume that, so long as she wasn't dropped off on their doorsteps, then she must be reasonably functional. Out of sight, out of mind, out of her mind—it was all okay by them.

The thing was, I didn't see how crazy she was either. It's not just that I was with her so much I had no perspective; it's that her craziness made her focus desperately acute and her conduct effectively manipulative. Crazy though she was, she knew just exactly what to do and how to do it in order to cover things up for the longest time. "Crazy like a fox" is no fiction. My ex knew that only she was hearing those voices in her head, and she knew it was not wise to let anyone else listen in. No no no. Even when she tried to step out of a moving car at sixty miles an hour, she convinced everybody it was because they'd overmedicated her, not because God had whispered

"Jump!" in her ear. As a result, the doctors cut back on her medication, if you can imagine.

I found out really how bad things had been for her and for me, in retrospect, after she was institutionalized and I looked around at the smoldering detritus of our so-called "life together". But, the day I first knew that things had gone too far was the day I found myself, fully dressed, locked in the shower of the downstairs bathroom, eating two Taco Bell "Taco Bell Grandes" standing up, hiding, escaping from my ex as she pawed and knocked at the door, calling for me. For minutes and hours and days and weeks she had paced into wherever I was, called my name, and then when I'd looked up expectantly, she'd turn and walk out, only to return a moment later and repeat the process. Endlessly. She'd made it impossible for me to work, to watch TV, to eat, to sleep, to live. But it was not until I stood there eating those tacos in the shower that it occurred to me that, if the authorities came into my house at that moment, they would think I was the crazy one. In fact, I was. But, as with the moment of my brother's death, my survival instinct suddenly took hold and snapped me out of it. That was the last time I ate tacos in the shower. It was also the last day I lived under the same roof as my first wife.

I don't know that Bill Suff ever had such a moment, such an opportunity, such a bona fide crossroads. As I said before, I don't much believe you have much choice in these things. Some people make it out of the wilderness okay, and others don't, and the seeds for return and redemption are sown long before you ever get lost. I suspect that the day Bill killed Dijianet was the day he needed to tell Teryl that he'd had it with her betrayals and he needed her to get lost. Instead, he wound up partnered with her at trial. He couldn't let go, and he still hasn't. He hangs on to everyone, dead or alive. You run away, but he's still there, sitting in the backseat, grinning at you in the rearview mirror.

Of course, arrogantly, I believed that my experience with my first wife had prepared me sufficiently for what would be my relationship with Bill Suff, convicted serial killer. I figured I could play cat and mouse with him, get him to reveal things to me that he wasn't even willing to admit to himself. I figured I could see his manipulations coming, and I could either pretend to give in to them or else counter them, depending on my strategy of the day. It didn't even bother me—although I was well aware—that I was objectifying Bill and about to treat him with the same detachment he'd had for his victims. Bill was a case study, not a human being— I didn't need to care whether he lived or died, so long as he lasted long enough to supply material for this book. He was commerce, man—nothing more.

And Donny agreed. Once I'd sold the book on the basis of the pitch—"lawyer/writer plays cat and mouse with killer/writer"— Donny's concern for content, for positive, revisionist family history, became a simple issue of "When do I get paid?" Suddenly, as far as his family was concerned, Bill "owed them", and this book was the first installment of the payback. Donny was the only one in touch with Bill at that point—he swore he'd make Bill sign the requisite contracts, by which Donny would assume all of Bill's rights and income and become owner of Bill's writings. Then the publisher and I would make our deal with Donny.

But, until that happened, until all the documents were signed and initialed, Donny insisted he wouldn't let me speak with Bill.

The problem was, once the contracts were slipped to Bill inside the jail, he balked. And Donny panicked—the miniseries was fading away. So, late one night in August of 1995, my phone rang.

"Collect call from . . ." said the chipper female monotone recording, and then a sing-song male voice, curiously spoken on a breath intake rather than exhalation, as if he was taking the words back rather than giving them up: "Bill Suff," said the man's voice.

At once I decided on a two-pronged strategy. First, as I saw it, "model prisoner" and "good son" Bill was responsive to authority. By the same token, his acquiescence in the face of superior firepower was dishonest. I knew that if I lorded over him, he might well say what I needed him to say, but I couldn't trust it. You can't trust anyone you put in a position of subservience. Bill's only honest

candor came when he had his hands around some girl's throat—
that was the real deal. However, if I backed off and didn't have
power over Bill in our interactions, he'd just take me for a ride and
get grandiose with his lies. Of course, you're probably wondering
how this could even be an issue—I mean *he* was the one in jail,
freshly convicted of a dozen homicides, and *I* was a free man who
could hang up on him and change my phone number and disappear
from his life if I wanted, so, by definition, didn't I unavoidably have
the upper hand?

What you have to understand is that Bill lives in a completely
egocentric, childlike world. Everything revolves around him, just as
any and every child thinks it does. His emotional growth stopped
cold somewhere in childhood, and he's still there. Everything that
has ever happened or will happen is at once his fault or his credit.
He is responsible for the breakup of his parents' marriage; he is
responsible for Teryl's betrayals. As a child, when he cried, his mom
and dad used to come running. So, when Dad ran out the door and
all the way to Michigan, sans Bill, it must've been because Bill had
proven himself an unworthy son. And Teryl had loved him and
trothed herself to him and gone away with him and craved salvation
from him even as she cared for him in sexual ways that no other
woman ever had, all because he must have been doing something
right. So, when Teryl up and cheated on him—for love or money—
it was because he hadn't been man enough for her. It couldn't have
been because she was a low-life, white trash whore whose own ability to love had been gutted by an incestuous stepfather. She had to
be a princess because Bill knew damn well he was a knight in shining armor who wouldn't have settled for a lesser mortal. And yet now
the suit was rusty and the lance was limp and the princess was on the
prowl and it was all Bill's doing—everything in Bill's world just had
to be Bill's doing, one way or the other. And so as everything he
wanted to hold on to began to float away from him and out into
space, as if the gravity had suddenly been turned off, his world no
longer spinning certainly on axis, of course Bill had to desperately,
voraciously seize control—control over life and death itself.

Not to be overly Freudian, but we're all locked into childhood impasses in various ways. I will always remember my father, driving me from the hospital where my brother was comatose, on our way to my mother's funeral, at a moment when I finally expected this World War II Silver Star hero to be crying, only to find that he was angry and self-righteous instead: "When your brother gets out of the hospital," he said, pounding on the steering wheel, staring straight ahead, refusing to turn toward me, "things are going to be different. *I'm in charge now!*" In the same breath, he was blaming my mother for our tragedy and himself for allowing her to put us in harm's way, as if he could have prevented that tire from blowing at high speed. He couldn't accept that his life had just been turned upside down by pure accident. To him, his failures as a husband and father were what drove my mother, my brother, my best friend, and myself to be on the road that fateful day without him. And, of course, she'd foolishly had faith in me as a driver, whereas he never would have. All my poor father could think of were all the times he didn't somehow find a way to make peace with my mother, to make her happy, to make her love and respect him for all time. He desperately wanted control, and now, absurdly, in his grief, he was asserting it over someone too dead to notice. This from a man who had what can only be classified as a "normal" childhood under the auspices of loving parents. Apparently "normal" includes plenty of unresolved "stuff". Apparently good intentions and love are not enough to save any parent from a kid's ultimately critical regard.

But, again, it's one thing to have unresolved "stuff" that makes your own life less than wonderfully happy, and quite another to be landlocked in a way that makes you into a serial killer. The stress of my mother's and brother's deaths brought my father's guilts and neuroses to the fore, and, I think, made him own up to things once the grieving was behind him sometime later. It's been many many years since "the accident", but I recently asked him if I could see the legal files which contained the various investigative reports as to the facts of the matter. My father told me that he'd thrown out the files some months ago, after an earthquake collapsed the shelf that contained them, but then he blurted out: "But why would you want to see them? *It wasn't your fault.*" He had apparently found a way to forgive himself, and me along with it. In that respect, I fear he's come farther along than me.

In the meantime, Bill Suff continues along as the most guilt-ridden "innocent" man in history. He insists he's never ever been guilty of anything, but you can feel the weight of the world—*his world*—on his shoulders. And you can read it in his writing. He's positively imploded, like a star collapsed into itself, a black hole. Now nothing can escape him, not even light—no wonder he can't find himself when he looks—he's infinite mass, too solid to be visible, defined only by his pull on the heavenly bodies that try to slip by. And, when he was in jail in Riverside for all those years before and during his trial, the authorities there only added fuel to his nuclear fire. They actually expanded the domain over which he rules.

When he was arrested, Bill was first imprisoned in Riverside's "old" jail while the new one was in the final stage of construction. The jailers were naturally worried about having this monster in their midst. *The Silence of the Lambs* was in theaters at the time, and I'm sure they thought they had their own homegrown Hannibal Lecter in custody. No one in Riverside really knew how to contain Bill, or rather their image of Bill. This was a guy who had eluded capture for years. This was a guy accused of killing more than a dozen women in this county alone, and there were other cases awaiting indictments in other counties. So penal anxiety ran rampant. While in jail, should Bill be shackled all the time? Should he be allowed to mix with other prisoners? Would he try to escape? Would he try to kill himself? Or would someone try to kill him, thinking it would be a commendable and noteworthy thing to do or else at least serve as some revenge for victims' families who had ties to both prisoners and jailers in this relatively small community?

The conclusion was to prep the "new" jail specially to house Bill Suff.

Now, I don't know if you've ever visited a jailhouse, but the fearsome claustrophobia you feel is as much the result of the tight quarters as the continuous, unnerving, unholy din of hollering, jabbering, and just plain noise that prisoners make, calling to each other from one cell to the next, all day long, a million conversations and complaints trumpeted all at once, interrupted by the occasional blast of orders from the guards over the public address system or the resonating clangs of doors opening and closing and the thud of footsteps as guards make their rounds. To a man, prisoners will tell you that the noise is the worst part of prison life. You can't sleep, you can't rest, you can't think, and, even if you're deaf, your body vibrates from the shock waves.

However, in an amazing demonstration of blind codependence, claiming that they were doing it to make the jail guards' jobs easier, the Riverside County authorities quickly handed Bill a "cell" that was really an insulated, oh-so-quiet, private, walled room where he could be free from the noise, the taunts, and the prying eyes of both inmates and guards alike, and, in that room, that "apartment", Bill was given both a color television set and a phone which he could use at all hours of the day and night. For his various allergies, aches and pains, and other real and exaggerated ailments, Bill had continuous access to the infirmary and the staff doctor, or else the nurse would bring him his pills in his room. This accused serial killer—arguably the worst criminal the county had ever encountered—had free room, free board, free medical care, free phone, and free TV. He probably could have gotten HBO if he'd asked. In all his life, he'd never had it so good.

And, of course, it went to his head. Now he knew how important he was. Now he knew that he'd worried needlessly all those years about being caught. He was a bigger deal in prison than he was in the outside world, and it only confirmed his egocentric view of things. Now, when people wanted to see him—and there were plenty who did—they had to come to him. This was his turf—he was the king on his throne—*he* decided who *he* would tune in or tune out, and, insomniac that he is, he could amuse himself till all hours, reading, writing, making phone calls.

So I knew that, when I would first be in contact with Bill, his view would clearly be that I needed him more than he needed me. And that meant I needed to find an opening to prove him wrong, otherwise I would just be a passing diversion for him. I needed to segue from diversion to lifeline in his mind if I was going to get anywhere with him.

The second prong of my strategy that first night I spoke with Bill was to connect with him in a way that was unfamiliar to him. I needed to throw him off his stride, yet keep him intrigued. I knew that he'd dummied up on his lawyers and everyone else who'd tried to get close to him. A lot of words came out of Bill—spoken and written—but none of them ever amounted to much in terms of revealing his true emotions.

"Wait'll you meet Bill—he's really something," Randy Driggs, Bill's codefense lawyer, had told me in his disarming drawl. "He just chats and rolls along like none of this is happening."

At trial, Bill's lawyers couldn't even tell if he was listening to the testimony, no matter that lethal injection was the prosecutor's goal. Sometimes Bill'd surprise Driggs and Peasley by passing them a written note, but usually it had nothing to do with what was going on at the time, and all too often it contained some fiction that he'd decided to float—like back in Texas when he suggested the CIA conspiracy. "It's not that you'd call him uncooperative," said Driggs. "He went happily to all the doctors and psychologists and everybody else we asked him to see, and he couldn't get enough of all our meetings and trial preparation, but he was non-responsive in that, no matter what issue was hanging fire that day, he'd just smile and say he was innocent and talk about the cookbook he was writing. He didn't give us any help; we basically prepared this defense in a vacuum."

So, I knew Bill was going to be noncommunicative as to anything that mattered, and I also knew that, when he did communicate, his goal was not communication. Rather, it was control.

See, when Bill was first arrested and stuck in the "old" jail, the authorities decided to bunk him with Riverside's other notorious accused, Jim Bland, who had kidnapped a young girl, taken her to the shack he'd prepared for the purpose, and then methodically raped, tortured, and mutilated her before finally granting her release unto death. Or maybe she'd actually died before he'd finished everything he had planned for her—we'll never know.

I was aware that Jim and Bill had become fast friends, and Bill delighted in telling people so he could watch them cringe. In fact, I was sure that most of the time when Bill said something—anything—it was to see how his listener would react. You can tell by his writing—both its content and presentation—that, at all times, he considers audience reaction. He's always experimenting, trying to find buttons he can push, trying to evoke a response. All writers do this, but Bill does it for a more sinister purpose. He's not trying to connect, he's trying to gain control. It's a test—*if you react at all, you lose*—and he keeps a scoresheet so he knows how best to get to you the next time. However, it occurred to me that if I could keep myself from reacting to his lead, but yet otherwise proactively present myself with emotional honesty and candor, then I could legitimately gain his trust. Or, at the very least, maybe he would find me to be a worthy opponent who would take a while to conquer. I correctly suspected that this was a man with whom no one ever dealt honestly and emotionally, going back to his youth. I might well pique his interest by treating the poor bastard the way he and every human being ought to be treated, even though he was more certain than ever that, due to his crimes, no one would dare treat him that way. He'd become a self-fulfilling prophecy, doing bad acts that perpetuated the very pain that crippled him. I hoped that if he couldn't read my reactions or if they threw him for a loop, then, for one of the first times in his life, he might well inadvertently project his own feelings outside of his killing fields.

Anyway, that was my pop psychology approach. What the hell, I couldn't do any worse than all the lawyers, doctors, and psychologists who'd gotten nowhere with him over the years.

"Press 1 to accept the charges, or 2 to say no," said the recording on the phone.

I took a deep breath, sat up in my chair, felt my heart pound, and pressed 1 on the keypad. A click, and: "William, nice to meet you," I said.

"William? That's my father, not me. Call me Bill," he said. He has a sort of jolly chortle to his voice even when he's trying to be serious, but I could tell that this time he was trying to break the ice and yet remain on guard.

The line gave a couple of odd, ominous clicks. Originally voluble, now Bill got real quiet. I heard him draw a breath to say something, but I cut him off before he could—I wanted to show Bill that, even though I meant business, I was going to be his protector first, and that he and I had a unity of interest in that intent.

"Hold on a minute, Bill, I want to give a notice here. To anyone who's listening in on this line, my name is Brian Lane and I'm an attorney licensed to practice in the State of California. Bill Suff is my client, and anything we say to each other during this phone conversation is privileged and confidential. More to the point, if you are listening, you shouldn't be—because you are violating Mr. Suff's rights *and you may very well be responsible for getting his convictions overturned.*" There was a pause, silence, and then suddenly the loud clunk-click of some eavesdropper disconnecting. Where there had been some static before, now the line was clean.

Bill laughed. "I was just about to warn you about that. But that's the first time they ever hung up."

I laughed too. A moment later I heard my office door slam, followed by the bedroom door just across the hallway. Apparently my wife didn't much appreciate that I was having a laugh with a serial killer after midnight.

"They're not allowed to listen in on you, Bill—that's ridiculous," I said.

"There's a lot of things they do here that they're not supposed to," said Bill. "Didn't you follow my trial?"

"I have to admit, I got hooked on O.J. and you stopped making the papers here in L.A. I remember when you got arrested, and there was never any question you did it, and then I heard you were convicted, and here we are," I said.

"Yeah, here we are," he said.

"Look, Bill, before we get into all that, I want you to know that the reason I want to do this book is because I admire your writing and I think we can talk writer to writer. I read 'Tranquility Garden' and some of your other stuff, and you're damn good. Your writing tells me that there's a side to you—a complexity—that never came out at trial. It tells me that, no matter what the prosecutor and the jury say, and no matter what crimes you've committed, you are a thinking, feeling human being that we should all take the time to get to know. I also think that if you and I talk about your writing, you're going to discover things in it about yourself that even you haven't recognized before. At least that's the way my own writing is for me."

"You liked my stories, huh?"

"I'm not gonna lie to you and tell you they're brilliant—I am going to tell you they are professional and they show promise and they made me want to see more, and that's not something I say to very many writers. I get a real sense that you work hard at your craft and you take on new storytelling challenges with each new piece, and that tells me you have the talent and the heart of a true writer. Anybody can write, but not very many people are really writers. And clearly you had to teach yourself to write, so you're not just mimicking a bunch of lessons people get in school."

"Thanks, I really do care about what I write." He seemed genuinely humbled, and humility is definitely not one of Bill Suff's usual personas.

We then proceeded to discuss and analyze "Tranquility Garden"—it was written when Bill was in jail in Texas, and it was his first short story, although he'd dabbled with poetry and incomplete writings when he'd been in high school. "Tranquility Garden" represented the first time Bill really believed he had the right to write, the right to memorialize some part of himself and expect others to pay it mind.

And, I have to tell you, all this discussion with Bill was embarrassingly normal and professional—I could have been talking to any of my non-murdering writer pals except for Bill's almost endearing trait of occasionally mispronouncing some sophisticated word. It's not that he uses the word incorrectly, it's that he says it wrong. His vocabulary is vast and growing, but I realized that he's picked it all up by reading rather than through conversation, so he's simply never heard many of these words spoken. There's never been anyone in his life intelligent or erudite enough to trade bon mots with him, and I can only imagine how he'd pronounce "erudite" or "bon mots".

During our chat, Bill even freely admitted that "Tranquility Garden" was about him, about his lost love. But, when I brought up the letters he'd sent to Teryl's parents—"I am dead now. I am alive, but I am dead."—he swore he didn't remember writing them. He wasn't denying their sentiment—he actually paused to think about it and then agreed that this was probably an accurate assessment of his emotional state back at that time, but it perplexed him that he couldn't remember having expressed it to anybody, let alone written it down and mailed it off. In any event, he insisted that he didn't feel "alive but dead" now, he simply felt alive and misunderstood. Then he quickly and nervously changed the topic to his favorite reading and his latest writings. Science fiction, fantasy, swords and sorcerers—he was a huge fan of the "Pern" fantasy books written by Anne McCaffrey, and he was just beginning to write just such a fantasy book based on a dream he'd had.

He explained that, like me, he stayed up late writing every night, and he suffered from insomnia, so he often had waking dreams. I told him that waking dreams were what writing is all about. He then went on to detail the "Pern" stories for me, since I was unfamiliar with them—he would later give me his copy of *The Complete Guide to Pern* for my edification. He's always been insistent that these sorts of dreams and fantasy worlds are crucial to him and should be crucial to my understanding of him, but I have to say that I don't believe him. While I do firmly believe that he fantasizes constantly, that a barren pockmark on a desert map could be a lush "Tranquility Garden" or a frothing cove at the beach could be a "Temple of Doom", I find Bill's formalization of fantasy worlds to be his least responsive writing. As you will see in "A Whisper From the Dark", his fantasy/adventure story, he's cribbing rather than giving. When he admits to fantasy, it's usually someone else's, some other writer's that he believes will be acceptable to his readers without really revealing anything deep about himself even though he is always ostensibly the protagonist/hero and even though that character always has a stated history drawn on Bill's own. His admitted fantasies are very artificial, too perfectly constructed, obviously manipulative, designed to help the next jury believe that if the evidence points to his guilt, then maybe he should be excused because he's insane. Of course, up until his conviction, Bill wouldn't even admit to the possibility of insanity. Like Don, he was strident in espousing his perfect mental health. But now, with a death sentence hanging over him, Bill's open to other defense strategies. Maybe. And, if he's not, wouldn't you have to call him insane? Wouldn't it be insane not to do anything and everything to save yourself from lethal injection?

The fact is that, as a matter of law, Bill Suff is insane, but not necessarily in a way that will get him off Death Row. He does know the difference between right and wrong, and he knows damn well what he's doing when he does it. It's just that there is absolutely no way in this or any world that he can stop himself. We will delve more into this later, but suffice it to say that Bill's terror is feeling that he's out of control, and so he kills to convince himself that he's in control, even as the very act of killing is proof positive of his lack of control. This is the orbit of horror which Bill's world circumscribes. Maybe I feel I can see this because I used to watch my schizophrenic ex-wife walk over to the afghan on our bed, tug it even, turn around, then step back to it and tug it even again, and then repeat the process endlessly until I yelled at her and frightened her only momentarily into stopping it because it was making me crazy. "I'm sorry," she would whimper, voice hollow and dry, eyes wide and unfocused, all pupil and no identity, making me feel sad and guilty beyond belief, "but I just have to do this," she'd say.

And then she would edge up to the afghan and do it again and again and again and again. It was the only way she could impose order on her chaotic universe, maybe hoping that she could silence the voices in her head by abiding rather than fighting them, or maybe the voices themselves were fictions that survival chemicals and neurotransmitters conjured in order to make sense of the senseless, irresistible impulses.

And where I come down is in believing that, while there are truly evil people in this world, the insane are by and large good people who, when they commit evil deeds, should be taken out of circulation to prevent further harm to the innocent, but should not be put to death. In a confined world, the insane have a chance at consistent productivity, periodic lucidity, and final atonement. I am not going to tell you that Bill Suff isn't evil, but I am certain that he is not going to kill or even threaten anyone at anytime in prison. And, regardless of him, we should not diminish ourselves by the delusion that we have the right to determine life and death even as we condemn others for exercising that same prerogative.

The "Pern" discussion with Bill led to anecdotes about my writing for *Star Trek: The Next Generation* and for *M.A.N.T.I.S.*, as well as other science fiction scripts and stories, although I don't read much sci-fi and haven't read any fantasy since a collegiate summer addiction to H. P. Lovecraft long ago. I explained to Bill that with science fiction and fantasy it's too easy to get caught up in the extrapolation, the "what if" sizzle, even as you distance yourself at warp speed from the emotional chords, the meat and potatoes, that bring real power and connection to storytelling. As my friend Gene Roddenberry had lectured me before he hired me, "Star Trek" is not science fiction—the stories are "people stories", timeless and real, which could be placed in any universe. As fans of the series know, Gene had created *Star Trek* as "*Wagon Train* in space", not some high-tech, whiz-bang hardware store.

Meanwhile, Bill was suddenly on cloud nine now that he knew somebody who'd had Gene Roddenberry at his last wedding. Bill was like a little kid, barely able to contain his excitement, wanting to know more, wanting to make sure I knew that he'd be watching the reruns to look for my episodes.

I had to laugh. I'd wanted to become Bill's hero in order to have power over him, but I'd figured that would be because he'd view me as a lawyer and writer who could champion his cause in the public forum—instead, it was because I could tell him "inside" stories about *Star Trek*.

Now that I finally had Bill's attention, I used *Star Trek* to turn our conversation to the real matter at hand: serial murder.

"'Elementary, Dear Data'—you remember that episode, Bill? That was mine. Data plays Sherlock Holmes on the holodeck, only he makes the mistake of ordering the computer to create an opponent who can defeat him. So the computer comes up with a Professor Moriarty that has real consciousness. A hologram that is more human than Data, the android. That's how you defeat Data's perfect capacity for deduction, not by programming but by emotion, not by logic but by the illogic that defines us as human beings. What we're about is the fact that we do things we shouldn't do, things that make no sense, things that are against our own self-interest. So this Moriarty believes he's real, knows he's real, and that belief in himself allows him to take over the Enterprise, to cross from the holodeck and into the real world." I took a breath and smiled to myself, and then: "Where he's willing to kill in order to become truly alive."

"I haven't seen that episode," said Bill Suff.

That was it. After all the in-depth talk which had come before, this was his only comment on an issue which had to have been, at least in part, a mirror of himself. Randy Driggs and Karen Williams had warned me—it's not like Bill would arm his phasers and fire back, it's just that the things which should have mattered most bounced off his deflector shields and out into space. My fear was that now he'd cloak and I'd lose sight of him altogether.

"Listen, Bill," I said, "I guess we should talk about the murders for a minute before we hang up tonight. I want you to know I'm not concerned with your guilt or innocence, but I accept the reality of your conviction and I have to write about you on that basis. However, as I get into this, the lawyer in me will carefully examine whether you had a fair trial and whether you have any issues for appeal. And I have to tell you I have a general queasiness about the way any serial killing case is tried—it seems to me inherently unfair to lump together a whole bunch of cases where you couldn't get a conviction in any one by itself, and then you wind up getting a conviction because the jury has all those dozen or more dead girls staring at them. I don't know of any serial killing trial that didn't end in conviction, do you?"

"I was tried and convicted in the press at the time I was arrested," Bill said, "and no one points out that since I've been in jail the prostitute killings have continued."

In fact, the prostitute killings had not continued, but in an honest relationship, you take a person at his word and you simultaneously demand that he take you at yours, even if you're contradicting him. That is to say, you don't argue; instead you try to find an explanation by which both of you can be right. I did an end around in response to Bill's statement.

"Didn't your defense lawyers try to bring that out at trial?" I asked.

"No one wants to hear it. No one wants to admit they got the wrong man. It wasn't that they conspired against me out of some personal dislike for me in particular. It's just that there came a time when they had to ease the public's mind by telling them that the killings were over and they could relax because they'd arrested the guilty party. So, of course, then they're not going to let on that the killings keep happening."

"Bill, unfortunately, prostitutes get killed all the time. In every city in every country. And it's always going to be hard to trace the killer," I said, "because something like ninety percent of the murders in the world are committed by people who are close to the victims— husbands, wives, friends, business partners—while hookers get killed by people just passing through who have no motive personal to the victim and therefore leave no evidentiary trail that makes sense. That's the statistic that keeps getting twisted around in the O.J. trial—while it's true that most abusive husbands don't actually kill their wives, it's about a hundred percent certain that when you find a murdered wife who's been previously and recently abused, her husband did the murder."

The O.J. defense was at the time presenting its case, and it seemed to me that their arguments were a virtual denial that Nicole had been killed at all. In the face of overwhelming evidence as to O.J.'s guilt and no straw man they could offer up as an alternative killer, the defense was attacking the LAPD for sloppy workmanship even though the results themselves were unassailable. "Garbage in, garbage out" only makes sense when you get inconclusive or contradictory results. However, when every result shouts "O.J.", then clearly there was no "garbage in"—the work had not been so sloppy as to have impacted the integrity of the evidence. And, as to the theory that the LAPD planted evidence according to some sort of *ad hoc* conspiracy that rivaled D day in its complexity and timing, how could such a "sloppy" police force have possibly pulled it off?

I ran through this analysis with Bill, thinking that he would be more forthcoming about someone else's crimes, but that anything he said would give insight into his own. As it turned out, he was disinterested in anyone else's crimes—he quickly brought the spotlight back on him.

"I had O.J.'s expert witnesses, you know," said Bill Suff. "Dr. Gerdes, the DNA man, he said I couldn't have done it, that one out of every five people in the world had the same characteristics."

There was virtually no biological evidence in Bill's case. Semen in a condom found in trash "near" a body by a dumpster. Mixed semen from multiple "donors" found in another victim. A hair here and there, but no such evidence anywhere in most of the cases. Results that were at best "maybes" and at worst could have fingered any number of alternative suspects. Bill was right—you couldn't convict anybody on that evidence. But, then again, he'd been convicted twelve times over. Somehow Dr. Gerdes and the other "experts" who were so incredibly credible for O.J. in Los Angeles lost all their persuasiveness after a two-hour drive down the freeway to Riverside. And, heck, there would have been a thirteenth conviction pinned on Bill Suff in Riverside were it not for one momentarily abashed and rational juror who hung that one last case at eleven to one for conviction—seems that while the cops watched, automatic sprinklers went off at the body dumpsite and every bit of evidence was washed away. *No evidence, and still eleven jurors voted to convict.*

"Bill, let's be fair here—forget the biological evidence—if you were on the jury and heard all the other evidence against you, wouldn't you vote to convict on at least a couple of the counts?"

He stopped to give this some thought, and then came back calmly and rationally: "Yes, I'd have to say that I would."

"Okay, having said that, let's look at the evidence that's most damning."

"Zellerbach said the last murder took place around noon—and I have an alibi for that time: my wife Cheryl testified that I was home in bed with her all morning until about one-thirty in the afternoon."

"But Bill, you and I both know that that murder took place the night before, and you admitted you were at the scene."

"But the jury didn't hear any of that. All they heard was Zellerbach saying the murder was at noon while Cheryl said I was home with her. So the jury believed Zellerbach rather than Cheryl. That's what I'm trying to tell you—the jury already believed I was guilty—it didn't matter what my defense was—the media had already tried and convicted me."

"Bill, the jury didn't believe Cheryl and your alibi because your tire tracks were all over the murder scene. The jury knew you were there—whatever time it happened—and trying to alibi it away only made you and your defense unbelievable."

Suddenly, the lawyer in me began to get fired up. With all due respect to Bill's lawyers, Peasley should never have proffered the alibi. The tire evidence was the strongest evidence in the case. It went like this: (1) For many of the murders, Bill drove his van. (2) Bill drove off-road a lot. Why? Because by day he'd hunt for potential body dumpsites that suited his fancy and fantasies, and then by night he'd go dump the bodies there. (3) Driving off-road caused Bill to blow tires fairly frequently. (4) Whenever Bill went to replace a tire, he'd go for the best deal, ultimately leading to four mismatched tires being on the van as of the time of the last murder. (5) Zellerbach adroitly produced tire tracks and Bill's tire purchase receipts so that with each progressive murder you could find the exact combination of tracks from old and new tires which matched what would have then been on the van, differing from previous tracks by the addition of whichever new tire had been purchased since the previous murder.

By the time of the last murder, Bill might as well have signed his name in those damn tire tracks.

Admittedly, this is "only" circumstantial evidence, but circumstances have to be pretty queer for a guy's van to keep showing up without him at scene after scene of sexual murder.

And then there were also shoe prints which came from shoes like the ones Bill owned—two different pairs of them—along with fibers from a sleeping bag like the torn one in Bill's van.

A bloody knife in the van, and ID and personal possessions of the victims found in Bill's apartment, workplace, and van, rounded out the physical evidence.

Of course, all this was nothing compared to what they had on O.J., and he's phoning for tomorrow's tee time right about now, while Bill's sitting on Death Row, insisting that the knife and the victims' possessions were planted by police determined to cement their case.

In fact, Bill's quite right in pointing out that the blood on the knife proved nothing, and much of the other evidence didn't "turn up" until second or third searches of places previously searched by police. It would have been easy for a "determined" cop to dip into the victims' effects, taking items from the victims' homes, only to then "find" them at Bill's; and I would be remiss were I not to mention that the lead cop on the case—the cop who arrested Bill and interrogated Bill in violation of his rights, denying him legal counsel even when he demanded it—Detective Keers was not long thereafter fired from the police force and charged with receiving stolen property in another matter.

Ahem.

But my belief, as I told Bill in our first conversation, is that the circumstantial evidence against him was weak to nonexistent in any one of the murders with which he was charged, taking on a cumulative weight only when all the cases were tried together; yet reasonable doubt always hovers in the wings of a circumstantial evidence case, which is why the cops dragged in Rhonda Jetmore.

Rhonda Jetmore was the linchpin of the prosecution's case. She was the one and only person who could point her finger at Bill Suff and say: "He did it—he tried to kill me, but I'm the one who got away." The basis of this testimony was her claim that, in 1989, she had been hooking to feed a hard-core drug habit, had been flagged down by Bill Suff, taken to a boarded-up old abandoned building where she plied her trade, and had barely escaped with her life by fighting him off when he had suddenly turned on her and tried to strangle her to death. She even remembered his big BILL belt buckle.

However—and it's a monumental "however"—after the alleged attack she left town, gave up hooking, finally gave up drugs, took up food, and put on about three hundred pounds, and only came back to testify after the cops tracked her down and showed her a pointedly suggestive photo lineup which included a current photo of Bill Suff that looked little like the man who'd supposedly attacked her all those years before. Her descriptions of Bill kept changing until they finally matched his present appearance and she took the witness stand, but her description of the BILL belt buckle was always wrong. You've heard of political assassin Dan White's "twinkie defense"? I like to think of Rhonda Jetmore as "the twinkie *offense*"—I think the cops and the prosecutor knew the way to her rather stout heart, and I think they all knew that, without a positive ID of Bill, he would walk.

Sorry to be so cynical, because as you know I am not maintaining Bill's innocence, I'm just telling you—as I told him in our first conversation—I don't much like the way in which he got convicted.

Bill greedily agreed with me, embellishing my points as we chatted, but what he never did was simply explain his innocence. He didn't even try, and that really bothered me. All he did was try to argue away prosecution evidence by undercutting its weight or alleging conspiracy. Then again, maybe I'm asking too much. Maybe I can't really put myself in the place of an innocent man unjustly accused. How dare I expect him to act one way or the other. Right? It's just that I think I would be angry and determined to prove my innocence rather than just counter the prosecution's arguments as to my guilt. It would not be enough to be acquitted; I would want to be declared innocent so that I could truly have my life back, without the whispers and funny looks and "Sorry, we're closed" signs swiftly turned to my face. If I were innocent, I would want the world to know it. I would stop at nothing to prove just how far away I was from any of these murders. And, the fact would be that the multiple cases would offer me more opportunity than ever to prove innocence—that's the double-edged sword of trying serial murder in one fell swoop—you can wind up convicted even if you've been clever enough not to leave enough clues at any one crime, and yet if you can legitimately alibi just one of the crimes, the whole pyramid of indictment comes crumbling down.

Indeed, defense would be easy . . . if you were innocent.

But Bill has yet to come up with even one genuine alibi for any of the thirteen murders with which he was formally charged, let alone the others informally hung on him.

And when you call him on it, he flies straight into absurdity without passing "go": "I have these close friends, the Schartons," he said. "They live in Elsinore. Anyway, Florence—that's Florence Scharton—she heard from a friend who overheard some cops talking about how the city's prostitution problem was getting better because every time one prostitute was murdered, then a lot of the others would leave town. 'Just like we planned it,' is what one cop said. And Florence said there's no question the cops themselves are killing the prostitutes in order to get rid of them."

Now I didn't want to burst Bill's bubble, but this was nuts. I decided on a literary response. "Bill, you know sometimes when we're trying to come up with clever mystery plots, we run into 'the vault door problem' without knowing it. The way that works, say you're writing a story about guys who want to break into a bank, so you plan a wonderfully elaborate, high-tech scheme which has them tunneling under the street and into the vault during broad daylight. You know, they pretend to be a construction crew, and they shut down the street and use these amazing lasers and robots and stuff. Very clever."

"Yeah? So what's the problem?"

"The problem is the vault door is always open during business hours, so all the robbers had to do was walk in the front door and point their guns. You understand what I'm saying? Why on earth would cops murder hookers in the hope that it would drive the rest out of town? Why wouldn't the cops just bust them and then dump them outside the city limits as the terms of a mass plea bargain? If you want to clean up prostitution, all you gotta do is do it, and you make a stronger case being up-front and very public about it. Let the media ride along with their video cameras, and the johns'll stop hiring the hookers. In every city where they publish the names of johns arrested with hookers, the business dries up. Fast. Trust me—you got a 'vault door problem' with your Elsinore theory."

The wind came out of Bill Suff's sails, and he was audibly pissed, which he shows by forcibly evening his tone—never up and angry, tight-lipped instead. "Easy for you to say—you're not in jail," he said, and I thought that was a very fair and pointed statement.

But I was drained—it was two-thirty in the morning, and I'd worked at being vigilant and methodical, albeit candid and honest, for far too long as our conversation had progressed—so now I opened my mouth and proceeded to put my foot square in it, all the way down the gullet. You just never know when to say when, I guess. "Bill," I said, "you're well-read and you're creative, and the way you're going to save yourself is by making use of those attributes. Since it's your life on the line, you know this case better than anybody, better than all the lawyers and all the reporters and all the victims' families. So, you tell me, if you're not the killer, then what kind of a person is he? What's your profile of him, taking into account all the evidence? Who is this guy? Tell me about him and then we'll go hunt him down."

Dumb dumb dumb. I still cringe when I think about it. All the trust that had been built up exploded all around me. I'd asked a fairly obvious trick question, and Bill put me between the crosshairs and pulled the trigger without even a nod to mercy: "I wouldn't have any idea about that," he said. "I wouldn't hurt a fly and I can't even imagine what a murderer would be like or how he'd think." It was an answer by rote, the standard response from someone whose fate had all too often been in the hands of cops and juries and jailers and parole boards. Name, rank, and serial number—that was all he was giving me—he'd totally shut down.

Of course, it would do no good to argue with him, to tell him that innocent people can well imagine and are manifestly intrigued by what killers might be like, while only the guilty refuse to discuss it out of fear that they might give away some truth about themselves.

In a backhanded sort of way, I considered Bill's response—or better, *lack* of response—to be a victory for me, but the cost had been too high. I knew his first shot at me was about to become a fusillade.

"This will interest you," he said snidely. "Before my trial, I told my lawyers to get a book—Mr. *Murder* by Dean Koontz. Get the book and read page 23. That's all I'll say."

"I'll get it first thing tomorrow," I said with real contrition, knowing that I was being played for a fool.

"Good," he said. And then: "I guess we should talk about our contracts."

"Sure—you have any questions about them?"

"I don't, but my copyright lawyer does," he said.

Now I was reeling. *His copyright lawyer? How in the hell does a convicted serial killer get a copyright lawyer?*

"Your copyright lawyer?" I asked.

"There's this lawyer who's been asking to visit me. She's got some interest in me and my case, although I'm not sure what it is. I think she's against the death penalty. Anyway, I've been phoning her the last few days, and when I told her about our contracts, she had me get in touch with a friend of hers who's a copyright lawyer, and I read him the contracts and he's got some changes—ready?"

Under California's "Son of Sam" law then in effect, Bill couldn't make any money from this book (although his family would get half)—the book was for his ego and perhaps to help him with his appeal by presenting another side of him, that's all, so what reservation could he have about doing it? It suddenly occurred to me that all the time I'd spent on this project and on the phone with Bill had been wasted. He was playing with me, had enjoyed my attention, and had now had enough. I was but a link in the growing chain of unwitting sycophants that surrounded him. He'd used me to manipulate someone else into introducing yet another person into his life. There he was locked in jail, the key all but thrown away, and he had more friends and advisors all the time, working for him for free. I'd have had to pay my own lawyer at least five hundred bucks for the contract revision notes this murderer had gotten for free! In fact, the advice had cost the copyright lawyer— he'd had to pay for the collect phone call!

Incredibly, Bill Suff, baby killer, serial killer, was about to give me revisions on contracts that I had drafted. I didn't need to give the matter much thought—he was going to get emotional honesty from me, like it or not—I figured I'd listen to his fucking notes . . . and then tell him to shove it. And that's what I did.

He read me the revisions, which basically consisted of him retaining both the copyright and the creative control of the book's content, and I said: "Bill, listen, I don't want you to be uncomfortable, and I don't want you to sign something you don't want to sign, but these are standard form contracts that protect both of us and the project, and I don't agree with these revisions you've just proposed. The publisher will never go for them. I have to assign the publisher all my copyright to the material, and so do you. So I'm thinking the best thing would be if we don't go forward on the project. It's been interesting speaking with you, and I want to encourage your writing, and we'll talk once in a while, okay? But I've got a lot of other projects to do, and this just doesn't work for me. Really, no hard feelings. It's cool."

"Right," he said, not so much cool as abruptly freeze-dried. "Nice talkin' to ya. I understand."

And we rang off.

I'd meant it when I said I would forget about this project, and Bill knew I meant it—you can't bluff this guy. Weirdly, I was relieved—dealing with Bill was too damn hard. But, by the same token, I now knew Bill would sign the contracts. A day would pass, maybe two or three, and he'd sign. He wouldn't let me abandon him—he'd spent his whole life trying unsuccessfully to deserve not to be abandoned. And I'd wind up stuck doing this book, no matter what *tsuris* it would rain down on me.

I got up from my desk, said good-night to my dogs, stretched and clicked off my office light as I opened my office door. The darkness was disconcerting. I gave my eyes a few seconds to adjust; and, gently, the invisible became fuzzy, grainy, clear—lines of light and shadow that showed me the way across the hall and toward the bedroom. I took one step, and my breath caught even before I knew why. I froze there, in the night, in the shadows, and a shudder ripped through my body. I heard something, not something in the house or yard, but something in my mind. My dogs all lifted their slumberous heads and eyed me—the chow's ears revolved around and aimed, all pinched and on edge and expectant. Maybe the animals were hearing it too, could that be possible? Could there be some unvoiced but incredibly clear thoughts that are so outrageous and alarming you can actually hear them screaming across time, space, and species—thoughts made palpable not by meaning but by intention? Because what I was thinking, what I had just realized, what I was hearing replayed louder and louder in my mind, was that oh-so-controlled, oh-so-inexorable, impervious, overflowing, burning glacier ice in Bill's voice, in his final words to me, words that were not words but sounds, precise and clipped and utterly devoid of human emotion, sounds I had misperceived as calm but now knew were threats and promises of pain and death. For suddenly I knew, without question or hesitation, that had that secretly livid man/monster been able to hitch up his big BILL belt and climb into his big BILSUF van just after our phone call, some innocent girl would have lost her life tonight. Like all the others, she too would have missed the signal, would have heard the words but not the sounds until it was too late.

So, like that, my virginity was lost. I had gotten in bed with a serial killer, and, by the mere sound of his voice, Bill Suff had shown me how the cycle for him begins.

CHAPTER 7

If There's a Tempest, Fugue It

On page 23 of Mr. *Murder* by the eminent and prolific Dean Koontz, the most likely circumstantial suspect in a homicide considers the possibility that maybe she did the crime but just can't remember it because she was in a fugue state.

A fugue state is a sort of wakeful unconscious, a sort of trance, a state where you are active and responsive but unable to will control over your acts and unable to remember what you've done when you later "come to". This is not simply amnesia where your memory blacks out but your behavior remains consistent; in a fugue state you are theoretically capable of acting out in ways that are "not you". Accordingly, under the law, you would not be culpable for your acts.

It's a pretty bizarre deal, and, by the most bizarre of coincidences, I just happen to know a lot about it. See, back when I was in law school, I was the defense attorney in a "mock" murder trial, and the defense I was saddled with was—you guessed it—fugue state.

My client had been accused of murdering his girlfriend. His story was that he was asleep, heard a prowler, grabbed his revolver, and fired one shot at the menacing figure coming into his room. This of course did not explain why his girlfriend had six bullets in her.

The prosecution put on evidence of premeditation and motive: after learning that his girlfriend was going to dump him for his rival, my client went out and bought the pistol that became the murder weapon. And then, after killing the girl, my client tossed the gun down his apartment building's trash chute. He first denied having anything to do with the killing, but then later "admitted" to the prowler scenario once the fingerprint-covered gun was reclaimed and a paraffin test turned up gunpowder on his hands.

I was definitely on the wrong side of this case, but lawyers have to make do with what they have, and fugue state it was. My client was a likable witness, but there wasn't much he could testify to— he remembered nothing after the first shot, nothing until he turned on the lights, went over to look at the body, and made the horrible discovery that it was his girlfriend.

My expert was a psychiatrist who insisted that, yes, fugue states do exist, and you prove them indirectly, by what the patient cannot recall and what he would not normally have done. Even better than "Nessie", the Loch Ness Monster, where absence of evidence is not to be taken as evidence of absence, a fugue state is positively indicated when other explanations go wanting. So, if you had the slightest doubt that a young man would throw away his life and murder his girlfriend out of simple jealousy, then *fugue you*.

That was the defense.

And so I presumed I would sooner be taking a ride on Nessie's back than hearing the jury come back "not guilty".

Incredibly, the jury hung at eleven to one for conviction. The lone holdout was a young man who later told me he could relate to fugue states because he'd once been in one.

Swimming near their little putt-putt in the Pacific just off Santa Barbara one summer, this juror and his brother were suddenly attacked by a great white shark. The deadly *Carcharodon carcharias* had the juror's brother in its grasp and was about to shred him for lunch when the juror somehow got to the boat, found the oar, beat the shark loose, and hauled his brother to safety. The thing was, the juror remembers none of it after the shark first struck. The next thing the juror knew, he was paddling for shore with a busted oar, his bloody brother lying at his feet.

Afterwards, doctors told the juror he'd been in a fugue state, exhibiting incredible focus and sense well beyond his usual capacities.

Of course, we all know stories of adrenalized moms lifting cars off their kids, but the moms in those cases generally remember doing it. However, a fugue state is more than an explosion of adrenaline; it's a trip to a different realm altogether. It's a "head" thing. *And if the head don't fit, you must acquit.*

But I didn't for a minute buy Bill Suff's hint that maybe a fugue state could explain his crimes. Peasley and Driggs didn't go for it either—they'd have been laughed right out of court if they'd even tried to suggest it.

The next couple of times that Bill called, I let the answering machine get it. I didn't want him thinking I was waiting by the phone—I wanted him to think that my life was moving along just fine without him, and it was.

But when I finally did pick up one night, I laid right into him about this fugue state business. "I read *Mr. Murder*, Bill, and you don't suffer from fugue states," I said. "If you're ever going to plead insanity or mental defect, you're going to have to admit to remembering the crimes. If you really couldn't control yourself, then that's 'irresistible impulse'; but if you try to say you still don't know anything about what happened, then no one's going to believe you. Too much planning went into these crimes—victims were not chosen at random, dumpsites were predetermined, trophies were taken for later reflection and enjoyment, and tracks were covered up after."

That's the thing about serial killers—the crime itself, the murder, the acting out, is only the first step. Next comes the real fun—mutilating the bodies, posing them obscenely, re-dressing them in odd ways. These are sexual crimes, but all too often the killer is impotent at the time of the killing—it's only later, when he's playing around or remembering back to what he did, that he gets off. This explains why there wasn't semen at most of the scenes. The pastiche, the freeze-frame the killer locks in his mind is that last look back at his handiwork as his van's headlights wash over the perfect staging, the perfect expression of his emotional bent that evening—that memory is what the killer takes away with him and fantasizes over later, again and again. And that's what helps fuel the next killing—next time he'll try a little variation, give vent to some creative thought or image which logically succeeds the previous, a challenge both to his art and his libido.

Not that I'm trying to maintain that serial killing is art. But it is expression, and although we are probably kidding ourselves to try to read too much into each detail of each crime, you have to agree that the crimes mean something, and each one speaks for itself. When pressed to explain why this pose, why this mutilation, why this choice of victim, the killer's answer might be as simple and complex as: "Because it seemed a good idea at the time." Pretty much the way Picasso justified his "blue" period.

But all this flows from the notion that, however irresistibly driven, the killer "knows" what he's doing when he's acting out. Forget the fugue. The killer's reptilian, limbic threshold is in the driver's seat, and its needs are basic and all-consuming and decidedly conscious.

Sex, aggression, and survival—survival of one's self now through dominance, and then forever through procreation. It's Darwin again—give the man a cigar.

So I was not surprised when Bill dropped the fugue business without argument—he knew it was bullshit.

And then, only a couple of days later, he told me about a "nightmare" he'd been having—he even wrote it down. Here it is:

Brian,

Here's one you've not yet been told about. At least, I don't think anyone has told you about this. I've only told a handful of people about this girl: Tricia, Mike Kania, maybe Frank & Randy, and one of the psychiatric doctors in the Air Force who was a personal friend of mine.

I've had this same recurring dream since I was in high school. As a senior, just before graduation, around the time of our senior prom, I first had this dream. It shook me up enough that I had decided not to go to the prom. The prom is another story and has no real bearing on this one.

Anyway, the first time I had "The Dream" was when I was a senior, as I've already said. I next had the dream (quotation and capitals, inferred) right after graduation when I began working for the Forestry Dept. as a fireman. Our cook was a family friend called Tom Sheehan (deceased some 10 yrs ago), I told him about the dream and he gave me some off-the-wall explanation about it being some kind of foretelling dream. Tom was into dream interpretation and related subjects. Then I enlisted in the Air Force and began to have the dream more frequently. Between January '69 and December 13, 1969, when I married Teryl, I must have had that dream a couple dozen times.

After Teryl and I were married, the occurrence of the dream dwindled down to maybe three times in five years. Now, Teryl made a claim recently that I kept trying to get her to cut her hair like an old girlfriend wore her hair. Not true. Fact is, she already wore her hair like Jeannie Bennett and Liana Little-feather wore theirs—the two serious girlfriends I had in high school. Actually, I was trying to get Teryl to cut her hair like that of my "Dream" girl.

When I went to prison I didn't have the dream for about a year or two. Then, all of sudden, it started up again with a slight variation that caused me to awaken screaming. For the remainder of my time in prison, I began to have the dream two or three times a month. Now—YOU figure it out . . . the same dream, with slight variations, two or three times a month for the next eight years or so and you've dreamed that dream one helluvalot! There's got to be some meaning to it!

Anyway, I got out of prison and the dreams stopped! Or so I thought! While Bonnie and I were together, the dream hits me four times that I can definitely recall. After Bonnie and I break up the final time, I start having the dream about every other month. Not enough to be *really* worried about it. I got married to Cheryl and they stop again for several months. Then they start up again about the time she gets pregnant with Bridgette. They again occur about every couple of months or so. Then I get arrested and I'm in jail.

The dream stops for almost a year. Then it's back with a vengeance. The dream hits me almost every night for two weeks. I talk to Mike Kania about it and I break down crying. I asked him if he thinks I'm going crazy. He replies, "Do *You* think you're going crazy?" (I just hate it when someone answers a question with a question!) Right then, I decided not to tell him anymore when I had the dream. Anyway, in answer to that question, I'm not so stupid that I don't know . . . If you can question your sanity, chances are you're not insane. Ergo—I guess I'm sane enough to know that I'm not crazy, just because I've had the same dream, or a variation of the same dream, about a thousand times since I turned 17 years old. ('67–'68)

After those wracking two weeks, the dream slacks off to the point that it only hits me once every five, six or seven months. The last time I had the dream was about two months ago. Until just awhile ago.

I awoke from the dream, a variation of it, shaking and sweating. I may have cried out, I don't know. Nobody hollered for me to shut up, neither did a guard come running in here. Of course, there's a few people in here that yell or scream every so often, I think just to keep in practice! It's more or less taken for granted that someone is going to break down once in awhile.

Well, by now, I've probably piqued your interest. So *what* is the dream? Here is the main dream that I usually have.

THE DREAM

She's facing me, so I can see her from head to toe. She's wearing a beautiful dress that comes down to mid-calf, below her knees, that is gently moving in a breeze. The dress is a light shade of green with a tint of blue throughout it. The top of the dress is just off her shoulders with short sleeves that puff out. It gathers tight, just below her breasts; not small or large—just right, in proportion to her size. I *know* that she's five foot six, but I don't know how I know this, because—I neither know her name or who she is. I cannot recall ever having seen her at any time in my life, outside of this recurring dream.

She's by no means a "raving beauty." Actually, she's rather plain, but with proper touches of makeup, she could be called very pretty. At 5'6", she looks to weigh about 90 pounds to 110 pounds, thin with curves in all the right places. She looks to be in her late twenties or early thirties, but I get the distinct impression that she's about 10 years older than she looks. Her hair is blond, cut rather short in short bangs that sweep off to the right of her head. She has a part in her hair on the left side of her head and the back tapers to a point just below the base of her head at the back of her neck. Her hair is very fine, almost like baby hair, but it's almost mannish in style.

Her face—clear and smooth in complexion, it looks like she's never had a zit in her life. Her face is almost "V" shaped with a nearly sharp chin. A small mouth with thin lips. A thin, small, slightly upturned nose. Her eyes are the prettiest part of her face. Emerald green, with flecks of blue; wideset with a slight trace of an asian cast to her eyes, and long, thick eyelashes. Her eyebrows are thick as slightly arched above her eyes. Her ears are not covered by her hair and they are very delicate, set close to the sides of her head. Everything about her screams "Delicate— Do Not Bruise."

She's scared, the fright is plain in her eyes. Both hands are stretched out in front of her, pleading for help. I don't know what's wrong, but I know she's in great peril. I know she's asking *me* to help her, but I don't know how I can do it.

I often wake up from this dream and I've been crying—not always, but often. I sometimes have the shakes like I'm cold, but I'm not because almost all the time I've been sweating.

The variation of the dream is worse. It's the one I've often awakened with a scream in my ears, my throat and I don't know if it's *me* that screamed in reality or me in the dream or her or whatever it is that's chasing us. In this variation, I'm holding her hand (my right in her left), we're running, with me a step in front of her. It's not like most dreams where when you're running, it's like you're running through molasses. She and I are running at what seems like normal speed, I can feel the shock of my feet hitting the ground. And that's a *very* strange sensation, because in reality, I *can't* run! Between my left knee and ankle, ever since my motorcycle accident I've lost my balance and have fallen when I try to run. I can walk fast and take extra large strides when I'm in a hurry, but after a short distance I start limping badly. So it's weird that I'm running in this variation of the dream.

I look over my shoulder at her, she glances over her shoulder at *something*. I can't see anything behind her, but I realize that there is something very dangerous behind us. She turns her head back to me and I can see the fright is even more intense in her eyes. She doesn't say anything, neither do I, but somehow the message is communicated to me that *IT* is getting closer. I say *IT*, but I know that sometimes it's singular, sometimes it's plural (more than one). All in the same dream.

One other strange fact about these dreams: Her age has *never* changed. Even back when the dreams first began, I remember she's the same age now as she was then. And when I've dreamt of *me* in the dream with her, I was the same age. My age has never changed!

Now—can you explain these dreams to me? I certainly can't come up with an explanation. Mike Kania didn't have an explanation. The psychiatric friend in the Air Force said it probably doesn't mean anything. But then I hadn't had that many dreams (of this dream) back then. Only Tom Sheehan gave, or tried to give, any kind of explanation: that what was happening in the dream was something that was going to happen in my future. My question: How? It hasn't happened yet. And I can't run like it appears I'm running in the dream. *So,* what *is* my subconscious mind trying to tell me? Clearly another case of "I'm the savior trying to save someone." A la Bonnie, Cheryl, Teryl, Cathy Sharp, Kristi, Bob Allen, Bobbie Hensley, etc, ad infinitum.

I've had other dreams. It's not as if I'm having *only* this one dream and the variation of it. In fact, a lot of my ideas for stories come from my dreams: "Crash Landing", "A Whisper From The Dark" and "The Archeologist". All came from a nutshell of an idea I had in a dream. But "The Dream" or "The Girl", it's not the same as the other dreams I've had. So, what does it mean? The question remains mysterious.

Take Care and God Bless.

Bill S

When Peasley and Driggs were assigned the Suff case, they were not happy campers. This was a case that would consume them for years, and the result was preordained: Bill Suff would be convicted, and he would receive the death penalty. The only suspense would be whether some other prisoner would slip a shiv into Bill's gut and save everyone the time and trouble of trial.

Nonetheless, Peasley and Driggs are damn good defense lawyers, and they were determined to do more than just go through the motions filing motions that had no chance at success.

Driggs bore in on the DNA, blood, trace, and tire track evidence, and he and his investigators and experts feel to this day like they pretty much rendered it all moot. Of course, the jury felt otherwise, but they'd decided they felt that way long before the evidence was ever presented.

As for Peasley, he tried to walk a tightrope. If there are no more than six degrees of separation between any two people in the whole wide world, then there were no more than one or maybe two degrees between Bill Suff, his victims, the cops, and the jurors in this case. Riverside is sprawling but close-knit, and Peasley knew for certain that it would backfire big time to invoke the usual defense strategy of putting the victims and the cops on trial, so he smiled and scowled and sat back and let the prosecution put on its case with virtually no objection. Throughout the first half of 1995, prosecution witness after prosecution witness took the stand, and

Peasley didn't even bother to cross-examine. Even at this break-neck pace, this was going to be a long trial—eight months—and Peasley wanted each witness in and out of there without any clash or histrionics that would be memorable come deliberations. Peasley wanted the jury to think that these witnesses weren't important enough to cross-examine, that their testimony amounted to nothing. He also wanted the jury to feel that he'd been a good guy in letting the prosecution attempt to make its case unimpeded, and so it would hardly be fair when the hotheaded Zellerbach later objected to every bit of defense testimony.

And, finally, Peasley and Driggs both wanted to give the impression that they weren't worried about the prosecution's case because they had a solid and stirring defense soon to be revealed.

Of course, they were bluffing—they had less than nothing to offer in defense.

From the beginning, what they'd desperately wanted was some sort of insanity defense. That would have at least given them something to try, something to make the jury go out and think about. But the psychologists and neurologists, the ink blots and CT scans, all came back negative, giving no basis for claiming insanity.

The problem was Bill Suff. He acted functional and sane, and he didn't want to go along with any insanity plea. He wanted to argue the evidence, which someone ought to have realized was a pretty darn insane idea, and the closest he ever came to confessing was just a suggestion of the possibility to Dr. Michael Kania, the psychologist who told him he'd feel better if he told the truth.

"Which is?" inquired Bill.

"There's no question you're guilty," said Kania.

"I don't know that," said Bill. "But then I've had blackouts since my motorcycle accident. I suddenly wake up sitting in my van parked in a parking lot somewhere and I don't know how I got there or where I've been the last few hours."

"Then you're willing to admit that you could have committed the crimes during these 'blackouts'?"

"No."

"But you could have?"

"I've never killed anybody."

In retrospect, Bill didn't need an analytical psychologist who wanted to fit him for clinical indicia and then try to help him get well; he needed a guy with a blowtorch, a can opener, and a scalpel, determined to peel back each layer of the onion until the rot fell out for all to see.

You might well want to insist that insanity shouldn't be a defense, but you just can't seriously maintain that Bill Suff, serial killer, is a sane guy. He doesn't kill in cold blood for money, jealousy, hate, wantonness, or other "understandably evil" reason that applies to the particular victim; he kills somewhat random but always objectified victims who fuel the compulsion and lust over which he has no control. And, as always marks the truly insane, he lives in complete denial of his insanity and is therefore unable and unwilling to help his own defense at trial.

How can it be right to try a man for his life when he acts like the trial isn't happening and he spends his time writing a cookbook instead?

Under the law as it now exists and has existed since we adopted and adapted it from the English, Bill Suff should not now be on Death Row. Neither should he be walking the streets.

So, as I review Bill's "nightmare" letter, I accept that it is at once a confession and a lie, proof of both his rational cleverness and his underlying insanity.

In the dream, a woman is being chased and Bill is running with her in order to save her. But, at the last, she looks up and sees the horror about to pounce. This is where Bill stops recounting the story. What happens next is all too obvious: Bill sees himself reflected in the woman's eyes. He is the horror. He means to be her protector, but he is in fact her killer. She has been trying to run from him, and he's not about to let her go except in death. This exactly defines his take on his relationships with his wives, his mother, his father, his brothers, his sisters, his children, and his murder victims. Bill means to save them all, to be their hero, but he always winds up failing them and they try to abandon him, their love now dead.

This "nightmare" is therefore very real and really insightful as to Bill's unbalanced state of mind.

However, the clever lie is that it's no nightmare.

I believe that Bill consciously truncated the story in its retelling in order to make it seem like a nightmare which snaps him awake at the moment of horror. While I am amazed that he would trust me so much as to give me even this small piece of the puzzle, he's not yet ready to trust the whole truth to anyone outside of himself. And the whole truth is that this is not a nightmare at all, it's a fantasy memory. The "nightmare" letter is really a letter to "Penthouse Forum". Big Bill Suff lies back in his bunk in the dead of night, many nights, and he consciously, intentionally, gladly, lustfully remembers the chases and the murders, the posed and positioned freeze-frames, the glossy centerfolds he created—some more exciting than others but all of them something to be proud of—and the man gets himself off.

That's what this is all about.

So, when you waltz through the words and pictures in this book, try to think about them that way, as Bill would, try to see what Bill sees, try to feel what Bill feels.

I know I tried, and I came perilously close save for that last, unbridgeable, quantum leap between sexual perversity and actual murder.

What happened was, I would speak to Bill late at night, and then I'd go to bed and have nightmares. Now, I don't usually have a problem with nightmares—that is to say, I kind of like them. I'm pretty good at remembering my dreams, but my nightmares I know in every detail. When I wake, I take time to mull them over, to try to understand what pea was under the mattress of my psyche the night before.

Luckily, my nightmares have never been particularly night-marish—the most recurrent is a rather tame affair, more disorienting than frightening. It always takes place in the present, when

I suddenly "realize" that, although I was awarded my Master of Fine Arts degree years ago, I still have courses to go back and take. It's like I was given the degree in error or on faith, and I have yet to really earn it. I guess I feel like I'm some sort of hoax. In the nightmare, I am embarrassed and never quite able to "get it together" enough to go take those courses and complete my obligation, no matter how hard I try.

The reality is that I was working on my master's at the time my mother and brother died. After "the accident", I took a one-year leave of absence from school. In fact, I took a longer leave of absence from life. Talk about fugue states—I still don't remember those years in any organized, systematic way. It's like I just jumped from a memory here and an event there, with huge gaps in between. Not even a haze, just big blank gaps. And although I'm pretty sure I went to graduation and got my master's one particular summer, I note that the framed degree on my wall is dated some six months later. I think that maybe my course work was done and degree earned that summer, but there was some technical "residency" requirement or "dissertation study" units that had to be accounted for later. I vaguely remember something like that. In any event, it unnerves me to think about it awake or asleep. It is of course just the tip of the iceberg for the real nightmare of the accident, which I guess I can't bear at all, even after all this time.

The other nightmare which I can't help but remember, even though I only had it once, is the nightmare that psychiatrists say you can't have. Supposedly you are unable to dream of your own death. I'm not talking about the sort of suicidal, delusional fantasy where you see yourself dead, as if you were still alive and outside yourself somehow—that's a common fantasy during depression, although I've never had it. No, the nightmare I had was a bona fide real scenario where I died. In it, I'm walking alone down a dark block, by some brick buildings. I'm thinking of nothing in particular—it's an innocent and not worrisome walk. But then I turn the corner and come face-to-face with the barrel of a revolver. I never see the person holding the gun—there's no time. I turn the corner, the gun comes up, pointed at my face (I think maybe the hand holding the gun is wearing a black glove, maybe), and BOOM! The gun goes off and everything goes black. And I jerked awake, knowing that I had just been killed in my dream. That's death, as far as I'm concerned. Forget the beckoning white light and the music and the voices/faces of loved ones—forget the bullshit. When you're dead, you're dead. It's black and without sensation. Nothingness. When you're dead, you don't even know it. You don't know nothing no more.

And the thing is, after dealing with Bill Suff for a while, I began to have nightmares that, for the first time in my life, I do not remember. I know I awoke sweating and frightened, but I have no idea why. Whatever the images were, they're either gone or locked away. And that really scared the hell out of me.

Either coincidentally or not, at the same time as I was having these unremembered nightmares, everything in my personal life started to go to hell. My marriage crumbled, and my wife was diagnosed with a chronic illness and some very nasty addictions that she denied. I got screwed on a house purchase, wound up in a half dozen emotionally draining lawsuits, and had to look for a new residence. The writing business looked good "on paper", except that my employers didn't pay me on time, and that led to more lawyers and legal machinations that cost me more than I could win.

And, as I "researched" the seamier side of the Suff story—as, for example, I interviewed hookers to try to find out how they could have been so stupid and unwary as to get into a van with a serial killer—I began to get downright obsessed with all sorts of sexual fantasies and adventures. Obsessed to the point of deciding to act them out. Feeling like I was living a boring life on borrowed time, and I'd better go "experiment" before it was too late.

Anyway, that's the "intellectual", ex post facto way of describing my head during that heady period. The simple experience of it was that I couldn't shake either the desire or the determination to live out these fantasies. I thought about them day and night, and I planned long and hard what I was going to do and how and when I was going to do it.

The foreplay of planning was incredibly arousing—the anxiety itself was arousing, and I was plenty anxious, that's for sure. By nature, I'm extremely conservative—I take risks in the privacy of my own mind, when I write, and sometimes even that frightens me. Many a time I've written a scene and then condemned myself for having been "sick" enough to have thought of it, wondering what cruel, twisted, atavistic part of me that scene could have come from. Luckily, every time I feel that way I read the morning newspaper and find out that someone has gone out and actually done something a hundred times worse than anything I could ever dream.

But here I was working on the Suff story, and I wasn't going to dream or write, I was going to go act out. Bill was my catalyst, my excuse for getting deep down and close to the primordial ooze of pleasure, pain, aggression, stimulus-response from whence we all come. Because I was certain that what separates Bill Suff from all the rest of us is a very very fine line indeed.

For those of you who know me, and everyone else who is meeting me for the first time in these pages, suffice it to say that I didn't go out and do anything too terrible, and I've got perversely proud Polaroids to prove it. Typically, I "acted out" more as observer and good listener than participant, but then omission, commission, and admission are all the same deal.

Right?

For the curious among you, the accumulated learning from this aberrational hiccup in my lifetrack boils down to: (i) it is indeed possible to have a giggling fit with a ball gag in your mouth; (ii) pantyhose has more uses than a Swiss Army knife; (iii) if you want to get filthy rich, open a dildo harness repair shop; (iv) no matter where you put a clothespin, it doesn't hurt when you clamp it on, it hurts when you take it off; (v) transsexuals invariably brag about how incredibly big they were; (vi) happily married men fantasize their wives being raped by gleaming black men, while the unhappily married envision their wives on their knees to their bloated, garlic-breath bosses.

Or so I'm told.

What I discovered about myself after I reined myself back in is that there were fundamental differences between my acting out and Bill Suff's acting out, even though my experiences did allow me to get a clearer sense of him.

First, as noted, I got off on the foreplay. Clearly, Bill does not. While I was nervous and had to whip myself into a frenzy in order to act out, Bill goes the opposite way. His planning is cool and methodical and affords him no release or enjoyment. His preparation is to establish more and more control, over himself and then his victim. My preparation was to find a way to lose control, to rid myself of a too-conscientious superego.

However, the primary acting out itself is probably similar for us both. You are completely focused on your senses, on feeding specific, insatiable sensory needs, and everything else around you gets lost, moving at a slower speed. This reminded me well of my fantastical perception of "the accident"—I heard the "bang" of the tire blowing, and I fought calmly and logically with the steering wheel and the brakes to keep the car on the road, and yet my sensation was of the car drifting gently towards the dirt median no matter what I did—meanwhile, all sounds blanked out except for the radio, which continued to play music at normal speed even as everything else went into slow motion—and, when the car began to flip over, it was a graceful, peaceful arc, with the blue sky reaching down to meet me—and then everything went black and red as I was knocked unconscious and awoke a half hour later to the sight of nothing but blood.

At the same time, none of this gentle recollection contains any of the emotionality—the sheer terror, guilt, and fear of imminent death—that I must have been feeling. Denial of this crucial negativity is precisely what empowers and preserves the fantasy. The fantasy is therefore not an end in itself; it is what protects me from a horror that I cannot undo. In fact it took twenty years—twenty years of self-destructive unhappiness, of a bruising pea under the mattress, failed marriages, and blown career opportunities—before

I finally allowed a psychotherapist to lead me into hypnotic, guided regression that loosed the pain I never knew I felt. Over the years, my left eye had begun to twitch during times of stress. When hypnotized, I zeroed in on that twitch. It was that left eye which had been bashed during the accident. The twitch proved to be my eye muscle finally running out of the strength to hold back the pain of death from my consciousness. Twenty years after the fact, and I wailed on a sofa in a doctor's office in Santa Monica as my life and the lives of my mother, brother, and best friend were being crushed by certain serendipity. No remorse, no bitterness, no artifice, merely the leer of the abyss. It was one thing to say I had died when the car was sailing off the road; it was something else again to feel it for the first time.

Incredibly, once I opened myself up to living that nightmare, I felt alive again. I was no longer dead but alive; now I was just plain alive. Being dead had been a self-imposed exile—a critical part of me had been butchered off, wrapped up, and shelved because I was afraid, and yet the fear proved to be worse than what I was afraid of. But, for all those years in exile, I had done things, acted in ways that would have been different had I known how to come back from disintegration.

I suspect that it's the same for Bill, even though he remains in denial and murder gives him the strength to maintain the mask. If, despite your worst intentions, the psyche tends toward becoming whole, then you must geometrically compound that which you must deny if you are to keep from ever facing your initial fear. So, as you act, as you become increasingly and necessarily more frequently criminal, the fantasy is more pronounced but the act is ever cooler, the focus more and more sharp.

Just think of Bill when he has his hands around a woman's throat. If Rhonda Jetmore is to be believed (and she may well have been primed by specialists who led her into "remembering" how serial killers act), Bill was so focused on killing her, so lost in his fantasy plan, that it was relatively easy to snap him out of it by surprising him with a punch to the face. She didn't just break his physical hold, she broke his glasses, his perception, and his concentration, and then he backed off and she escaped. After that, Bill added both a garrote and a knife to his repertoire, and no one ever fought him again.

Of course, fiction writers have to write it differently for the sake of drama, but the reality is that fantasy is tenuous, easily burst the more complex and circumscribed it becomes. Break Bill's cycle, and he has to crank it up and start all over.

In the end, while I fully enjoyed my sexual acting out and was doubly aroused at the time when I realized I was not so anxious or guilt-ridden as to not become aroused, the acts themselves occupy a dreamlike, unreal place in my memory. It's that they're non sequiturs—they don't fit in with the chronological, characterological line of the rest of my recollections, much like that business with the master's degree. Accordingly, I actually have to remind myself that, yes, they did happen, I did do that—otherwise, I could just as easily be convinced that they never took place.

By the same token, when I lie back and flip through the stack of mental images, they are incredibly juicy, almost liberating. The secret of it is also exciting, as in any taboo.

For Bill, and others like him, it seems that the act itself is not enough. When my acting out was done, I couldn't wait to get the hell out of there—I felt complete release, and later the pleasant memories were a total surprise. My acting out was a loss of control, and, once done, I needed to immediately regain control and get back to my life. I recall an adventure I had as a youth in Paris, a short time spent with an Irma La Douce in a seedy Pigalle hotel— trust me, she was in complete control and I was terrified and completely controllable, first desirous of paying to be with her, then ready to pay even more to get out. But Bill's acting out is about his control, total control over the woman of the moment, and it is not complete unless and until he reconfigures the scene to create the memories he needs—he kills and then he uses the body to create his fantasy memory. His act is no release, and may not even really be arousing. Later, it's arousing, but it's not enough. He's lost control when he's not killing, so he will have to try again; while I, having acted out a forbidden fantasy and then regained control afterwards, don't have any urge to try it again. My spell is broken even as Bill's is all the stronger and angrier, *yet we both have the exact same goal: we all move stridently in the direction of what will be for each of us control.*

So, perhaps the only real difference between serial killers and us is that, for reasons experiential and genetic, they never don't feel the terror of being out of control, while we take control—and serial killers—for granted. Much to our ultimate chagrin.

CHAPTER 8

Bill's Vittles and Fixin's

All through adolescence, Bill Suff was a big dork who played a big horn in his high school band. Speaking to the court just before his death sentence was pronounced, Bill even pronounced himself "a lovable nerd". You've seen the pictures—this was not a guy who partied down or played around, and he was the first to admit it.

But, having savvy, grace, and *cajones* in a social setting has nothing to do with whether you're playful and funny, and, were you to stop by the writers' offices on any hit TV comedy, I promise you would find nothing but a collection of geeks and malcontents and guys whose formative years were spent "accidentally" overhearing variations on the line "Hey, who invited *him?*" delivered *sotto voce*, more *voce* than *sotto*.

Yes, no matter how dorky, you get the last laugh if you have a sense of humor, if you work hard and overcompensate in order to accomplish while taking advantage of all those years spent observing, analyzing, and note-taking on the outside looking in. But bear in mind that no matter you're the funny one, if you're the writer rather than the performer, then somebody else is delivering your lines and continuing to get the public acclaim. You're funny but you still keep your distance—humor is at once your connection and your insulation.

And Bill Suff is one of those funny, playful guys who didn't much get into the game and has now learned to embrace that rejection. Accordingly, Bill doesn't ever sit down and tell you a joke—he always maintains a serious facade that he thinks is only appropriate considering the unjust circumstances of his imprisonment. Yet, he constantly sets you up and manipulates things for the sake of maximum irony, for reaction, so that you live the joke rather than just hear it.

I told you about his "friendship" with murderer Jim Bland. Same deal when Bill first got to Death Row at San Quentin. "Made some new friends," he excitedly told me by phone. "We're real good friends now—William P. Bonin and Randy Kraft—ever heard the names?"

I thought for sure that Bill Suff was about to explode with laughter, but he never did. Of course I knew of William Bonin, L.A.'s "Freeway Killer", so named because he dumped the bodies of numerous young men along our maze of freeways. And Randy Kraft was his own prize piece of work—when he was finally stopped and arrested for drunk driving, he would've been allowed to sleep it off and be released on his own recognizance in the morning were it not for the California highway patrol officer strolling to the far side of Kraft's car to ask his passenger if the latter wanted to drive the car home rather than be towed. That's when the officer noticed that the passenger was one very murdered Marine. It's one way to drive legally in the "diamond" carpool lane, I suppose. Anyway, Bonin died by lethal injection just a few weeks after Bill's arrival at Quentin's "D" Block. Kraft is presently trying to fake a psychological defense for his appeal.

"I know all about Bonin, Kraft, and all the others," I said. "Do they ever talk about their crimes?"

"Nope, never do—we all mostly avoid talking about why we're here—it's kind of an unwritten rule—you take a man for how he treats you here and now, not for anything he might've done outside of prison."

"Except for child killers, right?" I queried.

It was a nice little jab, I thought. "Riiiiiight," said Bill slowly and cheerily as if he weren't a child killer, dragging out the word, trying to buy time to think all this through before the conversation

BILL SUFF'S FAMILY ALBUM

Above, clockwise: Wm. Suff, Bobby, Kenny, Roberta, Donny, and Bill. 1961, La Mirada, California.

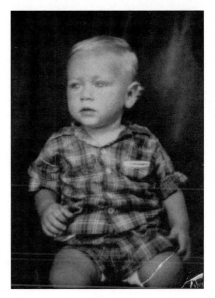

"Piss-poor protoplasm". Bill Suff, eight months old. See Chapter 16.

School Days 55-56

Bill in happier days.

"Dressed for success". Unfortunately, the uniform made the man. Bill in his band uniform with siblings (from left to right) Roberta, Bobby, Donny, and Kenny. See Chapter 10.

Above: Air Force cadet Bill on his 20th birthday in 1969. At right, clockwise from top left: Bobby, Donny, Roberta, and Kenny.

Bill's Boy Scout sash and numerous merit badges.

Bill and first wife Teryl on their wedding day, December 13, 1969. Not so happy as they appeared—Teryl was then pregnant with her stepfather's child.

Bill, Teryl, and Billy Jr.
The caption on the back of the snapshot
reads "A Lovely Trio," yet Billy Jr. was
beaten repeatedly and suffers permanent
brain damage.

Bill and Billy Jr.

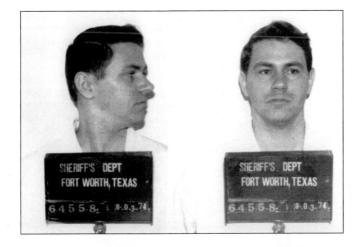

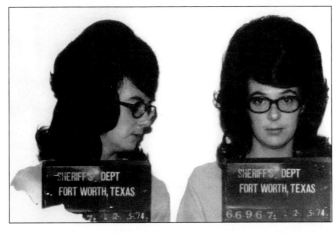

Bill and Teryl's
Texas mugshots
taken while
serving time
for the murder
of their infant
daughter,
Dijianet.
Model prisoner
Bill received a
seventy-year
sentence but
only served
ten before
being released
on "postcard
parole". Teryl
received a
seventy-year
sentence but
had her
conviction
thrown out by
the appellate
court.

The perfect couple in their perfect world—Bill, girlfriend Bonnie, and Myrtle the dog in 1984. Bonnie still believes that Bill began to kill when she broke off their relationship, but the evidence shows that he was sleeping with prostitutes as well as killing them even while he was living with Bonnie.

Above: Bill and second wife Cheryl during her pregnancy.

Right: Cheryl, Bill, and baby Bridgette, 1991. The more attention the baby got, the more angry Bill would become. He was murdering at least one prostitute a month by this period. Bridgette was taken away permanently by child welfare authorities at age four months.

Bill's bird drawings. In color, they're bright blue. They're the template for the bizarre re-dressing and posing of Tina Leal's corpse. See Chapter 14.

Bill, chili cook-off champ. See Chapters 8 & 9.

① TRANQUILITY GARDEN

The day had been warm and at 4:00 that afternoon, it was just beginning to cool off. A warm breeze blowing in from the ocean, coming over the mountains and through the open livingroom window.

Jeannie was sitting in a chair, facing the window to catch the breeze. She was totally absorbed in the magazine she was reading and didn't hear the knock the first time. The knock came again and she set the magazine aside. The knock came again as she reached to open the door.

The young man at the front door smiled and stood up straighter as the door opened.

"Hello, Jeannie. How are you?"

"Why, Lee! Hello. I didn't know you were home. When did you arrive?"

"Oh, a little while ago." He shrugged and looked down at the welcome mat. "Are your parents home?"

"Uh, n-no Lee. They went to Riverside. They'll be home soon. Why don't you come in and wait."

"No, thank you. I came to see you. Mom wrote me you're getting married soon."

"Yes, I am. Next Thursday. You remember Ricky. We went to High School together."

"Yes, I remember." He hesitated, then uncertainly asked, "Jeannie, can you come with me? Just for a walk. We'll be back before dark."

Above: Page one of Bill's short story "Tranquility Garden", written while in jail in Texas, 1974. See Chapters 3 & 4.

Opposite: Bill's daily logs of his life on San Quentin's Death Row. See Chapter 12.

193rd Day - Monday - 8/19/96
0700 - Breakfast - Omelet, Oatmeal, Milk, Grapefruit Juice.
0900 - Yard Time - 2nd Wave, 1st Out.
1300 - Recall - Sack Lunch - PB+J, Pretzels, Graham Crackers, Apple, Orange Drink.
1700 - Supper - Chicken Patty, Cheese Taters, Beans, Noodle Salad, Cake.
1830 - Phone - Florence - No Answer
2130 - Legal Mail Out - Brian w/ V.O. for Lee (Lea, Leah, Leigh), requested Paper & Pens.

194th Day - Tuesday - 8/20/96 - HAPPY BIRTHDAY (No PEARS)
0630 - Breakfast - Scrambled Eggs, Tortillas, Pear Pieces, Grits, Milk.
1000 - Shower/Shave
1100 - Sack Lunch - PB+J, Graham Crackers, Sunflower Seeds, Apple, Orange Drink.
1530 - Laundry Whites Pickup.
1700 - Supper - Burritos, Rice, Beans, Menudo, Salad, Cake.

195th Day - Wednesday 8/21/96
0630 - Breakfast - Oatmeal, Applesauce, Doughnuts, Milk.
0800 - Yard Time - 1st Wave, 1st Out (Moved to cell 1EB65 white out on the yard. Property in cell 65)
1300 - Recall - Sack Lunch - None when I came in.
1500 - Mr. Numera says too late to get a lunch now. Will get white laundry from 5th tier.
1700 - Supper - Hamburger, French Fries, Corn, Cottage Cheese, Apple Pie.
1730 - Mail - Mom.
1930 - Laundry Whites Returned.

196th Day - Thursday - 8/22/96
0630 - Breakfast - Farina, Boiled Egg, Bananas and Milk. 1st Out.
0700 - Hard Call - 1st Wave, 1st Out.
1300 - Recall - Sack Lunch - Cheese, Cookies, Sunflower Seeds, Bananas, Cherry Drink & Apple.
1530 - Mail - Tricia (B'day Card)
1700 - Supper - Chicken Breast, Rice, Salad, Cake, Koolaid.
1800 - Laundry Blues Pick up.

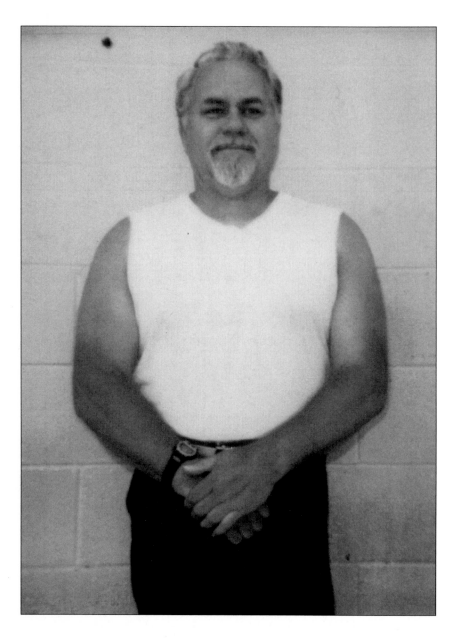

"The most wronged man on earth".
Bill today in San Quentin Prison.
A model prisoner, and jovial, gentle soul who easily makes friends with guards and inmates alike. Now more than ever he's convinced that everyone who meets him is convinced that he's not the sort of person who could harm anyone.
See Chapter 18.

continued, and then: "Actually, it's child *molesters* that have problems in jail." I know he thought he'd parried back pretty well, but what he didn't notice was he was suddenly speaking on the inhalation—it's what con men call a "tell", some unconscious action that gives away what you're really thinking, that proves you're worried even though you're saying you're not—and it occurred to me that maybe Bill wouldn't be able to fool a polygraph, after all.

"What about Bonin's impending execution—he ever talk about it?"

"Yeah—some—he's hoping it won't happen."

"It will—he's out of appeals and he's not a real sympathetic character—even the anti–capital punishment people have a tough time standing up for him," I said.

"Well, like I said, I like him—he says he didn't do it," said Bill.

"Riiiiiight," I said. "So when you're alone, you guys don't talk shop? You just compare notes on how you all got framed?" You could hear I was smiling.

Bill lowered his voice out of the reach of his tier-mates: "Maybe Bonin's guilty, I don't know. I just know the guards who've gotten to know me keep telling me they don't understand why I'm here, because now that they know me they know I have to be innocent. I don't ask them, they just volunteer that."

"And you think they're serious?" I asked. Out of the 440 or so guys on Death Row in California at that time, only a handful were serial killers—it's rarefied air, the top of the pyramid for felons trying to show they've got The Right Stuff. My goal with Bill has always been to make him see that I truly do accept him for what he is, so it would be cool for him to discuss it all with me. The only way he's going to get off Death Row, legitimately working an insanity plea, is to be candid with the world about what he did. I firmly believe that even the families of the victims will back off some if only Bill would give them their closure. Closure through disclosure. But San Quentin was dummying him up. Time and distance from the crimes was dummying him up. He'd pretty much confessed to me, shown me inside his world back when we'd met in person in Riverside in early October of 1995 as he waited for and worried about the death sentencing, but now that it was a reality he wasn't so scared anymore. Assuage Bill's worry and the truth goes with it.

"We can talk about all this when you come up here in person," said Bill insincerely, changing the subject since it hadn't exactly gone the way he'd planned it. So much for his little "surprise", his "joke" about his infamous, newfound friends. That's the thing to remember about Bill: if you don't play along with him he doesn't take his ball and go home; rather, he backs off and lets you run the show. He can be controlled. This is a man who causes no trouble in a controlled environment. In fact, he thrives there.

"He was a pleasure to deal with," said Randy Driggs.

"But he didn't give you any help preparing the defense," I pointed out.

"I meant, unlike my other clients, I never had to worry about Bill sticking a pencil in my ear. He was never violent, never aggressive. Hell, every other client I have, even their mothers bark at me and get in my face threatening I better get their sons off or else."

"And Bill's mom—Ann?"

"The only client's mother I ever had who didn't insist her son was innocent. She just insisted *she* was innocent."

"Any problems dealing with Bill?" I asked the guards at the Riverside lockup every time I visited.

"Nope" was always the answer. "Oh, he complains about things sometimes, gets impatient, gets kinda stubborn when you interrupt him while he's reading or writing, but we never worry he's gonna cause trouble or get violent. He's just not like the other prisoners. And he's definitely not like what we expected when they first brought him in. Sometimes it's hard to believe he is who he is. He always tries to be real polite and respectful."

"You know that when he's out of jail he's always gone around pretending to be a security guard or a cop, right? Guess he identifies with you," I would say.

"Heard that," the Riverside guards would say, oddly complimented.

"Surprised?" I asked.

"Maybe," they'd say.

On the other hand, the guards at San Quentin are surprised by nothing, and they're a whole lot less awestruck by their charges. "No, he's not like Richard Ramirez, he doesn't try to kill us every time we get near him, but a guy like Suff you gotta watch every second because he puts on such an act of acting cooperative."

"So you watch out for Richard Ramirez because he's out of control, and you watch out for Bill Suff because he's totally in control?"

"All these serial killers—they're totally different from the rest of the prison population. These guys have their own agendas—secret agendas—in their heads. And they're patient—time passes differently for them. Maybe, for his own reason, for reasons none of us will ever understand, Suff wants to get over to that water fountain over there. He might wait a year, five years, ten years, but I promise you there will come a moment when he makes his move to try to get to that water fountain. So you gotta watch out. You don't know what a serial killer is up to, but you know he's up to something, and today might be the day he goes for it, just because you let your guard down. Other convicts—they want to escape, they want to have sex, they want to hurt somebody. Serial killers—whatever they do, there's another reason behind it, there's always a bigger picture. Everything they say or do—every single thing—it's all a lie. You never look the other way, particularly when they treat you like a friend."

"Bill says sometimes he gets called on the carpet by the assistant warden—he just gets rousted out of his cell, hauled into some conference room and told he's a sex offender and a murderer. Then he gets sent back to his cell. What's that all about? Just trying to rankle him, see if you can push him to fight back?"

"Serial killers get too comfortable with the discipline here. They're smarter'n us. They learn the rules, they follow the rules, they expect that'll give 'em freedom to plot whatever it is they're plotting. So you gotta throw 'em for a loop now and again. You gotta let 'em know that the rules aren't the rules, the rules can change any damn time we decide to change 'em. You gotta remind 'em that they're the prisoners and we're the bosses. They tend to forget that."

The voice of experience—no bumpkins among the San Quentin guards—day in and day out, these guys live with Bill Suff—*and serial killers are not like other guys.* So, the questions remained: can any of us ever really understand how serial killers think? Is there any kinship? Are they even human? Why does some inner voice keep telling me that we're all closer than we want to be?

"I think you're gonna be surprised by me," Bill has said to me on several occasions, teasing me about something he'd written which he wanted me to read and respond to.

The first time was the first draft of the speech he was going to give at his sentencing, and the surprise proved to be his request that, if he was executed, then his organs and corneas should be harvested for transplant so that both his life and his death would not be in vain.

Of course, I wasn't surprised. Once I got to know Bill, he ceased to be surprising. As with my wives, my initial fantasy of what they *had* to be was more electric, exciting, unpredictable than their grounded, repetitive reality. I knew that Bill saw himself as eternal—alive, but already dead—a ghost who was not about to give up his playful haunts, determined to have the last laugh and maintain control of his victims from beyond their graves as well as his own. Bequeathing his organs was just another way of asserting that control—it was to be expected.

But, on the day of sentencing, everyone in the courtroom was plenty surprised. Surprised, stunned, and then incensed, in an instant. The words were barely out of Bill's mouth before members of the victims' families were hurling themselves forward to lynch him. One furiously apoplectic man had to be restrained and then ushered out by the bailiffs, while others screamed obscenities or burst into tears. The judge pounded his gavel and demanded order, and couldn't wait to ad lib that Bill was "evil incarnate" when he pronounced sentence. Yeah, Bill surprised all of them all right—he sat there and acted surprised at their surprise, the perfect picture of magnanimous menace, all calm and innocent, the eye of his own firestorm. It was wonderfully cruel and diabolical, and Bill laughed about it later when we met in private: "I guess they got a little upset," he said to me, "I guess they were pretty surprised."

"The one who's going to be surprised is you, Bill," I said, "because they really are going to execute you if you keep up like this."

He looked at me curiously, brow furrowed but eyes wide. He just didn't get it. I got the distinct impression that I was looking at a child who thought he could suddenly say "All right, game's over, let's all go wash up for dinner", and all those dead girls would rise, laughing, ready to play Bill Suff's game again the next day.

Read in court on 10/26/95:

BILL S STATEMENT TO THE COURT
PRIOR TO DEATH SENTENCE
BEING PRONOUNCED

Your Honor, I'd like to start out on a personal note to a relative of one of the girls, a girl I greatly cared for: Mr. Lyttle, I cared about your daughter, Kimberly, a great deal. Several times I gave her money for food and rent. Sex was often not involved. One Christmas, I even bought Kim and Sara presents to put under their tree. Four times I asked Kim to move into my two-bedroom apartment. There would always be food on the table, she wouldn't have to worry about rent, she could quit being a prostitute and, if she wanted, I'd use my county contacts to get her into a drug rehabilitation program. I'd even list her and Sara on my medical and dental insurance plans. Kim and Sara would never want for anything. Talk to Janice Farmer, Jan was at Kim's apartment the first time I invited her to move in with me.

The last time I saw Kim and Sara was in April '89 at her apartment when I again asked them to move in with me. She said she would think about it. The next time I heard about Kim was in January '90. I ran into Jan at a store in Elsinore and asked if she knew where Kim and Sara had moved to. Jan told me that Kim had been killed. Mr. Lyttle, I couldn't have killed Kimberly, I cared for her too much. I only wish that Kim was still alive to let you know what kind of person I am. Ever since her death, I've prayed that GOD is now caring for her. And I will continue to pray for Kim, and also that her true killer is found. I hope that one day you will come to realize that I did *not* harm Kim in any way and that I am *not* the person the news media and the prosecutor has portrayed me to be.

Your Honor, prosecutor Zellerbach and the news media have all painted a grotesque picture of me as a cold-blooded, heartless monster. They couldn't have been more wrong about me! I am a caring, loving and helpful person. Ask anyone who was close to me. I'm also a hopeless romantic. I fall in love easily and it's nearly impossible for me to fall *out* of love.

When I was in the Air Force, I was a medical corpsman working in a hospital pediatrics ward. Later, I became an ambulance attendant. While in prison I first worked in the prison infirmary and finally got into the computer industry as a keypunch operator. And during this total of 15 years, I saw so much pain, loss of hope, despair and death that my goal became one of helping people any way I could, no matter how far out of the way it took me. I gave people I barely knew money, food and even a place to live when they had no other place to go. I opened my home and myself to them, never asking or expecting anything in return. *THAT* is the kind of person I am, *NOT* what prosecutor Zellerbach made up about me!

Now, I don't blame the jurors for finding me guilty, nor assessing a death penalty on me. Given these circumstances, conditions and arguments, *whoever* was on trial would have been found guilty, not just me! The law says that the prosecution must prove, beyond a doubt, that the defendant is guilty. It's a good law, in theory. But, I offer this as a more practical truth: "A prosecutor need not *prove* anything. He only needs to make the public and the jury *think* he's proven it!" And prosecutor Zellerbach had lots of outside help on this case. Long before a jury was impanelled, I was tried and convicted by the news media. And they decreed a death sentence on me, though not in so many words. The people who read and listened to the news media immediately believed the worst. Three days after I was jailed, I began to receive death threats. If I had been acquitted, or if all charges had been dropped; someone, either related to one of these girls or not, would have killed me. Even if an appeal frees me, I don't stand a chance of returning to *any* semblance of my previous life. And any hope of romance is out of the question. No woman I might meet and begin to care for will make any kind of commitment to me. She would be wondering if anything reported by the news media was true.

During the Voir Dire, several people expressed their belief that I *had* to be guilty, because the prostitute killings stopped after my arrest. Sorry, but that's just not true. The prostitute killers were active here before I came home to California. Since my arrest, several more prostitutes have been killed, and as everyone has conveniently forgotten, I was originally charged with an additional killing, only to be absolutely excluded by DNA evidence. With all of the sorrow that's been brought on by these deaths, it's a shame that there is still more sorrow to come because the responsible parties are still out there killing! So, prosecutor Zellerbach, what's the whole truth with respect to the prostitute killings in Riverside County? The public *does* have a right to know the *whole* story!

As for me, a couple of people said that I seemed emotionless and unremorseful during my trial, never making eye contact with any of the family members who testified. Well, my response is, how can you look into the eyes of someone who is wrongly convinced that you killed their daughter, mother or sister? It was tearing me up inside, but I was forced to learn long ago that to show my feelings was a weakness and left me open to be hurt by others. I felt sadness, pain and empathy for what happened to these women, as well as sympathy for their relatives. Granted, this isn't feeling remorseful. But then, how can you show remorse for something you didn't do?

Prosecutor Zellerbach made a big show about certain items found in places associated with me. A summons issued to Ms. Hammond. Purses and a t-shirt belonging to Ms. Zamora. A map with locations of where Ms. Hammond and Ms. Zamora were found, marked by ink-dots. Well, none of those items were found on the first search or a second search. It wasn't until a third or later search that those items suddenly, and mysteriously, showed up in an obvious location where it would have been impossible to miss them in the first place! And, it was testified that a vehicle different from mine was seen and heard in the alley where Ms. Hammond was found. At a time when I was just leaving for work more than 50 miles away. To me, the only thing any of this sup-posed evidence proves is that the evidence was *planted* by some-one. Planted to link me with those two ladies. Planted because the police were under pressure to find someone, *anyone* guilty!

And then, there is Rhonda Jetmore. She identified me as the person who attacked her six years ago. And it was from a picture taken of me about four years before she was attacked. So she identified me from a picture 10 years old! Why didn't she iden-tify me when she was attacked? She says she was picked up in front of John's Service Center. Well, both before and after her attack, I was working inside that building, evenings and week-ends. My toyota was parked in front. She couldn't have missed seeing me inside or going to and from my car. *If* her story was true; *if* it was me who actually attacked her; she *should* have rec-ognized me back when she was attacked!

Now, another point prosecutor Zellerbach made a big thing of was what he thought I've been doing for the past 3½, now almost 4 years. Just what did he *expect* me to do? Rant and rave, kick the walls and cause trouble for everyone? That's what *he* might do if *he* was put in jail. But if I did that, I would have played right into his portrayal of what kind of person *he* says I am. Well, prosecutor Zellerbach, I wish you'd explain to me exactly how an innocent man is *supposed* to act in jail?

Did I write down most of my recipes as a cookbook? Yes, I did. It was a suggestion made by several people who cared enough about me to give me a means to retain my sanity under conditions and circumstances that would drive most people crazy. Did I watch TV? Yes. *Everyone* watched TV in jail. It's nearly the only source of news and entertainment. Especially if you're a people person and have to spend 24 hours a day in a cell, alone, with no outside contact. I also wrote . . . my cookbook, fantasy stories, romantic poetry . . . I even drew cute cartoons on the envelopes for the few people who would write to me, so I could show them that I hadn't *yet* lost my sense of humor. After all, writing and drawing is the best means I have to express what's in my heart and mind.

One last point before I close: People have said that I'm a "Homicidal animal and shouldn't be allowed near women." Well, believe it or not, during my stay in jail, there are several women that I've come into contact with that actually *like* me and trust me enough to be less than arm's length away from me. One lady in particular spent hours at a time alone with me in a 6 ft. x 8 ft. room locked from the outside with the nearest deputy out of sight and earshot. At no time was she worried that I might harm her. These are women who got to know me and *know* that I am *not* the person the prosecutor and news media portrayed me as being.

In closing, Your Honor, this last is addressed to this Court. No animosity intended, but I sincerely feel the Court was wrong in not granting a change of venue: All along I've said that I wasn't going to get a truly impartial jury *or* a fair trial. I also feel the Court erred by not sequestering the jury: It's human nature to read or listen to what the news media is reporting that was found inadmissable in the court—restricting order or not. And therefore reading or hearing things they shouldn't have. Now I hope that didn't serve to anger this Court, because I do have a last request. For I think I have proven better than any words can say that I am non-violent and can keep my word, in regard to a promise I made to Your Honor when this insanity began.

My request is that at the end, if I've exhausted all of my rights to appeal and am still facing a death penalty, that this Court make the following provisional order in regard to my execution:

"Laws at that time permitting, that my execution be performed in such a manner that my heart, corneas and other needed organs can be removed and donated anonymously to an organ bank for transplanting to a needful person or persons." In this manner, my death will *serve* mankind rather than being just another corpse in a graveyard. And finally, that the remains of my body be cremated and then given to a person I will name later to dispense with in an agreed manner. Thank you Your Honor for granting me this opportunity to express my feelings.

Sincerely,

Bill L. Suff

After witnessing the courtroom reaction to Bill's statement, it occurred to me that Bill's playfulness wasn't so much about getting one particular reaction from his audience; it was about getting any reaction at all—he simply wanted to be noticed, for any reason, good or bad. In his childlike desperation for affection, he was willing to settle for mere attention, and this clearly reflected his perception of his relationship with his parents: it's not that they either loved him or hated him, it's that they were inconsistent about it. What made them lavish him one day, made them punish him the next. From the beginning, try as he might, he had no control or at best imperfect control over his own life. No wonder then that when he had his own babies, he was at any and every moment equally ready to bestow a kiss or deliver a dropkick.

Serial killers are not made by "simple" abuse; they are born to confusion, to inconsistent love and ultimate abandonment. I had read that before, but now I was seeing it firsthand, in Bill Suff's lost eyes. Wounded by rejection, prevented from callousing by a burst of loving hope, then bloodied anew, the pain always fresh, never inured. While straightforward unrelenting abuse gives you a choice, a chance to fight, flee, or die, the confounding of love and hate determines your fate for you, guaranteeing your survival at the cost of your soul. You are alive and you are dead.

Think about it in your own lives—if you came from a loving home, like me, you were certainly disciplined now and again. I know I earned a spanking or three, none of which I recall with the slightest physical or emotional pain, although it was embarrassing and eventful enough to teach me the necessary lesson. In fact, my parents' preferred form of punishment was to tell me to "stand in the corner", facing the walls while I thought about what I had done wrong. This event lasted but a minute or two each time—although it seemed longer at that age—and, as I stood there, I definitely recall thinking that I was getting off awfully easy for whatever it was I had done. I was neither scared nor scarred by the experience, and I remember counting some two hundred little holes in the acoustic ceiling tiles just above me; but yet I discovered that the next time I was tempted to do the "wrong" thing, I automatically thought twice and then veered in a more correct direction.

On the other hand, twice in my childhood my parents mistakenly acted in a way that terrified me, and, although I've intellectually excused and forgiven them since, I still get a twinge of the emotional horror and hurt that originally derived therefrom. In both instances, my parents were acting from their own internal strife although it was couched as a reaction to something I'd done, with the result that I felt rejected, abandoned, and confused.

The first incident for me was when I was maybe five or six years old. The whole family was in our car—my brother and I in the back, father driving, mother next to him. I said something to my mom—something innocuous, but, surprise! my father reflexively reached around and gave me a swat across the cheek. It was the one and only time he ever did that. I was shocked and terrified and in emotional agony—the open-handed swat itself didn't actually hurt at all. My mother was even more shocked, and she began to yell at my father, which only scared me even more. As it turned out, he had whacked me because he thought I had said something terrible to my mother. In fact, he was deaf in his right ear due to war injuries, and he'd misheard what I'd said. Had he stopped to think, he also would have realized that what he thought he heard was impossibly out of character for me anyway. But he was feeling pressured that day about business concerns, and so he was on the ragged jagged edge to begin with. As I say, I understand all this now, but it doesn't take away the recollection of how, for one instant, the rug was yanked out from under my emotional world.

The second incident was years later, when I was a teenager. My mother was under incredible pressure that I had not recognized. She was having health problems, and she was desperate to get out of her marriage to my father but felt that she couldn't without jeopardizing his financial underwriting of my brother's and my educations. My mother, my brother, and I were all driving in my mother's car. I said something, and boom! my mother jerked the car over to the curb and told me to get out. She told me that she just couldn't take it anymore, that I was utterly selfish and ungrateful. At least, that's what I think she said—it's certainly what she ought to have said. All I really remember is her ordering me out of the car as she started to cry. In my heart of hearts, I knew she wasn't about to leave me there, but I was absolutely paralyzed with fear and refused to get out of the car. My brother burst into tears. Our saintly mother had suddenly become a monster or a Martian or worse, and I was to blame. Quickly, she caught herself and relented, pulling the car back out into traffic. I vividly remember the exact corner where this occurred in Van Nuys in the San Fernando Valley, and I still get a twinge anytime I drive near there. I also know that it was on a Wednesday in mid-April, and I always remember it when April rolls around. I know that afterwards my mother felt as bad about the incident as I did, but that doesn't mitigate the emotional reality that her momentary rejection and threat of abandonment was totally crushing.

Interestingly, my therapist recently pointed out that most if not all of the emotionally charged incidents in my life revolved around cars. I suggested that you spend a lot of time in cars in Southern California and they create an artificially confined venue from which there is no escape as interpersonal issues come to the fore. Cars heighten reality. They are also incredibly conducive to fantasy. They are worlds unto themselves, both a part of and apart from the rest of the world. The FBI profilers have postulated that serial killers can function more easily in modern times because the mobility afforded by cars gives them a wider killing field which makes them more difficult to catch. I think the truth is the converse: Serial murder is not at an all-time high because it's easier for serial killers to commit their crimes and get away with it, it's because the cocoon of the car actually fuels the crime. If you move too much you never root, you never connect, and it's insulation and fantasy which create the *mens rea* for serial murder.

Yet, once again my childhood traumas—car-related or not—may have held back my maturation and even glitched my chances for happiness, but they did not propel me to serial murder. So I get the chills when I imagine a child like Bill Suff whose entire emotional youth was manipulated and toyed with by his parents, taken to inexplicable extremes. We cannot ever justify the crimes that he committed as an adult, but you just have to accept as gospel that Bill Suff never ever had a fair chance, and, because of that, neither did his victims. Particularly once he bought his van.

Catherine McDonald had worked hard to get her life together. A pretty, thirty-year-old African-American from Los Angeles, she'd completely kicked a sometime drug habit and was employed as a domestic in order to provide for her two toddlers. She lived in an apartment not too far from the meticulously manicured middle-class house where she'd grown up and where her kids stayed during her workdays, taken care of by her proud mom and stylish sister. God was an important part of Catherine McDonald's life.

The problem was, God seemed to like to see Cathy pregnant, and, in mid-September 1991, she was in the last days of her first trimester for "child number three". Of course, Cathy had yet to nail down even a "husband number one".

With her pregnancy starting to show, Cathy had to explain the situation to her employers, and they made it clear that, once she got "too far along", they'd have to find someone to replace her. Permanently.

Panicked but practical, Cathy steeled herself and made a plan: she'd spend the next few weekends "moonlighting", making some extra cash that she could stash away, so that she wouldn't be a burden on her family when she was out of work.

The "moonlighting" would be a trade she thought she'd left behind but always knew she could and would resort to in a pinch: the world's oldest profession—work that's always there, skills that never get rusty. But no way would she let her family know.

So, on a Thursday afternoon, September 12, 1991, Cathy dropped off her kids at her mom's, made some excuse about a weekend holiday with a fictitious beau, and down the freeway she cruised.

To Riverside.

To where Bill Suff was proudly but nervously prepping for the Riverside County Employees' Annual Picnic and Cook-off.

Bill had a reasonably new wife, a very new baby daughter, and a lot of worries about how that baby kept getting so injured all the time. He also had several years of murders under his belt, and he was now moving at a pace of at least one per month. He had a very real fear that Texas was happening all over again, that his wife might leave him if this stewardess class she was taking actually led to a job, and maybe somehow it was all the baby's fault. Again. If you believed in omens—as he did—it just didn't help that this baby had the same birthday as the dead baby. He could have and should have viewed it as God granting him a second chance, but he saw it instead as a curse destined to revisit him again and again.

Thankfully, the cook-off would be a chance for him to socialize and prove to all the world that nothing was wrong, and he actually reveled in the pressure of concocting his sweet chili one more time, after having won the "best chili" ribbon two years running and the "best dish overall" two years ago. This year Bill was determined to regain that ultimate title and *take home the loving cup and ribbon that went with it. New trophies to add to his collection. Of course, the other "trophies" couldn't be displayed so publicly—clothes, jewelry, and other personal items from his murder victims: he had these "trophies" in his apartment, his van, at his workplace, little reminders that got him a little bit erect any time he thought about them, anytime he wanted, secrets hidden in plain sight, a trail of blood and agony that anyone could see but no one did. It's not that he wanted to get caught; it's that the threat of exposure was exhilarating. How then to take it one step further? How best to prove that he was in control, total control, of the living and the dead alike? Bill had the answer.*

When I first got involved in the Suff case, all everyone wanted to talk about was "Bill's cookbook". Bill himself brought it up to me in every conversation. He was playful about it, but he was also extraordinarily proud, and he wasn't lying when he told me that two of the jail guards had asked for the chili recipe on behalf of their wives who'd tasted the stuff at the cook-off. However, most people's reference to the cookbook was in the context of creepiness. The notion of an accused serial killer sitting in his jail cell and writing a cookbook was just plain "over the top".

As you will see, the cookbook contains both recipes and anecdotes. It's quite a sophisticated piece of writing—Bill's very distinct, folksy "voice", along with careful instructions and chitchat. I was amused to note that Bill even penciled in the trademark and tradename logos whenever he recommended ingredients by brand.

"But aren't you supposed to do that legally?" he asked me when I raised the issue.

"When you publish it, yes—but not when you're just writing it for yourself or your friends," I said.

"I'd like to see my cookbook published," he replied.

"We'll put it in our book."

"No, I'd like to see it published separately—I don't want it in our book. I'll get it published later."

This created an early dilemma for me. The answer was to submit the cookbook to my agent, Peter Miller, for review. However, when I suggested that to Peter, he wasn't amused: "I am not going to solicit the publication of a cookbook written by a serial killer—are you crazy? I won't even read it. Don't even talk to me about this. Just get your book done so we can move on to projects that don't make me sick."

But I pushed:

"Peter, just give Bill a read, a review—tell him the truth. What's happening is all this is going to his head because I complimented his writing. He needs an objective opinion—an objective kick in the teeth. Then he'll let us publish the cookbook in the real book."

"You want me to have one of my editors tell him his cookbook sucks? No way! I'm not having this guy mad at me."

"Peter, he's in jail, he's on his way to Death Row. Even if we get rid of the death sentence, he's never getting out."

"No. N-O. I don't even want this guy to know I'm alive. I don't even want him to think about me. I have little children. I have a wife that I love."

"You're being irrational."

Peter's response was silence.

"All right," I said, "what if I write the review of the cookbook, and I pretend one of your people did it?"

"No names—I don't want my address or phone number on there—you hear me?"

"Fine. I'll FAX you a copy of the review as soon as it's done."

"Don't. I don't even want it in my files."

Here's the memo I wrote:

TO: PMA EDITORIAL STAFF
FROM: J.G.
RE: "VITTLES 'N' FIXIN'S" by "Bill S"
COVERAGE: RUSH!

This is a cookbook "peppered" with the author's short personal anecdotes. The recipes can best be described as "personalized home cooking".

First, let me say that the recipes look okay, although they are not obviously special in a "signature" sort of way.

Second, let me say that the anecdotes and the structure were interesting, a good read overall, and it is the "folksy reality" of the author's voice and style that makes the book most endearing—this is a "guy next door" writing about his good cookin'.

By the same token, any promise in the writing is mitigated by grammatical errors and unintentionally unsophisticated syntax which clearly brands the author as an amateur (talented, but not yet professionally polished).

A lot of editing and rewriting would be needed to raise this ms. to a level where we could even consider pitching it.

And this brings me to my third point: as we know, mixed genres are always tough sells (no matter how well-written). The publishers and the audience both want to know whether a given book is animal, mineral, or vegetable, and everyone gets lost when an author tries different tacks in the same piece.

More particularly (and I write this after having contacted several publishers this morning to confirm it), cookbooks are only sold when the author's voice and identity are already known and valuable commodities. In other words, other than fad diet books, true cookbooks are only sold on commission, by a publisher asking an already successful and renowned chef, restaurateur, or food columnist to go ahead and write a book.

Even then, neither publisher nor author makes much money off the book — it's more of a "prestige" accomplishment that leads to other, hopefully lucrative opportunities.

Accordingly, none of the publishers I contacted would agree to read such a submission. Were "Bill S" actually Wolfgang Puck, of course, there might have been some interest.

My suggestion is to encourage "Bill S" to think about using the kitchen setting and the notion of cooking as the jumping-off points for a sort of fictional memoir, à la *Like Water for Chocolate,* or in the manner of *The Bridges of Madison County,* (or, for that matter, *Fried Green Tomatoes*!), particularly since you told me that he also writes short stories and novels.

In conclusion: we cannot sell this (or even submit it), but the author should be encouraged to put it aside and keep up his other writing. I sense he's got good writer's instincts, and, once he pays his dues, someday he'll put out a solid piece of work. I'm happy to review his future material.

ADDENDUM—MONDAY AFTERNOON:

I am absolutely floored by what Jeff just told me. "Bill S" is that creep in California! Amazing. Too bad his talent is going to such waste in prison. Anyway, obviously my coverage of the cookbook is secondary to the fact that never, under any circumstances, could we sell or be associated with selling the writings of a convicted serial murderer and baby killer.

Even if we used a pseudonym or a straw man, we would run too much risk of having our credibility destroyed should the publisher or public ever learn the truth. (And it would be illegal for "Bill S" to make any money, right? Doesn't California have a "Son of Sam" law?)

I'm afraid I have to take back what I said about encouraging "Bill S" to write—there is no point in giving him false hopes of publication or income. The only context in which his work could legitimately appear would be in a story about him, or some day posthumously (it's kind of macabre, but I suppose if he's executed, there might be some lurid interest in the writings he left behind—not that we'd want anything to do with it).

Sorry to be so blunt, but why was I given this ms. to read?

I immediately sent this bogus memo to Don Suff, knowing that he would get it over to Bill in the Riverside jail.

Predictably, Don did what I expected.

And Bill's response was equally expected—suddenly he was becoming predictable to me, suddenly I had the illusion of control over him, suddenly I realized I myself was thinking like a serial killer.

"I can't believe what they said about my cookbook!" Bill yelled over the phone at me—it was the first time I'd heard him actively angry. Maybe Peter was right to worry.

"Actually, Bill, they liked the cookbook, it was *you* they had a problem with," I replied.

"I cannot believe it!" he shouted. "What does one thing have to do with the other?! This is a good cookbook!" Suddenly I was Alice and this was Wonderland and Bill Suff was trying to make nonsense sensible.

Now, I have to confess that I've never "done" drugs, fearing the feeling of being out of control, so I have no firsthand experience with controlled delusions, but I have grilled friends about their drug experiences. One friend told me how LSD had turned a bowl of spaghetti Bolognese into a nest of wriggling vipers. After that, he always insisted on *al dente*.

At the same time, I once knew a girl—an actress—who didn't use drugs at all, but nonetheless saw a blue-winged demon trailing her whenever she was stressed, which was pretty much all the time. The only good news was that she didn't always talk about it. Not coincidentally, she was my first sexual partner, a onetime thing during which I was afraid to remove my black socks for fear everything else would slip out of place. I simply realized too late that the socks were still on. Logistics can be daunting, and mechanics are nothing short of a curse, but somehow it all comes out in the wash, as they say. Luckily for me, the actress didn't seem to notice the socks, her eyes staring up intently over my shoulder toward the scalloped, shadow-box ceiling, where the demon no doubt hovered. I didn't happen to notice the demon myself, but I was grateful for his distracting her.

The point is that the difference between the acid king and the actress was that his hallucinations were misperceptions of reality, while she was seeing something where in fact there was nothing there at all. I think.

My sense of Bill Suff is that, like the acid king, his fantasy world is just an alternative view of our own. This means he's grounded. This means he is conscious of his own imagination. If he is forever seeing vipers, then he can damn sure imagine them as spaghetti—either way, he knows he's got a bowl of something in front of him.

Accordingly, while murder may not be murder and dead may be alive, Bill is well aware of his acts and he can extrapolate from them or even see them through someone else's eyes when need be. I therefore knew I could make a point and have him "get it" despite his vocal denials. This seeming "sanity" is why we hate, fear, and are fascinated by certain serial killers—they appear to us to have rationally "chosen" their deadly avocation, and their victims are lured in by the same calm.

"Bill, we gotta face reality here—no one is going to publish your cookbook except as a footnote to your crimes. You want it published, it's gonna have to go in our book. It's up to you."

Only a serial killer would reply as Bill did: "All right, do it— put the cookbook in our book," he relented. It was more important to be published than to be innocent. Or, viewed from another angle: when you know you're guilty, there's a limit to how far you can maintain your act of innocence.

I was quite proud of myself.

"But the guy that wrote this stuff about me—what's his name and how do I contact him?" asked Bill icily.

Before Bill's formal sentencing, he was interviewed by a corrections and probation department official who made out an informational report for the judge. The jury had already voted for the death penalty, but the judge had a right to make it life imprisonment if there was some compelling humanitarian reason to do so. Bill had not testified at trial—now he could tell his side of the story to the corrections official, in the hope that he could sway the judge to spare his life.

Of course, Bill protested his innocence to every charge and every bit of evidence on which every charge was based. He was also innocent of killing baby Dijianet.

The corrections official—a woman—listened to Bill's story, took copious notes, and then eyed him with a smirk as she snapped her notebook closed: "You know something, Mr. Suff, you must be the most wronged man on Earth."

Bill thought about it for a minute, and then he nodded: "Yes, ma'am, I believe I am."

In her report, the woman wrote that Bill was unrepentant, remorseless, and a liar. She, too, damned him because he seemed more concerned with his cookbook than with his crimes.

In fact, they were one and the same.

September 12, 1991. The lights were on and nobody was home. The big pot was simmering on Bill Suff's stove. Only one more day to the chili cook-off. Bill had been a whirlwind of activity, dicing and slicing and grating and stirring—a pinch of spice, a tweak of condiment—tasting, tasting, always tasting, no wonder his spare tire now had a spare tire, but now he'd cleaned up all the pots and pans and utensils, cleaned them and hung them on their appropriate hooks, and tidied up the kitchen counter, and all that was left was the big crock-pot on the stove. And Bill was gone.

So was his van.

Cheryl was home, but she stayed out of the kitchen. Even with Bill gone, she could hear the growl he growled if she came near while he was cooking. He was gone, but the crock-pot was his alter ego, and it was there churning on the stove. The edge of blue gaslight watched her as she walked by the kitchen door. Bill would know if she went into the kitchen. He would know, and he wouldn't like it. He berated her for her cooking which was unarguably lousy, but she knew he would be even angrier if she ever actually learned to cook. He needed her to be incompetent so he could take care of her. And she needed him to stay busy and distracted— anything so he'd stay away from the baby.

Cathy McDonald was having a good evening. It was a weeknight, and she'd just expected to earn enough to pay for food and a motel room for the weekend (tomorrow, Saturday, and Sunday after church figured to be the big paydays), but some college boys, a couple of lawyers, and a farmer with a truckload of onions had all welcomed her full red lips to their groins and their wallets, so she was ahead of schedule and pretty relaxed. All she'd done was get driven around the block a few times, and she'd even been able to keep her clothes on except for the top, of course. No AIDS issue either, not that she ever made much of an issue out of it. What would be, would be. The only thing she caught herself wondering as she wandered the street for one last trick that night was how come the onion farmer didn't taste like onion. "You are how you taste!" was a cute homily she shared with friends and customers alike. But this farmer—how could you grow and sell onions if you didn't eat them? How could you sell a good or a service you didn't appreciate for yourself? Cathy liked sex, always had. Paid or not, it was warm and exciting and made her feel in control. Everyone gets off on control, don't they?

When the van pulled alongside her and the driver beckoned her over, he had a kind of half-smile, like he had gas. He looked like he was trying not to look nervous, which is exactly how you want your tricks to look. Too steely was scary. Too much to the point was a cop. Too twitchy meant he didn't have enough of a bankroll or a hard-on, so you'd just be wasting your time and you might get smacked, to boot.

Looking in through the window, the van looked almost homey— staged, but homey. There was a Bible on the front console, a sleeping bag in the back. There were other bags and rope and odds and ends all over, all carefully stowed. There was even an audiocassette recorder down behind the front seats. The driver was clean and his belt buckle shined, although his stomach slopped over it, held tight by the too-tight shirt. His jeans were pressed and that shirt was dark—it was like his personal uniform. This was maybe an ex-military guy, or maybe private security. On second thought, maybe he was a cop or a cop-aspirant, but this was no sting—he didn't want to bust her, he just wanted to get laid. He stated that he wanted sex and he would pay twenty dollars, no more.

Cops made sure you were the one to tell them what you'd do and how much it would cost—so, no, this was no cop.

Cathy McDonald had not heard a whole lot about the Riverside Prostitute Killer. The guy had been operating for years, a task force was pulling its collective hair out, and a German film company had even made a movie about it, based on the fiction that the killer really was a cop, but none of it had much to do with Cathy. See, Cathy was black, and the killer had only killed whites. A local newspaper had just pointed out that fact this week.

So, Cathy had nothing to worry about.

At least not until Bill Suff read that newspaper.

The German film crew goose-stepped into town about halfway through the killing spree. Like all foreign filmmakers, storytelling was going to get lost in political diatribe, and, to these particular filmmakers, this was obviously a story about a fascist, vigilante cop secretly terrorizing his beat, murdering hookers to scare the populace into granting the cops more power and authority in order to clean up the streets. This was a way for the Germans to pretend that the Nazis were all American now.

As noted, Bill Suff would later adopt this fiction as his "alibi", much as O.J. conjured up crazed Colombian drug dealers.

In the meantime, since the task force wasn't getting anywhere and the murders kept happening, the local press was hard-pressed to come up with daily angles for coverage, so they greedily glommed onto this low-budget movie production. No doubt Bill read about it in the newspaper—he read every article about the killings and clipped them out religiously.

So, when the papers indicated the location of the next day's movie shoot, Bill showed up and blended into the onlookers. Pretty soon he started acting like he belonged there, like he was local security for the crew. He kept the onlookers at bay and he advised the crew on the closest and best places for late-night coffee and doughnuts. Later, once the errand boys brought in boxes and jugs of the stuff, the crew politely offered Bill a bite. He didn't decline. Jelly doughnuts and crullers—even the crumbs were sweet.

Finally, after a few days, the film crew was ready to move on to the next location. They arrived bright and early, just after dawn, with all their big trucks of equipment and "honey wagons" for the cast. This was going to be the scene of a "murder". A "local hire"— that is, a Riverside girl/actress—was going to play the corpse.

She never got the chance.

The Riverside Prostitute Killer had marked his territory the night before.

There was a real live dead body waiting in the weeds for the film crew as they arrived.

They packed and finished the movie in Germany. Publicly, they pretended that they believed their fiction had stumbled onto the truth and the killer cop wanted them out of Riverside; but, privately, the opposite conclusion obtained—the real killer was pissed that a cop was getting credit for something a clever civilian was doing. The killer wanted the difficulty of his work to be appreciated.

When Cathy McDonald's nude, fully exposed body was discovered in a sort of dirt/rock field on September 13, 1991, the task force was not happy. There was no doubt this was the work of the Riverside Prostitute Killer. She had been posed on her back, knees wide apart but feet bottoms together, arms outstretched crucifixion-style except that one hand was up and one was down, fingers fanned and pointing. She could have been showing off the latest kitchen showcase on The Price Is Right, *or she could have been taking a formal stage bow, or maybe she was doing that ersatz "Middle Eastern" dance where the women slide their heads back and forth from shoulder to shoulder—it's more of an old vaudeville routine than a real dance—Steve Martin doing "King Tut". Whatever this pose represented, it was a new pose for the Killer, who seemed to be more whimsical with each outing. It's hard to say whether it's better or worse that Cathy's face was exposed rather than bent back under and buried in the ground like an ostrich as had happened to some victims, but Cathy's open eyes and the big bloody gouge through her neck suggested that the Killer had chosen to take more time toying with her while she was alive rather than just concentrating on posing her postmortem. Although*

*the killing might have started out innocuously, dispassionately enough,
something had pissed off the Killer, something had happened between victim and Killer after she was already in his clutches.*

*Indeed, unlike other victims, Cathy had not been re-dressed in some-
one else's clothes, no wildly striped men's socks going up her legs like a
clown or a chicken, nor were her arms stuffed inside a T-shirt, no coats
over her head or plastic bags over her torso. Cathy had somehow become
more personal to the Killer, her death mattered more than the ultimate
place she would come to occupy in his mosaic of murder. But, so there
was no mistaking the Killer's work, Cathy had been punctured between
the legs with a sharp knife, she'd been stabbed in the chest, and, like several other victims, her right breast had been removed.*

*With each breast excision, the Killer had gotten better and better,
more meticulous, more sure. Cathy had been cleanly sliced right down
to the fat, and this time he hadn't nicked the ribs. Mercifully, she'd been
strangled before the heavy cutting began, so there was little blood and
much unreality to the scene. And, unlike other victims, she had no cigarette burns on her, nor had her belly button been carved out so he could
look inside her and see what ticked. Cathy's sightless eyes and expres-
sionless face made her seem a mannequin rather than a mother.*

You can't look at dead bodies and talk about them or write
about them if you think they're real. You have to tell yourself
they're not people now, and they never ever were. Then, if you can
distance sufficiently while nonetheless remaining focused, you can
actually begin to see the victims through a killer's eyes.

I remember when my comatose brother went cyanotic and the
life force left him—he was technically alive but he was gone, and
although he still had a human shape he was no longer a human
being. His nurse in Neurological Intensive Care had made the
break from him before she'd even known him—after he died, I
chanced to see her daily log. In every entry she referred to him as
an "it".

More dramatic, simultaneously terrifying and comforting, was
my mother at her funeral. I'd wanted to see her one last time, so I

insisted on an open casket, until I saw her and realized it wasn't her, not anymore. Her soul had moved on, and mortuary makeup had turned her into someone else's hideously mistaken version of what she'd been. Had she still looked alive, I think I would have had to have killed myself.

Having seen her, I postponed the interment so she could be cremated and then buried. My father indulged me because he knew I was hanging on by a single emotional thread. I just didn't want her buried looking like that. We don't bury our loved ones so that we can forget them, we bury our memories of them so that we know where to find them when we want to remember. When I was to visit the cemetery, I needed to be able to see my mother as she had lived.

On the other hand, the serial killer doesn't see his victims for what was in life, only for what is in death, which is the killer's own eternal creation. I go to the cemetery and have to jog my fading memory of the past, while the serial killer exists easily in the present. He wanted the woman dead—that's when she would become his. He saw her dead before he ever met her. Alive, she was always an "it"—one potential victim could easily have been interchanged with another, so many potential victims never became victims at all, thanks to sheer circumstance—but dead, each victim is finally and irretrievably distinct. And now, since it's always the present, she exists for him forever—she's dead, but she's very much alive.

Cathy McDonald knew she was going to die. The Killer had her bound hand and foot in the back of his van, and he was driving her someplace, and she knew she wasn't coming back.

But she had to try to save herself—she owed that to her children, the ones waiting at home and the one she carried in her womb.

So, when the Killer parked by this desolate field, when he climbed into the back of the van and hovered over her, his eyes burning with hate, she swallowed hard and tried to speak to him.

She told him she would do whatever he wanted. This would not come as news to him, of course, since she was hardly in a position to resist, but she thought maybe he wanted to hear the words. Maybe he'd even believe that she was submitting by choice rather than by force.

But the Killer didn't take heed—he was too busy preparing his garrote, unwrapping his knife, cutting off her clothes.

Now she begged—she told him about her children, about her pregnancy. She was lucid and she was direct, and this he heard. The other women, they were all too drugged up to be so conversant, nothing they said amounted to much, but this one was intelligent and sensible, and he could listen because he wasn't so full of rage against her as he'd been with the others. The others had made him mad—some were women he'd known, women he'd loved, not random as the police thought—but this one, this black woman he was killing partly because he needed some relief tonight and partly because he needed to kill a black woman in order to thumb his nose at the police and their profiles.

Yeah, the Killer had read the newspaper. How dare they say he only killed white women? He could kill any damn woman he pleased. This would tell the police that they ought to give up, that they were to blame. This black woman wouldn't have died if the police hadn't done that profile.

For the Killer knew he'd been careful not to leave enough evidence anywhere at any time that could tie him to the killings, so he couldn't be found out and he couldn't be stopped unless he was caught in the act. To catch him they'd have to predict where he'd be and then be there waiting for him to show. But he was unpredictable. Killing this black woman would prove it. Maybe next time he'd kill someone orange, or green, or purple. Maybe he'd kill someone white and paint her purple.

And now that he had Cathy McDonald writhing at his feet, smooth dark flesh glistening, muscles striated, eyes wide and round like coals, he started to wonder, to really consider: does black skin look the same on the inside as out? Just how far did that pigmented skin extend? Black men had black penises; did Cathy have a black vagina, a black clitoris, black labial lips and folds? What was pink and what was black down there, and was it all hung the same as with white women?

These were questions he'd never pondered before, but then he'd never been alone with and in control of a black woman before. Sure, he'd "slept" with black hookers from time to time, but when it was business rather than murder they barely took the time to undress, let alone let you explore their bodies. Twenty dollars only bought you an orgasm, and that only if you were quick about it.

But tonight the Killer would have all the time he wanted with this mysterious black minx, and he could answer any questions that came to mind. Whatever he wanted to know, he could find out with a little probing, a little peeking, a little cutting with his knife.

Oh, and that business about her being pregnant—he knew she wasn't lying, he could tell by the desperate yet determined tone of her voice. But he wasn't sure how he felt about that, about killing a pregnant woman. There was no way in the world he was going to spare her because of the pregnancy, but he just wasn't sure how he felt about it. Babies frightened him. They ruined his life. Like his birth had ruined his parents' lives.

Yet, he liked babies. When you played with them and fed them and they were happy, they were great, like little animals. It's just that you couldn't keep them happy, and they demanded so much. Animals were easy to train. Babies fought you. They always made you feel like you couldn't do enough and you couldn't do anything right. And, to be honest, a baby wasn't really yours, was it? Maybe when it was growing in the womb it was part of the mother, but it was never really connected to the father. Fathers could have babies and never even know about it. Fathers could have babies, know about them, and then walk away from them at any time and never come back. Mothers could have babies that weren't their husband's. And, when mothers were pregnant, fathers didn't exist at all, they suddenly ceased to matter, they became phantoms. It wasn't "Wham! Bam! Thank-you, ma'am!," it was "Wham! Bam! Thank you, sir—now take a hike, I'm busy for the next nine months and then the rest of my life."

It was no coincidence that the killings increased in frequency and urgency the moment the Killer's wife got pregnant. The only thing worse than her being pregnant was her actually having the baby.

His baby would have to go.

But then Cathy's baby wasn't even a baby yet, or was it? The Killer wanted to know, he wanted to see. He was curious, he was stimulated. Boy, girl, black, white? Did it have hands and feet? How about a face? Or hair? Or a heart? In magazines and on TV he'd seen photos of babies in the womb—the doctors looked in through the belly button. Sure, the belly button—he knew what to do, he'd done it before with women who weren't pregnant—he'd cut carefully, precisely, and he'd look in, but this time he'd see a baby. It wouldn't hurt it, it would be okay. It would be like the Killer was a doctor. He would see things that only a privileged few earn the right to see.

But then Cathy noticed him looking at her stomach. She knew. She knew he wasn't just going to kill her, he was going to do something to her baby. It didn't matter that she and the baby were both already dead, that even though her lungs still breathed and her heart still pumped, her life was now in retrospect. There was no escape here, but she was not going to let him do things to her baby!

So she fought, tied up though she was. Maybe she kicked, or spit, or bit, or simply screamed. And he saw in her eyes that look of horror—not fear, horror, the look you have when you see a monster, the look the girl had in that dream he always had—the look his wives both had when they caught him hurting their babies—and so now the Killer got mad at Cathy McDonald. He saw himself in that look of horror, and he didn't like what he saw, so he had to destroy it, he had to destroy the monster even though the best he could do was shatter the mirror.

The Killer punished Cathy McDonald. She got strangled and she got stabbed. She got killed several times over. And somewhere along the line the Killer took down his pants and fumbled for a condom. He pressed himself on top of her, and he licked her face, then the blood on her torn neck, then her nipples, then took a gentle bite, careful not to break the skin or leave a tooth impression that could come back to haunt him.

And he was surprised to find that she tasted good. Not sweaty, not salty, not bitter, not bland. Cathy McDonald tasted sweet.

The FBI profilers try to be proactive; they try to force serial killers into the light before the next killing happens. It doesn't take much in the way of brains, balls, or gamesmanship to sit back and let a serial killer keep killing until he screws up and gets noticed, so you've got to somehow get yourself a step ahead of a guy who's been a step ahead of you ever since the opening bell. But, proactive can backfire. It's never like TV or the movies where the killer now decides to go after the cop, because that would require the killer to change his emotional rules of engagement—the killings would have to take on a different meaning for him—and, if he could do that, then he could stop killing altogether. No, proactive backfires when you piss the killer off. Then, as a profiler, you have to live with the fact that, although the killer would have killed again even if you'd done nothing, you are nonetheless responsible for his choice of victim and the final insults she suffered.

No authority in Riverside will confirm whose brilliant idea it was to publicize the Prostitute Killer's profile with respect to race, not that it wasn't obvious anyway just by listing the victims, but Cathy McDonald died because of it. In addition, her mutilation reflected a new and nauseatingly nasty "fuck you" from the killer.

In the previous killings where the right breast had been excised, the severed tissue had been found nearby or tossed on the ground. In the Casares murder—the next after Cathy McDonald—the severed breast would be hung from a tree branch, just another way for the killer to demean the victim herself or maybe make the authorities briefly think that these killings were not tied to the many others where the breasts were left intact. The killer walks a desperate tightrope of desire to "sign" his crimes even while he varies the signature so he won't get caught.

But, in Cathy McDonald's case, the severed breast was never found.

Why? What horror did this imply? Was it symbolic, artistic, or of practical necessity?

The first of the "excision" killings was in San Bernardino, a murder for which Bill Suff has never been charged, although he will be should he ever overturn his Riverside convictions. Right now, San Bernardino is simply saving itself the cost of a death penalty trial.

I asked Bill about the San Bernardino case and he waved it off: "They just think I did it because her right breast was cut off," he said.

"Good enough reason, don't you think?" I responded.

"I love women's breasts," he replied, "why would I cut one off?"

It suddenly occurred to me that not even in the lowest, drunkenest, ugliest locker room conversation I had ever had with anyone at any time, had I ever had a conversation like this. But then I had to ask myself: If you are innocent of atrocity, what exactly is the right way to answer when you are accused of it? If Bill would've thrown up at the question, would I have taken that as guilt, as remorse? If he'd laughed, would I have thought him nervous? Is there anything he could have said or any tear he could have shed that would have been innocent-seeming in the face of such guilt-loaded inquiry?

Perversely, my mother used to ask me what I'd say at her funeral, what sort of wonderful eulogy I would give, this "gifted" writer son of hers.

Of course, I was appalled at the question, appalled and terrified. I did not want to contemplate her mortality in any context. I told her that there was nothing I could say, that mere words could not capture her or the depth of my feelings for her, so her funeral would be the one time I would be tongue-tied, with a case of writer's block that could not be moved.

She seemed not to understand.

What I meant but could not express was that I would not use my talent and my heart to affirm her death. If I did not acknowledge it, if her death did not just pass like another sunrise and sunset, then it would be like it had not happened. And, if I told her in advance that I could not eulogize her, then maybe she would keep herself from dying. Of course, while she was alive I could not tell her that I was really insolently refusing to do what she'd asked of me, so I couched it as an impossibility, but promised to do the impossible nonetheless.

After all, she wasn't asking, she was expecting, commanding. So, when the time for her funeral was actually at hand, I knew I would have to say something; and I got up and made a fool of myself, saying that I could say nothing, saying that her life and her death were utterly personal to me and incapable of being shared, not that anyone understood a syllable I uttered as I sobbed away, completely distraught.

Later, I felt I'd done what I'd told my mother I would do, but nonetheless I had let her and myself down. I accepted the obvious—she was gone—and so I wrote poetry about her and to her, etched eternally on her gravestone in iambic hexameter. I did the same for my brother.

Yet, I still cringe when I remember her asking me what I'd say at her funeral. What should I have answered? It wasn't just that she was putting me in an emotionally impossible position; it was that she made me feel terribly guilty. I was responsible for her death even before I killed her.

"Bill, say something innocent," I suggested.

"I am innocent," he said.

How come I felt guilty and this convicted serial killer did not?

"Any idea why someone would cut off these women's right breasts?"

"Nope."

"No image comes to mind? No painting or story, some myth, anything?"

"Nope." Then Bill Suff cleared his throat, and: "But I do have a phobia about anyone putting needles, hypodermics, in my left arm—I tell you that?"

"This is the first time. Go on."

"That's all there is to it—I won't let 'em give me a shot or take blood out of my left arm."

"Why is that?"

"I have no idea. But it's for as long as I can remember."

"Anyone ever intentionally hurt your left arm? Anyone ever break it or burn it? Your mother or your father ever twist it, abuse it?"

"Not so's I remember—no."

"That's a weird deal."

"I agree. But it is my left arm and hand that were hurt in my motorcycle wreck. Were you aware I've got no strength, no good grip in my left hand?"

"Not enough to strangle anyone with?"

"Wouldn't know—never strangled anybody."

"Then . . . would you be willing to be hypnotized to find out what this left arm business is all about?"

"Sure. Maybe."

The human body talks to its owner. Emotional memories become visceral sense memories. My left eye twitched because it contained the emotional "data file" of the accident that killed my mother and brother. That eye had been fractured during the accident. Bill's left arm knows why he kills. Something happened to that left arm, or maybe it's just the killing arm. Maybe the phobic fear is that sticking a needle in that left arm will cause the truth to leak out. I don't think Bill's left arm has anything to do with severed right breasts other than, when you're facing a body straight-on and cutting with your right hand because your left hand is weak, then it's easier to remove a right breast than a left. If you're trying to excise the left breast, you have to twist your wrist down and then back up at a tough angle under the armpit, so you can't make a clean cut. But, a right breast you can just slice from right to left and down—piece of cake.

Never forget the practical aspects of a serial killer's pattern—it's not always so mysterious and psychologically deep. Killing is more often than not triggered by external stress—problems on the job or problems at home. Bill's killings escalated as soon as Cheryl got pregnant—a problem pregnancy that sent her first to bed and then to the hospital and otherwise made her unavailable for and inattentive to Bill. The details of the killings are influenced by the same sort of stressors. Cathy McDonald died because of the threat and challenge of the profile. Her breast was removed because it seemed like a good idea at the time and because the killer was enjoying his surgical brilliance with the knife in her vagina, neck, and chest—he was on a roll, and he kept on going, hand steady, technique improved from before, no people or cars around, nothing to impinge as he took his time to do whatever came to mind. Cathy wasn't hacked at; she was quite professionally operated on and then "dressed".

In all the other cases, the severed breasts were found nearby. In Cathy McDonald's case, the missing breast was never found.

Forensic experts, biologists, naturalists, and anyone who knew anything were all called in to comb the area in the hope of finding animal tracks, droppings, blood or tissue from the breast, or any other evidence to show what had become of it. Everyone wanted desperately to find the breast because it was the killer's pattern to leave it, and no one wanted to believe that perhaps this one murder had been committed by some not-quite-accurate copycat.

However, the only thing proved beyond a shadow of a doubt was that the Killer took the breast away with him.

Why?

On September 14, 1991, Bill Suff took his simmering "sweet chili" off the stove and served it at the Riverside County Employees' Annual Picnic and Cook-off. By acclamation, Bill's recipe won "best chili" and "best overall dish"—he was the grand prizewinner and he couldn't have been prouder. His picture appeared in all the local papers. He was a celebrity. His chili had been sampled by stock boys and supply clerks and truck drivers and jail guards and police detectives and their wives and children. In the midst of the Riverside Prostitute Killer's terror, the picnic was a way for the county to pull together and enjoy high spirits that would momentarily lift the pall. Members of the task force cruised in to enjoy the food and drink as they changed shifts.

And everyone wanted Bill's recipe.

It's in his cookbook, reprinted on the pages that follow.

As Bill notes, the key to great chili is the meat.

CHAPTER 9

Excerpts from

"The Cookbook"

written by Bill Suff

Bill's
VITTLES
'N'
FIXIN'S

written by
Bill Suff

DEDICATION

This book is dedicated to those whom have repeatedly asked the 'Starving Person's Question': "Is It Done Yet?" for keeping me at work on it and to those whom have kept encouraging me to keep writing (because they wanted copies of all my recipés for themselves). Most important is this dedication, because without her threats, encouragement and telling me that I should write down my recipés, this book would not be at all. Thank you, Patricia 'Tricia' Barnaby, for assisting me in, not only putting my recipés down on paper, but for giving me a way to retain my sanity when troubles surely would have caused me to leave it far behind. And, of course, without the following people, some of these recipés may not have ever come into being. Special thanks to: Bonnie A., Bobbie H., Gayleen, Kathy R., Karen, Tom, Cathy, Rebecca, Cheryl and their children. These people were the first to taste many of these recipés; my guinea pigs, as it were. They liked what I fixed and in most cases desired the recipé for their own use. In some cases, they were given copies of these recipés. The rest will be able to obtain them from this book. Hopefully, from my directions, they will come up with the same tastes I presented them with. To those whom are trying these for the first time, I can only say, "I wish I could cook the meal for you!" Eat hearty, or bon appétit, as the French say.

AUTHOR S NOTE TO THE READER/COOK

I first began cooking when I was 16 years old. My mother had to begin working when we lost my father and I became the family cook. For awhile, my brothers and sister were very unsure about eating my meals. I had began cooking strictly by package directions and still made my share of mistakes. The bad part was when I had to *eat* those mistakes. Needless to say, I learned very quickly what "exact measuring" meant. I only regret that I never took any cooking classes while in school. It wasn't until I was on my own that I began "creating."

As you read through these recipés, you may raise your eyebrows in surprise or wonder at some of the ingredients I have listed. Believe it or not, those ingredients work very well in those recipés if used in just the amounts I have listed. Questions have been asked of me as to why I put this or that in such and such recipé. My first reply is usually, "If you've never actually tasted this particular combination, please don't condemn it." Granted, my tastes (and those for whom I've cooked these recipés) may differ somewhat from yours. For instance, not everyone relishes the taste of Malt Vinegar like I do. Usually, you'll find Malt Vinegar used (and sold) in fast food restaurants specializing in seafood. But when combined in the right proportions with the other ingredients, it adds a certain tang that greatly enhances the flavor of the food. That brings to mind the only rules I have when cooking. The first, being: *"Try it, the taste may grow on you!"* and second: *"Don't be afraid to experiment with different tastes and ingredients—you might create a winner!"* That's how the majority of my recipés came into being.

You may notice that in nearly every instance, I've refrained from the use of egg yolks. Usually, only the albumen, or eggwhite, finds its way into my recipés. The reason for this is my fear of the outright consumption of the cholesterol that resides in egg yolks. The egg yolk contains over 90% of the cholesterol found in eggs. I've been asked, if all I use is the albumen in my cooking, what happens to the left over yolks? Let me put it this way—My cat comes a-running when I cook and she's got the shiniest, prettiest fur in the neighborhood.

Like many non-professional cooks, I use a lot of brand name ingredients (®) in my recipés. I've always tried to give credit where credit is due. The companies that make those brand name ingredients can make them a lot better than I can—faster, too! I suppose a different brand could be used, according to your own personal tastes, but I'm faithful to the brands that I use. For instance, I prefer Best Foods® Real Mayonaise over, say, Miracle Whip®, whether I'm making a turkey sandwich or my Deviled Eggs.

Another preferred choice is the butter I use. Shedd's Spread Country Crock® tub Butter is my personal favorite. I feel compelled to stress, however, that whichever brand name you use, butter or margarine, I recommend the soft, tub butter over *any* stick-type butter for your meals. The reason, which I cannot go into in these pages, involves the manner in which the butter is processed in making it "hard" to retain its stick, rectangular form even when it gets soft. (You can check with any health store or local Health Department to find out exactly what the process actually is.)

One of the recipés included in these pages is my prize-winning chili. And yes, my chili *did* win some chili cook-off contests. Three of them consecutively in three years. I've been repeatedly asked for my recipé and upon reading the list of ingredients am asked, "Don't you put *beans* in your chili?!" Like it's a sin to leave out the beans. I have to emphatically reply, "No! Beans don't belong in chili!" As far as I am concerned, anyone who puts beans in their chili, is doing so to hide the taste of their chili. Their chili won't stand up to others on its own merits! I've attended some chili cook-off contests where chili containing beans were disqualified. And I agree with those rules. The way I see it, beans are a dish you eat out on the trail swapping ghost stories while the cattle are asleep! Don't misunderstand me, I don't *dislike* beans. In fact, my favorite are Pork and Beans, Lintel Beans, Black-eyed Beans and Green Beans. Some of the others I'll eat, but I wouldn't cross the street to get them.

Before each recipé is a brief history of how I came about creating that particular recipé. In most instances, the dish was created because of someone or something. A few were specifically created for someone and one or two just happened by accident while fooling around in the kitchen. However they came about, though, doesn't matter. What *does* matter is that the time was taken to experiment with new tastes and mixing of ingredients. After all, who ever would have thought to put cheese *inside* fish, or mayonaise and mustard in chili or to barbeque chicken in the oven, or . . . You get the picture? Don't be afraid to try something new or to do something different from the usual, accepted way of cooking something!

In closing, remind yourself that just because you were taught to cook corn-on-the-cob by boiling it in water, don't be afraid to wrap it in aluminum foil with butter and toss it on the barbecue grill with those spare ribs! Barbecued corn-on-the-cob tastes surprisingly good.

Enjoy reading, enjoy cooking, and savor the tastes!

BILL SUFF

BILL S RECIPES
(ALPHABETICALLY)

Baked Beans plus
Side Dish - Meat

Barbequed Cheeseburgers
Main Dish - Meat

Beer-Batter Shrimp
Main Dish - Seafood

'Burger "Secret Sauce"
Condiment - Sauce

Cheddar Perch
with Beer-Batter
Main Dish - Seafood

Cherry-Apple Muffins
Dessert - Snack

Chicken and Mushroom
Casserole
Main Dish - Meat

Chicken Cacciatore
Main Dish - Meat

Chocolate-Peanut Butter
Fudge
Dessert - Snack

Coffee Cake
Dessert - Snack

Country Barbeque Sauce
Condiment - Sauce

Creamed Beef and
Mushrooms
Breakfast - Meat

Deviled Eggs
Appetizer - Snack

Egg Salad Sandwiches
Lunch - Eggs

Fricasee Chicken
Main Dish - Meat

Giblet Gravy
Condiment - Gravy

Holiday Whipped
Potatoes
Side Dish - Vegetable

Lasagna
Main Dish - Meat

Marinated Ribeye Steak
Main Dish - Meat

Mushroom and Cheese
Casserole
Main Dish - Vegetable

One-Eyed Flapjacks
Breakfast - Combo

Oven Barbequed Chicken
Main Dish - Meat

Pizza Biscuits
Appetizer - Combo

Sautéed Bell Peppers and
Mushrooms
Side Dish - Vegetable

Shrimp and Pasta
Chowder
Soup - Seafood

Soda Swirl Cupcakes
Dessert - Snack

Spice Muffins
Dessert - Snack

Strawberry Turnovers
Dessert - Snack

Stuffed Bell Peppers
Main Dish - Meat

Sugar Cookies
Dessert - Snack

Sweet Chili
Main Dish - Meat

'Tater Boats
Side Dish - Vegetable

Vege-Meatloaf
Main Dish - Meat

Vegetarian Pizza
Main Dish - Vegetable

Western Clam Chowder
Soup - Seafood

Western Omelet
(w/Quail Eggs)
Breakfast - Eggs

Wild Gumbo
Soup - Meat

Spicy Tuna Patties

Tuna Casserole

A SAMPLING OF BILL S RECIPES

SWEET CHILI

Serves 8 to 10

T his recipé has a long and extensive background. I first began attending chili cookoffs in Texas while working for Uncle Sam. I've tasted everything from rabbit and game bird chili to 'possum and rattlesnake chili. The overall theme was a hot and spicy chili. As I got older, my stomach began to rebel at those hot spices. So I had to modify my chili. After many, many different variations, I finally settled on the version that appears here . . . An award winning one. For three years running, this is the version that took First Place awards in its division. The first two of those three years, it also won the Overall Best Chili—Grand Prize Award. But the biggest compliment I ever got for my chili, came from an old girlfriend. She hated chili! Couldn't stand it, wouldn't even try it. One evening, I fixed up a pot of it. It cooked all that night and the next day. That evening I was going to have a couple bowls and take the rest to work the next day. When I dished up a bowl, my girlfriend suddenly decided she wanted a taste. Half of the chili disappeared that evening and she took the rest with her the next day for *her* lunch. After that, she still professed a distaste for chili—but she sure had extra helpings of *my* chili. Now! You must realize that there is a lot involved in making this chili, and it's best if it gets a chance to cook a minimum of 15 hours. It *can* be fixed in a couple of hours if you're willing to sacrifice some taste. But if you have the patience to let it cook all night and into the next evening, it's well worth the wait. And please, I beg of you—don't spoil the chili by adding beans! As I've stated many times—"Beans don't belong in chili!" Beans may help the chili to go further in feeding, but it ruins the pure taste of the chili. If you want the chili to feed more people, make more chili! Of course, there are some people who never understand that and will add beans anyway. Well, I say "Line 'em up downwind of those people who ate those beans!"

½ pound Lean Ground Beef
¼ pound Stewing Beef, cut to half bite-size
¼ pound Shredded Beef, cut to half bite-size
¼ pound Ribeye Steak, cut to half bite-size
16 ounces Tomato Purée
¼ cup Sweet Pickle Relish
2 tablespoons Malt Vinegar
2 tablespoons Lemon Juice
½ cup Budweiser® Beer, allowed to go flat
½ Hickory Smoke Barbeque Sauce
¼ cup Hunt's® Catsup
4 tablespoons heaping Best Foods® Mayonaise
2 tablespoons heaping French's® Mustard
6 tablespoons Country Crock® tub Butter
2 pkgs Lawry's® Chili Mix Seasoning
1 large bag Frito's Corn Chips
1 small Green Bell Pepper, chopped
1 small Stewing Onion, diced
½ cup Green Olives w/Pimentos, quartered
8 large fresh Mushrooms, sliced and quartered
1 large Jalepeño Pepper, diced
3 Bay Leaves, crushed
2 cups Sharp Cheddar Cheese, shredded
2 tablespoons Chili Powder
1 tablespoon Corn Starch
2 teaspoons Salt
1 teaspoon Black Pepper
1 teaspoon Minced Onion
1 teaspoon Orégano
1 tablespoon Hickory Smoke Salt
1 tablespoon Garlic Salt
1 tablespoon Paprika

In a skillet, cook the Ground Beef thoroughly then pour off and discard the grease. Add half of the Bell Peppers, Stewing Onion and Mushrooms, plus 1 tbsp. Malt Vinegar, 2 tbsps. Butter, 1 tbsp. Chili Powder, 1 tsp. Salt and 1 pkg. Chili Mix Seasoning. Cook for 10 minutes over medium heat, stirring occasionally. Pour juices into a saucepan after spooning the meat and vegetables into a 2-quart crockpot set on low heat. Place the saucepan juices, covered, over low heat to simmer. Next, cook the Ribeye Steak, Shredded Beef and Stewing Beef in a skillet, then discard the grease. Follow above directions to cook the second half of the above ingredients with the meat. Again, pour juices into the saucepan to simmer and the solids into the crockpot.

To the saucepan, add the Pickle Relish, Garlic Salt, Hickory Smoke Salt, Lemon Juice, Minced Onion, Corn Starch and Orégano. Bring heat up to medium, stirring until mixture begins to boil, then add mixture to the crockpot. To the ingredients in the crockpot, add the Flat Beer, Tomato Purée, Mayonaise, Barbeque Sauce, Catsup, Mustard, Jalepeño Pepper, Black Pepper, crushed Bay Leaves, 2 cups of crushed Frito Corn Chips, remaining Butter and 1 cup of the Shredded Cheddar Cheese. Cover and let cook on medium for 2 hours, or on low heat for minimum of 15 hours, stirring occasionally. When through cooking, pour remaining Cheddar Cheese over top of chili, cover and let sit for 10 minutes with heat off. Serve hot with Paprika sprinkled over top and remaining Fritos on side for dipping. Salt and pepper to taste.

(Author's note: I've also made this chili using beef, as shown, chicken, pork and rattlesnake meat. In my opinion, the rattlesnake chili tasted the best—followed closely by beef, chicken and pork. Of course, personally, I do not care for pork. Hence, my ranking it last, far down the list.)

CREAMED BEEF AND MUSHROOMS

Serves 8 to 10

When I was in the Military, our great 'Uncle Sam' fed us an old perennial favorite—S.O.S.—and those initials didn't stand for 'Save Our Ship!' What it actually was, was Creamed Sausage on Toast. I liked it, but since then, I've cut back on my intake of pork drastically. So, I came up with my own version of this filling breakfast. Of course, like most foods, it can be eaten anytime you want it, rather than only for breakfast.

1½ cups Ribeye Steak, (see below for slicing)
¾ cup fresh Mushrooms, thinly sliced
8 tablespoons Country Crock® tub Butter
8 tablespoons Lemon Juice
1 small Stewing Onion, diced
3 tablespoons sifted Flour
1 tablespoon Best Foods® Mayonaise
1 cup Lowfat or Nonfat Milk
2 large Egg Whites
8–10 slices toasted Wheat Bread, buttered

[When you purchase the Ribeye Steak, have the butcher slice the meat wafer thin. Then cut the steak into smaller pieces (about 1" x ½").]

In a large skillet, brown the pieces of Ribeye Steak in 2 tablespoons of Butter. Remove and discard the greasy butter. To the cooked meat, add the Mushrooms, Onions, Lemon Juice and 3 tablespoons of Butter. Sauté for 5 minutes over medium heat. Remove and discard remaining liquid.

In a large saucepan, melt the remaining Butter, stir in Mayonaise and Flour. Cook over medium heat until bubbles begin to appear and then add the Milk. Bring to a slow boil, stirring frequently.

Spoon skillet ingredients into the saucepan, stir to mix well. Allow to simmer while whipping the Egg White with a wire whisk (about 2 minutes). Spoon egg into the mixture and heat until mixture begins to boil. Remove from heat and allow to slightly cool, then liberally spoon over buttered toast. Salt and pepper to taste.

ONE-EYED FLAPJACKS

Serves 6

A close friend that I lost in an auto-accident could never decide whether she wanted eggs or pancakes for breakfast and always left the decision up to me. A few times I ended up making both, but as neither of us ate large breakfasts, we always had leftovers. So I came up with this idea and it cut our breakfast bills in half. It solved her problem of making that decision, also. The combination of the two tastes good, too!

12 large Eggs
2 cups Whole Wheat Flour
1 tablespoon Baking Powder
¼ cup Powdered Milk
2 tablespoons Brown Sugar
½ teaspoon Salt
¾ cup Buttermilk
¾ cup Warm Water
2 tablespoons Warm Honey
1 cup Country Crock® tub Butter, melted

In a large bowl, combine the Flour, Baking Powder, Powdered Milk, Sugar and Salt. Thoroughly mix all of the powders. In another bowl, crack open all eggs into bowl (try not to burst the yolks), then dip out 3 tablespoons of the albumen (egg white), adding it to the dry powders with the Buttermilk, Water, Honey and a half cup of the Butter. Mix the ingredients into a smooth batter. (Batter should be very thick, nearly a paste. If too thin, add tablespoon at a time of Whole Wheat Flour. If too thick, add tablespoon at a time of albumen or warm water. Keep adding until proper consistency is achieved. There should be very little running of the butter when it is poured on the griddle.) Pour batter onto a hot griddle in the shape of a doughnut about 6 inches across with a 2–2½ inch open center. (That takes a little practice.) Drop one teaspoon of butter into the center of the ring, then scoup out one egg yolk and enough albumen to fill the opening in the batter. (If desired, yolks may be broken and both egg yolk and albumen beaten like scrambled eggs.) Flip batter and egg center together as one. When done, serve warm with salt and pepper to taste for the egg center. Syrup to taste for the whole thing.

For added taste, add items like bacon bits, diced ham, cheese, etc., to the egg center.

WESTERN OMELET (WITH QUAIL EGGS)

Serves 4 to 6

S ome people may panic at the thought of using Quail Eggs (or any other egg) in place of Chicken eggs. However loathsome it may seem to those people, I hope this will temper those feelings. First of all, there is no appreciable difference in taste between the two. In comparable amounts, quail eggs have more than double the amount of protein and about one-third the amount of cholesterol that chicken eggs have. The only significant drawback, is that it takes two to three quail eggs to equal the amount obtained from one chicken egg. You can locate quail eggs at most places that advertise to sell live quail in the want-ad section of your local newspaper.

24 Quail Eggs
¼ cup Cold Water
¼ cup Lowfat or Nonfat Milk
4 Green Onions, white portion only, diced
1 small Green Bell Pepper, diced
1 small Jalepeño Pepper, diced with seeds removed
3 fresh Mushrooms, thinly sliced and quartered
1 teaspoon Garlic Salt
1 teaspoon Hickory Smoke Salt
2 tablespoons Barbeque Sauce
2 tablespoons Country Crock® tub Butter
1 teaspoon Chili Powder
2 teaspoons Parsley Flakes
3 cups Sharp Cheddar Cheese, shredded

In a skillet, cook the Onions, Bell Pepper, Jalepeño and Mushrooms in the Butter over medium heat until the Bell Pepper bits are soft. Empty ingredients into a saucepan, cover and keep warm over heat on the lowest setting. In a large mixing bowl, whip the Quail Eggs with a wire whisk until yolk and albumen are well blended. Mix in Water, Milk, Garlic Salt, Hickory Smoke Salt, Chili Powder, Parsley Flakes and Barbeque Sauce. Beat until all ingredients are completely dispersed in egg mixture. In a large non-stick skillet, pour about ⅓ to ½ of the egg mixture to cook over medium-high heat. Stir the mixture (like scrambling eggs) until clumps begin to appear, then stop stirring. Sprinkle ⅓ to ½ of the shredded Cheese and saucepan ingredients over the egg mixture. When egg mixture begins to solidify around ingredients fold omelet in half. Cook another one to two minutes, turning omelet over once. Remove omelet and place in warmer. Repeat above instructions with remaining ingredients. Slice in equal portions and serve warm. Salt and Pepper to taste.

(Note: Real diehards may substitute 10 regular chicken eggs for the quail eggs. However, the cholesterol tends to rise 30 to 60%.)

DEVILED EGGS

Makes 2 Dozen

veryone has got their own version of making Deviled Eggs and I'm no different. If you use this recipé to serve to your guests, *don't* tell them beforehand what *all* of the ingredients are. Some of my guests dislike certain ingredients, regardless of the food those ingredients were used in. . . . But those same people played a very large part in causing my Deviled Eggs to disappear. WARNING: These eggs are rather high in cholesterol and fatty carbohydrates. Try not to eat them all yourself!

24 large Eggs plus 1 large Egg White
3 tablespoons Best Foods® Mayonaise
2 tablespoons Thousand Island Salad Dressing
1 tablespoon Kraft® Mustard
1 tablespoon Sweet Pickle Relish
3 teaspoons Parmesan Cheese
2 teaspoons Salt
1 teaspoon Garlic Powder
1 teaspoon Hickory Smoke Salt
1 teaspoon Chili Powder
1 teaspoon Malt Vinegar
Paprika, to taste

Hard boil 24 eggs in water with 1 teaspoon Salt. Drain and discard water, then rinse eggs in cold water. Remove eggshells, then rinse again in cold water. Slice each egg length-wise, cutting off top third of the egg. Remove yolk from the larger portion of the egg and set eggwhites aside. Put top third of eggs and bottom half yolk into a large bowl. Slice yolks and egg tops into small chunks, or mash with tines of a fork. Stir in all ingredients listed above, except for the Paprika. Combine all ingredients to form a thick paste.

Spoon paste into yolk space of eggwhites set aside earlier. Sprinkle Paprika over eggs, salt or pepper to taste. May heat slightly before serving. Serve warm or cold.

(NOTE: Any remaining egg paste can be used to make egg salad sandwiches.)

CHERRY-APPLE MUFFINS

Makes 18–20

A dear friend of mine had three rambunctious boys and an equally active daughter that I would care for every so often when she had no baby-sitter. I was not above bribing them when movies, games and toys began to bore them. I created this recipé as an extra-special treat that was as good for them as it was tasty. The problem with these muffins is that if there are more available, you (or the kids) want to continue eating them until they're all gone.

1½ cups Granny Smith® Apples, skinned, cored and diced
1½ cups fresh Bing Cherries, pitted and diced
2½ cups sifted Flour
¼ cup Country Crock® tub Butter
2 tablespoons Cinnamon-Sugar
½ cup Lowfat or Nonfat Milk
2 tablespoons Baking Powder
4 large Egg Whites
1¼ cups Brown Sugar
1 teaspoon Dark Cane Syrup

In a large bowl, blend together the Flour, Cinnamon-Sugar, Baking Powder, Brown Sugar, Butter, Egg Whites, Milk and Syrup.

Stir to combine all ingredients to a thick, batter-like texture. Fold in diced Apples and Cherries, mixing them thoroughly into the mixture. Spoon mixture into paper-lined cupcake or muffin pan, filling each cup ⅔ full. Bake at 400° for 25–30 minutes. Serve warm or cold, with or without butter spread.

SPICE MUFFINS

Makes 2 Dozen

I have to be honest, I didn't come up with this recipé by myself. A lady-friend and I were trying to come up with a bedtime snack to eat while watching T.V. while waiting for sleep to overtake us. I thought up the basic recipé from one I learned while in the Air Force. My lady-friend came up with a few other suggestions. Some we used, some we rejected. The idea of putting Ginseng into the mixture came from my taste for Ginseng Tea. You can get Ginseng capsules in nearly any health food store. I personally favor the Korean Ginseng over the other varieties available.

3½ cups sifted Flour
4 oz. Ginseng Powder
1 tablespoon Baking Powder
2 teaspoons Ginger
2 teaspoons Cinnamon
2 tablespoons Brown Sugar
1¾ cups Lowfat or Nonfat Milk
6 oz. Semi-Sweet Chocolate Chips
4 oz. Country Crock® tub Butter
4 large Egg Whites, lightly beaten
⅔ cup Honey
2 oz. Apple Cider

If you get your Ginseng in capsule form, empty about 32 capsules into a large mixing bowl. This should be close to 4 oz. of powdered Ginseng. Mix in the Flour, Baking Powder, Ginger, Cinnamon and Brown Sugar. In a double-boiler, mix together the Chocolate Chips, Butter and Honey. Heat them until they combine together in a thick syrup. To the powder mixture, stir in the Milk, Egg Whites, Apple Cider and heated syrup. Mix until well blended. Pour into a paper-lined or well greased muffin tin and bake in a preheated oven at 400° for 20–25 minutes or until muffins spring back to the touch. (Sticking a toothpick into the center of the muffin, it should come back out clean.) Allow them to cool about two minutes, then serve warm, topped with butter. Eat away with someone you love.

SODA SWIRL CUPCAKES

Makes 3 Dozen

Everytime I would make these cupcakes, they'd seem to just disappear without any apparent help. I lived alone and I'd swear that *I* didn't eat them all. So I figured that the story a friend of mine once told me must be true. You see, refrigerators are strange places. . . . there's a Black Hole in each and every one of them! You put something in the refrigerator and then next thing you know, it's gone. "The Black Hole ate it up!" And for some strange reason, the more people there are in the home, the more that Black Hole eats!!

Cupcakes
2 cups Brown Sugar, packed
1½ cups Lowfat or Nonfat Milk
1 cup Flour
1 cup Sprite® Soda Pop

¾ cup Hershey's® Hot Chocolate Mix
½ cup Country Crock® tub Butter
3 large Egg Whites
1½ teaspoons Baking Powder
1½ teaspoons Baking Soda
1 teaspoon Vanilla Extract

Icing
3 cups Confectioner's Sugar
2 cups Hershey's® Hot Chocolate Mix
1½ cups Country Crock® tub Butter
⅓ cup Lowfat or Nonfat Milk

Cupcakes: Open the soda pop a couple hours ahead of time to let it go flat. In a large bowl, mix together the Brown Sugar, Flour, Baking Powder and Baking Soda. Add in the Milk, Sprite® Soda and Butter. Stir until batter is creamy and smooth. In another bowl, mix together the Hot Chocolate Mix, Egg Whites and the Vanilla Extract. Mix until this group is creamy and smooth, also.

Frosting: Mix together the Butter, Milk, Sugar and Hot Chocolate mix. Stir together ingredients until they are thick and smooth. Set aside until cupcakes are ready to frost.

Cooking: Preheat the oven to 350°. Line a muffin tin with cupcake liners. Pour cupcake batter into each liner ¾ full. Spoon 1 tablespoon of Chocolate mixture into each liner and using a swizzle stick, swirl the mixture into the batter. Bake for 20 to 25 minutes, or until cupcakes spring back when touched. Remove muffin tin and cupcakes from the oven and let cool on a cooling rack. When cool to the touch, frost with chocolate icing. Then eat all that you want before the "Black Hole" gets them.

STRAWBERRY TURNOVERS

Makes 1 Dozen

I really like strawberries! Always have—always will. A lady friend I used to see a lot had a presence that exuded strawberry. She wore strawberry perfume, strawberry earrings, strawberry incense in her home, strawberry knick-knacks, strawberry everything! But she couldn't cook worth beans. I altered another recipé to come up with this one for her. Talk about someone being in seventh heaven . . . !

4 cups fresh Strawberries
3 cups sifted Flour
2 large Egg Whites
1 cup Granulated Sugar
1 cup Brown Sugar
1 cup Country Crock® tub Butter
½ cup cold Water
½ cup Lowfat or Nonfat Milk
1 tablespoon light Corn Syrup
1 tablespoon Vanilla Extract
Cool Whip® Whipped Cream Topping
Betty Crocker's® White (Vanilla) Frosting

Filling: Remove green crowns from the strawberries then slice them in half. Place them in a large mixing bowl, add the Granulated Sugar and Corn Syrup. Stir to disperse sugar and syrup throughout the mixture. Refrigerate until ready to use.

Shell: In a large bowl, combine 2½ cups Flour, Egg Whites, Brown Sugar, ¾ cup Butter, Vanilla, Water and Milk. Mix all ingredients into a thick dough. Divide dough into four equal parts, placing one fourth on a flour dusted surface. Dust flour lightly over dough and roll it out to about ⅛" thickness. Cut three rounds out of the dough about 6" across, dust again and set aside. Repeat with remaining dough.

Assembly: Preheat oven to 350°. Spread butter on ¼" border of each round, then scoop 2 spoonfuls of strawberry mixture into the center of each round. Fold the rounds in half so the buttered edges can be pinched together. Arrange each turnover on a non-stick cookie sheet so edges do not touch. Place cookie sheet into oven and bake for 30 to 40 minutes, or until shell turns a golden brown. When done, allow to cool or serve immediately. Top with either whipped cream or frosting. May wait until turnovers are cold before frosting is put on and refrigerated until later.

CHOCOLATE-PEANUT BUTTER FUDGE

Makes About 2 lbs.

In college, I took a course in effective communication in which one requirement was to write a resumé. On it, I was to list my attributes pertaining to the job as well as the areas in which I was weak. The imaginary position I was applying for was one in which I was overwhelmingly qualified. I thought and thought for a weakness that would apply, because I was told that I *had* to list something. I finally wrote down my greatest weakness: Chocolate! I *love* chocolate, in nearly all of its forms. This recipé came about because of my love for chocolate and after my first taste of a Peanut Butter Cup.

1 cup Hershey's® Unsweetened Cocoa
2 cups Salt-Free Peanut Butter
2 cups Lowfat or Nonfat Milk
2 cups Sugar
½ Country Crock® tub Butter
½ cup Semi-Sweet Chocolate Chips
2 tablespoons Cinnamon-Sugar
1 teaspoon Vanilla Extract

In a large saucepan, combine the Cocoa, Peanut Butter, Milk, Sugar and Cinnamon-Sugar, heating over medium heat. Stir until mixture is smooth and creamy. When mixture begins to bubble, remove from heat and add in Butter and Vanilla Extract, stirring until well blended. Allow to cool for 20 minutes, then fold in Chocolate Chips. Pour mixture into non-stick pans to about 1-inch depth and allow to cool to room temperature. Once at room temperature, place pans in refrigerator for a minimum of ½ hour. Cut into squares and serve cold.

COFFEE CAKE

Serves 12

I used to avoid Coffee Cake like a cat avoids dogs. Having a severe allergic reaction to coffee, I wouldn't consume *anything* that I thought had coffee in it. And I believed that Coffee Cake was made with, naturally, coffee! To my great pleasure, I found that Coffee Cake was nothing more than Spice Cake. So, after coming across a Coffee Cake recipé, I cooked one up. While it was good, it didn't quite have the taste I liked. Once again, I began experimenting. After a few inedible results—one which not even wild birds would touch—finally I came up with the following recipé. My roommate almost became my girlfriend because of this recipé. Hope you like it, too.

3 cups sifted Flour
½ cup Brown Sugar, packed
¾ cup Country Crock® tub Butter
1½ cups Lowfat or Nonfat Milk
5 large Egg Whites
1 tablespoon Baking Powder
1 tablespoon Baking Soda

2 tablespoons Cinnamon
½ teaspoon Salt
1 tablespoon Vanilla Extract
¼ cup Molasses
2 tablespoons unsalted Peanut Butter
1 cup Applesauce
4 tablespoons Cinnamon-Sugar
¼ cup Confectioner's Sugar
Cool Whip® - Whipped Cream

Combine the Flour, Brown Sugar, Butter and Milk in a large bowl. Stir in Egg Whites, Baking Powder, Baking Soda, Cinnamon, Salt and Vanilla Extract. Mix well until all ingredients form a smooth, but thick batter, then set aside. In another bowl, combine the Molasses, Peanut Butter, Apple Sauce and Cinnamon-Sugar. Mix into a smooth sauce, then set aside. Pour half of the batter into a non-stick, 9"x15" cake pan. Swirl the sauce through the poured batter. Do not mix the sauce into the batter so much that the sauce combines completely with the batter. Bake in a preheated oven set at 300° for 60 minutes. During last ten minutes, check often with a toothpick to verify inside is done (toothpick should come out clean if done). Let finished cake cool about 15 minutes on a rack. Top each slice with a large dollop of Cool Whip and serve warm or cold.

WILD GUMBO

Serves 6

I'm not ashamed to admit that I'm a fan of The Carpenters music. Often, I would sit in a candle-lit room listening to the soothing sounds of Karen and Richard. When I heard their song

"Jambalaya," I began to wonder what it was . . . not to mention 'Crawfish Pie' and 'Fillet Gumbo.' After an opportunity to taste all three, I decided I liked the first and last, but could not quite acquire a taste for crawfish. Upon coming up with my own version of the two, I found many of my friends liked it, too. So here it is.

2 cups Wild Brown Rice
2 cups Boneless Chicken, cooked and chopped
1 cup Shrimp, deveined and shelled, chopped
1 can (8 oz.) Minced Clams, drained
1 cup Green Chili, sliced diagonally
2 stewing Tomatoes, chopped
½ cup Country Crock® tub Butter
1 medium-sized Hot Italian Sausage, diced
½ cup Okra, sliced in ½" lengths
1 small Bell Pepper, chopped
3 cups Water
2 tablespoons Minced Onion
2 tablespoons Hickory Smoke Salt
2 tablespoons Paprika
2 tablespoons Orégano
2 Bay Leaves
2 teaspoons Minced Garlic
1 teaspoon Cayenne Pepper
1 teaspoon Barbeque Seasoning
1 teaspoon Worcestershire Sauce

Cook the Rice according to package instructions. In a large pot, combine all ingredients except the Hickory Smoke Salt, Onion, Paprika, Orégano, Bay Leaves, Cayenne Pepper and Barbeque Seasoning. Cook over medium heat for 15 minutes, stirring occasionally. Reduce heat and drop in Bay Leaves. Let simmer another 10 minutes. Add in remaining spices mentioned above and let simmer an additional 5 minutes, stirring to keep ingredients turning over.

Remove from heat, cover and let sit for 5 minutes. Discard Bay Leaves. Serve warm with Parsley as garnish (if desired). Salt and pepper to taste. (Crush one or two Saltine Crackers over gumbo for additional taste, if desired.)

COUNTRY BARBEQUE SAUCE

Makes 2 pints

My grandfather had a recipé for a terrific barbeque sauce he created. I finally found a combination that came very close to his. I have no idea what was in his recipé, he would not tell anyone. But I don't mind telling people what goes into my meals. Enjoy the taste of this one on your 'burgers.

1½ cups Tomato Purée
¾ cup warm Water
¼ cup Malt Vinegar
⅜ cup Hunt's® Catsup
3 tablespoons Brown Sugar
1 tablespoon Hickory Smoke Salt
1 tablespoon French's® Mustard
1 tablespoon Cinnamon
1½ teaspoons Garlic Salt
½ teaspoon Chili Powder
1 fresh Mushroom, finely diced
2 whole Bay Leaves

In a saucepan, combine all of the ingredients except the Malt Vinegar, diced Mushrooms and the Bay Leaves. Cook over medium heat, stirring occasionally, until the mixture begins to boil. Reduce heat and let simmer. Meanwhile, in a skillet, cook the mushrooms in the vinegar over meadum heat for five minutes. Add mushrooms and vinegar to the saucepan mixture. Drop in the bay leaves and raise the heat to medium. Stir often and cook until it begins boiling, then reduce the heat again to low and to simmer for 15 minutes. Remove from heat and allow to cool. Pour into glass jars and refrigerate until needed.

NOTE: This Barbeque Sauce goes well with every recipé in this book that calls for a barbeque sauce in the ingredients.

EGG SALAD SANDWICHES

Serves 6

When I was growing up and carrying sack lunches to school, I always hoped that my lunches would include these tasty sandwiches rather than bologna or PB&J sandwiches. These sandwiches were so much more delicious. But I had to discover this recipé for myself. I have to admit that the first couple tries were rather tasteless and one try was completely inedible! I *was* successful, though, and can credit this recipé as my first real creation. Hope you like it as well as others have.

6 large Eggs, hard boiled
¾ cup Best Foods® Mayonaise
2 tablespoons French's® Mustard
2 tablespoons Catsup
¼ cup Sweet Pickle Relish, drained
1 tablespoon Malt Vinegar
1 tablespoon Garlic Salt
2 teaspoons Hickory Smoke Salt
2 teaspoons Minced Onion

2 teaspoons Paprika
½ small Green Bell Pepper, diced
¼ cup Sharp Cheddar Cheese, finely shredded

Sauté the diced Bell Pepper in the Malt Vinegar until soft. Slice the Eggs into very small bits (or finely dice). Stir together *all* ingredients in a mixing bowl until it becomes a thick paste. Spread the paste liberally between two slices of bread and garnish with sliced tomato, lettuce, American sliced cheese, etc., and chow down!

'BURGER "SECRET SAUCE"

Makes 10 ounces

A certain fast food restaurant hasn't got anything on *my* secret sauce! Try it on *your* 'burgers or any other kind of meat. Believe it or not, it even tastes good on salads! A little like 1000 Island Salad Dressing.

¾ cup Best Foods® Mayonaise
2 tablespoons Hickory Smoke Barbeque Sauce
1 tablespoon French's® Mustard
1 teaspoon Salt
2 tablespoons Sweet Pickle Relish, drained
2 tablespoons Bacon Bits
1 teaspoon Malt Vinegar
1 teaspoon Garlic Salt

Mix all ingredients together to form a thick sauce. Store dispensing container and keep refrigerated until needed. Use like a normal condiment spread.

THANKSGIVING/CHRISTMAS WHIPPED POTATOES

Serves 6 to 8

When I was young, we always had the same old mashed potatoes and gravy during the holiday season that we had every other day of the year: Lumpy mashed potatoes. I don't know about you, but I believe the holiday season should be accompanied with a very special meal—from meat to potatoes to vegetables. That belief led me to come up with these two recipés for my holiday dinners.

5 medium to large Russett Potatoes, with skin, diced
4 tablespoons Country Crock® tub Butter
1 tablespoon Malt Vinegar
1 tablespoon Brown Sugar
½ cup Lowfat or Nonfat Milk
½ teaspoon Salt
¼ teaspoon Nutmeg
½ tablespoon Cinnamon-Sugar
¼ teaspoon Garlic Salt
2 tablespoons Paprika

Boil Potatoes (with skin) until soft. Drain and mash until most lumps are gone. Add Butter, Vinegar, Brown Sugar, Milk, Salt, Nutmeg, Cinnamon-Sugar and Garlic Salt. Whip to a smooth and creamy texture. Sprinkle Paprika over potatoes and serve warm with Giblet Gravy. Salt and Pepper to taste.

'TATER BOATS

Makes 8

I've always liked Baked Potatoes, but could only get them the way I liked them when I fixed them myself. I came up with this method of making them because the toppings always ran out before I was done with the potato. I turned them into "Boats" to entertain a friend's youngest daughters. They like "Boats" a lot better than baked potatoes. The main point is that all four girls and their mother ate all of their 'Tater Boats!

4 large White Potatoes
2 tablespoons Country Crock® tub Butter
4 large fresh Mushrooms, diced
2 tablespoons Sweet Pickle Relish, drained
2 tablespoons Best Foods® Mayonaise
¾ cup Sharp Cheddar Cheese, shredded
½ tablespoon Onion Powder
1 teaspoon Garlic Salt
Sour Cream, to taste
Paprika, to taste
8 Parsley Sprigs
Additional Toppings, per personal choice

Wrap each potato and one teaspoon Butter in aluminum foil, then bake them in an oven preheated to 350° for thirty minutes. Remove potatoes from their wrapping and slice in half, lengthwise. Scoop out most of the meat of the potato, being sure not to break through the skin. In a large bowl, mix the potato with the mushroom pieces, cheddar cheese, onion powder, garlic salt, mayonaise, pickle relish and remaining butter, using a mixer set on low. Mix thoroughly to a coarse consistency. Spoon this mixture into the potato shells. Place back into oven, uncovered, for fifteen minutes.

When done, remove from oven and sprinkle paprika over the top of the potato. Spoon a healthy dollop of sour cream atop the center of the potato and a sprig of parsley atop that. Add any desired additional toppings. Serve hot; salt and pepper to taste. Usually serves two per person.

BAKED BEANS PLUS

Serves 6

A young lady already mentioned in these pages swore that her momma's Boston style Baked Beans were the best ever cooked. I wasn't about to argue with her, but I had this recipé locked away in my brain from when I worked as a short order cook. I served it only to those of my friends who knew about it. When I served it to this young lady, she said that I *had* to give the recipé to her momma. Well, that never happened—so, if she still wants it, here it is.

4 cups Red Beans
4 All Beef Frankfurters, sliced into ¼" lengths
4 slices Bacon, chopped
1 cup Malt Vinegar
⅛ cup Brown Sugar
¼ cup Hunts® Catsup
⅛ cup Molasses
¼ cup Hickory Smoke Barbeque Sauce
2 tablespoons Best Foods® Mayonaise
1 tablespoon Garlic Salt
1 tablespoon Orégano
½ tablespoon Country Crock® tub Butter
1 teaspoon Cinnamon
3 Bay Leaves

Place the Red Beans, Malt Vinegar and 2 Bay Leaves in a large pot with enough water to cover the beans. Cook over high heat until it begins to boil, then reduce heat to low, cover and let simmer for 30 minutes. Drain off the liquid and set aside, covered. In a skillet, sear the Bacon and Frankfurter pieces, then add those to the pot of beans. Place the pot over low heat again and stir in the Catsup, Molasses, Barbeque Sauce and Mayonaise. Cover and allow to simmer through the rest of the preparations. In a mixing bowl, blend together the Brown Sugar, Garlic Salt, Orégano, Butter and Cinnamon. When this mixture is thoroughly combined, add it and the remaining Bay Leaf to the pot of beans and stir the mixture until the ingredients are completely intermixed. Cover and let simmer for an additional 20 minutes. Salt and pepper to taste. Optional topping of Sharp Cheddar Cheese is especially tasty. Serve as side-dish to any red or white meat.

MARINATED RIBEYE STEAK

Serves 4

This one goes back to the days of youth, when I was working as a short order cook at a fancy restaraunt. A certain lady-love of mine would come in for dinner a few times each week and would have me fix this dish for her. I didn't know that the restaurant manager was watching me on these nights. I didn't get in trouble or anything, but she did appropriate my recipé and began offering it on the menu. Eventually, I quit working at that restaurant and my lady-love began coming over to my place every few days so she could still enjoy this dish. She said that I must be doing something different, because those at the restaraunt just didn't taste as good. By the way, these are fixed on a barbeque grill for the Out-of-doors, Flame-cooked taste!

4 Ribeye Steaks
8 long Bacon Slices
16 wooden toothpicks, round type
¼ cup Soy Sauce
¼ cup Apple Cider
¼ cup Worcestershire Sauce
¼ cup Smirnoff® Vodka, 110 proof
2 oz. Lemon Juice
1 tablespoon Brown Sugar
1 tablespoon Garlic Salt
1 tablespoon Molasses
1 teaspoon Basil
4 teaspoons Cinnamon
2 whole Bay Leaves

Wrap two strips of bacon tightly around the edge of each steak and pin in place with 4 toothpicks per steak. Set aside until marinating sauce is ready. Combine the Soy Sauce, Worcestershire Sauce, Lemon Juice, Brown Sugar, Garlic Salt, Molasses and Basil in a saucepan and cook on medium until sauce begins to bubble. Reduce heat to low and stir in the Apple Cider and Vodka. Drop in Bay Leaves and allow to simmer 5 minutes, covered, stirring often. Remove from heat and allow to cool, then pour sauce into a wide plastic container with a lid.

Pierce both sides deeply, several times with the tines of a fork. Place bacon-wrapped steaks into a container with marinating sauce. If sauce doesn't cover the steaks, spoon sauce onto top of meat. Cover and let sit in refrigerator for minimum of four hours (I usually let the steaks marinate overnight). Place steaks on barbeque grill directly from marinating container. Sprinkle ½ teaspoon Cinnamon on each side of steak and cook to desired degree (rare, medium, well-done, etc.), then remove and serve hot. Salt and pepper to taste. Garnish with a sprig of Parsley.

FRICASEE CHICKEN

Serves 6

A ladyfriend and I wanted Chicken for dinner one evening, but we didn't want it barbequed or fried—and we were tired of Fast-Food. I recalled a dish I used to cook when I was younger. I hadn't fixed it in many years, but as I began to prepare it, the recipé came flooding back into my mind. The dish practically fixed itself, so my ladyfriend and I busied ourselves with other amusements. When the dish was ready, the meat literally fell off the bones and melted into our mouths!

2 complete Chickens, cut up
16 oz. (one pkg.) wide Egg Noodles
3 Carrots, thickly sliced
4 fresh Mushrooms, sliced
2 stewing Onions, chopped
2 Celery Stalks, chopped
2 small Russett Potatoes, cut into small chunks
1 small Bell Pepper, seeded and chopped
1 tablespoon Minced Garlic
2 tablespoons Orégano
1 teaspoon Crushed Thyme
1 teaspoon Sweet Basil
¼ cup fresh Parsley, chopped finely
1 tablespoon Salt
4 cups Water
Paprika, to taste

In a large pot, place the Chicken, Carrots, Mushrooms, Onions, Celery, Potatoes, Bell Peppers, Water and Salt and start cooking on Medium-High heat until water begins to boil. (Depending on size of Chicken, more or less water may be required.) Reduce heat to medium, add in the Garlic, Orégano, Thyme and Basil. Cook for 20 minutes, stirring often. Reduce heat to low, stir in Parsley, cover and simmer for one hour. Drain off enough water from pot to cook the Egg Noodles in and proceed to cook the Noodles according to package instructions. Afterwards, discard that water. Scoop a healthy portion of Noodles onto serving plates. Ladle vegetables on top of Noodles, with Chicken pieces placed on side. Sprinkle Paprika over vegetables and Noodles. Salt and pepper to taste.

SPICY TUNA PATTIES

Makes 2 Dozen

The mother of a girlfriend in my youth made the most delicious Tuna Patty Melts I had ever tasted. I practically begged her for the recipé, but nothing I said would get her to share that secret with me. I had left that girlfriend (and my youth) far behind before I attempted to duplicate that wonderful taste I remembered. Friends who have eaten these (*and* enjoyed them) will possibly curse me if they find out what one of the ingredients are. That they ate them of their own accord is beside the point. The fact is, they hate that particular item. My remedy—? Don't tell them what's in it, just let them try it. If they like it, fine! If they don't, there's more for me!

4 cans Chicken of the Sea® Tuna Fish in Spring Water
2 cups seasoned fine Bread Crumbs
1 Jalepeño Pepper, diced
4 Anchovy fillets (flat type), chopped
2 large Egg Whites, slightly beaten
1 small stewing Onion, diced
1 tablespoon Parsley Flakes

2 tablespoons Garlic Salt
2 teaspoons Ginseng Powder
1 tablespoon Chili Powder
1 tablespoon Barbeque Sauce
Country Crock® tub Butter

In a large bowl, combine all of the ingredients and 1 tablespoon of the Butter. Mix thoroughly until all ingredients are damp and form into balls easily. Using waxed paper, form the mixture into 24 patties, separated by small stretches of that waxed paper. Fry lightly, in a large frypan, adding butter as needed, until both sides of the patties are golden brown. Patties can be frozen and microwaved before eating. Serve warm with salt and/or pepper to taste or eat cold as a snack. Can even be placed between slices of bread with cheese and other condiments.

OVEN-BARBEQUED CHICKEN

Serves 4

I came up with this recipé one night when I lit the barbeque for the chicken and it was put out by a sudden rainstorm. Unfortunately, I didn't have a lid for my hibachi and the chicken was already cut-up to cook. My girlfriend said she'd fry it. I said no, that I had promised to cook barbequed chicken. She was mystified, but she left me to what she considered an impossibility. When I served dinner, she raved about the taste and how the meat just fell off the bones. From that point on, she preferred barbequed chicken barbequed this way!

8 pieces Chicken
½ cup Hickory Smoke Barbeque Sauce

¼ cup Country Crock® tub Butter
2 tablespoons Best Foods® Mayonaise
1 tablespoon French's® Mustard
¼ cup Sweet Pickle Relish, drained
4 fresh Mushrooms, diced
¼ cup Green Olives w/Pimentos, quartered
1 tablespoon Lemon Juice
1 teaspoon Malt Vinegar
3 tablespoons Honey
Chili Powder, to taste
Onion Powder, to taste
Barbeque Seasoning, to taste
Hickory Smoke Salt, to taste
Garlic Salt, to taste

Into a saucepan, stir together the Barbeque Sauce, Mayonaise, Mustard, Lemon Juice, Malt Vinegar and the Honey. Stirring often, heat over medium heat until bubbles begin to appear, then remove from heat. Place two stretches of aluminum foil in an "X" on your work surface with three or four pieces of Chicken in the center. Liberally brush the chicken with the barbeque mixture. Spoon Butter around the pieces of chicken, then sprinkle the Pickle Relish, Mushroom and Olive pieces over the chicken. **OPTION 1**—Sprinkle the five seasoning spices over the chicken now. (Or wait 'til option 2.) Fold foil over chicken, double-wrapping it completely. Bake in oven preheated to 350°, for fifty minutes. After 50 minutes, carefully open the top of the foil, exposing the chicken, but allowing a reservoir around the chicken for the juices to remain. Daub barbeque mixture over chicken again. **OPTION 2**—Sprinkle the five seasoning spices over the chicken now. Place chicken, left open, back into the oven for 10 minutes. Remove chicken from foil and place on platter (salt and pepper to taste). Pour juices from foil into saucepan with barbeque mixture. Reheat sauce for 5 minutes over medium heat, stirring often. Remove from heat and use as dip for chicken.

BARBEQUED CHEESEBURGERS

Serves 6 to 8

That's right—Barbequed 'Burgers! I know, everyone knows how to fix these and has their own way of doing it. Well, it's entirely possible that not everyone will like the way *I* fix them. No bragging intended, but I haven't met them as yet. The way I cook 'burgers even converted one very stubborn young lady from eating only those made the way her Daddy cooked them, to preferring mine instead. When she saw the way I was making up the patties, she claimed her Daddy didn't make them that way, so she wouldn't be having any. She changed her mind when guests began raving about the taste and wanted my recipé. She said she'd try just one bite . . . She ate four! Then she tried to tell her daddy that *he* was making them wrong!

1½ pounds Lean Ground Beef
½ cup fine Unseasoned Bread Crumbs
½ cup uncooked Oatmeal
3 large fresh Mushrooms, diced
¼ cup Sweet Pickle Relish, drained
¼ pound Monterey Jack Cheese, finely shredded
American Cheese, 2 slices per 'Burger
1 tablespoon Minced Onion
1 cup Hickory Smoke Barbeque Sauce
1 ounce Lemon Juice
1 tablespoon Onion Powder
1 tablespoon Garlic Salt
2 tablespoons Barbeque Seasoning
2 tablespoons Hickory Smoke Salt

In a saucepan, combine the Barbeque Sauce, Lemon Juice, Onion Powder, Garlic Salt, Barbeque Seasoning and Hickory Smoke Salt. Cook the mixture over medium heat until bubbles begin to appear, stirring often, then reduce heat and simmer 10 minutes.

Remove from heat and cover. Place Ground Beef in large bowl and knead in the Bread Crumbs, Oatmeal, Mushrooms, Pickle Relish, Minced Onion and Monterey Jack Cheese. Add ½ cup of the barbeque mixture and knead it thoroughly into the meat. Form meat mixture into patties about ¼ inch to ½ inch thick each. Cook over a barbeque grill to the desired texture (rare, medium, well-done). Brush additional barbeque mixture on each side of the patties as it is cooking. Place 2 slices of American Cheese on each pattie 30 to 45 seconds before removing patties from grill. Serve on heated buns or bread slices. Salt and pepper to taste.

Special Sauce Garnish: Mix together ¼ cup of Thousand Island salad dressing, 3 tablespoons Catsup, 2 tablespoons Best Foods® Mayonaise, 2 tablespoons French's® Mustard, 1 teaspoon Worcestershire Sauce, 2 teaspoons bacon bits, 1 teaspoon Chili Powder, 1 teaspoon Hickory Smoke Salt and 1 teaspoon Malt Vinegar. Blend all ingredients with mixer set on low for five minutes. Spread generous dollop on both sides of buns before placing cooked pattie on them. Store sauce in sealed container in refrigerator. Makes enough for 2 dozen cheeseburgers.

VEGE-MEATLOAF

Serves 6 to 8

Mothers everywhere run into problems getting their kids to eat certain vegetables. A friend of mine had that problem with four daughters. She asked me if I knew of any tricks to get kids to eat vegies. I told her to disguise them so they looked and tasted like something else. I came up with this recipé for her. Almost any vegetable can be incorporated into it. Those which I have listed here are vegetables that I'm fond of. By the way, broccoli and cauliflower just don't make it!

2 pounds Lean Ground Beef
1 cup fine unseasoned Bread Crumbs
2 large Egg Whites
8 ounces Tomato Sauce
1 small Stewing Onion, finely diced
1 small Green Bell Pepper, diced
4 fresh Mushrooms, diced
2 tablespoons Corn Starch
1 ounce Lemon Juice
1 ounce Malt Vinegar
1 teaspoon Orégano
½ teaspoon Sage
2 ounces Worcestershire Sauce
1 tablespoon Brown Sugar
1 teaspoon Garlic Salt
4 tablespoons Alfalfa Sprouts, finely chopped
½ cup Hickory Smoke Barbeque Sauce
1 tablespoon French's® Mustard
2 tablespoons Best Foods® Mayonaise
4 tablespoons Country Crock® tub Butter

In a skillet, cook the Onion, Bell Pepper, Mushrooms and Alfalfa Sprouts in the Lemon Juice, Malt Vinegar and Butter over medium heat until the pepper pieces are soft. In a large bowl, knead together the Ground Beef, Bread Crumbs, Orégano, Sage, Worcestershire Sauce, Garlic Salt, 4 ounces of Tomato Sauce, ¼ cup Barbeque Sauce, Egg Whites, and 1 teaspoon of Corn Starch. Fold in the cooked vegetables, making sure the ingredients are well dispersed throughout the meat. Form the meat into a loaf and place into a standard, non-stick loaf pan. Form a cover over the loaf pan with aluminum foil and cook for 55 minutes in an oven preheated to 350°.

Sauce Topping: In a saucepan, combine the remaining Tomato Sauce, Barbeque Sauce and Corn Starch with the Mustard, Brown Sugar and Mayonaise. Simmer on low for 15 minutes, stirring occasionally. When meatloaf has finished cooking, remove the foil and pour the sauce evenly over the loaf and replace in oven for five minutes, uncovered. Allow to cool slightly before serving. Salt and pepper to taste. May sprinkle Parmesan Cheese over each serving and garnish with sprigs of Parsley. (Note: Listed vegetables can be interchanged with other vegetables, as preferred.)

VEGETARIAN PIZZA

Serves 6 to 8

This is another meatless dish I used to make for my vegetarian friends. It's even good for people who are watching their weight. Except for the butter, cheese, and the barbeque sauce, this pizza is low in the fatty solids and cholesterol. The toppings can be interchanged to suit your own tastes. The crust dough is easy to make, a slight variation of a breadloaf recipé I had. One word of warning, however; unless you have the experience, I don't recommend that you spin the pizza dough over your head. You could have disastrous results like I did. Especially if you have a low ceiling like I had.

Crust Dough
3½ cups sifted Flour, plus extra for dusting
2 tablespoons Rapid Rising Yeast
1 tablespoon Log Cabin® Light Syrup
1½ cups Warm Water
2 tablespoons Country Crock® tub Butter, melted
¾ tablespoon Salt

Sauce
16 ounces Tomato Purée
2 tablespoons Worcestershire Sauce
2 tablespoons Hickory Smoke Barbeque Sauce

2 tablespoons Barbeque Seasoning
2 tablespoons Orégano
2 teaspoons Garlic Salt
1 teaspoon Sweet Basil
2 Bay Leaves, halved

Toppings
16 ounces Mozzarella Cheese, shredded (more if desired)
4 ounces fresh Bell Peppers (Red or Green), chopped
4 ounces Black Olives, pitted and sliced
4 ounces Cherry Tomato, chopped with seeds removed
4 ounces fresh Mushrooms, thinly sliced
4 ounces Onion, finely chopped

Sauce: In a large saucepan, add together the Tomato Purée, Worcestershire Sauce, Barbeque Sauce, Barbeque Seasoning, Orégano, Garlic Salt, Basil, Bay Leaves and 1 teaspoon of Butter. Simmer over low-medium heat, stirring often, until ready to use (at least 30 minutes). If sauce begins to boil, reduce heat to low and continue to stir.

Pizza Dough: Combine 2½ cups of Flour with Yeast, Salt, Water, Syrup and 1 tablespoon of Butter. When those ingredients are thoroughly combined, fold in remaining flour until last of flour must be kneaded into dough. Dough should have a thick, smooth texture when done. Cover dough and let sit for 25 minutes. Lightly dust flour over work surface and place ½ of the dough on it. Flatten dough with hands, dust dough with flour and then flatten the dough further with a rolling pin until large enough to fit a 12-inch, non-stick pizza pan. Place dough on pan and dimple with fingers. Repeat instructions with second half of dough for second pizza.

Topping the Pizza: Brush remaining Butter over top of pizza dough. Spread sauce liberally over dough, leaving about a ½-inch border around pizza. Spread cheese atop the sauce, followed by sliced and chopped toppings over the layer of cheese. If desired, add more cheese over toppings for a final topping for the pizza. Bake at 400° for 15 or 20 minutes, or until crust is a crispy, golden brown. Serve hot, garnished with grated Parmesan Cheese. Salt and Pepper to taste.

STUFFED BELL PEPPERS

Makes 2 Each

I used to buy Stouffer's® Stuffed Bell Peppers so much that my grocery bill was almost as large as a week's paycheck. I had to either cut down on eating one of my favorite foods or learn to cook it from scratch. Since I had ideas for adding more ingredients, the choice was simple. I usually only cooked these for myself, so I didn't figure the recipé for a large amount. This recipé only needs to have the quantities multiplied by the number of people eating and you'll have a nearly complete meal in this one by itself.

2 fresh Green or Red Bell Peppers
1 cup cooked Rice
1 cup cooked Ground Beef
1 cup Tomato Sauce
¼ cup Barbeque Sauce
2 fresh Mushrooms, diced
1 small Stewing Onion, diced
1 tablespoon Hickory Smoke Powder
2 teaspoons Garlic Salt
1 tablespoon Steak Seasoning
1 tablespoon Chili Powder
½ cup shredded Sharp Cheddar Cheese
¼ cup Green Olives w/Pimentos, diced
1 Bay Leaf

Cut the top off the Bell Peppers and scrape out the shell, discard top and seeds. Cook the rice as directed on the package. In a large skillet, cook the Ground Beef, pour off and discard the grease. To the skillet, add the Mushrooms, Onions, Olives, Barbeque Sauce, Tomato Sauce, Bay Leaf and the seasonings. Cook over medium heat, stirring often until bubbles appear, then reduce heat to low, cover and let simmer for 20 minutes. Place Bell Pepper shells into a casserole dish. Stir Rice into Ground Beef mixture, remove from heat and spoon mixture into shells. Pour remaining mixture and sauce around the shells. Cover and cook in oven preheated to 350° for 50 minutes. Then remove cover and spoon juices over Pepper shells and meat filling. Return to oven and cook an additional 5 minutes, uncovered. Serve two stuffed peppers per person with cheese sprinkled over top. Discard Bay Leaf. Salt and Pepper to taste.

CHAPTER 10

Dressed for Success

Plumage, manes, and bright orange butts. The males of the "lower" species get all the cool garb. While every male would jump every female, given the chance, the females try to be selective and the males vie amongst themselves to see who will be top dog. Generally there are more males than females, and so survival of the fittest is always also survival of the prettiest. The king of the jungle always looks like the king and never like the jester.

However, once you "rise" to the human race, females outnumber the males. Suddenly, female looks matter, or at least the females think so. The truth is that when push comes to shove, every male would still jump every female, given the chance, but one-night stands and approaching from behind don't do much for evolution. For real propagation and nurturing, particularly bearing in mind the long odds of human impregnation and the very long period of human gestation, the female's got to look good enough to come home to even when morning sickness lasts well into the night.

So, in humans, the females get the feathers and the charge accounts. In the case of the second ex-Mrs. Lane, she believed that shoes were the attractor of moment. Imelda Marcos was a K-Mart shopper compared to my ex. When we split, she had to rent a mini-storage for the seasonal overflow, and Polaroid stock skyrocketed as she cleverly slapped photos of the shoes on the sides of the boxes so she could differentiate between two dozen pairs of bone pumps. I had no idea that bone came in so many colors.

At the same time, human males are hopelessly lost. Most mistakenly think that they have to look good—a vestige of our lesser ancestors combined with misleading instructions from females—and only an insightful few males realize that looks don't mean shit. How many times have you said "How in the heck did that troll wind up with that supermodel?", as if you were surprised. The answer is not money or power or brains or brawn; the answer is that any male can still have any female if he thinks of himself as king of the jungle. The difference being that a human male can look like the jester and still be king because there will never be enough kings to go around, while supermodels have become pretty much a dime a dozen thanks to cable television.

I am no king. Neither is Bill Suff.

When I was a teenager, I went with my friend Rob—the one who died in the wreck—up to an Oakland A's game, where I was determined to make a play for the adorable blonde ballgirl. Rob and I had press passes, field passes, courtesy of me conning the A's management, and so we were on the field in ballgirl territory as the players warmed up pregame. I assumed that our mere presence on the field would bespeak "importance" to the girl, but I knew I could cement our relationship once she noticed how nicely I was dressed. I was wearing a handsome, plaid, cashmere sport coat, bought for me by my mother, who had told me that you need to look good, stand up straight, and give girls nice presents—the basic marching orders for Jewish males.

When my conversation with the ballgirl went nowhere—"Hi, how are you?" "Fine. Could you move so I can watch batting practice?"—I resorted to pointing out my fine sport coat. Rob pretended not to know me. The girl looked right through me, sport coat and all. Maybe another of those blue-winged demons had winged in.

Nonetheless, pathetic though I was and rejected though I was, I didn't pull out a knife and gut the cute little ballgirl. To this day I've never even had a negative thought about her. If she'd responded positively to my "advances", I know I would have later concluded that she was pretty stupid.

Subsequent dating and marriage followed a more complex pattern, but underneath it all was the same insecurity and the same misplaced reliance on packaging. Essentially, I bought two wives, paid for by vast amounts of money and even vaster amounts of physical and emotional caretaking, all for naught. There is no more foolhardy or just plain wrong mission than deciding that your only goal in life is to make someone else happy. It is a manipulative and terribly selfish motive, dripping in honey, and I apologize.

Bill Suff was an even more terribly shy youth, particularly when it came to girls, and he didn't have a cashmere coat. He couldn't even get close enough to girls to get turned away. How then could he gain their affection?

Bill did not have a plan exactly; he just operated on instinct, instinct that would later become a conscious pattern by trial and error.

A pattern that would bring him wives and girlfriends and women to murder.

Try this scenario: You're eighteen years old. You go to the Rose Bowl for a high school football game. One bus you see is filled with a group of wayward girls from a church "home". Your emotional antennae point you toward one girl in particular—you know nothing about her but you find her attractive.

Emotional antennae are weird deals. If you drop me into a crowded room, I will be instantly sucked toward people who lost their parents at any early age. I feel it as attraction, only later finding out anything about their backgrounds. Somehow they exhibit loss or pain that I instinctively want to heal. I dated a paralegal for a time many years ago, and, when I broke up with her, she sobbed, "But I thought we had a future together because you'd lost your mother and I'd lost my father!"

I was stunned. I truly had no idea that this had formed any basis of my attraction to her, but of course she was right. Suddenly I realized that my previous girlfriend filled the same bill. From that point on, I was at least wary of that particular parameter. But then how do you know when you meet someone whether you are attracted to them for good reasons or self-destructive reasons? As you get older, everyone you meet has lost a parent or two, everyone is suspect, everyone proves a letdown. At least when you're younger and more insecure you can delude yourself into thinking that people have more to offer than they really do. You fictionalize them and relate to the fiction. Reality is always such a drag.

Anyway, Bill first met Teryl Cardella at that high school football game at the Rose Bowl in the fall of 1968. She was fifteen and he was eighteen, but he was too shy to speak to her. However, after a while he came up with a gambit that allowed him direct ingress into her soul.

Bill had dressed in a light blue shirt, dark blue pants, and a glitter belt for the game. He also had a gold sweater which he was carrying rather than wearing this early on a warm Southern California evening. He thought of himself as a sort of mysterious dandy, a kind of hip Johnny Cash. He also thought the outfit was more or less adult and authoritative. If he was too shy to speak, then the outfit could speak for him. Years later, in the Air Force, he would even come to be known as "Hollywood" because of the blue and silver glitter Nehru jacket he wore.

Too timid to hang around his peers at the game, unsure what to say to them, Bill cruised down to the front of the stands, by the field, where the ushers and security guards prowled. He struck up a conversation with one guard who was trying to tell him to go back to his seat.

"In all those blue clothes, you're dressed a lot like me," said the guard.

"I always wear clothes like this," said Bill.

"You oughta head on back to your seat, son," said the guard.

"The kids are pretty rowdy up there," said Bill.

Just then, some peanuts, chunks of ice, and berries pelted down. Bill looked up into the crowd and spotted Teryl—she was smiling at him—she and her friends settled into their seats, acting like they hadn't thrown the peanuts, ice cubes, and berries, but nonetheless wanting to make sure that everyone knew they had.

"Tell you what," said the guard to Bill (at least this is what Bill told me he said), "since you're dressed like one of us—one of the security guards—why don't you take charge of this section and see if you can keep these kids in line."

And so Bill did—he became an *ad hoc* security guard for the night. And Teryl kept taunting and teasing him by tossing stuff to get his attention, and then acting all innocent as he scolded her. Then the minute he'd turn away, she'd climb up on the wall and grab some berries off the vines there, and she'd hurl them at him. They were going to mess up his nice clothes. Finally, he had a flash of inspiration. He went to Teryl and asked her—ordered her, actually—to mind his sweater for him. He gave her his sweater and she sat down and was a good girl for the rest of the night. Clearly, she liked the attention. She liked Bill's attention. She liked that he would trust her with his sweater. By the end of the evening, she let him walk her to her bus and she wrote her address and phone number on his hand. Then she kissed him, just a peck. Her mates taunted her to give a real kiss, but, before she could respond, Bill did: he grabbed her, dipped her, and kissed her full and deep. Like in the movies. "Great kiss," Teryl said. Everyone cheered. Bill Suff had never done anything so forceful, so impromptu in all his life. It was the happiest moment of his life.

When he thought about it later, he knew what had happened: It was the uniform. The uniform made him bold. And it made people do what he asked.

So, from that night on, for the rest of his life, Bill was never out of uniform. Prior to that he'd worn his high school band uniform, extending the costumed hours before and after performances, but the night at the Rose Bowl proved that even "civilian" clothes could have the urgency and authority of a uniform. From high school to the local fire/forestry department to the Air Force and the Medical Corps, to prison in Texas, then to Riverside, county service and the prostitute killings, and back to prison—Bill's uniform of each period defined him, empowered him. Clothes didn't make the man; they spoke for him, they were him.

When he met Cheryl Lewis in 1990 in Lake Elsinore—she was then only seventeen, working at night in a Circle K minimart—Bill had scouted her, decided to move on her, and showed up in an "unmarked" security guard's uniform—sheriff's shirt without the patches, pressed khakis.

"Don't pay me any attention," he whispered to her, "just go on about your business. The store management has hired me to keep watch on you and make sure you're all right here working so late at night."

And she believed him. After all, he was more than twice her age, just barely younger than her parents, and he hung around for endless hours all night long—no one would do that if it wasn't his job, right? Or, more importantly, he really did make her feel safe even though before he first showed up she couldn't actually say that she really felt unsafe. She sort of felt unsafe in retrospect, after he'd made her realize what a fool she'd been to have been unwary. It's a dangerous world out there. And she was important enough to deserve protection.

When Bill was arrested in Riverside in January 1992, much was made of the sheriff's shirts hanging in his closet; when he was tried, much was made of his personalized belts and tourist T-shirts and caps. The prosecutors tried to identify him through his clothes and the recollections of witnesses, but they missed out on the real point: *his uniforms predict his conduct*. Put him in prison garb, and he's harmless. Put him in a guard's clothes or firefighter's clothes, and he's helpful.

Then again, when he pulls on his killer's clothes, look out.

Contrary to any profiles or prosecution theories, there's no evidence that Bill wore crypto-cop clothes when he killed. I think the hookers would have been wary of it, and I think Bill had a different mind-set in such clothes. I even think there was a different "uniform" for the nights he simply dated hookers, as opposed to the nights he killed them. No biological or trace evidence turned up on any of Bill's clothes, yet there's no way he could have cleaned everything up so thoroughly. I think that somewhere out there he hid a bag of killing clothes, as well as the clothes he sometimes re-dressed his victims in.

What then were his killing clothes?

I suspect there were two stages of dress for the nights of the killings.

First, the clothes Bill wore when he stopped for the girls and enticed them into his van. These would be a slightly understated version of his dating clothes—long-sleeved shirt, plaid or dark; trousers, dark denim or maybe khaki; boots or maybe sneakers if his bum leg was bothering him, the one hurt in the motorcycle accident; and a big belt, but not the "BILL" one or any other so memorable.

Second, the actual clothes that Bill had to be wearing in order to commit "the sacrifice". These would be clothes that were at once practical, erotic, and priestly. Think "wizard", "hangman", Bob Guccione, and Velcro . . . and there's only one outfit that comes to mind: a jumpsuit. Bill wore them in the Air Force Medical Corps. He wore them in prison in Texas. The Air Force jumpsuits had been sent home and were waiting for him in Elsinore when he got out of jail for killing his baby. They already had blood on them from those ambulance calls in the Corps. Now no one much looked for those jumpsuits after he was arrested for the Riverside Prostitute Killings, but then again no one ever found them, either; and between the cops and Bill's family, his stuff was scavenged through and picked at like chicken pox. Of course, he might have ditched the old jumpsuits years ago and replaced them with brand-new or even government surplus clothes made out of parachute material that doesn't shed trace evidence. No matter where he got the damn jumpsuits, the fact is he had 'em, and once he had his victims in tow he'd dress up in the jumpsuits, and then he was able to kill.

Practically speaking, jumpsuits are easy to get in and out of, even in the dark. They also cover you from neck to ankle, catching your loose hairs, sloughed skin, and all other biological evidence. If you're wearing clothes underneath, the jumpsuit protects them from arterial spray, spitting, or any other messy act by your victim.

Erotically, jumpsuits zip or Velcro-rip open all the way down the front, allowing you to be fully dressed yet fully exposed, ready to "perform", and the fully encasing, unbreathing nylon feels really slicky and sweaty and second skinny should you be buck naked inside.

Meanwhile, the look of a jumpsuit is decidedly mystical, authoritative, and reverential. If you're medieval, it's a robe and hood; but modern means jumpsuit. It's what all the high priests wear.

But why is this relevant?

You will recall I previously knocked Bill's Dungeons and Dragons stories, but now you should take a look at the unfinished "A Whisper From the Dark", which follows shortly. The death-dealing villain is Zernebock, defined as evil incarnate—the same description the judge used on Bill when sentencing him to death. Zernebock is timeless . . . and be-robed. If you're going to be Death, you have to dress the part.

See, Bill lived in the environs of Elsinore, but it was really his self-made Pern. It took me a while to convince myself of this, because his fantasy writing seemed so obviously contrived to make that very point. I kept thinking this was all misdirection—a sensible fiction to mask the true delusion. I kept thinking that Bill would be cleverer and less open, that he came up with Dungeons and Dragons because that's what he knew people would expect to hear, much as he knew the cookbook would play into the Lecter stereotype.

Indeed, similarly, when Bill and I contemplated an insanity defense should his convictions be overturned and his case retried, I pressed him for any possible abuse or death-traumas he might have suffered as a youth. He said there was nothing, but then proceeded to write me a letter that contained, among other tales, a dream he had in which he was accusing his parents of abuse. He then wondered aloud whether the dream was some repressed memory fighting its way into his consciousness.

I read all this as fraud. I assumed he was just inventing what I needed in order to defend him.

However, I changed my mind about all this after he made a very real Freudian slip in discussing the last murder.

Bill was still in jail in Riverside, and his death sentence was due to be pronounced in a matter of days. He would then be taken immediately to a "safe cell" where he would be under suicide watch. Some night thereafter—it could be days or even weeks later—he would be spirited out without warning, tossed into a secure police vehicle, and transported to San Quentin. His days of high living in Riverside would be over, and the days of his life would be numbered.

Accordingly, he was at his lowest ebb emotionally, and I had just gotten a court order in order to see him alone without a guard looking in. I had to sign on as his civil attorney in order to get the order.

My friends and family kept asking me if I was frightened at the thought of being alone with Bill unmonitored, but I have to say I wasn't worried he'd try to kill me. Although he would have nothing to lose and was certainly plenty angry at all the world, I just didn't see him hurting me. Perhaps this was my shortsightedness, since I just can't relate to blind or irrational rage no matter how hard I try—I mean it just always seems so false to me when I see it depicted in film or on TV as some Charles Foster Kane trashes his wife's room—it makes me cringe because I don't quite believe it, Welles or not. He just seems to be thinking, *Okay, as I reach to sweep everything off her dresser, what'll look good for me to destroy next and how do I keep my best profile toward the camera?* In life, the times I've seen rage, it came across as entirely volitional and calculated. People do trash things, but don't they have a purpose in doing so? As they're flinging and stomping and punching, isn't there a consciousness that says "I know exactly what I'm doing and even though it's self-destructive and childish I'm going to do it anyway"? Isn't rage more a matter of punctuation than text?

Paralleling this to other emotions and motivations, when you're in the throes of hot sexual foreplay, doesn't the thought cross your mind that you ought to reach into that drawer and get that condom even though you wind up letting lust overrule the thought? Bill had nothing to lose by killing me, but he had much to gain by treating me well—from legal advice to friendship to, most important, my telling his story in this book. So, no, I wasn't fearful of him.

I was, however, worried that he would be a waste of my time, that he just wanted my company and would give me no legitimate or usable insight into his mind.

The Riverside guards put me alone with Bill in a conference room that doubled as the jailhouse law library. Before we did much else, I gave him a crash course in using a law library, so he could help himself with his own appeal. I also wanted to see just how smart he really was—not unexpectedly, he learned in twenty minutes what it takes most law students an entire semester to pick up.

And, as I moved around from bookcase to bookcase, I wanted to see how Bill watched me from his chair, how he moved, how he focused—I wanted to judge whether this was a man capable of concentrating on and mentally and physically overwhelming so many adult women without any slipups.

I remembered that years ago a friend of mine was working for a film director who'd gotten possession of two tiger cubs. I was invited to come play with the cubs, and they were amazing. Cute and cuddly and kitten-like, and then ZAP! a bird flitted out of a tree and the cubs' eyes and ears snapped to attention and their claws came out. It was like someone had turned on a switch. And, just as quickly, the cubs became cuddly and relaxed again . . . except now I'd seen their true, instinctive, unalterable, predatory nature and I didn't find the critters so cute and cuddly anymore. Even as cubs they could cause damage, and, six hundred pounds later, adulthood would make them downright terrifying and extra hungry.

So the question was, would Bill show his predatory nature in the context of me showing him the whys and wherefores of legal research?

Answer: yes. He listened and he learned, with a vengeance. Nothing escaped him. I saw him observing me as well as the law books and cases. He was the student, but I was the subject rather than the teacher.

Of course, being focused and judgmental did not mean that Bill was a killer, but then again, if he hadn't been able to be so focused he certainly could not have been guilty of anything. If he'd been dumber or more scattered, he'd have to have been innocent.

Now I sat down next to him, mere inches away.

And I admit that, all the time we chatted, I kept looking at those ham hands of his. I kept imagining the sensations they had experienced. Those thick, stubby fingers had crushed throat cartilage, burst veins, torn flesh. They had killed grown women and they had killed a baby. What had that felt like? What was it comparable to? You know how people always say any mystery meat—from rattlesnake to dog—tastes like chicken? Well then, what does strangling someone with your bare hands equate to for those of us who haven't taken that dark path?

I cannot even imagine. I don't even like forming hamburger patties.

However, I do have to say that as I sat with Bill, I had the odd sensation of talking to him and being outside myself watching myself talk to him at the same time. I was trying not to be tricked into his world—I was there to manipulate him, and not vice versa—and yet I realized later that my paranoia and focus split me in a way not unlike the way Bill sees the world. I personally had no incentive to violence, but at that moment the world had become a different place for me simply because I was now looking at it differently than before. I was now in Bill's world after all. The serial killer exists on multiple planes of consciousness and focus that require utter vigilance and complete emotional detachment at the same time. Killing results from a singular release/burst of pain, confusion, and concomitant rage that suddenly floods through this intricate, geometric, high-rise reality, not unlike orgasm I am afraid to say. And that is as close as I can get to seeing that murder could get you hard.

"Bill," I said after we'd been talking for a while and he was starting to get anxious, seeing the clock winding down and knowing that our visit would soon end and his trip to Death Row would not be far behind, "let's be real. Let's say we get your convictions thrown out on appeal because it was prejudicial to try all these cases together. Then you get retried on the strongest case. So you get convicted of that last murder, Eleanor Casares."

"And Cheryl Coker, too," he said.

"Really?"

"I'm not saying I did it, I'm just saying the evidence—the evidence the police planted—is strongest in those two cases."

"I see." I wracked my brain to see what was most damning about Coker—both Casares and Coker were breast-removal cases—and then I realized what had Bill so concerned: Coker was the case where a condom had been found nearby. The DNA match to the semen in the condom was no big deal, it matched Bill but it was a low-percentage match. That is, it didn't eliminate him, but it did include about a few million other people in the immediate vicinity, like most white males. So why was Bill concerned about it?

Because leaving the condom there had been a mistake. He'd been so careful in all the other killings, but this time he'd left behind actual evidence. Out of haste or neglect or arrogance, that condom had gotten knocked out of the back of his van when he was carting out the body to toss her and pose her atop the pile of branch clippings in a dumpster bay.

Bill had fucked up, and that made him feel out of control, and that made him feel guilty. Not guilty of murder, guilty of screwing up "perfect" murder.

Maybe this was one of the only times he'd actually even come during a killing rather than later. Maybe he'd lost his bearings and then lost the condom because the whole sexual experience with Coker had been so WOW! Certainly something had happened to take his mind off his meticulous post-homicide rituals during which he carefully stowed condoms, garrote, bonds, knife, and the other tools and trophies of his trade.

I eyed Bill—he was far away, no doubt back at the murder scene.

"The condom, Bill?" I suggested.

"Never use them. Can't come in them," he stated emotionlessly.

Right. So it was the condom that had him spooked. I decided to play along but press any other button I could find. "Maybe the right breast being cut off then, think that damns you somehow?"

"I've been thinking about that since you asked before. You know, there is the myth of the Amazon Women—maybe that's what it's all about."

"Yes?"

"An Amazon Woman would cut off her own right breast so it wouldn't get in the way of her using her bow and arrow."

Of course, how silly of me not to have thought of that before. "So we've got a killer into mythology? What's his point, cut off their breasts because that makes them seem like Amazons and then he's a bigger deal for having brought them down? Or is it just his way of saying that, no matter what they are, he's bigger and badder and he can hurt them anytime he chooses? And why cut some but not others?"

"I have no idea," said Bill Suff, but he was fidgeting and fidgeting and fidgeting, nervous as a cat.

"All right, let's talk about Casares," I said.

The Casares case was the one where tire tracks at the orange grove murder scene matched all four of Bill's mismatched tires. This was the case where Bill admitted to the cops that he'd been at the scene and seen the body, but she was already dead. His story was that he'd stopped to pick fruit late at night, saw the body, and panicked because he rightly surmised that everyone would think that he—convicted baby killer—must have been involved. The problem with his story was that he had taken home Eleanor Casares' clothes and then laundered them, and even Bill Suff couldn't really explain why he would have done that.

The naked body had been discovered with a coat draped over its head and face. According to Bill, her clothes were piled alongside her, and he just grabbed up the pile and fled.

None of this nonsensical story was admissible at trial, as previously noted, because the cops ignored Bill when he begged for a lawyer before he answered any questions. He now says he was so tired and scared by the cops, he would have said anything. But he still can't explain why he took home Eleanor Casares' clothes. Maybe he just thought she didn't need them anymore, so why let them go to waste.

"I've read your own defense investigator's report on this, Bill," I said, "and even though Tricia Barnaby's a big ally of yours and thinks you got a raw deal by the illegal way you were arrested and then tried, she's got a real problem with your story about seeing Casares' body in the orange grove."

"I admit I was there. And I admit I saw it."

"The problem is, Tricia showed you photos of Casares in life, and you said they didn't look like her."

"I couldn't really tell if they were her or not."

"Yeah, but when you saw her in the orange grove—the only time you ever saw her, according to you—her face was covered up by a coat. So how do you know what she looked like?"

Bill didn't skip a beat. "It wasn't Casares that Tricia showed me photos of—it was Kelly Hammond."

Tricia Barnaby had showed Bill photos of every victim, and her reports were quite clear. She had specifically advised the defense lawyers about the "problem" with Bill's identification of Casares because, up to that point, Tricia had almost convinced herself that Bill was innocent.

Bill and I stared at each other. He knew that I knew he had just lied to me.

"Bill, I don't care if you're guilty or innocent, and I'm just here for the story. Not the truth, not the lies, just the story. So you can say that Tricia Barnaby is wrong, and you can say you're innocent, and I'll make sure that your words get published in our book. Even more, I'll help you with your criminal defense just because I want to keep the system honest and because I hate the death penalty. But, if you really want to get off Death Row, then you're going to have to be candid and truthful and make a jury see you as a human being. Juries don't put human beings to death. Even the families of the victims will let up on you and get back to their lives if you just give them closure. What I'm telling you is that my best advice, based on my experience, is that if we get your convictions overturned, then you are going to need to plead up to at least Casares, and maybe Coker, as you say. You are going to need to tell the world you're guilty, but your mind is such that you couldn't help yourself—whatever the truth is of your psychology. Because sane people aren't serial killers. And, in prison, you are not only not a harmful person, you are productive and sensitive and you can contribute to society through your writing. So that's the deal. That's the only way I can help you. This book will humanize you in the public's eye—they never heard from you at trial, so it was easy to stereotype you as a one-dimensional monster. But now once they are surprised to find that there's more to you than they know, that you actually might have some worth, that your voice is important to be heard, then it's up to you to give credibility to that voice and that humanity by being honest. You won't be forgiven, and you shouldn't be, but maybe people will conclude that it's not up to them to decide that—that's God's job."

It was quite a speech, and Bill was twitching by the time I was done.

"So, tell me about Casares," I said.

He started to speak, and then he cut himself off, and then, stammering, out of breath, he lurched into: "I just remember that when I was back in my van and I was pulling out, and my headlights washed across her lying there in the graveyard—*I mean in the orchard!*—I saw her face in the light shining under the coat."

I don't know if I looked faint, but I sure as hell felt it. An orange grove wasn't an orange grove: *it was a graveyard!* And Bill knew he'd just given himself away. It was more than a Freudian slip: it was a pratfall, a swan dive, Earth reentry, a shine a light in his eyes and count the fingers what fingers KO—"yes, Houston, we have splashdown!"

Suddenly, I was awash in my recollections of all Bill's innocuous little stories about all the secret little places he used to scout

out and then take Cheryl and Bonnie and this or that girlfriend to. As well as the various Tranquility Gardens where he'd go alone.

Suddenly, his fantasy writing became real for me. And his previously grounded science fiction tome, "Crash Landing", took flight. In that piece, however, refugees find themselves marooned in an unknown world in an uncharted universe. Our world—Earth—becomes a parallel world where any given space, any room, any cove or dune or field or orchard can simultaneously be something else entirely. It wasn't that the place looked any different in each universe, it's just that each universe had a different meaning and a different set of rules, and people could cross over at the intersection points, finding themselves the victims or heroes of agendas quite opposite from anything they just left behind.

And that was why Bill Suff could never harm a fly, let alone be a serial killer and baby destroyer. Murder was wrong in our world, and death was permanent and to be avoided. But, in another world, murder wasn't murder at all—sometimes it was even mandated for the greater good and for unrelenting destiny—and death simply didn't exist.

Suddenly, I had understanding to go along with the impression that Bill had always given me that there simply had been no crimes in Riverside, that accusing him was not wrong, it was absurd.

The deaths of all those young women had happened in another world where they weren't dead at all, but they had nonetheless been sacrificed for their own good.

And the person taking the sacrifices was not a killer but a priest, a holy man, a wizard, salvation incarnate.

Which was why Bill had to have dressed the part.

"Where'd you hide the clothes, Bill?" I asked. "The jumpsuit, the robe, the clothes, the surgical tubing, the knife, the engraving tools, the paint, the condoms, all the stuff. There must be a bag or a box somewhere, like that tackle box you used to have." He said nothing, so I went on: "It's all out there, and it can help save your life. It explains you. First we humanize you by showing the good side, the writer, romantic side of you—the truth. Then we explain what happened by showing what really happened—no more guess-work by cops and profilers—we show the aberrational side as it really exists—again, the truth. Truth and closure. Once we know you, we stop fearing you because we know you can be controlled. And once you know you, maybe you don't feel like killing any-more. Either way, we no longer have to kill you. We don't have to *snuff the Suff*."

Snuff the Suff was the chant of the victims' families during the penalty phase of the trial.

"Where's all that stuff hidden, Bill? It's been waiting out there for years now, and the elements can only be ruining it. We're already going to be accused of planting it to create a scam defense—we need to dig the stuff up before there's nothing left of it to find."

"I ever tell you how much I enjoy Shelley Long?" he asked. "And Bonnie Bedelia, too. Here—I even keep track of their birthdays."

With that, Bill opened a manila envelope and pulled out news-paper clippings about actresses Shelley Long and Bonnie Bedelia, along with a sheet of legal paper on which he had handwritten their biographies and other pertinent facts.

We then spent the next half hour discussing his favorite Hol-lywood stars and reviewing his outline for what he hoped would be the next *Die Hard* movie. He called it *Die Hard: Dam Hard*. In it the venerable Bruce Willis and his movie wife—*Bonnie Bedelia*—had to stop terrorists from blowing up the Grand Coulee Dam.

As for the killing clothes and the killing kit, they're still out there somewhere—in the desert, by the sea, under a rock, by a tree, in a cove, behind a wall—and someday someone will come across them and wonder what they mean. Hopefully, that person won't try the clothes on for size—who knows what they could make a person do.

CHAPTER 11

Excerpts from

"A Whisper From the Dark"

and

"Crash Landing"

Two unfinished novels written by Bill Suff

A Whisper From the Dark

ONE

Sheathed as it was, the sword called "Daystryker" would not cut. But I have a powerful, strong arm and the blow should have felled any man. As Daystryker landed at the juncture of neck and shoulder, Lupien acted as though he had been hit by naught but a feather. As he reached for me, I upended the table and flung it at him. It halted him only long enough to swing an arm sideways and shatter it like so much kindling wood. However, it gave me enough time to dash through the doorway and into the next room.

I slammed the door and threw the bolt. That should hold Lupien long enough for me to attain my desire, I thought to myself. But never before had I seen Lupien exhibit such strength and it would bode much ill for him to lay hands upon me. Ordinarily, his sinews were near the power of mine own. But now his might could be my bane.

I crossed the room in half a dozen strides and stood between the window and the blazing fireplace. Barely had I begun to trace my portal when a mighty crash sounded from the doorway. Turning from the wall, facing the bolted door, I saw Lupien's arm protruding through it and into the room. Slowly, his arm bent at the elbow and drew back. The door splintered and fell away from its hinges, littering the stone floor. Lupien strode through the now open archway and raised his huge hands toward me. Behind him a hooded figure moved into my sight, and quickly I realized who my real adversary actually was. The creature held a small crystalline sphere in his claw-like hand and I knew Lupien for the puppet he was and from whence his strength had come. The meaning of the clouded look in his eyes now became clear to me, also. Taking two steps to my right now placed me within arm-span of the fireplace and I raised my voice aloud, speaking plainly in the gnome's own language.

"Hear me well, Wick! Stop him or I'll throw this into the fire. Verily, you can see just how hot it is, and you'll get naught but slag for your efforts."

Being born in the fires of a sun, no ordinary flame could harm Daystryker. But Wick didn't know that. I held Daystryker toward the fire and Wick's evil eyes grew wide. He hurriedly covered the glowing sphere he held, and, slowly, the vacant look in Lupien's eyes cleared. Then they closed and he limply folded to the floor, oblivious to everything happening around him. Wick slowly advanced further into the room. He had slipped the crystalline sphere into his cloak, but had not yet brought his hand back into sight. I knew he now had his hand closed around something else. But I had no idea what other tricks this strange gnome had available to him, nor was I curious enough to find out. I softly spoke a few words in the tongue of the Ancients, and Wick must have guessed what was coming, for he brought his hand out of his cloak empty and threw both arms up to cover his eyes. As I spoke the last word of the incantation, an invisible weight gathered itself and settled in my left hand. Tossing that weight forward, I willed it to fall at Wick's feet. As it hit the floor, there was a soft pop and a cloud of smoke instantly formed about the gnome. The power of the spell would hold him for the nonce, so he could neither move nor see.

Quickly, I slung Daystryker across my back and returned to the wall, where I finished outlining my portal. After completing the tracing, which would open my path through dimensions, I turned and hurried to Lupien, hoisted him to my shoulder and again returned to the portal tracing. I couldn't leave Lupien in Wick's clutches because the gnome would inflict grievous vengeance upon him if I did.

After placing my hands on opposite sides of the tracing, the space inside the portal suddenly became a mass of shifting, kaleidoscopic colors. As I took my first step forward, passing through the wall, I envied Lupien his unconsciousness. Colors could now be smelled; sound could be tasted; odors had rough textures and the force of pressure, and that pressure was painful. My senses were being assaulted in ways which would send most people into the world of insanity.

Luckily, it only lasted the few seconds it took me to take my next couple steps. My third step brought me into a world of bright sunshine, clean air and soft grasses 'neath my sandalled feet. The portal I had stepped through winked out of existence without a sound and could not be reopened by anyone, save myself. This world and the world in which Wick lived were in two different planes of existence. Even if Wick *could* open a portal, he wouldn't be able to find out which plane of existence Lupien and I had entered among the thousands that are possible.

I stooped to lay Lupien on the grass and then moved back several feet to await his return to consciousness. I wasn't about to take a chance on his dislike for me causing him to make a mistake when he came to. Slipping Daystryker from where it hung across my back, I settled down upon the veldt grass myself and began my meditation ritual. Sitting cross-legged, I spanned Daystryker across my knees and rested my hands upon it. My eyes slid half closed and I muttered softly to myself the litany I had learned under very unusual circumstances. For that matter, this whole affair came about because of some very, *very* unusual, *painful* circumstances.

Six years ago and worlds away, I was an irrelevant cog at a computer firm. Worlds away, not in time and space, but in what can only be described as dimensions. Now I dress in animal hides and sandals, carry a sword, and have, at times, even found myself speaking in languages I've never heard before. And I was now being considered as the savior of a race of a troubled people. Many times in my life I had heard that the brain is the most mysterious organ in the human body. Little did I know *how* mysterious until that moment six years ago when I was awakened by a whisper from the dark.

TWO

M y name was Michael Dermott, born in St. Charles, Illinois, in the year of Our Lord, nineteen hundred and sixty-five. Six years ago, I was twenty-two and holding down a promising job at Compnet Research Corporation, one of the best computer research and development companies in Southern California. At five foot eight, a hundred and seventy pounds soaking wet, with blond hair and green eyes, I was often mistaken for the typical California 'Beach Bum', although I'd spent very little time at the beach. A bit of a computer nerd, I lived alone in a one-bedroom apartment near the beach in the city of Oceanside. I'm perfectly aware that I'm not much to look at, as far as women are concerned. In fact, I've always been kind of intimidated by good-looking women. For general information, good-looking women are as numerous as the stars in the sky in Oceanside. Needless to say, this fact was the primary reason for my self-imposed solitude.

However, once I began life on my own, I began to go out on camping excursions. Quite often, three-day weekends would find me in nearby campgrounds. Being unattached, I wouldn't have to make plans very far ahead of time. On spur-of-the-moment occasions I'd just pick up and leave.

On the weekend of January 17, 1988, I had done just that. That cold winter Sunday, I was on my way back home after spending a wonderful two days camping on Palomar Mountain. Sleeping bag, tent and miniature campstove were all tied down on the back of my motorcycle. My backpack held the other sundry items that I had packed for the weekend away from the noise and problems of city life. The weekend was very relaxing for me; however, maybe it was a little *too* relaxing.

That morning had been exceptionally cold with a film of frozen dew glazing everything. By noon, the sun had most of that glaze melted and nearly had everything dried out. I started out from the campground around 1:30 that afternoon, riding along at a leisurely speed, gliding through the curves smoothly. Ahead of me was a curve bathed in the shadows of the surrounding vegetation, so I eased off the gas and began to lightly apply both brakes, suspecting ice in those shadows. Just as I entered the curve, I saw the ice and heard a racing engine. Applying more pressure to the brakes, I attempted to stop before I reached it. But at that moment, the oncoming car came around the curve, skidding out of control. Time seemed to creep by then, seconds expanding into pregnant minutes.

The car was a candy-apple red Camaro with a pair of scared teenage faces showing behind the windshield. The driver's eyes were shifting wildly left and right, seeking an escape or some way he could stop the insane ride they were on. The girl riding shotgun had both hands locked on the dashboard and I even believed that I could see her knuckles showing white from her fierce grip. Her eyes were wide with fright, but when she saw that I was in the path of their careening car, her eyes grew even larger. She had realized in that instant that I was the only thing that stood between them and the edge of the road. An edge which disappeared into the vast open space where the mountainside dropped away from the road.

My forward momentum had almost ended and I saw that if I hadn't braked, I'd have been out of the car's path now. As those items were registering in my brain, so were a number of other things: A deer was frozen in its place by the sudden onslaught of noise, a pair of doves were scared into flight, and a squirrel down the road stood up on its hind legs to see what all the ruckus was about.

As my mind collected all of this data in those few minute-long seconds, I realized the amount of noise was inappropriate for the tires on my bike to be causing. Almost as an afterthought, the answer came to me: A truck behind me was nearly standing on its nose as the driver slammed his foot and brake pedal to the floor, causing the tires to scream their protest out to the pavement. Added to that noise, was that caused by the Camaro's tires as they left the ice and were crying out their own misery at traveling in a direction they were never meant to travel.

The next moment, the right front fender of the Camaro smashed into the front end of my bike, bringing me to a bone-jarring stop and immediately altering my direction of travel. In that instant, my eyes and mind registered several things moving in the slowest of slow motions. Sort of like a motion picture moving by one frame per second. The eyes of the girl in the car locked with mine, and, in those eyes I read the terror and sadness at what was happening. The front tire on my bike instantly blew apart, while the front end began folding in upon itself. My left leg smacked against the car, while my right leg and hip hung up on the handlebars which threw me back down onto the seat. My left hand cracked against the windshield right in front of the girl, causing her to blink tears out of her eyes. Throughout all of this, I knew that my left leg had broken in two places, my right hipbone cracked loudly as it broke and my left hand broke in several places. Surprisingly, though, I felt no pain from any of these injuries, which made me begin to wonder if all of this was only a terrible dream. But no dream I'd ever had was this vivid or intricate.

I'd like to believe that it was hitting me which slowed down the car enough to keep it from following me over the side of the mountain, but it was probably the railing. The car pushed my bike, with me still on it, backwards to the edge of the road and the protective railing. When my bike hit the railing, it stopped, catapulting me over the side and into the air. As I tumbled, I could see the ground, then my bike hung up on the railing, then the empty sky and then the ground came around again, followed by a tree that was flying toward me at a crazy angle. Just as the bike and railing came into view again, a terrible weight crashed into my right side under my arm and then something clubbed me along the right side of my head. At that moment, everything disappeared . . . The day turned into the darkness of dreamless sleep.

THREE

Questions were being asked of me and a light flashed in my eyes. I didn't like the light or the questions, so I shook my head. *Big mistake!* Immediately, I regretted that movement as pain began to explode through my head, neck and shoulders. Flashes of pain and fire caused my eyes to shut tight. Only that caused more pain and then I was visited by the darkness again.

When I next became aware of things, I heard a soft, insistent, feminine voice in my head. It was a pleasant voice filled with musical tones and harmonics that were hard to place. And there was an odor that I couldn't place any more than I could place the voice. It was a pleasant, almost sweet odor similar to apple blossoms with a faint taste of cinnamon behind it. But I don't think I was actually *smelling* them. The odor was just there . . . in my head.

"Awaken Chalder. Ye must awaken. Ye be needed verr' much!"

I questioned the voice dreamily: "Who's Chalder? And what am *I* needed for?" The voice immediately came back to me.

"Ye be Chalder! Remember, oh please remember, Chalder! Ye must remember. Ye be th' way. Two hands will open th' door. Ye're hands, Chalder. Daystryker awaits ye."

Again, dreamily, I responded. "Yes. I remember. My hands will open the door. My hands. Daystryker awaits my hands. *I am* Chalder!"

"Yes, yes! Ye be Chalder!" The voice was excited now. *"Ye're hands open th' door. Daystryker does await ye."*

A face then became visible from deep in the darkness. A feminine face, coming closer to me until it was right in front of my dream eyes. Her face was angelic, with wide, violet-shaded eyes set in an oval face of alabaster skin. Her hair floated like a nimbus around her head, filaments spun from gold casting an aura of misty colors that circled her, cutting off sight of everything below the neck and beyond. Even the surrounding darkness seemed to disappear. Her face seemed to hover in front of me with nothing to support it. Turning my head to the left and then the right, I hoped to get some kind of idea as to where I was. But her face moved with my eyes, always before me in the center of my vision. My neck muscles told me that my head was turning, while my eyes were saying differently. I glanced down to see just what kind of surface I was standing upon: Ground, floor, stage, *space* . . . I don't know what, but my body position, I knew, was one of standing. Once again, however, her face still moved with my eyes so I could see nothing but her face! I was aware that by now I should be afraid of *something*, but for the life of me, I couldn't figure out what. Meanwhile, she had continued talking and I found myself paying more attention to her.

"Ye must relearn things, Chalder, 'tis of great import. For 'twixt ye're skill at this and ye're art with Daystryker, ye're life and th' lives of others shalt be preserved."

An intense, urgent look came into her eyes as they locked on mine. The urgency took up residence in her voice as well.

"Nou, repeat all of which I tell ye. And try, Chalder, try hard."

As she continued to explain what I was to do, images began to form in my head. I could see the delicate lines that traced a door in the air. Though the lines were invisible, I could still see them. I learned that the door being traced in my mind was a portal through which I would be able to move between dimensions. A doorway between the world I was a part of and the world I desired to be a part of.

"One thing further I must warn ye of, Chalder. There be dire peril 'twixt one world and the other. Ye must continue moving forward once ye enter th' portal. Madness and pain await any who should falter. Th' terrors entering a mind that bides too long 'twixt what was and what 'twill be, shalt drive a hale mind to be consumed by the chaos. Even a closed eye is of nae use. Ye must keep moving!"

At that moment, a gruff voice filled with impatience entered my mind. It *had* to be in my mind because no external sounds met my ears.

"LYNARRA, YE MUST LEAVE TH' ORRIHAN NOU. IF HE HAN'T LEARN'T BY NOU, HE BE NAE USE TO US. LEAVE HIM BE NOU 'FORE TH' HODEKIN CATCH SCENT OF YE!"

"Lupien, I'll nae be listening to ye talk abou' Chalder that way! This person be Chalder and he is th' only one can wield Daystryker. Th' spatha wilt allow naught but th' Albyn to swing it. As well ye be aware, Lupien. Remember ye're hands 'ere ye attempted to lay hold upon it?" This last was said with a certain amount of smug satisfaction that brought another surge of anger in the voice I now identified as Lupien's.

"YE HAE NAE PROOF THAT THIS ORRIHAN IS TRULY TH' ALBYN! HOW DOST YE KEN THAT HE CAN WIELD TH' SPATHA? YE'RE NAE SEER NOU, BE YE?!"

"Dinna be glaikit, Lupien! Dost ye think a seer just suddenly becomes? Bear I th' mark of a seer?! Daystryker itself was th' sway to Chalder. And if ye once more name Chalder an orrihan, I'll mark ye well, me ownself. Nou leave me to this working."

The argument between Lynarra and Lupien lasted only a few moments before a burst of outrageous anger filled my mind, I suppose directed at me, and then the gruff voice and angry presence was gone. Only the serene presence of Lynarra now remained. Again, her soft voice came to me and only now did I realize that although her lips were moving, no sound issued from those delicate arches. She reminded me of a person who mouths the words while reading. Her actual words were somehow projected directly into my mind, as had Lupien's.

"Chalder, ye must hasten to mend, for when ye be hale ye must open th' portal and come unto Chiréon. Save ye take up Daystryker, th' Hodekin wilt be upon us and I fear th' enmity of Zernebock, th' wicked one, shalt cause our destruction. He is our bane. Only ye can be our salvation."

Then, for an instant, impatience and fear filled my mind, and Lupien's gruff voice returned with an edge of panic to it.

"LYNARRA! YE MUST COME NOU! 'TIS TH' HODEKIN . . . WICK HIMSELF! HE'LL SLAY TH' BOTH OF US WITHOUT A WIT OF GRIEF! HURRY!"

"Chalder, remember this, too! It may be of aid to ye: 'Aperient Oriel Fenestra!' Remember. Come, Chalder, come! We need ye."

With that said, Lynarra's face was gone. So was everything else that was associated with this dream. And I felt that it had to be a dream. Surely none of it had been real, it couldn't be. I was thinking all of this and also still remembering every bit of the dream as I opened my eyes. Instantly, the sterile odor of a medical atmosphere informed me that I was in a medical environment. A blurred, white form moved to my left and then I heard buttons being pushed. Next came a soft, feminine voice. Different from Lynarra's, but still pleasant to hear.

"Doctor Welles? Nurse Mandell. Your patient in 416 just awakened." Then came the sound of the phone receiver being returned to its cradle.

The white form moved closer to me, so I shut my eyes and started to shake the cobwebs out of my head. I say 'started to' because as soon as I moved my head a fraction of an inch, bright flares began going off behind my closed eyes. That soft voice came back with a tone of insistence. "Don't move your head, sir. Try to remain very still. You're still in traction and it may hurt if you move too much at first." I wanted to tell her that I wasn't about to move anymore, that the pain had already taught me that particular lesson very well. But I couldn't get my voice to work.

I opened my eyes as the bursting flares began to subside, and then blinked a few times to clear my vision. My eyesight began to improve almost immediately and I got a clear view of the nurse attending to my welfare. She was young, petite, though a bit on the thin side, shag-cut blonde hair, wearing a pants-type nurse's uniform with a nametag above her left breast that read: 'Maggie Mandell, R.N.'. I croaked out something unintelligible, but she understood me anyway. She turned to the bedside table and picked up a cup, filled it from a water carafe, grabbed a straw, then put it all together and held it for me to drink.

"Just take small sips first. You need to get used to swallowing again."

That worried me. I wondered how long I'd been here. After lubricating my throat a little, my voice worked better. "How long?" Swallow. "How long here?"

She hesitated in making her reply. Then, "Mr. Dermott, sir, Doctor Welles is on his way up here right now. He will tell you everything. He was on call in the emergency room when you were brought in and has worked everything in regard to your injuries. He is the best one to ask your questions of. You'll get your answers and the reasons behind them from him." Another moment passed in silence and then the aforementioned doctor walked in. He was an old man, tall, a little on the heavy side with white hair, deep wrinkles and dark-framed glasses.

"Mr. Dermott, how are you feeling this afternoon?" He waited for a reply, so I gave him one.

"Perhaps you're in a better position to tell *me* that answer." My throat felt better by the second and it became ever easier to talk. "I've got minor aches and pains just about everywhere. The major pain is behind my eyes, in my head. It feels like someone has been using it for sledgehammer practice. When I woke up, I tried to turn my head and wound up watching some 4th of July fireworks behind my eyes. And will you please stop calling me 'Mister' Dermott? I don't like any sexist appellations like Mister, Master, or even Sir. Please, I'd much rather you called me Michael."

"Very well, Michael. What can you remember of your days before your accident and coming here?"

I thought for a moment. Accident? An accident that put me under the care of a doctor and a nurse? This place had an emergency room and I was in room 416, which meant there were at least four floors in this building. Probably a basement, too. Therefore, I had to be in a large medical care building or, more probably, a hospital. Thinking back from this point, I remembered every bit of the dream about Lynarra and Lupien. But I didn't want to talk about that. They might begin to think that there was something more wrong with my head than just the good knocking around it got.

Before the dream though . . . There were misty scenes that floated around in my head. I answered the doctor's question by talking it through. "The last clear thing I can recall is the camping trip I took up near the Palomar Observatory. I also remember breaking camp and loading everything onto my Kawasaki, a 750-full dress. But everything after that is kind of fuzzy. I remember a girl's face . . . scared . . . crying, I think. A green sports car. Maybe a Camaro." Then some more of the mists cleared. "It hit me and I was thrown from my bike. I was falling away from my bike. I seem to recall seeing a big tree flying through the air, but that can't be right. That's about all," I said, with a half shrug that brought tears to my eyes.

"That's good, Michael. You remember a lot more than I expected you to be able to remember."

I interrupted him at that point. "I've got a number of questions for you, doctor. Like, how long have I been here and what injuries have I, for starters."

"All in good time, Michael, all in good time. First, I want to examine you." I closed my eyes in resignation and submitted to his examinations. I've never been a very patient man, but I knew that it was no use to protest. He looked into my eyes, ears and mouth. He probed at my right shoulder and the ribs under my arm. He next probed at my right hip and kept asking if there was any bad pain in any of the places he was probing. I told him about dull aches in each of those places, except for the hip. The hip was very tender and made me wince a bit. I added that there were also aches along my back, left leg, left hand and wrist. "Well, that's to be expected, Michael. Your left hand was broken in six different spots. We're still not sure whether or not you'll have full range of motion return. You'll need some extensive physical therapy for your hand. You'll need it for your leg and hip as well. You may have to learn how to walk all over again."

I began to get even more worried now. If I was going to get that much physical therapy and maybe even have to relearn the ability to walk, I had to have been in a bed and immovable long enough for some of my muscles to atrophy. How long that was, I had no idea, but I did know that it took awhile.

"Now, as to your questions. Your injuries weren't half as bad as they could have been, considering your accident. But, while your injuries could have been worse, those you did sustain were, for the most part, bad enough to put you down for the count. Do you remember the date of your accident? When you broke camp and started down from your campground?"

I only had to consider the question for a moment. "I went up to Palomar and set up camp on Friday afternoon, the 15th of January. I broke camp around noon Sunday and started right down the hill. So the date would be the 17th of January. What's today's date?" The answer to that question was more important to me than what had happened in the accident.

Doctor Welles made a few notes in the chart he had brought in with him, then put his pen in a pocket and closed the chart. "Michael, today is Wednesday, the 14th of July. You've been in a coma, or at least deeply unconscious, for the last six months." I was able to work out how long it had been faster in my head than he could tell me. I shut my eyes at the amount of time I had lost. I wondered who had been doing my work, who was feeding my birds and fish. The doctor's voice was suddenly sharp with concern. "Michael? Are you all right?" I opened my eyes and looked at him. "Nurse, some water!" Nurse Mandell instantly gave the cup of water to the doctor and he held the straw for me to sip. After a couple draws of water, he took the cup away. "Are you all right now, Michael?"

I took a couple deep breaths and felt better. "It just had me startled for a moment that I've lost six months due to this accident. I realized that some time has passed, but not how much."

"Well, I'm going to have a physical therapist come up to talk with you and set up a schedule for you. The traction on your head and neck will be removed tomorrow or Friday. Your physical therapy should begin next week and I'll be checking in on you several times between now and then. The nursing staff will be in and out of here even more often. I'm going to leave an order for a painkiller, in case the pain in your hip or elsewhere gets too much for you to handle. That will give you some relief from your headaches, too. I'll stop back by for a minute before I leave this evening." He then left my room and the nurse stepped closer to my bed.

"Would you care for some more water?" I didn't, so she set the cup back on the nightstand. Then she turned back to me. "You know, you're something of a celebrity in here. You survived an accident that most people wouldn't have. The fact that you were wearing a helmet probably says a lot for your still being alive. You're a very lucky man."

I gave her a half-hearted smile. "To be perfectly honest with you, I don't really feel very lucky. Losing that much time out of a person's life kind of puts a damper on everything."

She smiled back at me and I noticed for the first time just how pretty she was. She had a beautiful smile and her blonde hair was a perfect frame for her face. "Listen, Michael. There are a few non-medical questions I'd like to ask you. Do you mind?" I couldn't look her in the eyes, I was getting tongue-tied. So I just said okay and stared at the ceiling. "Several times during your unconsciousness you spoke, as if you were carrying on a conversation with someone. You kept mentioning the names 'Kaldeer,' 'Day Striker,' 'Hod Ken' and 'Len Ara.' A few times you said something about your hands opening a door. And through it all, you often mentioned the phrase 'Aperient Oriel Fenestra.' Do any of those words mean any thing to you?" She waited politely, not saying anything about my not looking at her.

I was contemplating whether or not I should tell her anything about my dream. I didn't know if she would think I was crazy and would call a psychiatrist to start filling my head with nonsensical claptrap about me hating my parents and seeing sexual innuendoes in everything. I had even heard of a couple cases where a psychiatrist had brainwashed patients into thinking they had been sexually abused as children. No siree, no psychiatrists for me. After deciding, I quickly glanced at the nurse to see if she was staring at me, then back to the ceiling. I knew that I was coloring with embarrassment, but I couldn't help it. Quickly, I gave her an answer. "A dream, th- that's all. Just a dream I, uh, I had before I woke up."

I could see her smile grow larger from the corner of my eye, and I felt like I was faintly trembling in the nearness of her presence. "I see. You know, it's highly unusual for a person to dream or speak aloud while in a coma. That's why Doctor Welles told you that you may have been in a very deep state of unconsciousness. I just wanted you to know that this has happened several times during the past couple months." She stopped talking, I guess to give me a chance to reply, then: "Well, I've got to get back to the nurse's station. I'll check in to see how you're doing every so often. The call button is pinned close to your right hand. If your pain gets to be too much for you, give the button a push and I'll be right in with your medication. See you later." With a slight wave, she was gone, leaving faint traces of perfume swirling in the breeze of her departure.

FOUR

The pain in my hip was bothering me, but not so bad that I couldn't bear it, if I tried. The pain in the back of my head was slightly worse, but I was pretty sure I could cause it to diminish without having to resort to drugs. I had never cared to try any kind of drug. In a way, they scared me. I'd heard of patients being given drugs for one reason and then getting addicted to them. I wasn't about to get addicted to any drugs. So, if I could keep the nurses from giving me a drug for the pain, that was just another step to my goal. I've read a lot of self-help books and have studied some techniques of hypnotism. I called upon these techniques now trying to pacify the pain receptors in my head and hip. My eyes slid half closed as I coaxed myself into the trance, whereupon I could convince myself that the pain I was feeling was actually something else.

In this instance, I pictured the different points of pain as overfilled sacks of water. The pain slowly ebbed away as I mentally emptied the sacks. Soon, I pictured the sacks emptied of water and the pain was nearly gone. But it happened much quicker than it ever had before. When the pain had diminished to the point which I could handle it, I became aware of a faint tingling left in the back of my head. The sensation grew to the point that it enclosed my entire brain. It wasn't an unpleasant sensation, yet it wasn't exactly welcome either. It felt like after my foot would fall asleep and before the feeling returned. I felt no pain in the sensation at all, but now I realized that there was no pain anywhere in my body.

Then another sensation filled me and I began to feel a great fear. It felt like somebody . . . no, not somebody, some *thing* was hunting for me with deadly intent. I was beginning to get very scared now. I still couldn't move my head because of the traction, so I began to search the room as far as my eyes could reach. At the same time, I reached for the call button to summon the nurse. Before I could touch it, though, there came a contact.

There was a distinct sensation of terror. There was also a worry that the thing I had sensed before was going to discover the person I was now sensing. Then the feeling of self came. The person was female and she was scared that if the thing found her, the best she could hope for was that it would kill her. The real terror, though, was that it would have a far worse fate in store for her. I could feel her fear and it was as real for me as it was for her. Trembling with that fear, I could feel sweat forming on my forehead. I closed my eyes, and, as the room was cut off from my vision, another source of input flooded into me. With it came an identity: Lynarra! I had thought the previous conversation with her had been a dream. Now I was beginning to believe otherwise. After all, I had never before had contact with a dream character while I was awake.

In my mind's eye, I could see that Lynarra was trapped. A gnome was coming into the room in which Lynarra was crouched behind a huge block of stone. The gnome had not yet seen her, but discovery was bound to come soon. Five yards away was a window, the only means of escape, yet too far for her to attempt to reach. The gnome would have her as soon as it caught sight of her. I stared with my mind's eye at the gnome and felt my sense of contact with Lynarra fade away. Swiftly, contact with the gnome came to me. Feelings of pain, anger, carnage, malice, and many other forms of evil intent caused me to reel with dizziness. Only because I was lying down in bed, back in my hospital room, did I keep from losing my balance. I clenched my teeth and grasped the sheets under my hands with all the pitiful weakness I had. Never before had I known that much evil could reside in any one creature.

I braced myself against this feral malevolence and sent tendrils of my consciousness at the gnome. I was staggered with surprise when I found myself inside this creature's mind—if it could be called that. It was like I was in a hallway with corridors branching off in various directions. One corridor led me to a memory of this creature bowing down to an evil that paled its own evil in comparison. A name came with this memory and it shocked me because I knew the name: Zernebock—Master of the Hodekin. I rapidly backed off and turned into another pathway. Here I found another memory, a memory of a race called the Ancients. Instantly, the spells and enchantments, charms and sorceries, the mantras of magiks, all of the things the gnome had learned became a part of me. I knew that I could defeat this creature if we ever faced each other in battle. But I knew that I would also be placed in great peril by such a battle.

The next corridor led me to a buried memory of this creature's birthing. I found myself suddenly present at that awful event. An old woman, old in years and experience, was lying on a cot, near death, wracked with pain, unable to pass the oversized newborn through her withered birthing canal. A midwife had been called, but she was at a loss at giving any aid to the old woman. Two other people were present in the room with the old woman and the midwife. Two men: one clad in mail and armor, dirk and sword hung at his side; the other, the old man who owned the wayhouse. The armed man was speaking, angrily.

"I tell ye Lucinda, it bodes evil that this child comes this night! Th' storm outside be but an omen that ill comes with this birthing! Dinna be party to this!"

"But Swordmaster Kierkin," the old man pleaded, "if Parcaminia dinna birth soon, she'll die."

"Look at her, Cauponis! Durst ye ken that 'twould be relief to her?!"

At that moment, the door crashed open and a cloaked and hooded figure entered with a swirling fall of raindrops. Swordmaster Kierkin's hand was instantly on the haft of his sword as the wayhouseman and midwife cringed away from the figure in the doorway. Before Kierkin could draw his sword, a bony hand emerged from the cloak and pointed at him. A horrible voice boomed forth from the hood.

"Stay thy hand, swordmaster, or die before a new breath be drawn!"

Kierkin looked up at the figure and must have realized that the threat had not been an idle one, so he dropped his hand away from his sword and bowed his head. The figure then buried its bony hand back in the cloak and addressed the three people standing around the old woman.

"Yon babe shall be birthed this eve to the woe of many! It shall be mine bondsman and many wilt bend knee before it! Nou leave this room 'ere thy lives be worth naught!"

Thoroughly cowed, all three walked out into the rain as if all will had left their bodies. Without a hand touching the door, it swung closed behind the cloaked figure. As the figure approached the old woman, her rheumy eyes opened and she warily watched it come nearer. The hood slowly slid back of its own accord, and, as the old woman saw the face that, until then, had been hidden, she gasped and then lost consciousness. The figure looked dispassionately at the dying woman and then moved to stand next to the cot. Raising its hands, the figure began to make intricate designs that glowed in the air above the old woman. The unconscious woman drew a breath, a second one, and then, before her chest could rise a third time, the figure closed its left hand in the air and the old woman's chest sank, never to rise again.

Suddenly, the cloaked figure froze and the head slowly turned to look directly at the point from which I had been viewing everything thus far. I flinched before I remembered that I couldn't possibly be seen, that this was nothing more than a memory of the creature that was stalking Lynarra. But the figure *did* appear to be staring directly at me. The eyes glowed with a sickly, pale-yellow, and pupils that were thin slits of bright red. The skin of the centuries old, wrinkled face was a mottled shade of putrescent green that had a decidedly unhealthy glow. The bald pate was shiny with a sheen of febrile dampness that gave it a look of decayed death. The figure then brought its thin, liver-colored lips into a hideous, humorless grin and began to mumble.

At first, the words seemed to be random phrases of nonsense, but, as I listened, I began to recognize the language as one long dead on both this world and mine. Somehow I knew this person to be one of the Ancients. A member of a race of beings that made a study of alchemy, the working of magiks, sorcerers and wizardries. These Ancients had wandered the various dimensions at will long before mankind had begun to proliferate on my own world. And I also knew somehow that this Ancient one was the outcast known as The Wicked One—Zernebock!

I began to withdraw from the memory, while still watching the smile and pure evil intent of the eyes. Suddenly, the figure flung its left hand in my direction and a wave of inky darkness flew toward me. As the darkness seemed to wash over and through me, I felt nothing, but the macabre tableau before me was blocked from my view. Then the darkness passed by me. Once again I could see what was happening in the room.

The belly of the old woman was now split open and Zernebock was pulling the child out of the woman's womb. There was surprisingly little blood spilled, as if the body had been completely drained of blood before the child had been removed. From my viewpoint, the old woman's body now looked like nothing but an empty husk. The body now forgotten, Zernebock cradled the infant in the crook of one arm and started to turn around. As the malevolent eyes passed my viewpoint, Zernebock froze. Once more this Ancient one appeared to be staring into my very soul. A frown turned the thin-lipped grin into a terrible grimace, and again the strange language was spoken. This time I had no trouble understanding it.

"I dinna ken how thee be able to bear th' Death Spell or from whence thee comes. But thou shalt surely fall into mine hands if thou shouldst become a physical form, Shade! Thou shalt then bide th' agony I wilt deliver upon thee! Be wary of this, Shade!"

While Zernebock spoke, I took a quick glance at the child stolen from its mother. I gasped in shock as I saw the infant, wondering what kind of creature could have been the sire. The infant's head was much larger than the rest of its body. Its face was one of a very old man with deep creases of old, old age, beyond the cute wrinkles of a newborn. As I looked at the infant, the eyes opened into huge, pale, depthless orbs that reflected the pain of being born and much, much more.

I knew that I had to get away from these two beings, so I began to withdraw from this memory. I felt uneasy with the way Zernebock was able to detect me, even though I was not really there. I didn't know if Zernebock would be able to touch me with one of his spells through time and dimensions, and I wasn't about to take any further chances. But, as the scene began to fade, Zernebock spoke to me once again.

"Heed this augury, Shade! This babe shalt wreak grievous privations upon yon peoples. Then wilt thine world be laid bare to mine enmity. Thou shalt also become mine bondslave, Shade! Know this and tremble with thine fear!"

Anger immediately filled me as I was withdrawing, and I shouted, hoping Zernebock would hear me. "Nay! Thou shalt *never* meet thy designs whilst breath yet quickens within me!"

Those words surprised me. They weren't what I had intended to say, though the meaning was the same. I was about to add more to this loathsome creature, but once again I found myself in the strange mind-hallway of corridors, passing those branching pathways leading to other memories. Quickly, I also began to withdraw from the Gnome' s mind, just wanting to be as far away from the evil that I had so far been mute witness to. But, as I began leaving the Gnome's evil mind presence behind, Zernebock's horrible voice seemed to follow me out, alerting the Gnome to my presence.

"Wick," the evil voice echoed around me, "a Shade leaves thine memories. Yon female dost not possess an interest to mine purposes. Snare yon Shade before it canst make leave and bind it unto mine will!"

The Gnome quickly spun on its heels, searching the very air surrounding it. I immediately sent my thoughts toward Lynarra, hoping to make contact again. It came at once with an air of amazement in her mind.

"Chalder! Be ye here nou?" she whispered.

"Lynarra, be calm. I am only speaking to you in your mind, much as you did to me before. Think your words to me. We should be able to speak one to the other well that way."

Her thoughts then came to me clearly. "Chalder, we need ye. Where be ye?" The fear was very evident in her thoughts.

"As I said, be calm, Lynarra. I am yet in an hospice. I merely shut mine eyes and found myself with ye. Yet, I think I can be of aid."

"Be ye able to aid when ye be there and nae be here?"

"Be ready to escape out yon window as I attract Wick's note."

"But Chalder, Wick has enmity toward all who interfere against his will. Ye shall hae nae chance against him lest ye take up Daystryker."

"Harken unto my words with care, Lynarra. Already once I've faced Zernebock's death spell and bore no ill. Wick canst do nothing to me. I am only with you in the form that Zernebock calls a shade."

"Be it so, Chalder, ye know best in this matter. But please, take care. Wick kens magiks which are beyond a person's reason. And, he has . . ." Her thoughts ended in a gasp.

I quickly backed my presence away from her and caught sight of the gnome moving around the corner of the stone block. I began to feel an anger at his finding Lynarra, and focused my presence at his mind again, leading with all of the anger I could amass.

Wick's mind opened up to me once again, the force of his evil washing over me with a foul stench, and I had to fight off a brief surge of panic. I had to keep in mind that he couldn't touch me because only my thoughts were here. My body and true presence was still in bed, in room 416, in a San Diego hospital. Abstractly, I wondered if I appeared to be asleep and what would happen if someone there tried to awaken me. Then I refocused on the problem at hand. Wick's thoughts were filled with anticipation of evil and he grinned an evil smile when he spotted the young girl crouched behind the stone block.

"Aha! Ye hae nae hope o' getting away nou. Ye belong t' me!" His voice was grating on my nerves; slightly low-pitched, with the sound like rocks grinding together. The glee in his voice was almost too much to bear. As he raised his hands toward Lynarra and took another step forward, I yelled as loud as I could with my thoughts.

"Hold!!!" I calculated my thoughts to ring in his ears, making it impossible to tell exactly where the sound was coming from. He immediately spun on one toe, searching for the source of the voice which was ringing in his ears. Of course, no one was there, but it took him a moment to verify that. Lynarra took that opportunity to make her escape and leapt for the window. The sound of her footsteps made Wick spin back in her direction, so, once again, my thoughts crashed into his mind, making him whirl about.

This time however, he started moving his arms in an intricate motion, like he was tracing a design in the air. Then the lines became visible to me as a faint glow, but there was something wrong with it. When I looked directly at the design, it faded out of focus, causing my eyes to work hard at trying to refix it. If I turned my gaze to one side, though, the design came into crystal clarity, visible only to my peripheral vision. Wick had been mumbling all the while he was tracing the motions in the air. And the words which reached my ears sounded vaguely familiar, though I couldn't exactly place them.

Suddenly, I caught the meaning of the words Wick was muttering and I started to get scared. Quickly, I once more began to withdraw from this world, but then Wick threw his arms out in my direction. The design that glowed in the air started moving rapidly toward me and I immediately spoke a counter-spell. Exactly where the words I spoke came from and what they meant, I didn't really know; neither did I care. But speak them, I did, and just as I knew that these particular words would stop this particular threat, I knew it was time for me to leave Wick and his malevolence, now that Lynarra had made her escape.

Just before the scene in my mind's eye vanished, I saw a shimmering aura appear in the air before the glowing design. I knew that I had been the cause of this new appearance, but again, I really wasn't sure where it had come from. Only that it had appeared at my summoning. Then both spells came together and were gone with a resounding thunderclap that hurt my ears, and a smell of ozone burning my nose.

FIVE

When I opened my eyes, I found myself back in my hospital room, still secured to the bed by the neck and head traction. Everything that I had seen in my mind's eye was now gone. The quiet, murmuring sounds of the subdued atmosphere of a hospital ward came to my ears and I knew that I was where I was supposed to be. Still, though, there was the echo of that thunderclap from my counter-spell wiping out the spell Wick had thrown at me. That, and the ozone smell from the explosive burning away of both spells. Now the echo and smell was causing a slight throbbing pain in the back of my head, but I was almost afraid to use my self-hypnosis trick to reduce the pain. However, the last time I did that I ended up inside Wick's evil mind. I wasn't ready to return to Wick's world, yet. I decided that this one time I'd let medical science take care of the pain. So I reached for the call button and gave it a push, hoping the nurse would respond quickly.

A few seconds later, Nurse Mandell responded by entering my room. Three steps into it, she stumbled to a stop. Her mouth dropped open and then was covered by her hand. Her gaze was directed to the wall above my head. I craned my eyes upward, trying to see what she was seeing. However, because of the traction, I was unable to see any part of the wall above me. Nurse Mandell hurried to the side of my bed and placed her hand on my arm.

"Michael, are you all right? What happened in here?"

I looked at her, unsure what she was talking about. My voice must have confirmed my uncertainty. "Why? What's on the wall?"

She looked up at the wall again before answering my question. "There's a huge burned area on the wall. It looks a little like something exploded against the wall. Do you know what happened up there that might have caused that?"

I thought about that question for a long moment and then gave the only answer that I *could* give. "I—I think I can give you an answer for it, but it's not going to satisfy you or anyone else. First, though, could you give me something, that's *not* a narcotic, for a terrible headache? Then, if you've got a lot of spare time on your hands, I'll try to explain something that seems to be a dream that's more real than dream."

She hesitated a moment, then, "All right, I'll get you some pain medication right now. But your explanation had better be good. Maintenance is going to be very upset about this." Then she walked back out of the room.

A little over a minute later, Nurse Mandell came back into my room. This time she was followed by another nurse. They were still talking as they entered.

" . . . looks just like someone threw a blob of ink against the wall, but it's burned in." The second nurse gasped in shock as she saw the area above my head. Then she walked up to where the bed met the wall and I could just barely see her stretching to reach the spot with her hand. Then she backed away, re-entering my vision, looking at her hand.

"It's cold, real cold and it *is* burned." There was the color of black soot on her fingertips. "How did this happen!"

Nurse Mandell had, in the meanwhile, approached the other side of my bed and poured a fresh cup of water. Then she held a small medicine cup to my lips, dumping two tablets into my mouth when my lips parted. When the end of the straw sticking out of the cup was placed between my lips, I pulled hard and got a satisfyingly cool drink of water to wash down the medication. She then addressed the other nurse. "Michael said that he might be able to shed a little light on what happened." Then she gave me a questioning look with raised eyebrows.

I was still a little skeptical about telling them the exact truth, but I started anyway. "Uh, earlier you asked me about something you heard me say while I was unconscious. I told you that it was only a dream." She nodded. "Well, I've begun to think that it's a little more than just a dream." I began at the beginning, when Lynarra first contacted me, telling me that I was Chalder, and ending with the explosion of the two spells. In the middle of my discourse, the other nurse left the room shaking her head unbelievingly.

Crash Landing

PRELUDE

The year was 2005. No longer was one country fighting against another country. All of the countries had abolished their respective governments and formed the World Benevolent Government: a worldwide government that served the people of the world. However, after ten years of peace and prosperity, conditions began to get worse. The resources on Earth were dwindling precariously low and the world population had grown too large for this small globe of earth and water to support. Raw food sources had to be augmented by man-made products in order to feed everyone. Chemical additives made sawdust taste like steak, but it hadn't improved anything. The people thought up a nickname for the government: it became known as the 'WoBeGone' Government. The world leaders were unable to come up with any new answers to solve the problems of the growing population. Out of pure desperation, they began to look toward space and the possibility of colonizing other planets in the Solar System. Of all the planets, only Mars and one of Saturn's moons could sustain life. But it was hard work there and not many people were that strong.

Then, in 2017, scientists perfected the process of suspended animation. They were then able to travel further distances. Small, four-man ships were sent to all of the neighbor star systems with the hopes of finding habitable planets. By 2045, great shuttles were taking off to three different systems. The ships would first make the trip from Earth to Sol Base-Saturnia. From Saturnia, they would travel in one of the three directions to their final destination. Each trip only took a few days in 'ship time.' 'Ship time' involved the couple of days to leave the Solar System and then the few days to enter the destination system and the planet the ship was heading to. Actual 'Real time' could take anywhere from twelve to twenty years, depending on which destination they chose.

A few years after the Rigel System was opened to colonists, an alliance of scientists decided to make that their destination. The fourth planet out, CT-1030M, was named Panora and had been settled by a small colony. Panora was much like Earth, but had very little animal life on the planet. So the colonists were encouraged to bring their pets along. The alliance obtained four large ships to carry the technical, medical, and scientific staff along with other strong and hardy people. Also recruited for the trip was the designer of those ships and several of his co-workers and technicians. Doctor "Doc" Cephus Triskan had a very diverse background: Animal husbandry, physics, chemistry, architectural design and electronics were among the many fields in which he was conversant. He had also been the person who had designed and built the first somnambulance, or shipboard sleeping pods.

Doc Triskan decided to leave on the third ship and was given his choice of crew. It came as a surprise when he learned that the ship had been named after him: "The Triska." As time to leave came closer, he interviewed all of the passengers that would be carried on the Triska. He wanted to know everyone that would be on board and which pets they would be bringing. He agreed with the policy that colonists bring their pets. The transition to a new home was made easier when those familiar were included in the move. He was bringing his cat. The love in his life was Doctor Phall Beccera. She was to be the medical person on the ship and she was bringing her cat as well.

The command staff, Captain Ross Kalm and his second, Kandyce Skandgel, were to be pilot and co-pilot. The navigation tech was a very accomplished young man by the name of Balth Mystral. These three had worked together before on runs to Mars and Saturnia. They had a close working relationship and it was rumored that they could read each others' minds. At least, when they were working together each one seemed to know what the other needed without any words being spoken. And it had saved them before in many tense situations.

The day the first ship left for Rigel, the Triska was loading passengers and pets into their sleeping pods. Farm animals and all of the supplies had been loaded the week before. All of the passengers were asleep on board the ship the day the second ship left. Two days later the Triska was ready to lift off. Upon arriving at Saturnia, all of the final checks were made. Then the ship moved itself away from Saturnia station, heading for deep space.

After the Triska had cleared the Solar System, the crew said their 'Goodnights' and 'See you in twelve years', then climbed into their own pods. Doc Triskan made one last tour of the ship, checking all of the pods, and then climbed into his own somnambulance. He activated the pod and saw the injector slide out of a slot near his head and position itself against his neck. Automatically it found his blood vessel and then injected the somnambulant serum into his system. A moment later he drifted off to sleep and the somnambulance sent him into the deep sleep of suspended animation.

As the Solar System fell further behind the Triska, the four great engines shut off. The computers would keep the Real Time clocks accurate so the engines would re-fire at occasional intervals to maintain the coast that was set up with the lift-off thrust. In twelve years the ship would be just outside of the Rigel System and the computers would awaken the crew. A couple days later and the Triska would be planetside on Panora. And five hundred new residents would see their new home as the four ships unloaded their contents.

CHAPTER 1

"**H**it the stabilizers," she yelled, "or we'll never make it past that asteroid!" Kandyce was busy at her console, hitting one contact point after another, activating one directional thruster then another, trying to stop the Triska from her end-over-end tumble. "Four planets with one damned asteroid on an elliptical orbit and we have to start tumbling right into its path. Balth! What about those stabilizers?!"

"For crying out loud Kandyce, one's gone down and the other two are overheating trying to compensate!" Balth Mystral was worried, very worried. He'd never been in this kind of situation before. He had entered Spacetech Services when he was 18, and now, at 32 years old, he'd become one of the top techs to leave planetside anywhere in the known systemic arm.

Ross Kalm just sat in his pilot's chair, taking everything in. The readouts flashing in front of him told him everything he needed to know. Every couple of seconds he'd glance at the viewscreen to see the sun of the system they were entering pass within range of the forward scanners. "Simmer down Kandy, it's not all that bad. Our tumble is slowing some." *Nobody* called her 'Kandy'! Aside from Ross, that is. What started out as a practical joke between them had turned into a term of endearment. And nobody else was invited into it. "Balth, take the stabilizers off line. Kandy, run the thrusters as I call them out, ending each one as I call the next. . . ." He then began calling out numbers and Kandyce responded. Slowly the great ship began to steady itself and the sun in front of them gradually centered itself on the scanners. The screen automatically brought the focus into sharp clarity. "Kandy, hit the even thrusters for six seconds, then replace them with nine and ten for fifteen seconds." Kandyce immediately followed his directions, while at the same time watching her scanners which showed the star system ahead of them and the asteroid. "Alright Kandy, now add the forward thrusters to the engines."

"Ross, it's going to be close. Are you sure . . . ?" Abruptly she stopped speaking when she noticed something on her readouts. "Ross! This isn't Rigel! And I don't know any of these star systems I'm reading. We are *not* where we're supposed to be!"

"Let's not worry about that right now, Kandy. Just keep those thrusters firing." Ross had an uncanny ability to calm people down whenever panic seemed to threaten. He had that effect on people, whether they knew him or not, just by his voice and presence. It was no small wonder why he had been chosen for this voyage over hundreds of other pilots.

'This Voyage' had begun twelve real-time years ago and they were supposed to come out of their somnambulance pods when the ship entered the space near the Rigel System of planets. At that time, they were to make final checks in preparation to landing at Panora Base. Their passengers were 120 medical, agricultural and technical staff with baggage. The rest of the cargo included personal pets, food from Earth, medical supplies, building materials and general living supplies for a new colony. All were destined for the nearby city of Rigellia, a short two kilometers from Panora Base.

There were a total of four ships on this voyage, each spaced two days apart. The Triska had left Sol Base-Saturnia third in line. Three years after launch, the Triska passed through the tail of a black comet. The tail was composed of chunks from the comet, ranging in size from large to microscopic, any of which could do damage to sensitive instruments. One large rock took a chunk of the ship's tail off while another smashed its way into one of the main rockets, fouling another on the way, leaving the ship with only two functioning rockets. At the same time, much of the rear sensor array was removed. The comet and the rocks were enough to pull the Triska off its course and into a tumble. Nine years later, when the computers awoke the crew, the ship had long since left the known sphere of space. The other three ships had arrived safely at Rigel, only then becoming aware of the loss. In the collision, the Triska's telemetry antennae had also been smashed out of existence, so not even the receiving stations along the normal shipping routes knew the location of the Triska and her complement.

All three crew members in the control cabin had their eyes glued to their viewscreens and readouts. As the asteroid came closer, Ross checked another readout at his console, typed at his keyboard, and then turned quickly around. "Balth, check our main rockets. Have they fired?"

Balth's eyebrows raised in astonishment as he checked. "The board says that they are all firing. But the whole rear scanner array is off-line."

Kandyce quickly checked her panel, also. "I don't know, Ross. My readouts say 'Firing'. But the entire scanner array back there is blank." She didn't have to be told what to do next. No one had to tell her. Quickly she began to hit contact points across her panel and then hit them again in the reverse order. Suddenly, there was a faint roar coming from the direction of the engines and a distant shudder vibrated through the ship. A great smile painted itself across Kandyce's face as she turned back to Ross. "Does that help any, Captain?"

Ross glanced from the screens to readouts and back to the screens again. "Okay everyone, don't trust the readouts at face value. Recheck everything. Those rockets were definitely what we needed. Look at your screens." The asteroid began slipping back from the ship. Then it was noticed that the sun began to slip lower on the viewscreen. "Kandy, two-four-six, now and stay with it!" Kandyce followed suit and the sun stopped drifting off the screen as the three thrusters readjusted the ship. The sun of the system in front of them began to find the center of the screen as Ross spoke again . . . "All right Kandy, cut out four, keep two and six firing. Let's see if that holds us steady."

As Kandyce complied she double-checked, making sure that the directional thrusters were continuing to fire. Satisfied that all was well with them, she glanced at the ship scanners. The same screen was repeated at each station in the control cabin. It showed a central blip and the surrounding area within ten kilometers in a 360° readout. The problem was with the view of the rear of the ship. An area representing 45° was totally black. That meant that four or five of the sensors around the rear end of the ship were out. So were the two cameras that would have allowed them to look at the rockets and rear thruster array. She was also aware that along with the sensors and the cameras, the telemetry instruments and communication antennae would be out. So they would be unable to broadcast their position or receive any information from home. At least, until they could exact some sort of repairs.

Ross was speaking again. "Balth, check the telescopes. Make sure they're still in working order, then get Phall and Doc up here. I'll be in my cabin. Kandy, notify me immediately if there's any change at all." He then rose out of his chair, rechecking his instruments while he did so. He placed his hand on Kandyce's shoulder as they passed each other, she heading for his vacated chair. He disappeared behind the door to his cabin as Balth entered the corridor to the interior of the ship.

Phall was bent over a log sitting on her desk when Balth entered the med-lab. Doc was nowhere in sight. Phall started with a jump when Balth spoke. "Excuse me, Dr. Beccera. I'm sorry to disturb you, but Capt. Kalm needs to see you and Doc Triskan as soon as possible. Is Doc very busy right now?"

"Not at the moment." Phall Beccera was a tall woman with clear, green eyes and short cropped blonde hair. She had a soft, sultry voice which was usually spoken just above a whisper, but was never hard to hear. "I'll get him and we'll be there shortly." With that, Phall picked up her log and walked out of the med-lab, turning to the bays. Balth followed her out and turned to the observatory and the telescopes housed there.

CHAPTER TWO

I was just closing the door to the freezer unit at the outer hull when Phall came from behind wrapping her arms around me. "I found two more. Numbers 88 and 90. Same problem. Cracked shield." I shook my head and disentangled myself from Phall's arms. "I just don't understand it. There's 120 sleepers out there, five of those have cracked shields and the people that were in them are gone. When their shields cracked, the computer should have awakened me and them, too. And there's nothing wrong with the computers." I banged my fist helplessly against the door behind which were five people I knew.

Phall turned me to face her and took my face into her cupped hands. "Ceph, there's not a thing in the world you could have done. It's not your fault." She saw the tears in my eyes and pulled my head to her shoulder, again wrapping her arms around me, holding me close. "It's not your fault" she repeated. "Now come on. Pull yourself together, Ross wants to see us. He probably needs our report before we land at Panora. I've got the log on the desk, let's go check the animal pods and then we'll go see Ross." I nodded and followed her into the secondary bays.

As soon as we opened the door the odor let us know something had gone wrong in there. Immediately I shut the door and accepted the mask Phall was extending in my direction. Slipping it over my nose and mouth, I adjusted the airflow and then slipped the bottle into my pocket. Seeing that Phall had done the same, we turned back to the bay and entered.

As we walked into the bay, the lights brightened, the sensors reading us as we passed through the door. Littering the floor in front of us and along the walkways was evidence that more than one animal had somehow awakened and been released from their sleeping pods. We both went into the anteroom to the desk. Opening a drawer, I picked up a pair of stunning wands and handed one to Phall. Activating them, we turned back to the bay and entered the walkway between the sleeping pods. I heard something moving far down on the right side of the bay, near the food stores. Phall pointed to a spot midway on the left side, but I couldn't see anything when I glanced in that direction. "I don't know what it was," she said in response to my question. "I only caught a glimpse of it when it jumped or fell behind one of the pods."

"Okay. Let's walk the aisle, checking each pod and between

pods. Note damages, deaths, and if any are empty." I moved to the right side of the aisle and started working my way forward as I checked my side of the bay. Phall kept even with me along the left side of the walkway, performing her search as effectively as I was mine. About a quarter of the way down, I came upon a pod with the shield cracked from top to bottom. Looking into the pod, I could see the remains of six cats. And they had died some time ago. Taking the label card from the end of the pod, I read the names of the owners. One of them was Cali, my calico kitten. I felt a lump rise in my throat. One of the others was Phall's siamese kitten, Andromeda. She was going to be very disappointed, because she loved him as much as I loved Cali. But I couldn't worry about that anymore. There was more important work to do. Glancing over to Phall, I could see that she had collected two or three label cards from pods herself and had them in her pocket. So there were some damaged pods on that side of the bay, also. I doubted that she had found any of the pods to be empty, otherwise she would have brought my attention to it. I slipped the label card into my pocket and moved on to the next pod. I would wait for a better time to tell her about Andromeda and Cali.

I had just leaned over to check pod 46 when an ear-shattering, shrill screech resounded through the bay, startling me. I brought myself upright, glancing over to Phall who was frozen in fear, her wand forgotten and hanging from the strap around her wrist. I quickly stepped over to her side and slipped the wand back into her hand. "Phall, whatever it is, it can't hurt us any. We don't have any dangerous animals on board. Domesticated and farm animals are all that anyone was allowed to bring aboard. Let's find whatever it is and deal with it so we can get on with the rest of our work." She nodded and brought her wand up in a defensive position. We started walking along the aisle again, this time more interested in the spaces between the pods rather than the pods themselves.

Three pods further, Phall softly called to me. I was beside her in two quick steps. On the floor, between the pods, was a dead chimp. Chimpanzees had long been family choices for a pet. Especially families with children because they were perfect playmates for the children. The chimps were naturally adaptable and easily trained. This was a larger loss than the cats. Chimps were much harder to breed and were valuable not only for their relationships with children. They were also helpful in homes, workplaces and labs after being taught simple chores. We hadn't found this chimp's pod yet, so we had to find it and its mate. There were two chimps per pod and they were mates. Now I knew what had caused that unearthly screech. I turned to Phall and was frozen by her terrified scream. At that moment, something hit me in the middle of my back, knocking me forward, off my feet.

Everything seemed to be moving in slow motion. I felt myself falling toward Phall with a terribly heavy weight on my back. A searing pain began to make its presence felt at my right shoulder, while a rather strange warmth began to flow across the right side of my chest. I felt myself hit against Phall, knocking her sideways as her left arm swung up to catch me and her right hand, holding the wand, snaked towards me. The thought entered my mind: 'Why is she going to stun me?' Then I felt the side of my head strike the edge of the sleeping pod. In the next fraction of a second, I felt the overpowering and nerve shattering sting of the wand surge its way through my body, sending me into the sense-deprived world of unconsciousness.

CHAPTER THREE

Balth had followed Phall out of the med-lab and walked the short corridor and into the observatory that held the telescopes and the relays to the control cabin. Moving to the first of four telescopes, he flipped the switches to activate the telescope and put his eye to the viewfinder. Sighting it in on the nose of the ship, he then raised it to look directly ahead of the ship. The sun of the system ahead came into view, dampers automatically filtering down the harmful rays of the sun to protect the viewer's eyes.

Smiling with satisfaction, Balth moved to the second telescope and repeated his actions. This telescope had a wider field of view encompassing half the system that they were entering. He adjusted the telescope to the left and caught view of an asteroid belt, and, farther away, a blue planet. Faintly, he could make out some land masses with clouds dotting the surface. He left it focused in that direction. Moving to the third telescope, he activated it and aimed it in the direction of the asteroid they had so narrowly missed. That asteroid was a mean one, easily a hundred times the size of the ship, it looked like it was a piece of a world that had broken up. When Balth turned to the fourth telescope nothing happened. He threw the switches again, but still the viewfinder remained black. He was disappointed. With the telescopes situated near the front of the ship, he had been sure that they had escaped the damage that had been delivered to the tail section. He finally gave up on the telescope and turned to the relay board. Throwing the relays necessary to transfer control of the telescopes to the control cabin, he then turned and left the observatory, heading back to the front of the ship.

Kandyce was just sitting back in Ross' chair when Balth entered. She turned to glance over her shoulder at him and smiled. "Just like a Sunday ride in the park, huh?" Balth smiled back at her and moved to his navigation section. Sitting in his chair, at his station, he suddenly felt better. This was his domain, his expertise. He was comfortable here. He began working his panel, activating the relays that would complete the connections between the observatory and his station. Kandyce arose from where she was sitting and stood behind Balth as he hit the contact points that activated the screen the relays were connected to. Instantly the screen lit up to show the sun that was sitting before them.

"Evidently one of the 'scopes has been damaged. I could only activate three of them." Balth was explaining when Ross came back to the cabin. "The first three 'scopes are set for the sun as you can see right now." He hit a contact and then two more as he continued talking. "A planet that looks quite a distance away and the asteroid. The fourth 'scope is out, so I figure it may have been damaged along with whatever happened to the tail section." He turned in his seat, saw Ross and spoke directly to him. "Captain, I'd like to EVA as soon as possible with Doc so I can assess the damage we've sustained and see if any repair work is feasible."

Ross closed his eyes and nodded. "I was going to mention that when Phall and Doc got up here. I want them to know what's going on also. And then I want the report on our passengers and cargo at the same time. How about some printouts on this system, huh?"

Balth turned back to his console and started hitting other contact points and a small printer to his left came to life. It continued printing for a few seconds, and when it stopped he tore off the data sheet, then he hit the contacts again making the printer start up.

Ross scanned the sheet, smiled and started talking. "The sun is much like the sun at Rigel and Earth, but larger and hotter. I'd hate to get too close to it." Balth handed him the next sheet and he paused to scan it. "The planet the second telescope is aimed at looks inviting. Oxygen-Nitrogen based atmosphere, oceans, lots of land to crash on." He chuckled a little. "On the whole, it looks a lot like Earth, a little like Saturnia, but not as much water. There's plenty of clouds, so it looks like there's rainfall. And, unless I'm reading these figures wrong, there seems to be a hurricane in the northwestern hemisphere."

Balth hit another contact and the screen produced the planet they had been talking about. He hit yet another one and the image doubled in size. Reaching forward, he tapped the screen with his forefinger. "There's your hurricane, captain. Looks like it just made landfall, too." He touched contacts again and this time the asteroid appeared on the screen. "There's the little item that almost cut our trip short. I'm glad we missed it."

Kandyce gave a little gasp. "That thing's a lot bigger than I thought it was."

Balth handed Ross the sheet that was just printed up. "That thing's almost a planet. It's 207,000 miles long and 93,000 miles at its widest point. It's even got a bit of an atmosphere. I don't know what those two gases are. The computer can't make heads or tails of them. But the asteroid itself is pretty interesting. Gold tops the list, with silver, nickel and gallium close behind. There's minor traces of iron ore and some carbon in it. And with its orbit, I'd be willing to bet that some of that carbon has formed into diamonds. That asteroid is a miner's dream." He gave a slight laugh. "I'd like to get my hands on a large chunk of it myself."

Kandyce smiled at Ross and then to Balth she said, "What about the other three planets and that asteroid belt?"

Balth starting touching contacts again and the screen changed back to the planet they had been studying before. "You can see some of the asteroid belt here." He began tapping a contact point and the view on the screen began tracking to the right. "Okay, here's some more of the belt. It looks pretty extensive. I shouldn't be surprised that we'll find it describes its own orbit around the sun. The way the asteroids are spread out, and the number of asteroids, not to mention the size of some of the individual pieces, I would guess it was at one time a planet that broke up. As you know, that's the case with the belt of asteroids in our own solar system between Mars and Jupiter. In the survey of '96 they found that the asteroids were at one time a planet. The scientists discovered that there were other asteroids that didn't match, different from the majority of the asteroids. The supposition was that a rogue planetoid entered the system eons ago and collided with the planet, thereby breaking up both spatial bodies and forming the asteroid belt. Over the many years between the time of the collision and when mankind started to look further into space, the pull of the different gravitational bodies spread the asteroids across space in the orbit around the sun. I think this is going to be the case here."

Ross was absorbing everything Balth was saying. Finally, "Balth, focus in tight on that extra large mass of asteroids and give me a printout." Balth followed the instructions and the screen showed the result. On the screen, a large body of asteroids leapt into their view, then doubled in size, then doubled again. The printer chattered briefly and then went silent. While Ross read the printout, Balth was at work again. He swung the telescope forward from the asteroid they had narrowly missed; forward to the asteroid belt and focused it on the same section of asteroids they had been looking at before. This telescope was able to get a much closer view of them though. Balth touched the contacts that brought the view in closer. The screen showed the asteroids speed in to a very closeup look. A couple more seconds and they were looking at individual asteroids. He then started tapping the contact point again and the scene on the screen slowly panned to the right. The asteroids slowly drifted from the right to the left. Suddenly, Ross spoke up again, "Hold right there a moment, Balth. This printout says that there are artificial, or man-made, items out there. Can you bring that view any closer?" Balth's fingers flew across his panel and the view on the screen instantly changed to a very craggy, torn section of an asteroid. As Balth started tapping once again, the asteroid slid off the screen to the left. This continued for a short while. Then suddenly, as the screen showed an asteroid slowly spinning, passing to the left, an object, or piece of an object, appeared from behind the asteroid. "Balth, run a tape!" Ross spoke fast, but quietly. "I want to be able to review this later!"

Balth smiled and said "Already rolling, captain. I anticipated this."

Kandyce leaned forward to look at the screen closer. "It's artificial, but I can't make out what it is. Can we get a printout on this?" In answer to her question the printer came alive again.

Ross quietly looked over the printout when Balth handed it to him. He shook his head and spoke: "It's a form of metal, but it's got a base the computer doesn't recognize. I'll bet that whatever it is, we'll find the same substance laced through the asteroids themselves. All right. We can come back to this later. Let's see the next planet."

Balth switched telescopes and panned to the right while a planet appeared on the screen. It was small and speeding along in its orbit. He activated the printer again. After he gave the printout to Ross, and, receiving a nod, he panned the telescope to the right again. Suddenly, two planets appeared on the screen, one behind the other. Kandyce gasped "It's beautiful. It's even more beautiful than any other planet I've seen. It looks like it's mostly water." Ross read the printout Balth handed him, smiling while Kandyce kept going on about the planet. "Is that moon circling this planet or is it part of that planet in the background? With that planet in the background, I'll bet the evenings are simply spectacular."

Kandyce finally stopped raving about the planet and Ross interjected what he had read from the printout. "Oxygen rich atmosphere, very few minor gases, nitrogen count is lower than the first planet. It's even lower than Earth's. No pollution in the air and the moon belongs to this one. Oceans cover the majority of the planet and don't read as being very salty. And here's one for you— it's got a reverse rotation. So, the sun will rise in the west and set in the east. The moon is just the opposite. Its orbit rises in the east and sets in the west. Well, we're going to have to set down on one of these planets. I'd rather not have to negotiate that asteroid belt, so I think we'd better head for that planet right there. I think we'd better be thinking up some names for these places if we're going to be here any length of time." Ross folded all of the printout sheets together and tucked them into his back pocket. He looked at the screen for a few seconds and then continued speaking. "As far as that fourth planet goes, it probably has a slower orbit than this other planet. So, we can wait awhile and get a readout a little later. Balth, plot us a course for an orbit, then . . . "

Ross was interrupted by a shrill clang and then Phall's terri-fied voice came over the speaker. "Medical emergency! Captain to med-lab immediately, please!" Then the speaker went dead. Ross and Kandyce looked at each other and then turned as one for the corridor to the med-lab. Ross called over his shoulder, "Balth, take care of everything. I'll let you know what's hap-pened." Then they entered the corridor to the med-lab and dis-appeared from Balth's view.

CHAPTER FOUR

Phall was still shook by the sound of that piercing screech echoing in her mind. Even the calm words of Doc didn't still all of her fears. She had passed two more pods when she saw the cracks that laced the shield of pod 49. Reaching out, she snagged the I.D. card and slipped it into her pocket with the clutch of other cards she had already accumulated. She took another step, coming past the pod to look at the space between the pods, and froze. Flipping the stun wand into her hand, she called to Doc and he was instantly at her side. Together, they studied the dead chimp, then Phall turned to him as her eye caught a blur of movement behind him. As she recognized a large shaggy chimp with a look of wild anger on its face, her fright turned into pure terror. Doc had just started to turn towards her, when her terrified scream made him falter. The chimp hit him in the middle of his back, pushing him into Phall. She tried to catch him and bring up the stun wand at the same time. She saw the chimp sink its fangs into Doc's shoulder, and then heard the dull thud of his head striking the sleeping pod.

Phall was off balance from Doc falling into her, so, when she tried to stun the chimp, she missed, the stun wand going wide and away from the chimp. Doc and the chimp hit the floor before she did. As she landed on her back she saw the chimp raise itself from Doc and jump towards her. She screamed again and brought the wand up between her and the chimp. It landed on her stomach, knocking the wind from her. Then the wand came into full contact with the chimp's chest. It screamed a savage bellow before lapsing into unconsciousness, and fell off of Phall and lay on its side. She just lay where she was for awhile, out of breath and unable to move.

Finally, Phall was able to move and was able to take more than a gasping breath into her aching lungs. She rolled over to her side and raised herself off the floor and then remembered that Doc had been bitten and was bleeding. She was moving much faster now. Crossing over to him and rolling him to his back, she first checked his shoulder. It was bleeding from two deep wounds and half a dozen more shallow ones. Then she looked at his head where he had hit it on the sleeping pod. There was no bleeding, but one very large bump. He shouldn't be unconscious, she thought, so she did some further checking. It wasn't until she moved his arm that she found out his wand had discharged itself when it hit his thigh. He had been stunned by his own stun wand. She grabbed his arms and pulled him to a sitting position, then stepped behind him to lift him and drag him out of the bay.

When Phall reached the doors to the bay, she hit the panel to open them with her elbow and pulled Doc into the next bay. She laid him on the floor, removed her mask, but left his mask in place. The oxygen in the bottle would be good for him. She then turned to a small anteroom and rolled out a stretcher, positioning it beside him. Getting him onto the stretcher was a struggle, but eventually she had positioned him safely upon it. She almost ran as she rushed him the length of the bay and into the med-lab. Turning to the ship-wide intercom, she palmed the switch and spoke swiftly: "Medical emergency! Captain to med-lab immediately, please!"

Phall then grabbed a surgical pack from the sterile cabinet and moved back to Doc. Picking up a pair of scissors, she quickly cut through his jumpsuit to bare his right shoulder. Pressing a gauze pack to the wound to stem the flow of blood, she began to fumble with the surgical pack, trying to locate the items she needed. Finally locating another gauze pack, she discarded the blood-soaked pack and pressed the new one into place. She then taped the pack to his shoulder with as much pressure as she could apply. Turning away from him, she reached for the doors to the cabinet that held the injectables. Pulling out an injector with a full load of propellant, she began assembling the meds that she needed to inject into his system. Those meds would fight infection, aid in the process of healing, help him to recover from the stun quicker, and force his body to replenish the supply of blood that he had lost. She started to have trouble reading the labels on those meds and quickly swiped her palms across her eyes as she realized she was crying. 'This won't do,' she thought to herself. 'I've got to remain objective or I won't be able to function properly.' She blotted her eyes dry again and picked up the meds and the injector. Loading the first med, she pressed the injector to the junction of neck and shoulder where the blood vessel was located. It took a fraction of a second for the injector to read that there was a vein there before the medication was administered. One after another, Phall removed a vial and loaded the next one into the injector and pressed it into place at Doc's neck. Finishing that, she went back to the wound itself.

Phall used the injector again, administering antibiotics directly to the site of the bites. The bleeding had started to slow down some when she began to probe the two large wounds. The chimp's teeth had sunk more than half an inch into the shoulder. It would require deep stitching to close up where the muscle and skin had torn. She grabbed a sterilizer and gently probed each of the incisions with it, making sure that every inch was covered. Next, she used the cauterizer to stop the bleeding that still oozed from the wound.

Ross and Kandyce entered the med-lab at that instant, Ross taking everything in at once. Phall kept working on the injuries Doc had sustained while she gave a concise description of what had happened. Kandyce inquired if Phall needed any assistance, and, upon her negative reply, turned and followed Ross as he walked out of the med-lab heading for the secondary bay where the accident had happened. Phall had completed cauterizing the wounds before she had finished explaining the incident to Ross and Kandyce. She began closing the wounds from the inside, working out as they left the med-lab. After she had completed stitching up the wounds, she gave the injury the last injection that would speed the process of healing. She then covered the entire injury site with a living bandage. The living bandage was a recent discovery the medical profession found invaluable. Nearly invisible on the skin, it slowly became absorbed by the injury site. This eliminated the need for bandage changes and precautions against getting the injury wet or dirty. It also prevented the formation of scar tissue, so there would be no tenderness or stiffness after it healed. All that was left to do now was to get Doc into one of the med-lab recovery-monitoring beds and wait for him to recover from the effects of the stun wand.

Ross hit the panel that opened the door to the bay, entered and reached for a pair of stun wands. They could see the chimp lying halfway down the bay in the aisle. There were no sounds in the bay, except their breathing through the masks they had donned before entering. Then Kandyce pointed with her wand to the back of the bay. Ross saw the chimp and took a step backward. Kandyce did exactly the same thing and reached with her left hand to re-open the doors that had closed behind them. At their movement, the chimp screamed a blood-curdling challenge and leapt off the pod it had been sitting upon, rushing forward on all four appendages. Both Ross and Kandyce passed through the doorway before it reclosed, then Ross reached for the seal button that effectively locked the doors from being opened by anything on the other side.

Stepping to the right of the doors, Ross removed his mask and began to read the list posted on the wall. "We're going to have to flood the bay with a knockout gas to make sure we get everything that's loose," he said. "I'm not about to face even one chimp with just one of these." He held up the stun wand and then handed it to Kandyce. Turning back to the panel, he hit a series of contact points. Above the panel, a viewscreen came to life showing the inside of the bay. The chimp that had rushed towards them was with the stunned one lying in the aisle. Another chimp had joined it, but this one didn't look right. It seemed to be leaning heavily to the left and looked like it was dragging its left arm.

Kandyce spoke for the first time since they had made their abortive entry to the bay. "Looks like it broke its arm or shoulder and possibly a leg or ribs, and nothing healed back correctly. We'd better put them to sleep so we can get to work up front."

Ross agreed and hit a couple of contact points on the panel and then watched the viewer. "Shouldn't take but a few seconds." The scene began to get foggy and soon the crippled chimp fell to its side, followed a second later by the first chimp.

They waited another minute and then Ross activated the panel again. Soon, the fog in the bay had cleared out and a light appeared next to the viewer. Ross donned the mask again and joined Kandyce as the doors opened for her and they stepped through. They walked quickly to the sleeping chimps and began to move them, one at a time, to a holding pen at the rear of the bay. Ross and Kandyce were breathing hard when they finished. Ross looked the bay over one last time and then turned to Kandyce. "We'll have to leave the rest of this until later. We've got more important business up front. And I want to see how Doc is doing." Kandyce gave her agreeing nod, then turned with him, and the two of them headed back to the med-lab.

CHAPTER 12

Now You See It, Now You Don't

Before we begin this chapter, I want you to take a look at Bill's prison logs—these are from San Quentin.

290th Day - Friday - 8/16/96

0700 - Breakfast   -   1 Boiled Egg, Grits, Milk.

0900 - Shower/Shave

0945 - Phone   -   Brian - 4 times - No answer. Patty - out till the 26th. Tricia - Wants a Visitors form so she can come up for a visit, will talk to Frank about Cookbook and to Randy about Comp.

1100 - Sack Lunch   -   Meat, Cookies, Pretzels, Banana, Lemon Drink.

1505 - Laundry Blues Returned.

1700 - Supper   -   Chicken Breast, Beans, Peas, Salad, Watermelon, Bun.

291st Day - Saturday - 8/17/96

0700 - Breakfast   -   2 Boiled Egg, Sausage, Tater Cakes, Oatmeal, Cantaloup, Milk.

1100 - Sack Lunch   -   Cheese, Corn Nuts, Cookies, Banana, Fruit Punch.

1700 - Supper   -   Fish, Cheese Noodles, Green Beans, Salad, Cake.

292nd Day - Sunday - 8/18/96

0700 - Breakfast   -   Waffles, Dry Cereal, Milk.

1000 - Shower/Shave.

1030 - Sack Lunch   -   Meat, Cookies, Corn Nuts, Apple, Cherry Drink.

1100 - Phone   -   Brian - Will be up on the 26th, Lee may be up with him, will draw-up new contract between him and me only, Don is cut out of the loop, will pick up my stuff then, Gave me Mom's new #.

Mom - Hopes to send pkg. This coming week, will try to get pens for me, coffee and cigarettes are in pkg. Bernice received Award in school for excellence.

1700 - Supper   - Turkey Ham, Mashed Taters, Peas & Carrots, Salad, Cake.
2100 - Legal Mailout   - Tricia.

293rd Day - Monday - 8/19/96
0700 - Breakfast   - Omelet, Oatmeal, Milk, Grapefruit Juice.
0900 - Yard Time   - 2nd Wave, 1st Out.
1300 - Recall   - Sack Lunch - PB&J, Pretzels, Graham Crackers, Apple, Orange Drink.
1700 - Supper   - Chicken Patty, Cheese Taters, Beans, Noodle Salad, Cake.
1830 - Phone   - Florence - No Answer
2130 - Legal Mail Out - Brian w/V.Q. for Lee (Lea, Leah, Leigh), requested Paper & Pens.

294th Day - Tuesday - 8/20/96 HAPPY BIRTHDAY (46 YEARS).
0630 - Breakfast   - Scrambled Eggs, Tortillas, Pear Pieces, Grits, Milk.
1000 - Shower/Shave
1100 - Sack Lunch   - PB&J, Graham Crackers, Sunflower Seeds, Apple, Orange Drink.
1530 - Laundry Whites Pickup.
1700 - Supper   - Burritos, Rice, Beans, Menudo, Salad, Cake.

295th Day - Wednesday - 8/21/96
0630 - Breakfast   - Oatmeal, Apple Sauce, Doughnuts, Milk.
0900 - Yard Time   - 2nd Wave, 1st Out (moved to cell 1EB65 while out on the yard. Property in cell 65 when I came in.)
1100 - Recall   - Sack Lunch - None
1500 - Mr. Numera says too late to get a lunch now. Will get white laundry from 5th tier.
1700 - Supper   - Hamburger, French Fries, Corn, Cottage Cheese, Apple Pie.
1730 - Mail   - Mom.
1930 - Laundry Whites Returned.

296th Day - Thursday - 8/22/96
0630 - Breakfast   - Farina, 1 Boiled Egg, Bun, Banana, Milk.
0700 - Yard Call   - 1st Wave, 1st Out.
1300 - Recall   - Sack Lunch - Cheese, Cookies, Sunflower Seeds, Banana, Cherry Drink.
1530 - Mail   - Tricia (B'day Card)

1700 - Supper   - Chicken Breast, Rice, Salad, Cake, Koolaid.
1800 - Laundry Blues Pickup.

297th Day - Friday - 8/23/96
0600 - Breakfast   - SOS, Biscuit, Dry Cereal, Honey Dew Melon, Milk.
0800 - Yard Call   - 2nd Wave, Last Out.
1300 - Recall   - Sack Lunch - PB&J, Corn Nuts, Cookies, Banana,
                         Cherry Drink.
1700 - Supper   - Spaghetti, Pizza, Salad.
2030 - Phone   - Brian - Appointment made for Tuesday. Mom -
                         Will try to send pkg on Monday.

298th Day - Saturday - 8/24/96
0600 - Breakfast   - Sausage, Tater Cakes, 2 Boiled Eggs, Doughnut, Milk.
0930 - Shower/Shave
1000 - Sack Lunch   - Meat, Cookies, Pretzels, Peach, Cherry Drink.
1700 - Supper   - Turkey Ham, Cheese Taters, Beans, Salad, Cake,
                         Iced Tea.

299th Day - Sunday - 8/25/96
0600 - Breakfast   - Waffles, Dry Cereal, Melon, Milk.
1100 - Sack Lunch   - PB&J, Cookies, Corn Nuts, Apple, Orange Drink.
1100 - Phone   - No answer at Brian or Florence.
1700 - Supper   - Baked Chicken, Black Eye Peas, Rice, Green Beans,
                         Salad, Ice Cream, Koolaid.

As you can see, "meticulous" is an understatement, "compulsive" is only half the story, and "obsessive" barely scratches the surface.

Bill Suff doesn't just keep track of things, of everything, he sees things, details that none of us knows exist. He sees the forest, he sees the trees, he sees the leaves, and he sees the atoms that make up the leaves. He lives in a paradise of microcosm. Nothing is too small for him to fixate on, everything is relevant, and it's absolutely critical to chart it. If Heisenberg said you can't predict the exact location of an electron in its orbital shell at any given moment in time, then Bill would say "There! Right there! That's where it is!"

And so it would be.

You keep track of things because they matter now and they might matter more later, because they keep the uncontrollable and the frightening from creeping across your consciousness now, and because you might need to know for sure what's going to happen down the road.

So, you must ask yourself about Bill: With this kind of record-keeping, how come he couldn't alibi himself for the times of the murders?

Zellerbach says that Bill dazzled his interrogators by his total recall of all of his life except for those times when hookers were being slaughtered. That more than anything convinced Zellerbach that he had his man even before the scientific evidence came back from the lab.

When I visited Bill in San Quentin, he gave me his logs. He told me they helped him keep his sanity. I suggested they were more indicative of sanity long ago lost.

Bill laughed.

During his time at San Quentin, Bill had become increasingly hardened to the notion of confessing and exploring a psychological defense. He'd convinced himself that he'd convinced people here at the prison—guards and convicts alike—that he was an innocent man. As I had suggested to him, he'd shown these people his writings and now they knew him as a different person than they'd expected. Of course, I simply want people to understand that there is a humanity to Bill, despite his deeds, while he believes that to like his writing is to like him, and if you like him then you believe he's innocent.

It's childhood mathematics.

"I'm in the middle of this hideous divorce, Bill, and my feelings are really hurt that my soon to be ex-mother-in-law—a woman I was quite close to for years—now she won't talk to me."

"Well, that's understandable," he said, "she's got to take her daughter's side."

"I didn't think you'd say that," I said. "My position is that she can back her daughter without damning me. In fact, she can even believe all the lies her daughter tells her about me and yet still believe in me. You can believe *in* someone without having to decide whether you believe anything they have to say. So my mother-in-law can stay out of the middle, still defend her daughter, and still know me for the person I am now and always have been—a person she very much liked, a person she trusted with her daughter. You get my point?"

Randy Driggs had told me that he thought Bill had been more forthcoming with Frank Peasley because Bill didn't like Peasley but he felt that Driggs was a friend. You didn't just gain friends by being innocent, you lost them by being guilty.

"I've given it a lot of thought," said Bill, "and I just can't plead guilty to something I didn't do. I'm not afraid to die, if that's what has to happen."

So that was it: Bill felt he was deemed an innocent man here in the world in which he now lived, and he would die an innocent man. Zellerbach and the cops and the judge and the jurors and the victims' families—they would get their scalp but not their revenge.

"All right then, so if you're not guilty, then you must have an alibi—out of all these murders, give me one alibi."

"I can't think of any that I could prove."

"Then there's only one other tack: if you're not guilty, someone else is. Therefore, our task on appeal is not to try to refute evidence against you that even you admit makes you appear guilty beyond reasonable doubt; no, our mission is to point the finger at someone else who could be guilty of even one of these murders. If we can legitimately inculpate someone else for just one murder, then the whole house of cards will crumble because there wasn't enough evidence in most of these cases to convict you, you just got convicted of them all because they were all lumped together. Put up a dozen photos of dead girls, and whoever's in the defendant's chair gets the death penalty."

"Donny," said Bill Suff, "my brother, Donny."

"Donny?"

"There were red hairs found on one of the victims—I don't remember which anymore. Donny's got red hair."

"You really think Donny's capable of murder?"

"Yes. He was convicted of raping that prostitute in Las Vegas, so it's not a big step up to killing 'em."

Don Suff—he was definitely guilty of trying to cash in on his brother's infamy, but he's just not a serial killer. Don's like the little birds that sit on the backs of hippos—they wait for crumbs to float off the hippos' teeth and they munch bugs out of the folds in the hippos' skin. These birds are nothing to aspire to, but the hippos'd probably miss 'em if they were gone. Or not. It's hard to know if they evolved to their station or just flopped there and got overlooked when nature took a head count. But what was interesting here on the human side of the fence was that Bill clearly had a mad-on for brother Don, and this was the passive-aggressive way he was handling it.

"You mad at Donny because he wanted to sell your van to that guy that collects serial killer memorabilia?" I asked.

"I'm mad at Donny 'cause of what he said on *Leeza*," said Bill.

In October of 1995, Don and Ann needed money. I was friends with the then-executive producer of *Leeza*, and so I pitched her the idea of doing a show where the serial killer's family would get together and make peace with the families of the victims.

However, the victims' families refused. Instead, the show became "My Son Is a Serial Killer", starring Don and Ann along with Mr. and Mrs. Dahmer. Don and Ann got $1000 and a night at a posh hotel for their trouble.

It was the highest-rated show *Leeza* ever had, and, once it aired, Zellerbach and the victims' families demanded their own "Victims Talk Back" show so they could go "on air" and call all the Suffs every name they could think of.

Which they did.

The taping of the original show—"My Son"—was delayed for a half hour when Ann broke down and cried in the "green room". Leeza Gibbons tried to comfort her, and she too was reduced to tears. Ann was lamenting the loss of her son, the loss of her grandchildren, and the loss of all those poor dead girls. She was very sincere, however disloyal to Billy. Then again, she had cooperated with Zellerbach and the cops when Billy was first arrested. She'd even knit them a toy yarn octopus. She'd also turned over to them Cathy McDonald's library card and another victim's ring and necklace which she'd found in Billy's apartment after the first police search.

I like Ann, even though nobody else seems to. After she testified at the death penalty phase that Bill was a good kid who never hurt anybody or anything, the jury decided that she was "cold as a glacier". After listening to her, they said they could understand how Bill turned out as he had.

In any event, Ann went on television and spoke about Billy as if it were fact that he was a serial killer. Then Donny chimed in. He said he did not want to believe that Billy could have done these things, but, based on the evidence at trial, he had to accept that it was true.

Then Leeza asked him if he forgave his brother for his crimes.

"How can you forgive somebody who won't even admit to himself what he's done?" asked Don in perhaps the only rhetorical question he's ever posed.

"Can you believe he said that?!" Bill snarled angrily at me. "Even the guards at the jail couldn't believe it when they heard!" To Bill, his prison guards are the ultimate authorities—whatever they think is gospel, particularly when they're on his side. I wonder if they know quite how much he quotes them.

The bottom line is that Bill has not and will not ever forgive Don for *Leeza*. Ann he will not condemn—in fact he makes sure that she is taken care of financially and otherwise—but Don betrayed him in some profound way. I'm not exactly sure why what Don did was so bad in Bill's eyes—didn't Bill admit to me that even he would have voted to convict had he objectively viewed the evidence as presented?—but I do know that, prior to Don's appearance on *Leeza*, Bill had been exhorting him to stand up and make his brother's case for the defense, miniscule evidentiary point by miniscule evidentiary point.

Now that I think it through, perhaps the answer is that Bill knows the evidentiary points do not work in his favor, and all he

could ask for are people to stand up and swear to him and his character, for people to say "I don't care what the evidence is, the Bill
Suff I know would not have done these things!"

And maybe Donny should have said that.

I would have said it for my brother, God rest his soul.

Then again, my brother was not a serial killer, and no one's
invited me to appear on *Leeza*.

Funny how Ted Kaczynski's weirdo snitch brother is now a
hero, while Don Suff is a pariah.

"I find it hard to think Donny did these killings, Bill," I said,
"and I'd bet he has alibis for at least some of them."

Once again, that was the issue: no matter who you are and how
hard you are to keep track of, you ought to be able to alibi yourself
at least once out of more than a dozen crimes. Plus, Donny was out
on the streets all this time, and Riverside prostitutes were no
longer getting murdered and mutilated and posed. Circumstan-
tially, only Bill fit the bill. And Donny has a naiveté about him
that, while not innocent, nonetheless augurs for spontaneous
rather than premeditated guilt. He says he didn't rape that Vegas
hooker, he just didn't pay her, and then they got into a tussle and
she called the police.

I almost believe it.

In fact, Donny made a big confession of it to me when we first
met in person in Riverside. He told me he wanted me to hear it
from him first, since I was bound to hear it from others. There were
a few other things I would hear about him also. Let's just say that
the Suff boys all got into trouble in various ways, and women were
pretty much a common denominator.

Considering my failed marriages, I am not one to comment any
further on this.

So, when Donny fessed up to me, I told him it was irrelevant to
this book. I was then on my way to visit Bill, and that was the story.

"Need a microcassette recorder to take with you?" Don offered.

"Thanks, but I've got a tape recorder," I said, "and anyway I
don't think I'm allowed to take it into the jail."

"The one I've got is Bill's," Don said.

"Really," I said, this being my favorite response.

"The police missed it the first time they searched his apartment while Mom and I were there. So I took it, along with a bunch of tapes."

"Anything interesting on the tapes?"

"I've only listened to one or two, but there's nothing important on 'em."

"Like what?"

"Like Bill driving around in his van talking to Cheryl. And another where you hear a bunch of guys cheering as they watch a football game on TV."

"Huh?" This was my second favorite response.

"It's just like Bill had the tape recorder on, recording, while he did other stuff."

It was, as they say, déjà vu all over again. Like when Don had told me about Billy bringing used clothes and jewelry to Don's wife.

"I've kind of taped over some of the stuff," said Don sheepishly.

"Don't tape over any more, okay?"

"Okay."

"You know what I'm thinking?"

"Yeah. I know."

I was thinking that if Bill drove around in his van with a tape recorder going, then it was because he was taping his trysts and his murders. Listening to them later would definitely be arousing for him.

Donny brought me the tape recorder and the tapes—I listened to them all.

Sure enough, one was a tape of a bunch of men sitting on metal chairs in a hollow-sounding room watching Super Bowl XVI—Cincinnati and San Francisco—on the TV in 1982. None of the men said anything to the recorder, they just cheered and reacted to the game—they had no idea they were being taped. There was less conversation than one would expect among friends watching a football game together. Since Bill was in prison in Texas at that time, I assumed that was where he recorded this.

But, when I asked him about it, he got nervous. He denied making the tape and he denied watching the game. And his denials started to get long and complicated and explanatory. It's not just that he didn't make the tape, he couldn't have made the tape, and here's why—blah-blah-blah-blah-blah.

I didn't bother to listen to his explanation—it was obvious he was lying. The truth was that he had broken the convicts' code by secretly recording his fellows, even though nothing incriminating was going on. He'd also broken prison rules by having the tape recorder outside of his workstation—in Texas he'd been a computer operator, much privileged after being a model prisoner for so many years.

But why on earth would he care now about transgressions of prison ethics more than a decade ago? Because once a con, always a con. You know you could go back, you know you probably will go back. Somewhere sometime you will encounter your fellow cons again, and time doesn't pass for these guys. If you owe them, you will pay. Time served might pay your debt to society, but cons trade in different specie. Ditto, if you've made a fool of a guard. The cons and the guards are all waiting for you, and they will always remember not to forget.

"What was it like in Texas, in prison?" I asked.

"Oh, it was fine," said Bill.

"You know that if your California convictions get thrown out and you don't get retried, Texas will haul your ass back and make you serve the rest of your seventy-year sentence, right?"

"Riiiight," he said.

Bill's conduct in Riverside included numerous acts that would constitute violations of his Texas parole, so he is toast one way or the other. That was why it's so morally easy to help him with his appeals—Bill Suff is going to spend the rest of his life in jail somewhere, bank on it. He will never again walk the streets and be a danger to anyone.

"Tell me a little about Texas," I requested.

Bill proceeded to recount how violent the place was, how a new young inmate, in for the short term on a drug offense, was brutally and repeatedly gang-raped until he killed himself. Apparently the guards were bribed to leave unlocked the appropriate cell doors so that the cons could get at the boy each night.

And, where Bill worked, in the computer center, inmates were in charge of inputting State and County filings into the State mainframe database. That is to say, no more tinking out license plates. Now prisoners were given stacks of files that contained records of property transfers, deeds of trust, automobile registrations, driver's licenses, welfare benefits, marriage licenses—every kind of State and County filing respecting the assets and property and ultra-personal doings of private citizens.

Of course, the prisoners would secretly jot down the names and addresses of anyone who looked interesting—people who had rich homes and expensive cars—that way, when you or a friend got out, you'd know just where to go to steal the best stuff.

Nice work if you can get it.

"You know, Bill, I listened to these other tapes, too—what's the deal? They were obviously made in your van—I can hear you opening and closing doors, shifting into gear, accelerating, braking, traffic around you, your radio 'on' playing music, and then there's you talking with Cheryl at one point—she clearly didn't know she was being taped—you weren't talking about anything important."

"Don't remember taping Cheryl, but I could've. See, I drove around a lot for my work, as you know, and, well, I love music . . ."

"Yeah?"

He was thinking, trying to come up with an explanation. There were indeed hours of tapes of Bill just driving around. Clicks on the tapes told me that he had recorded over them repeatedly. I played them for an audio expert and he thought he could recover some of the underlying, earlier tracks, but it would cost a lot of money I didn't have. Plus, maybe I didn't want to know the truth, particularly if I was right. I'd been able to keep my emotional distance by telling myself that the crime scene photos were fake and staged and the people in them were actors or wax dummies—"Naw, these people were never really alive, so now they're not really dead"—kind of the inside-out version of Bill's thinking—but if I actually heard one of these poor girls screaming on a microcassette tape, well, I don't even want to think about it.

However, if we ever find the killing kit, don't bet that there won't be tapes in it. Like Nixon, Bill very much sees himself as significant to posterity and certain to be better understood and appreciated then than now.

"The deal with the tapes was . . ." said Bill, ". . . well, see, sometimes I'd hear a song on the radio and it'd become a favorite of mine but it wouldn't be on the album so I couldn't buy it."

"So you'd tape the radio playing all day long, and that way you were certain to catch this song at some point?"

"Exactly."

As you know, sometimes I would back off Bill when the conversation got a little *Alice in Wonderland*-ish. But not this time.

"Let me understand this—you'd tape the radio while you were driving in your van where it was noisy and you could barely hear the song on the tape later, rather than, say, taping the radio at home."

"If I was in the van taping, then when I heard the song on the radio I'd know where to find it on the tape. Otherwise, I'd have to listen to the whole tape."

"Bill, I say again: you could have done all this better at home, and it makes no sense that you didn't, other than it makes no sense that you would do any of this in the first place."

"It makes sense to me. Didn't you ever tape things off the radio?"

This is where Bill hopes to get you, when he finds the points where his world intersects with your own, where the parallel universes flow together and so what he does seems acceptable because you've done the same things. Sort of.

He was right—as a kid in the days before VCRs I'd used my audiotape recorder to record off of radio and TV. I'd taped Ted Kennedy's eulogy for slain brother Bobby. I had Dick Enberg's call of the Rams blocking a Packers' punt and winding up in the play-offs for the first time since I started following football. And I even had the audio portion of a TV retrospective of the Army-McCarthy hearings.

THE VICTIMS OF BILL SUFF

CHARLOTTE PALMER
Born October 17, 1962 • Died December 10, 1986

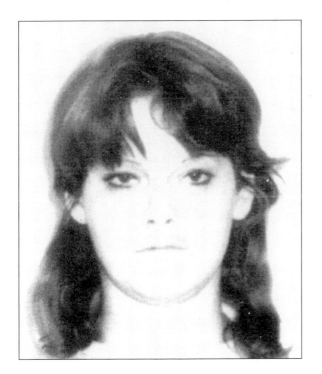

A perfect murder (no clues), but a signature work of murder as art. Bill wasn't formally charged in Charlotte's death, but police consider it "case closed" now that he's on ice.

KIMBERLY LYTTLE
Born June 27, 1961 • Died June 27, 1989

Bill says he loved Kimberly and wanted her to move in with him. When she refused, she got a fatal birthday present.

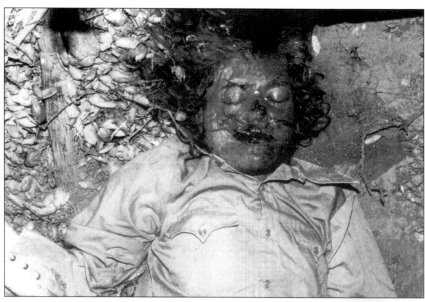

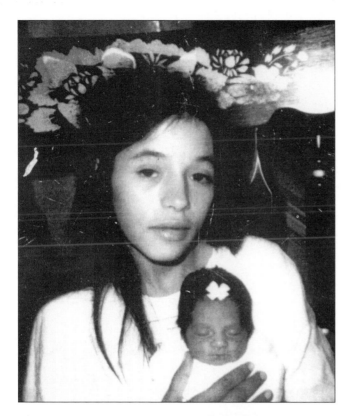

Tina was killed, mutilated, re-dressed to look like a cartoon character; and then Bill placed a lightbulb up into her womb. Why? See Chapter 14.

DARLA FERGUSON
Born July 29, 1966 • Died January 17, 1990

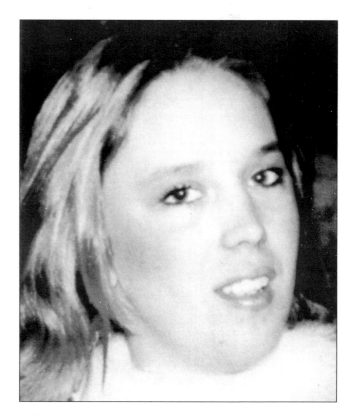

Bill's mom babysat and cared for Darla's daughter. Bill showed his own "special" care for Darla.

CAROL MILLER
Born June 20, 1954 • Died February 8, 1990

The killer posed Carol's corpse, stood back, admired his handiwork, and then calmly peeled a grapefruit. Was he just famished after a hard night's labor? See Chapter 17.

CHERYL COKER
Born April 24, 1957 • Died October 30, 1990

The repertoire of mutilation evidenced a now familiar horror: Cheryl's right breast had been removed and placed nearby.

SUSAN STERNFELD

Born February 6, 1963 • Died December 19, 1990

A nice girl who fought valiantly against a not-so-nice drug addiction, she was surprised by her killer and had no chance to fight back before being strangled and carefully posed in an empty dumpster enclosure.

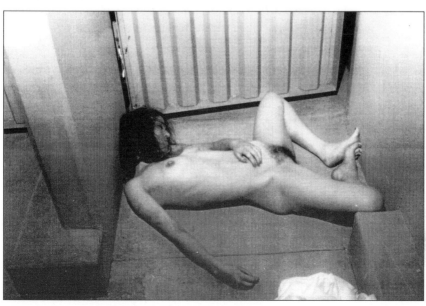

KATHLEEN MILNE PUCKETT

Born August 23, 1948 • Died January 18, 1991

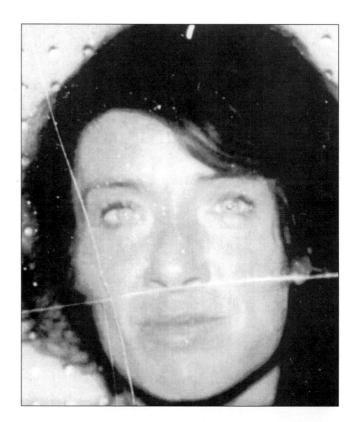

Bizarrely posed with her face twisted into the ground and her hair teased out.

CHERIE PAYSEUR
Born November 7, 1966 • Died April 26, 1991

Left in a flower bed in the parking lot of a bowling alley where Bill often bowled. The police stood by the body and watched as automatic sprinklers washed away all the evidence. The jury hung at eleven to one in favor of conviction— meaning that eleven jurors voted to convict even though there was not one shred of evidence against Bill.

SHERRY LATHAM

Born January 23, 1954 • Died July 2, 1991

Sherry's right thumb and index finger were wrapped around the branch of a bush, and the other three fingers were clenched. The killer thought she was dead when he dumped her here just off the side of the road, but she apparently had one last gasp and tried to crawl for help before succumbing.

KELLY HAMMOND
Born July 2, 1964 • Died August 15, 1991

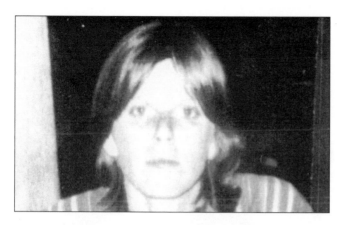

Bill was feeling more than a little ignored as his brand new baby daughter had become the center of attention for family and friends. Kelly made the mistake of being the first person Bill ran into after another prostitute scammed him. Note the demeaning pose of the body— head bowed into a trench; rear end upraised; legs, feet, arms, and fingers bent under or fanned and pointing with particularity. Aspects of the pose are identical to Bill's description of his own crumpled body after his near-fatal motorcycle wreck in 1988. See Chapters 13, 14 & 15.

CATHERINE McDONALD
Born November 4, 1960 • Died September 13, 1991

Bill's championship chili was simmering on the stove in anticipation of the Riverside County Employees' Picnic and Cook-off, but Bill knew he needed one last ingredient for his "special" recipe. That night, he went out alone in his van. The next day, Bill won the chili cook-off, and Cathy's strangled, stabbed, sexually mutilated body was discovered in a field. Her right breast was missing. It's never been found.

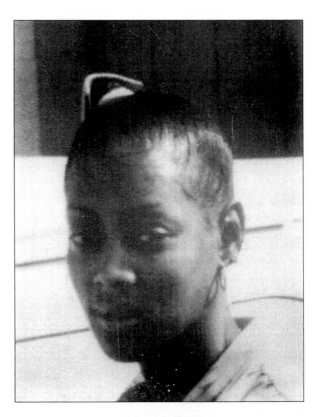

DELLIAH ZAMORA
Bron June 19, 1955 • Died October 29, 1991

*Delliah was
splayed out by
the roadside
like she was
thumbing for
a ride.*

ELEANOR CASARES
Born August 2, 1952 • Died December 22, 1991

Eleanor was found in an orange grove that Bill refers to as a "graveyard". Her right breast had been removed and hung from a tree branch.

DIJIANET SUFF
Born July 20, 1973 • Died September 25, 1973

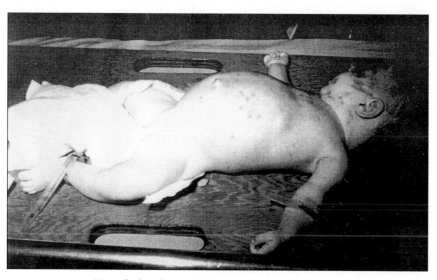

Note the handprint on Dijianet's head. She was battered, broken, and burned with cigarettes. The cause of death was a burst liver. The instrument of death was Bill Suff.

LISA LACIK
Birthdate unknown • Died January 18, 1988

Lisa was found in San Bernardino County, her right breast excised and tossed nearby, her head bent forward and buried in the ground like an ostrich.

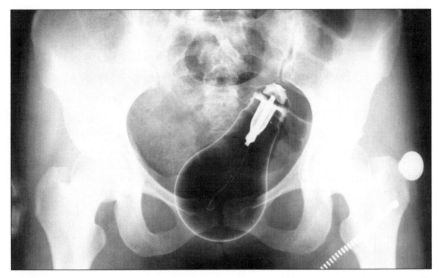

"It didn't break!" X-ray of the 95 watt GE "Miser" lightbulb Bill placed in the womb of murder victim Tina Leal, "the chicken girl". See Chapter 14.

RIVERSIDE COUNTY SHERIFF
PHOTO LINE-UP

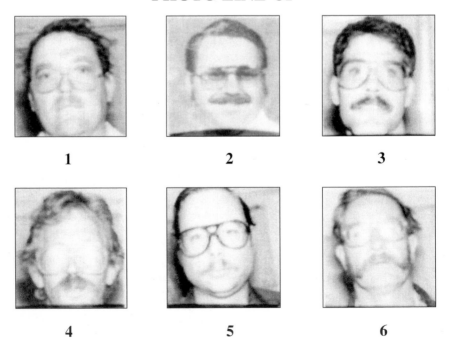

After Bill's arrest, this photo line-up was shown by police to the only living eyewitness, Rhonda Jetmore. She supposedly pointed to number two, Bill Suff.

But all that was experimentation—I was just playing around with my new tape recorder, my first tape recorder, trying to figure out what good it was. And, after a weekend or two of making such tapes, I never did it again. Tape recorders were for specific purpose, where people intentionally talked into it, for interviews or at family get-togethers or if you were doing some creative skit or such. You didn't just turn on a tape recorder and leave it running and then keep the tape like it mattered.

However, if I really thought about it . . . yeah, my brother and I did tape the radio now and again, to get new songs since we could hardly afford to go out and buy every record that got released and since you sometimes liked a group's single but knew you'd hate the rest of the album, and since, in those days, the pop playlist changed almost daily and you might decide some song was your favorite song only now they weren't playing it anymore. Then it would be good to have a tape of yesterday's playlist.

And, suddenly, I realized I was looking at the world through a child's eyes. All this seeming logic was kids' logic. It didn't apply to adults and it didn't apply to modern times, to the computer and CD age. I was seeing the world through Bill's eyes.

See, Bill Suff isn't just living on another planet, he's frozen in time there. He truly did stop living a very long time ago. Dead, but alive. Alive, but dead. Something happened to him in his youth, and his emotions, his worldview, stopped maturing. So his reactions and his emotions—his ability to love, his feelings of rejection—are as a child feels them, in black and white, utterly good or bad, supportive or devastating.

This explained why, when Bill was caught red-handed doing something he shouldn't have been doing—taping people secretly in his van—the best lie he could come up with was a child's lie. He was supposedly taping music off his van radio even though he prided himself on the stereo, the computer, and all the other state-of-the-art electronic goodies he had at home.

But emotional immaturity still did not explain why he killed people. Being a kid did not make you a killer. Something ugly had flown into the mix, and I still didn't know what.

"Bill, maybe you were taping yourself in the van, okay? Maybe it's just part of your record-keeping, your diary."

"Kept that on my computer," he said matter-of-factly.

According to Bill, his last apartment—with Cheryl—was neat, tidy, and organized, but according to everyone else it was a mess. The eye of the storm was his computer. It was his lifeline, his connection to our world, and he spent hours on it daily. He wrote his fiction on it, he kept his thoughts and philosophy on it, he played games on it, and now he was telling me that he kept his diary on it, too. He'd become proficient on computers in Texas, and then expert in Riverside when he was a computer salesman for the Schartons before girlfriend Bonnie Ashley made him quit since he had so obvious a crush on Florence Scharton.

"If your diary was on your computer, how come the police didn't find it, and how come it didn't provide you with an alibi?" I queried.

When I recounted the rest of this story to the D.A.'s lead investigator just after Bill's death sentencing, I thought the big ex-cop would deck me right there in the courtroom. A vein thickened up and pulsed in his forehead like a rattlesnake uncoiling. The upshot is that the cops blew the Bill Suff case. When they finally suspected him, they shouldn't've busted him, they should've tailed him, in which case they would have caught him in the act, would have recovered the killing kit, the killing clothes, and all the trophies. They would have closed more cases than they ultimately tried him for and there would be more families out there who could finally rest easy.

But the cops had run out of patience.

They also just did not understand their man.

Unlike the guards who chatted with me at San Quentin, the Riverside cops didn't get that Bill was cleverer than them, and this was all something of a game to him. A kid's game.

So, when the cops searched Bill's apartment after they had him in custody, they really didn't know what to look for. They thought he'd be like Dahmer with a fridge full of heads.

So the cops basically found nothing incriminating during their first search. Only on searches number two and three did they "find" effects and clothes from the murder victims. As noted, Ann says she found some of the items, and that may be what led the cops back. But other items mysteriously appeared during the later searches, even though Ann and Don had previously searched and not found those things. When cops really and truly believe they've got their man, they definitely try to make the proof easier for the prosecution, if you catch my meaning.

However, one thing the cops weren't smart enough to take during the first search but then wised-up and took during the second search was Billy's computer.

"See, I don't have a hard drive on my computer," Bill said, "I kept my machine running twenty-four hours a day, put some data encrypted onto floppies, and kept everything else in RAM."

Translated, this means that Bill saved some data—like his fiction writing—on diskettes which you could only access with a password. The way Bill had it, if you tried to access three times with the wrong password, then the information on the diskettes would automatically self-destruct.

So consider all that stuff gone—the cops blew it by trying to access it back at the police lab. But, again, that was his writing, not his diary.

The diary was another matter.

Imagine for a moment the scene in Bill's apartment. Piles of books and magazines and newspapers all around. The computer gently humming, glowing, in the center of the room, an unavoidable altar.

"My diary I kept in RAM," said Bill.

In the computer, in electronic blips that lived and breathed only so long as the computer stayed "on" was Bill's diary, in Random Access Memory. Turn off the computer, and the diary vanished into space, never to return. Everything the police and the world needed to know about Bill Suff and his life and times, life and crimes, was right there at their fingertips, just waiting to be asked to unscroll on-screen. No encryption, no password, no security. All you had to do was change windows to the open file of your choice. Like all Bill's manipulations, this was his test, his booby trap. Were you man enough? Were you Indiana Jones— clever and brave enough to pass the test and snatch the golden idol—or were you some bumpkin who would let treasure slip right through your fingers?

So near and yet so far.

And then gone with the wind.

The searchers turned off the computer and schlepped it down to their lab. And everything you wanted to know went away. Poof!

"Too bad," I said to Bill, "that diary could've given you an alibi. Right?"

He laughed.

"Let's just say things would have been mighty different," he said.

CHAPTER 13

Profile of a Serial Killer

My great-uncle Al invented the crash helmet. A humble man, he insisted that his inspiration was not brilliance, it was merely numbers. During the early days of flying, he started keeping statistics as to the type of flying and crash-related injuries that were keeping Navy pilots from going back up into the skies. Head injuries topped the list. Ergo, protect the head and you keep the pilots flying.

So they can go to war.

Ironically, Bill Suff owes his life to my great-uncle, I guess. In 1988 Bill had a motorcycle accident that should have left him dead. He pulled through, much to a lot of people's present regret. Had he not been wearing a helmet, there wouldn't have been this book.

However, like the crash helmet, profiles of serial killers are also nothing more than statistical inductions, and it wouldn't hurt to wear a helmet when you do profiling. This is not to discount the brilliant FBI profilers any more than I discount Uncle Al. It's easy to say you're just crunching numbers, but then only a special few people truly have the insight and the focus to see how the numbers really add up. Profilers are a combination of Sherlock Holmes and The Amazing Kreskin. They won't just tell you that you're looking for an angry guy with a daunting deformity that he feels isolates him from the rest of society; they'll tell you that he's got a stammer rather than a limp, that he wears briefs rather than boxers, and that he never puts lemon in his tea.

But the profilers might be wrong.

And the profilers couldn't tell you anything—right or wrong—

were it not for their mental database of previous serial killers. That's why no one caught Jack the Ripper. He left plenty of clues, but no one knew what they meant at the time. The whole deal was just too new. No one had the experience that would allow them to apply their intuition in the right direction. You have to reduce possibility to a reasonable number before insight can take hold.

Just by examining the crimes, the Riverside Prostitute Killer seemed an easy profile to make. You start with the obvious: This guy keeps getting away with picking up victims in the same small area, so he must be a guy who blends in and seems nonthreatening or acts authoritative. Since he's careful, meticulous, and organized, clever to cover his tracks, he's probably a guy who holds down a job and acts normal around his peers. He probably has a girlfriend or wife. And some stressor in his life—some problem at home or work—has exacerbated his rage and urge to kill. Next, as with virtually all serial killers, he has an abandoning father and a confused love/rejection relationship with his mother. From the git-go, this guy couldn't win.

You want more detail? He'll be a white male, mid- to late thirties, slightly overweight, slightly under average height, and no Mark Harmon. Why? Because that's what the statistics say.

But stop for a moment. Stop and look at this profile. It describes an everyman. It describes someone who is absolutely normal and whose life appears normal and extremely average . . . except for those moments when he kills. So how does this profile help you catch your killer?

It doesn't. In fact, it tells you that this guy is going to get away with murder after murder unless you just plain get lucky and happen to be in the right place at the right time to catch him.

That is, unless you try to manipulate him. Unless you put out the word of how you see him, and hope that he hears it and reacts to it in a way that reveals more about himself.

Hence, the Cathy McDonald debacle, which, as I say, none of the authorities will cop to.

But D.A. Zellerbach did recently admit to me that Bill Suff surprisingly did not fit the profile he and the task force had been working from. Nonetheless, Zellerbach tried to get that profile admitted at trial, and back then he was prepared to say that it fit Bill to a T.

According to Zellerbach today, where the profile went wrong was in describing the killer as a man certain to be overtly aggressive and threatening, particularly when cornered. He should have been a dominating presence, something more on the order of John Wayne Gacy, or that Glen Edward Rogers character, the accused but as yet untried cross-country serial killer, whom I find scary to look at even in pictures. A blue-collar Mr. Hyde.

The profilers were basing this conclusion on the mutilations, the rage, the clear and deep hatred of women which was being expressed. This had to be a man who had to grit his teeth in order to pretend to be calm between kills. This guy had to work out on the heavy bag, mountain bike, raise barns, or do something strenuous to blow off steam each and every day.

But Bill Suff was a weenie. A wimp, a whiner. When Zellerbach first saw him in custody, he almost thought they had the wrong man. "He was just such a crybaby," says Zellerbach. "He was not what we expected."

Zellerbach and the profilers had expected a man. What they got was a child.

The profile said that the killer did not know his victims prior to killing them. He would pull up, strike his deal, drive away with the girl, and kill her. She was an object, her killing was impersonal, when he was mangling her he was seeing someone else in his mind's eye.

Wrong.

In fact, Bill killed prostitutes that he had "dated". He regularly slept with the same girls. And, in the case of Kimberly Lyttle, he fell for her and decided he could rescue her and her child from a life of drugs and sex-for-hire. He told himself that he loved her. He offered her money *not* to have sex for money, *not* to have sex with him or with other men. And then, on her birthday in June of 1989, he made the grandest gesture: Bill asked Kim to move in with him.

Her response was rather less than he'd expected. Kim rejected Bill's offer, preferring to live on her own, wanting to keep her relationship with him "at arm's length", business and nothing more.

So that's when she had to die.

It's pretty damn insulting when you can't even pay a woman to quit being a hooker, when you want nothing from her but to allow you to help her. That's the very definition of rejection.

It's also the definition of control. What he was really trying to do was to control her, to own her, and she was too strong a person to go along with that. So she died.

To be noted is that she was the first of the series for which he has been convicted. There are other bodies that predate Kim, but not enough evidence against Bill, even though the police closed the cases upon his death sentence. Granting Bill his overdue presumption of innocence on those cases, we can say that Kim's rejection of him was the final straw. If he couldn't control this hooker, then he could hardly be expected to control himself—he became a killing machine. I know that some of the women in Bill's life— from first wife Teryl to Riverside girlfriend Bonnie—all want to believe that their rejection is what pushed Bill over the edge, but if anyone is entitled to take that dubious bow, it's Kim.

Love—or seeming love—becomes murder.

That's the equation that, at a gut level, we all "get", even though none of us—average Jills and Joes, profilers, psychologists, and cops alike—none of us can never quite really understand it. We know it can happen, but we just wouldn't do it. We know that men have a natural tendency toward wanting to take care of and control women, but how really does that simple, endearing insecurity turn into madness, obsession, and murder?

Early on, I went out to interview hookers for this book. Insight into their minds might give insight into their relationships might make sense of the death equation. Plus, I wanted to hang with hookers. My ostensible purpose was to ask these women how come hookers kept getting into a van with a serial killer. The question turned out to answer itself: because what hookers do for a living is get into vans with guys. If you work at the post office, you go to the post office. If a serial killer turns out to be driving the van, you lose.

And if the letter carrier is pissed because he didn't get credit for all his overtime, then you lose there, too. You can get yourself killed anywhere. Probably will.

Anyway, when I was making the rounds of the hookers, I came across a guy I remembered as a crew person at MTM Studios back when I was writing for *Remington Steele*.

The guy is now a pornographer and a pimp. And he's loaded with money. He lives in a strange substrata world where he is at once overt and yet unknown. His Hollywood Hills house appears normal from the outside, but inside it's a dungeon. Pillories and whips and chains and enema bags, and all that stuff. A beautiful, raven-haired UCLA medical student works for him, available at an hourly rate for customers who want their scrotums professionally slashed with razor blades. Of course, you first have to sign a release and waiver drawn up by the pimp's high-priced Westside lawyer.

If big toys are your thing, the pimp's got a yacht which you can hire, and he'll stock it with anything you want, living or dead, chemically active or inert, just so long as it all takes place in international waters. No questions are asked upon your return to the dock, and the cleanup crew is exceedingly thorough.

Into music or movies? The pimp's also got a state-of-the-art, high-tech, art deco, audio/video recording/editing studio. It's behind a buzzer-locked iron door in a seemingly abandoned tenement motel in the worst part of town. You have to know it's there to know it's there. And you have to know the password to get in. Then you get offered beer and quiche by a girl who's wearing gold mules. Gold mules. That's all she's wearing. They're great-looking mules.

Meanwhile, the pimp's latest deal is recruiting beautiful young girls in Latvia and the other former Soviet republics. He meets them in dance clubs and signs them to "services contracts", also drawn up by his Westside lawyer. The girls are brought over here, billed as "Swedish", told to say that they are in college and studying economics and international relations, and then, having learned to say that, they are rented out to men to whom they can say it. The girls are told that their earnings will be split fifty-fifty with the pimp, but then he later mentions that he forgot to mention that the costs he advanced to fly them over and house them have to be deducted. Oh, and he should hold on to the rest of their money since they don't have bank accounts yet and the green cards he's promised them have been delayed.

The girls pretty quickly get the picture, but they would still rather be here than there, so they put up with it. Besides, the men are rich and showy, and these girls get shown. Shown and traded around. And they don't realize that the pimp is so clever he knows that, sooner or later, these poor creatures will spill their guts to their johns. And then the john will rise up to protect the girl, to defend her and get her out of this mess. The john will fall "in love", and he'll go to the pimp to save the day. And the pimp will be waiting. No problem, the girl can be let out of her contract. For a price. Believe it or not, in case after case, the john then buys the girl and marries her.

However, the most amazing aspect is the warranty: If you get tired of a girl you've purchased, you can trade her back in and upgrade. Again, at a price.

The returned girls then seem to vanish off to other venues, or maybe they just vanish altogether. Names and IDs come and go and get duplicated between girls. I met and got to know a girl named "Coco". When she went away, another "Coco" took her place and used exactly the same fake ID. I never slept with "Coco", but I was told that I could buy her for the special price of $20,000.

I declined.

But nonetheless I felt the tremendous urge to help this girl out. I actually referred her to friends in the entertainment business who could help her get work as an actress—anything so she could buy herself away from the pimp.

She declined.

It never occurred to me to murder and mutilate her. When she spurned my help, I wrote her off. Whatever she gets she deserves, I told myself; she'd made a choice. Right. Like she had a choice. But I had no choice either: Although all us males want to be saviors, we can't be. It's a delusion. It's just that it's so damn hard to sit back and be loved or rejected for who we are rather than what we can provide.

Bill Suff, wimpy though he is in captivity, is apparently one man who just can't sit back and let himself be judged by these women. He's determined to make them love him, determined to make them see the goodness and value in him, even if he has to kill them to open their eyes.

This is another reason I have a problem with Rhonda Jetmore's testimony. Remember, she's the one who lived. And she said that Bill was supposed to give her twenty dollars, but then he suddenly refused, telling her she'd only get a dollar, and before she could respond, his hands were around her throat.

That story just fits too well with the profile, but not with the reality. Bill was always willing to pay for sex, love, attention. You pissed him off by telling him that that wasn't enough, you wanted something more, something he didn't have to offer, that other things were more important to you than him and his money.

Kelly Whitecloud hopped into Bill's van one night in August of 1991. She quoted him a price of twenty dollars, but then she told him she wanted to stop for some fast-food first. You get the munchies when you've just shot up with heroin, and Kelly needed to munch. It's a sad commentary when you crave McDonald's as much as you crave drugs.

At the drive-up window, Kelly got Bill to order her a Big Mac and a caramel sundae with the nuts on the bottom. Got that? Nuts on the bottom. Kelly leaned across Bill and hollered at the microphone/speaker to make sure the burger boy inside understood.

But, of course, when Bill and Kelly were pulling out of the parking lot, Kelly looked at her sundae and discovered that the nuts were on top.

I'm not making this up.

Moments later, Bill and Kelly were storming into McDonald's on foot, the accursed sundae held aloft like it was on fire. Like it was manure on fire. Like this was a HAZMAT matter. Bill demanded to see the store manager, and, without further ado, the sundae was replaced. Nuts on the bottom, you can be sure.

Back in Bill's van, Kelly powered through the food—they were barely out of the parking lot when she got down to the nuts. Sated by drugs and food, Kelly was no longer in the mood for a date, and she didn't need the money until she would need her next fix. She realized she could be quite content having scammed this joker for the food and leave it like that. She was in the mood to kick back and feel all the shit oozing through her veins. Drugs, sugar, and cholesterol—nothing like it.

So, Kelly Whitecloud suddenly turned on Bill Suff and told him angrily that the food was in addition to the twenty bucks he had to pay her for the date. She figured he'd balk and that would give her an excuse to back out of the deal. After all, when you work the streets you can't let yourself get the reputation of being a scammer; you had to stage things so it looked like you were honest and forthright at all times.

But Bill didn't balk. He wasn't happy about the added expenditure, but he'd just made a very public display of being with this woman, of defending her and getting her nuts right, and now he wanted to get his nuts right. He wanted to get laid. He deserved to get laid. If it cost him more, well, that was all right. Tonight he needed attention. He wanted to be allowed to suckle. He wasn't planning on killing anybody tonight, and he wasn't wearing the killing clothes. In fact, he was wearing his big BILL belt buckle. It was okay for people to see him and remember him, because this hooker was going to come back alive, and then no one would think of him as the Riverside Prostitute Killer. Kelly Whitecloud was going to be his alibi.

Unfortunately, she didn't see it that way. When Bill shrugged okay to the notion of paying the full freight plus the food bill, she'd had enough. She threw a tantrum, pretended he was giving her a hard time, and jumped out of the van just as he was pulling into traffic. Then she yelled at him as he drove away, just to make a show in case any of her peers were watching. Gotta make it look like she wasn't the one reneging on her deal.

In the van, Bill was devastated, humiliated, rejected. He'd done everything expected of him, everything a man could do, and now he was alone. And, in the rearview mirror, that crazy bitch was waving and hollering at him.

You know, in the seven years I was married to the second ex-Mrs. Lane, she told me continuously that she was unhappy. She never sought a divorce; she just kept beating me up emotionally by telling me how unhappy she was and how it was all my fault. Whenever I'd pin her down on what I could do to make her happy, she'd tell me something that was impossible to deliver. For the first few years, she told me that the only way she could be happy would be if I hadn't ever been married to my first wife. Yeah, it's pretty impossible to make your mate happy when happiness is predicated on changing the past.

It took me until just recently to realize that it wasn't my job to make her happy, nor was it within my power. When I realized that, I filed for divorce. You have to eliminate unhappiness from your life.

But you don't have to kill it.

After Bill drove away from Kelly Whitecloud, the bad thoughts welled up in his brain. A cacophony of anger and pain, pain and anger. He knew the tune.

Suddenly, it didn't matter that he wasn't wearing the killing clothes.

He picked up another hooker, Kelly Hammond, a few blocks later. She never came back. She was found posed in a particularly demeaning manner with her head dipped forward into a trench, her arms twisted and splayed at her sides, her butt up in the air, and her legs folded under her.

Some detailed aspects of the pose mimicked Bill's own "pose" when he was left KO'd on the roadside after his 1988 motorcycle accident.

Profile? What profile? The profilers always hedge their bets with the simple statement that the killer's pattern can be altered by an external stressor, by circumstances. When that happens, it's easier to predict a tornado than predict the moves of a serial killer.

Darla Jane Ferguson was another victim who didn't fit the profile but did fit the reality.

Bill's mom, Ann, baby-sat for Darla's daughter, and the little girl actually lived with Ann for several months in 1987. Remember that Ann had a child-care license and was quite active in that business up until Bill was arrested and Ann's license was revoked. Back when Ann was taking care of Darla's daughter, Bill happened to show up at a birthday party that Ann was having for the girl. There's no evidence that Bill had any direct contact with Darla, other than when he killed her in January of 1990, but there can also be no doubt that he had to have recognized her when he pulled up and said "Hop in!"

The profile said he wouldn't kill women he knew. But, while Kim Lyttle rejected him directly and got her comeuppance, Darla had inadvertently trod into the very heart of Bill's need to kill.

Darla had weaseled her way into Mom's life. Darla and her daughter had supplanted Billy Boy in Mom's field of view. Bill hadn't gone out looking for Darla that night, and he'd tried to forget her transgressions for years, but then destiny had placed her squarely in his path, in his headlights, and the killing clothes were on and the graveyard was waiting, and he knew he had to live up to his fate.

Other victims were friends and acquaintances of Kimberly Lyttle and other hookers that Bill dated. He didn't really know these victims, but he would have looked familiar and okay to them when he stopped to pick them up, and that just made things easier. "Hey, guy, you know Kim, right? What's your name? What'd you have in mind? How much you wanna spend?"

It all makes sense in retrospect, right?

We should have known.

But we couldn't have known. The most crucial piece to the puzzle, the enigma that is Bill Suff, is that he is not who he is.

No profiler in his right mind could have had the slightest inclination that the Riverside Prostitute Killer was a sensitive, spiritual, loving, passionate, caring, childlike person who could well express himself and gain a large measure of release through his writings. When maintained in a confined and disciplined environment where creativity is the only allowable release, then Bill Suff is harmless. The Bill Suff I know, the Bill Suff that Zellerbach knows, the continuously incarcerated Bill Suff who was tried and convicted for murder, is in fact *not* a murderer.

There is no profile for that guy, because that guy is an innocent man.

The Prostitute Killer only exists when he's back in a world big enough and free enough to incorporate his fantasy universe where women must be sacrificed to a higher and more complex destiny over which he alone is master.

So put that in your pipe and smoke it.

But rest assured that Bill Suff is now a statistic which the profilers will use to help them better pinpoint the next Bill Suff.

And there will be one.

According to the profilers, there already is.

It's just a matter of finding him.

CHAPTER 14

Posing

Whenever possible, I tried to draw Bill into discussions about sex and his sex life. I don't know what I was expecting him to say, but, at trial, the prosecution had made a big deal out of some hearsay that quoted Bill as saying that he hated prostitutes and would sooner kill them than fuck them. In fact, if you remember, it was Bill's brother, Bobby, who gave the testimony. Somehow it sounded sensible, seeming to explain the unthinkable, but everyone who knew Bill knew that Bobby was lying and just wanted an excuse to take the stand and squint into the spotlights. Bill's trial was a bully pulpit, and sibling rivalry reared up with fierce determination. *It just wasn't fair that Bill was getting all this attention*, thought Bobby, prepared to assume any position that anyone with a video camera wanted to see and hear.

For me, talking about my sex life is unnatural. Well, maybe not unnatural, let's say uncomfortable, let's just say that I keep it to myself and figure I can only get disheartened if I compare notes. In fact, in my experience the supposed macho male locker room chatter doesn't much happen. The only guys I know who partake are gay but closeted, and they seem to think that if they do this unintentional parody of talking about hammering this or that "babe" then no one will realize they have no idea what they're talking about.

Accordingly, since I'm not a big "sex talker", I can't really judge Bill's talk. He always seemed to enjoy the opportunity to talk about sex, and, once he got started he seemed to go on and on, even though it was pretty conservative stuff. It may well be that he was just trying to convince me that all his sexual inclinations were perfectly normal and hardly those expected of a serial killer. Or, as a prisoner who hadn't been with a woman in years, talking about sex in any context might have given him a needed release.

I won't dwell on what he told me, but, for those of you taking notes, he loves to give head to a woman but worries about receiving it. Apparently when he was in the Medical Corps they picked up a guy who'd been bitten off down there, and Bill's been squeamish ever since. Straight sex, missionary position, that's his bread and butter, or so he says. I already mentioned his distaste for condoms, and he insists he's not prone to any particular fantasies, fetishes, or experimentation.

Of course, his first wife, Teryl, disagrees. She swears all he ever wanted was to be sucked off, and he took her by force, fury, and punching power whenever the urge struck. She swears he bites, burns, and has all sorts of nasty little needs.

And the Riverside Coroner will tell you that the Riverside Prostitute Killer definitely left his mark with teeth and cigarettes, in addition to the carving knife.

But what I ultimately wanted was to spark Bill's sexuality. Forget the talk, I wanted to see what his sexual reactivity was. I wanted to see if he had normal impulses or if perhaps rage and other aggressiveness and weirdness would slip out.

So, one day, when I was alone with Bill in the Riverside jail, I snuck in a photo of Coco. She didn't have any photos where she was wearing clothes, and in this one she was stretched upright, like she was climbing an invisible but obviously massive beanstalk, twisted and smiling and looking back at the camera, flexed to maximum effect. Man, she had great musculature. And she was, by coincidence, exactly the sort of woman that Bill had described as his "dream woman"—very young, with blonde hair, small breasts, etc., etc. I wanted to see how Bill would react—would he slaver and lick his lips, would he ask to keep the picture, or would he grab it and eat it or stuff it down his pants or wipe his ass with it or shred it into a million pieces? Who the hell knew—anything was possible.

All my non-serial-killing friends had been quite impressed by the picture and had asked for copies—they were the control group for this exceedingly scientific experiment.

Didn't Masters and Johnson start out this way?

Interestingly, Bill reacted to the photo just the same as the controls. He was appreciative and clearly attracted. I can't swear it, but I know his own "Johnson" shook off its cobwebs—Bill shifted in his seat, in his prison jumpsuit. However, no serial-killing, evil-incarnate, sick motherfucking monster man came out and introduced himself. All that happened was that, after his initial receptivity, Bill quickly became concerned that the guards might see him with the photo, so, after visibly committing it to memory, he gave it back to me and asked me to put it away.

"Now that's exactly the kind of girl I like," he said.

This was another of those times when I felt like I was the pervert. I mean, what sort of man thinks it's really fun and exciting to show a picture of a naked girl to a serial killer?

Later, I got my redemption—as I'd hoped, Bill brought up the picture.

"You know," he said out of the blue, "that was a very nice pose for that girl."

When you read Bill's letter to me recounting his brushes with death, you will find that he describes the out-of-body experience he had due to the motorcycle wreck. He describes how he floated over his crumpled body and entered the tunnel of souls that would open onto heaven. However, forget about the mystical and spiritual aspects of his story. Focus instead on his exquisitely precise, geometric, figurative, long-winded, word drawing of the exact positioning of the molted body he left behind on the ground.

There's no mention of any emotional aspect to that body, merely details as to the angle of the turned head and bent arm and crossed legs.

Of course, who are we to judge what a person should notice when he's having an out-of-body experience and about to die, but yet . . . since Bill is admitting to us that body positioning is something that matters to him, then you would be remiss not to analyze the possible connection between him and more than a dozen dead women whose bodies were carefully manipulated into "interesting" positions. You decide whether any of these women were posed in a way that mimics Bill's description of his own body after the wreck, and you decide what the various body posings look like to you. They each seem to tell a story, to reflect an "artist's impression" of what each woman meant to him, what he saw in her or what she reminded him of. Once he'd killed them, these poor women were clay that Bill could mold into what he preferred them to be or what he believed they ought to be. He undressed them, re-dressed them in clothes that weren't theirs, stuffed a sock down the throat of one, and a lightbulb up the vagina of another. Then he carefully twisted them and posed them.

After wrestling with whether this book should contain any photos of the bodies, I had to include them because the posing is so truly important to interpreting both the killer and the killings.

I will offer my thoughts on one victim, on Tina Leal, the girl who's on the cover of this book. As you can see, she was found wearing clothes that weren't hers—striped men's socks up her legs, purple sweatpants with the legs tucked into the socktops, and a dark blue T-shirt with her arms folded inside the shirt. What you can't see is that she had that GE Miser lightbulb placed up inside her, clear into the uterus. There's an X ray that shows the lightbulb, and it may be the single eeriest thing I've ever seen.

Everyone associated with the case still trades thoughts about the meaning of that lightbulb, but everyone's first impression is always the same: "Wow, it didn't break!"

I actually think that's the answer to the mystery.

Since we know Bill had a "problem" with babies, I'd spent months wondering whether that lightbulb was a surrogate fetus, or whether there was some symbolic illumination of the womb intended by it. Was Bill looking up there, trying to ask why and what for? Or was he merely trying to make the point that he needed to come first to "his" women, not some child who would displace him? Was he trying to reclaim his male identity by pointing out that unless a man expends his seed, then a woman can't become a mother, no matter how much she wants to? Was this just the industrial-tech version of Adam's rib?

No, the answer lies in a different direction altogether.

Bear with me on this.

After Bill got to know and trust me, he told me about his happy life with girlfriend Bonnie Ashley, who he dated off and on from 1985 until 1989. He still professes to love her incredibly. She's still "the one" for him. And there's no question but that, by anyone's standards, the life he led with her was a high-end fantasy that he never could have thought he would achieve. She was also not only the prettiest woman he'd ever dated, she was pretty without qualification.

Bill and Bonnie lived in a terrific little house with a yard and a garden and pets; Bonnie worked and made a good income, while Bill held down a job but also made it his job to make this house a home, to contribute in artistic, aesthetic, sensitive, and husbandly ways.

Bonnie was "the rose" and Bill "the hollyhock", and they lay together in their "flower bed".

This was Disney, folks.

And, crucially, the rose was crazy jealous and possessive of her hollyhock.

Now this was the highest compliment Bill had ever received. For the first time, he had a woman he knew would not cheat on him, and yet she loved him so much she was worried about him cheating on her! His love actually mattered to her. This was a stunning turn of events for Bill. Bonnie followed him around, kept track of him, made him jettison the various other lady friends he had. Bonnie cried and got angry when she fretted that Bill might be wavering in his love for her, which of course he was not. But it was just so incredible that she would be so paranoid—she wanted him at any cost, and she constantly wanted to win him anew.

And, to top it all off, Bonnie had to have a hysterectomy, so she couldn't have kids. Bill could be her whole world to her, and vice versa, without interference.

Of course, we will ignore the fact that, despite his happiness with Bonnie, Bill was still dating and murdering hookers. Once again, throw out the profile—no one could have profiled this.

So, as the story goes, one day, in the midst of their perfect little existence, Bill and Bonnie decided they wanted to add chickens to their menagerie. They would start with a hen. They went to a chicken farm, to a woman known as "The Chicken Lady", and they bought a small incubator and they carefully and jointly picked out one fertilized egg. The Chicken Lady dangled a needle and thread over the egg, watched how the needle swayed and circled, and then she told them that she divined a hen in the egg rather than a rooster—this was a trick that, like others, the Chicken Lady could do with pregnant humans as well.

Bill and Bonnie took their egg and their incubator home, carefully set it all up and monitored it, and, lo and behold, the day came when a crack appeared in the egg. And then the little chick's egg tooth and beak appeared—Bill and Bonnie couldn't have been more excited.

Not one just to stand by and let nature take its course, Bill got out the "chicken birthing kit" he'd prepared for the occasion, and he helped the chick out of its egg, helped crack away the shell using cold water and a small paintbrush to brush away the blood where the chick was attached to its yolk sac.

And Bill and Bonnie had themselves a fine and healthy hen.

Bill immediately lay down and let the chick nestle in his chest hair.

Of course, the chick imprinted on him and followed him around like a dog. "Chicken Girl" is what he and Bonnie named it, and Chicken Girl was the perfect pet for the perfect lives of this perfect couple in their perfect house.

Chicken Girl quickly grew and learned to go in and out of the house through the doggie door, and Chicken Girl would fly up to your hand and gently take a bite of meat when proffered, and, as Bill watched with rapt fascination, she would lay eggs inside the house on the kitchen counter. Chicken Girl would even let the real dog, Bonnie's dog, Myrtle the spaniel, carry her around in its slobbery dog mouth. Yes, everyone and everything was smitten by Chicken Girl.

And, finally, when Chicken Girl was old enough, Bill and Bonnie went back to the Chicken Lady for another egg—a rooster—which was similarly incubated and hatched by the perfect couple in their perfect house. Tellingly, the rooster never acquired a name, but he did do his duty, and soon Chicken Girl's eggs were hatching with dozens of Chicken Girl-ettes, all of which she would lead around the house and yard, following Chicken Dad Bill. Yes, the rooster may have been the biological father, but he was treated as a nameless, spiritual zero, and this finally led to a confrontation.

The rooster spurred Bill.

And Bill tossed the rooster clear across the yard.

Shaken, the rooster steered clear of Bill after that, but he did fly at Bonnie whenever he had the opportunity, so the perfect couple gave this not-so-perfect rooster away to friends.

And life at the perfect house became perfect again.

Until Bill and Bonnie came back from a camping trip and found Chicken Girl gone.

Of course, there was the remote possibility that she'd just up and flown the coop, angry at Bill and Bonnie's absence, but the profile said that either a possum or a ground squirrel was to blame, and both had lately been seen acting fat, full, and sassy in the immediate vicinity.

So Bill was out there waiting when the killer came back for another meal.

It was the possum, and it was making a beeline for the hen house, intent on easy pickings.

What it got for its trouble was the blade of Bill's ax. By the time Bill was done, there were too many possum pieces to count.

And then, a few nights later the ground squirrel made its move, foolishly thinking that the turf was fair game since the possum had abandoned it.

Bill took a shotgun to the ground squirrel, liquefying it.

"Those're the only things that I've ever killed . . . that I can think of," said Bill Suff to me.

Think again, Bill.

And look at the photos of Tina Leal. With all sincere respect to the living person whom I never met, the corpse, as dressed up and posed, looks like a chicken. A costumed, cartoon chicken. No question. It's "Big Bird", it's "Foghorn Leghorn", it's "Rhode Island Red" from Bill's own drawings. Bill was big on drawing birds—the blue and purple clothes on Tina Leal match the colors in Bill's drawings of blue jays. The long, thin, "bird" legs with the stripes all the way up, thanks to the socks. And Tina's arms are inside the T-shirt because chickens don't have arms, they have wings—Tina's arms are placed inside the shirt so that they bulge up like a chicken's breast and wings. Tina's small, angular face with the tiny beak nose—did she look like a chicken to him in the first place, so that he knew he'd be obligated to complete her transformation?

Think I'm mad, or just worried that I can see things through Bill's eyes?

But now even you know why the lightbulb is there, don't you? Bill had seen Chicken Girl lay egg after egg, and it was always both miracle and mystery. *How come the damn things don't break? How can such a big thing grow inside that tiny chicken and then get squeezed out of that tiny hole?*

Ain't life grand.

We'll never know for sure why Tina Leal got "the chicken treatment" any more than we know why any artist suddenly gets one image in his head instead of myriad others. The magic of the creative process is that you begin with infinite choices, and yet you are able to choose. The only difference between the nonartist and the artist is that the former can't make a choice, doesn't see one choice because too many of them run together into a vision whiteout.

The day Tina Leal died, Bill Suff had his beloved but tragically lost Chicken Girl on his mind—in his killing kit the "egg" and the chicken clothes were waiting for their moment—and so what he inflicted on Tina was the one thing he had to do above all others.

Oh, and the "egg"—the lightbulb—it didn't break.

Damnedest thing.

CHAPTER 15

"I Shouldn't Exist But I Do"

The Letters of Bill Suff

Brian,

This is the 'Near Death Episode' paper I wrote just after my arrest. You'll probably need some explanations as to certain names or incidents mentioned in the paper. So, I'll do that here. I've told you about Dijianet's death, my Aunt Judy's death and Cathy Sharp's death. Earl's death, you can probably learn more from Mom or Don than you can from me. But one thing *they* don't know about, is something that happened *before* Dad died. Cheryl and I were at the hospital and he was supposed to be in a coma. Cheryl was about seven or eight months pregnant then; she was standing beside me and I was holding his left hand. Granted, his eyes were shut, but I believe that I still was able to reach him on some conscious, or *sub*conscious, level. Tears were in my eyes and I was telling him that he couldn't die before the baby was born (we didn't know the sex beforehand). Asking him to please hold on until *after* Cheryl gave birth, I felt him definitely squeeze my hand in reply. From that squeeze, I got the message that he would see the baby, regardless. And yes, I believe that happened . . . that he *did* see Bridgette when she was born.

Now as to other things and names mentioned:

A Bugler in the Air Force:

When I was assigned to the hospital at Carswell AFB in Fort Worth, my commander found out from my records that I played the bugle (trumpet). I was given a choice: Have 'Grounds Duty' or 'Funeral Detail.' Grounds Duty consisted of one week every three months of mowing the grass or trimming the shrubs on the hospital grounds. In retrospect, Grounds Duty would have been an easier duty. Most of the enlisted personnel only served on Funeral Detail: once every ten to fifteen funerals. Because there were only three buglers, I caught every third funeral and every third week I caught either the weeklong reveille or evening taps. Needless to say, between that and my regular ward medical duties, I didn't have a lot of free time to spend with Teryl.

As to 'Nita Severson and her ex-husband:

I worked as a typist for Nita for about two months after working for the Schartons and before going to work for John's Service Center. One day, when I got to her home for work, she told me to forget work that day and to drive her over to her ex-husband's home to talk to his widow. She asked if I would accompany her to the funeral. I guess it was because she considered me such a good friend. Bonnie came with me and Nita was little upset because she wasn't really invited.

As to Jesse Brown:

Jesse Brown was the supervisor of the Supply Services warehouse when I went to work for the county. When he died, we almost shut down the warehouse for the afternoon so we could go to his funeral. Bonnie was not present for that one.

The auto accident when I was 17:

I was working for the Perris Volunteer Fire/Rescue department when I was a senior in high school. We were called out for an auto accident on Temescal Canyon Road. A car being paced by an Elsinore Police Car crashed into a cement embankment for a railroad underpass. The two girls in the car were instantly killed. When I arrived on the scene, I saw that the driver was a girl I had dated a couple times when I was at Elsinore High.

The house fire:

After I graduated from High School and went to work for the Fire Dept. in Perris, we answered a call for a structure fire. The wooden frame house (shack, really) was totally engulfed. The babysitter and one child got out of the house. The three younger children didn't. When we got the fire out we found the children huddled together in a bedroom.

Charles Brown:

Charlie was a very good friend of mine while in prison. He was a very intelligent man that always asked my counsel on many matters. He wound up going to the infirmary because he felt sick. They diagnosed him with viral flu. It was later discovered that he had double-pneumonia. When he was transferred to the Huntsville Hospital, I lost my lead operator on the computer system he and I worked on and a very good friend. His sister wrote me two weeks later saying that he had passed away. I wrote a letter back to her telling her that he had been misdiagnosed, but I never heard back from her again.

The rest of the paper is self-explanatory. We'll talk more about it when I next see you.

Take Care
Bill S.

Twice in my lifetime I've had 'near-death' episodes. I've *never* told anyone about them for fear of being thought crazy. Because of those two episodes, death does not bother me as much as it may bother others. In my life, I can only recall four deaths that moved me to tears: Dijianet's, my Aunt Judy's, my dad's and Cathy Sharp's. I've seen a lot of death in my life: as the bugler playing 'taps' for military funerals in the Air Force; Nita Severson's ex-husband's funeral; Jesse Brown's funeral; an auto accident when I was 17; a house fire when I was 18 where the children died in the flames; the Casares girl that I am wrongly accused of; and those previously mentioned above. When I became aware of the deaths when I was 17 and 18, I was very upset at the unjustness of death coming to someone so young. It wasn't until 1971 that I came to terms with the passage of our corporeal lives.

Both Bonnie and Cheryl know a little about how I feel about

death. Cathy Sharp and I were sitting in my apartment one night listening to some music and watching the fish in my aquarium. She asked me how I felt about death. I asked her 'why'? She began a discussion that went on into the early morning hours. We spent all night talking about death, GOD, UFOs, paranormal experiences and more. I found out that she shared almost the exact same thoughts that I had on the same subjects. Like me, she was in no way fearful of death. Again, like me, she was concerned about the *manner* of her death: She didn't want a lingering death. (I don't want a painful death.) Cathy got what she wanted: Death came instantly. A dream she told me about was fulfilled. In her dream, she said, death would come with collapsing metal and glass. (Her thought was that she was going to be caught in a building damaged by an earthquake.) She also said that she would die alone: "A singular death." Less than a week later she died in a traffic accident. The driver of the other vehicle was drunk and survived the accident. I've only had this type of discussion with one other person. A month afterwards, Charles Brown was dead of a mis-diagnosed medical problem in prison. He was told that he only had stomach flu.

The first time I had a 'near-death episode' was in 1971: About 3:00 in the afternoon my appendix burst. I was gotten to the hospital by 3:30 pm. I was not operated on until after midnight. For more than nine hours poison circulated throughout my abdominal cavity. I don't know if it got into my blood or not. According to Riki Mandel, my nurse, a weaker person would not have survived what I went through. I *knew* why I was still alive.

While I was unconcious, I left my body. But I was sent back. However, before I was returned to my body (after the surgeons finished operating on me), I found out what happens to us when we die. I also found out a lot more. And that's why death doesn't scare me.

The second time I experienced a 'near-death' episode was when I had my motorcycle accident in 1988. Again, while I was unconcious, I left my body. Once more, I found out what awaits each of us when we die. This time I was told that it was still too soon for my 'arrival.' I was told that I have much more to accomplish before I am to be 'called.' I'll never forget the words or the voice that explained many things to me.

Several times after my motorcycle accident, Bonnie would *remind* me that I could have died in that accident. I told her that I would never die in any kind of automotive accident. I will not die a violent death. I will die in my sleep, flat on my back. And according to what I've learned, I will meet death no time soon. Death is still far from me. And I saw the deaths of others whom I know. I was saddened when it was revealed to me that my Dad would not live to see my daughter born. When I last saw him in the hospital, he was in a coma. I knew that he would never recover from it. I 'saw' his death back in 1988. In my family, my mother's death will come next, then Bobby's and Kenny's. Don, Roberta and Deena will live long after I'm gone. I'll not go any farther into this though. *Nobody* should know *when* they are going to die. It has a detrimental effect on a person's sanity.

I've told Bonnie, Cheryl and several others, when talking about my motorcycle accident, that I didn't die because something more is expected of me. What that something is or when or where I'm supposed to do it, I have no way of knowing. Yet, I *do* know that I will not die until I've accomplished whatever it is I'm supposed to do. Events are supposed to take place that I will have a direct bearing upon—events that will have a direct bearing upon me!

As I've already explained, in 1971, my appendix burst and I was rushed to the hospital by private car. When I got to the hospital, I was informed that all of the operating rooms were in use because of a shootout on the north side of Fort Worth. I was told that the only thing that could be done for me was to run IV's into me and keep me hydrated. Sometime later, a nurse came in and gave me a shot, to 'help' me sleep. I found out later that it was to help ease the pain. Evidently I went to sleep because the next thing I knew Teryl was telling me that it was midnight and that I'll be going to surgery soon. Finally, someone comes to take me to the operating room. I notice a clock on the wall is showing after 12:30 am. Before I'm wheeled into the O.R. though, I'm out again.

I suddenly feel very light, like I'm floating. I open my eyes and notice that I'm floating near the ceiling, looking down on myself and several people in green. I am unable to understand exactly what they are saying, but something seems wrong. A nurse is injecting something directly into the tube attached to my arm. Someone quickly places a mask over my face and I see someone else, like he wants something in a hurry. I think this is a weird dream, that the medication must be making me hallucinate. Then I feel something pulling at me from behind. I turn toward the pull and everything seems to go dark. I was suddenly rushing forward, moving without trying to. I could sense a couple other people near me, but I couldn't see anyone. I was experiencing a sensation of very rapid speed, when I saw a light far ahead of me. As the sensation of speed increased, the light took on a bright glow and seemed to be getting nearer.

I don't remember feeling any fear, but I *was* intensely curious. When I finally passed through the light, I felt a strange sense of wrongness. Like something was not quite right. Many realizations flooded into my mind: I had been here before; this was not the end; friends were here; many things awaited me. Most of all and clearest of all was the thought 'You don't belong here yet!' That was the wrongness I felt: I wasn't supposed to be there yet. The next instant it was dark again. When I opened my eyes, I was in a room with a nurse asking me how I felt.

In 1988, on my way to work, I was involved in a near-fatal motorcycle accident. By all rights, I should have been dead. The type of accident I had, the injuries I *did* suffer, and by the reports I've heard and read; I should have died as a result of that accident. Everyone admits that it was surprising that I survived it. That accident erased all memory from the time I went to bed the night before, until around 3:30 that afternoon. However, what

I've never told anyone is that I *do* have a memory of something happening while I was unconcious.

This memory begins shortly after the accident. I'm several feet above my body, looking down on the scene. Dust was still settling around me as I had ended up on the shoulder of the road. I could see a couple of people approaching my body and could faintly hear some voices: "Is he dead?" "Someone call 9-1-1." I could hear other voices, but was unable to make out the words.

As I was moving backwards, away from the scene, I continued to look at my body. The edges of my vision were blurring—vanishing into darkness like I was looking through a tunnel. I could see that my helmet had come off and my head was covered with blood. My body was lying half on my back—half on my right side. My left leg was bent at the knee with my left ankle lying under my right leg. My left forearm was folded up under my body. My right arm laid out like it was pointing back towards the accident. My vision began getting smaller, the blackness rushing in from all sides, when I began to feel the familiar pull from behind.

As I turned around, I could feel myself rushing forward at a tremendous rate of speed. I seemed to be in a large tunnel, rushing toward a dazzling glow that sparkled ahead of me. Again, I was able to sense others around me, but not all of them were moving towards the light as I was. The rest were just waiting around and I got the feeling that they were afraid to enter or go near the light. But I didn't feel any fear. After all, I had been in the light before and knew what awaited me. Those of us who *were* moving, seemed to start moving ever faster as we neared the light. I sensed another presence near me, but I couldn't take my eyes off the dazzling glow in front of me. The presence seemed to take my hand and began to plead with me. I can't say that I actually *heard* the words, but they were in my mind, nonetheless. I got the meaning of the thoughts of this other presence: I was needed by others and should not enter the light. I was unable to understand *why* I shouldn't enter the light, because I had entered it before. I tried to ask the presence next to me as to the reason I was needed. The thoughts came back to me disjointed and seemed vaguely distressing. Those thoughts became almost a painful uneasiness in my head, but I knew that I could not stop. I had to get to that light, with or without my companion. I begged that other presence to come into the light with me, but once again it claimed that I shouldn't enter the light because I was needed. I felt myself being slowed by the presence that was clasping my left hand. I cried out *"NO!"* and shook myself free. I felt a shock of pain shoot up my left arm and explode in my brain as the other presence fell away from me. Then I shot forward and entered the welcoming, dazzling glow.

Several impressions made their way into my mind at once. The pain in my head was gone; love was paramount here; all who came were welcome; I knew others here; I was *known* by others here. I *had* been here before; not once, but many times and I knew each of those occurrences.

Thoughts were coming to me again, this time from a brightness right in front of me. I was welcomed here, but it was again too soon for my 'journey.' I was still needed elsewhere. I had to return to my body to accomplish the task set for me. And then I was suddenly not there any longer.

I suddenly became aware that I was lying on something soft, on my back. Pain entered my awareness—my left wrist; my left leg below the knee; my right leg, inside thigh; my back; and more than anything else, my head. I sense someone near me and try to turn my head in that direction. I can't, because of a neck brace and pillow braces on each side of my head. I open my eyes and see Bonnie standing there. I recognize her, but nothing else.

I have a hard time talking because my mouth is so dry. Finally, Bonnie is able to understand me. I want to know where I am, what happened to me and can I *please* have something to drink?

Bonnie replies that I can't have anything to drink because *"they"* don't know if I have any internal injuries. She also says that I've asked those exact same questions over and over again since she got there. I don't remember saying anything before now. She lets me know that I've been in an accident and where I am. I ask her for the time, she tells me. I close my eyes and groan. She gets concerned. I ask her to call my work and let them know what has happened. She says that she's already done that.

Bonnie asks me what do I mean when I asked: "What is needed of me? What do I have to do?" I recall looking at her for a few seconds and then say, "I don't know." I'm not about to tell *anyone* about the light, the presences or anything else. I have a great fear that someone will think I'm crazy and put me away, lock me up in an asylum. I don't know if I could take it if people thought I was insane. I also have an overwhelming fear of not being in full control of all my capabilities. I'm certain that if I'm put in an asylum, I'll be given some kind of drugs that will make me unable to do for myself. (That's the one, main reason why I don't take drugs, drink heavily or smoke grass. I won't take any foreign substances into my body, unless they are prescribed by a doctor. And I have some reservations there, too.)

I know what questions are going to be asked by anyone who reads this. They are the same questions that everyone asks of those who relate near-death experiences: "What's on the other side of the light? What happens when we die? Is there a God? Is there an afterlife?" All of these questions are important and the answers are complex. I don't know if I can answer them to anyone's complete satisfaction.

For instance: *"Is there an afterlife?"* Life after what? Life—Death—some form of limbo? An afterlife for what? The body—the soul—the conscious being of each of us? What part of me started on that journey? My soul—my consciousness—or my *un*concious being? *I* certainly don't know!

Two questions can be combined, and answered the same way: "What's on the other side of the light?" and "What happens when we die?" The other side *IS* the light. Light is everywhere. Everything is the light. When we die, we go into this light. We become the light. The light becomes us. Once we have entered the light, though, that is not our final destination. That final destination is each person's own interpretation—Hell— Heaven—Valhalla. The end result is what each person perceives it to be . . . at the end of their journey! And their own perception may change many times throughout their journey. Each journey is over when it is *perceived* to be over, and not until.

I didn't so much as *see* what happens to us as receive an *impression* of what happens as soon as I passed into the light. Memories flooded into me. I recalled many wonderful things. When I was returned to my body, some of those memories remained. Only traces of other memories remained. Unfortunately, I lost much more than I was able to remember. But what I do remember is very uplifting.

We go on. We live again. Over and over. Call it reincarnation if you want; although that word doesn't explain it all. Time doesn't exist there. I experienced no passage of time. I could have been there for years—I could have been there for a fraction of a second. I was there and then I wasn't. The memory of thoughts were in my mind and I knew that they were from the presence of light that was in front of me—barring me from going any farther.

Is there a GOD? This question has baffled mankind for many centuries. Those religious powers that be claim we have to take HIS existence on faith. I don't. *Yes*, there is a GOD! GOD is benevolent, powerful, caring, onmi-everything . . . Must I go on? Yes, GOD is there—and GOD is here. GOD *IS!* Is GOD masculine or feminine? Yes and no. GOD is both and neither. It cannot be explained any further than that. There is no equivalent word for what I know.

When we "live" again, do we come back as ourselves, a doorknob, an animal . . . ? Do we come back to this place or travel on to another level? The questions go on and on. I am unable to answer them. I *do* know that we don't necessarily come back to the next proceeding "timeline". If I die today, I may not come back tomorrow; I may come back yesterday.

I do know one other thing that sticks out in my mind: The very nature by which GOD exists—solar systems, galaxies, suns, planets, our lives as we know them, should not exist! But they do—*we* do! That is why death itself does not frighten me. *I shouldn't exist, but I do.* And I will again, when I die. We all will, because GOD wills it to be.

....

27 November 1995

Hello Brian,

Well, there's so much to tell you, I really don't know where to start. Guess I should start with what else was in the envelope. There are 3 Visiting Questionnaires. One is for Bonnie, *IF* she wants it! Tell her that if she decides that she'd like to see me, I'm only an hour away from the exit we took into Pleasanton when we visited her brother, Dennis, in December '85. If I remember correctly, visits are between 9:00 a.m. and 5:00 p.m. on weekends. (Legal visits are allowed seven days a week at the same times.) I'll verify that next time I go out to the exercise yard and let you know next time I call.

I just got a "Legal" letter from the legal officer—a letter from Patty that she wrote while awaiting a plane to LA. Says she gets most of her work done in airports on her laptop. (See . . . Everyone has a laptop. Why not me?) She told me a lot of the same things you told about having an attorney appointed to me to handle my appeal. However, I've been doing some legal researching of my own and have already come across some pleasant surprises. I don't want to enumerate those surprises here, so they'll have to wait until I see you in person. She *did* say that she was happily surprised to hear that I was in the Air Force (I mentioned it in my letter to her from the AC). She says that her *dad* was one of the Tuskeegee Airmen! (Believe it or not, I didn't even know she was black! Jim Bland told me that when I went out to the exercise yard. But all of the times I spoke to her on the phone from jail, I never *once* suspected she was black. I didn't take it for granted that she was *white*! I was thinking

Oriental or Latin American.) But it was *very* interesting to find out about her dad, though. I wish I could meet him to get some first hand info on the Tuskeegee Airmen. I remember first hearing about them while I was at Lackland Air Base after my Basic Training. Anyway, she hopes to get over here to see me the first week of December. Maybe you'll run into each other?!

Now, I told you I got three letters last Monday, the 20th. One from Ron Peterson; one from his friend in Tampa, Fla., Ken Karnig; and one from my mother. I wrote back to both Ron and Ken, sent the letters out last night, the 26th. And I answered, almost, my mother's letter. But I'm not going to mail it! I'm afraid if I do, she'll blow up and so will Don and the rest of the family! And I believe; I'm *convinced,* that they can still hurt me terribly with both my appeal and any chance for a new trial. To put it bluntly: I'm scared of what they can say and do.

As I told you when I talked to you briefly on the phone this morning, I was on the phone with Don for about an hour and a half. I was talking him through some of my diskettes so he could read them. There's something wrong with my "Applewriter II" program that he's been using. It won't allow him to scroll through my text files. He can get to the beginning and to the end but not the middle. And since I don't have the documentation to the program in front of me, I can't remember how to do it. He has located, however, one of the disks that has "Death.Stalks1" and "Excerpts1" on it. "Death.Stalks1" isn't anywhere close to how much I had written on the story. Somewhere, on another disk is more of the story. I told how to boot the computer with a program that will allow him to 'catalog' all of the other disks to see what's on each one. Hopefully, he will find the other copies that are more complete. But! All I had written of "Death Stalks On Four Legs" is chapter *one.* And it takes place only in VietNam! Chapter two was to begin in California—Perris and Elsinore area. The "Excerpts" file contains a lot of scenarios that I was going to build the story around. It's so frustrating to be so close to all of that stuff, yet to be unable to put my hands on and pull up exactly what I *know* is there. At one time I had a computer print-out sheet listing every single disk I had, showing each and every program I had stored on each disk.

There is a problem, though. He found my disk that has the game TAIPAN on it. Just like me, he's gotten hooked on it. Both he and Bobby have been playing it and leaving other things undone. That was *my* problem. If I decided I was going to spend some time on the computer to work on a program or one of my utility programs, I had to hope that I found what I *wanted* to find before I came across Taipan. The lure was tremendous and there were times when I'd turn on the game and a week later I had the same game going. Fighting several hundred to a couple thousand pirate ships and selling my loads of Arms, Silk, Opium or General Cargo. Don't get me wrong—I had enough will power to avoid Taipan and work on some program, but that temptation was always there. Bonnie used to curse that program. When I'd call up that game, she'd just shake her head, knowing that I was going to be occupied for a few hours. Before I got her initiated in using the computer to help her real estate work, she'd write me off as a lost cause whenever I sat down to the computer. But one thing she'll *have* to admit to, is that no matter *what* I was doing on the computer, if she wanted to do some real estate work on it, I immediately got out of whatever program I was running and logged on to her real estate bulletin board and helped her with it! I *never* put her interests second to mine! She was always number *one* with me. Yet, that wasn't good enough for her, I guess. She still left me. I'd be willing to bet that she doesn't even know that to this date I would do *anything* in the world for her just to hear her say that she still loved me. If it meant that my death was the only thing that would bring happiness eternally to her, I'd do what is morally repugnant to me. I *would* commit suicide for her, if it was required to make her happy. And you *know* how I feel about suicide! (Man! I sure didn't want to get into my feelings about Bonnie in any letter. But now that it's written, I'm not going to retract it. Brian, <u>please</u>! Don't tell Bonnie how much I still feel for her. With her being married, and with Myrtle's death, finding out just how much I still cared for her can only bring her more pain. And more than anything else, I don't want her to suffer more pain. She's had enough because of me already.)

Now, topics that I was wanting to cover before I got side-tracked.

Do you remember a Robert Heinlein book I was telling you about while still in Riverside? It involved a time/dimension traveling device with a six-pronged activating device. The name of that book is "Number Of The Beast." I heartily recommend it to anyone just getting interested in Science Fiction. I wish I could read it again, but it's not in the library here. Maybe when, if, I get enough money ahead, I can order it from whichever approved vendor I'm allowed to order books from.

Just recently read a great short novel here called "Trace of the Werewolf." No, it did not involve the creature. (Have I already written you about this? I don't recall.) It was about the supposed heir apparent to Hitler's Third Reich, code name "Werewolf." The hero of the book was supposed to find out if this, now grown man, was going begin Hitler's atrocities all over again. During his investigation, he asked a great line: "In the words of Pontius Pilate: 'What is truth?'" I thought that line fits so very well with my final statement. And to answer it, *I'd* say "It's what Zellerbach has made up in his own twisted little world and has force fed to the public!" You know, when he spoke up after everyone else exploded at me, he said that I must not like him very well. If an understatement was *ever* spoken, he said it. But it's not just that I don't like him very much, it's that I don't care for the position he has where he can take any little bit of a whisper and turn it inside out, into a scream! I've heard of making a molehill into a mountain. But he's taken a speck of dust (my case) and turned it into the largest dung heap with him sitting at the top thinking it smells like roses! Everytime he opens his mouth, the worst bit of flatulence I've ever heard comes out when he speaks his bombastic praise of what he did to me. (And by flatulence, I'm not talking about his pomposity!) Do I dislike him? Maybe. Do I hate him? No! Am I afraid of him? Resoundingly <u>yes</u>! I'm afraid of what he can do with his office behind him to other people who are unfortunate enough to be in the wrong place at the wrong time.

I have been having some awfully weird dreams of late.

1. I was in some kind of visiting room and so was the Zamora family. They asked me, "We want to know the truth—Did you kill Del?" I started shaking my head, saying *"no"* when out of the dark to my side, Del herself appears, smiles to me *and* her family and says "This man had nothing to do with my death!" The family asked how the evidence was found against me. I said it should be obvious that it was *planted.* Then Del speaks again, "It was *put* there!" When the family next asks a question, "Then who . . ." I was awakened by breakfast call. I haven't had the dream again.

2. I was in an office somewhere (highrise) and I'm holding a gun. Check to see that it's loaded, cock it and say, "Now you can come out *father!*" Out of another room a man walks out and sits on a couch. He's not *my* father. From another door comes three more people, one of which is "father's" wife (not *my* mother). I proceed to tell everyone how "father" had sexually abused me for years (?). "Father" admits it, then his wife says, "I can't fault him, because *I* did, too!" Now this dream scares me because, first, I don't recognize any of the people in the room. Second, one wall is a mirror and I can see that it's *me* holding a gun, I'm about 10–11 years of age and standing behind me with her left hand on my shoulder is Bonnie! And she looks to be about 45, the same as when I first met her! That's all there is to that dream and again, I've only had it the one time (so far). What really scares me about it (besides I'm holding a gun) is that I don't know that I was *ever* sexually abused at any time in my life. I have no memory or other evidence of such a thing ever happening. So where is this dream getting its ammo (so to speak) from? One reason *why* I'm scared is because I've read and heard that dreams have a nutshell of honesty that the

subconcious is aware of, and that nutshell is what the subconcious builds the dream on. The fear I'm feeling from this dream is the same one you can imagine upon biting a chunk out of an apple, enjoying the taste and then go for a second bite. But to your dismay you see half of a worm drop out of the apple. Only one thought enters your mind "What happened to the *other* half of that worm!?" If you understand *that* fear, you'll know the fear I have from this dream.

3. I'm in a field, trees a few yards to my left and back. To my right, the grassy field slopes gently away. In front of me is a cliff that drops off to the ocean. Far out to sea, there is a huge wave building and it's coming towards me. But I know I'm safe because the wave won't crest over the cliff. Next to me, lying on a blanket is Florence (Don't you *dare* tell her!) and she's saying, "Come on, we've got just enough time." She's fully clothed and so am I. (I don't have dreams where I or a girl are nude. *Never* have!) I know what she's talking about (so do *you*!), but I can't bring myself to make love to her. Not that I wouldn't *want* to. But I don't. Suddenly, *Bonnie* drives up in a pickup truck, gets out stands at my left side, holding my hand and Florence drives off in the truck. Bonnie and I sit down on the blanket and watch the wave splash against the cliff face. From the spray that washes over the top of the cliff, Myrtle the dog comes to us completely wet and lies down to the right of us on the blanket. And here I awoke! Explain *that* one to me, if you can! What I wouldn't give for a good Dream Interpreter!

Well, it's now 2300 hrs (11:00 p.m. to us civilians) and I'd better attempt to get some sleep. Maybe I'll get lucky and have an *important* dream. Good Night and I'll write more tomorrow.

(signed)
Bill S

30 November 1995

Hello again,

Sorry. A few days have passed and I'm just now getting back to your letter. I just re-read what I've already written and see I left out who the other two visiting questionnaires are for. I told you about the one for Bonnie and then got side-tracked (that's been happening a lot lately). Anyway, I mentioned to you *several* times about a nurse at the county jail I became friends with. She testified in my behalf during the penalty phase of my trial. Her name is Janet, her husband's name is Ed. Would you please try to call the jail to talk to her. She usually works second shift (7:00 a.m. to 3:00 p.m.). Find out from her where you can send the other two questionnaires. She expressed a desire to visit me when she comes up here to San Francisco. I'd kind of like to see and talk to her again, *AND* meet her husband.

Now—what's been happening to me since I arrived here. Not much good. I've been to the Law Library *once*. Was told about an interesting case and decided to look it up. A Federal case: *Donald O. Coe v. Otis Thurman, Warden* #90-55128, I *think* it was a 9th Circuit case, but I'm not sure. Anyway, case cite is: *922F2d528*. Submit date was Nov. 5, 1990 and the decision date was Dec. 28, 1990—Reversed and Remanded. I was told that it had to do with the excessively long time it took to appoint an appellate attorney. I don't know, I didn't get a chance to get into the case. I had to *tell* the librarian what case I was interested in, then he had to find it and bring me the book. I had time to write down the case name, the decision and then a few of the cites mentioned. Next thing I know, it was time to leave and I had to give the book back.

And I received my first visit: Patty Daniels came over and saw me for about an hour and a half yesterday (Wednesday, the 29th). They put me into the booth as Patty came out (after she visited someone else). Then she asked me what I wanted. ???!!! I didn't have any idea what she was talking about. I finally replied, "I was called out here by *you*, what do *you* want?" She laughed (a *beautiful* laugh) and said "No, I mean what do you want to eat or drink?"

Then I remembered something Jim told me earlier, so I asked for a Pepsi. She wanted to know if I wanted a sandwich or anything and I said that I didn't feel comfortable about her spending her money on me. Again she laughed, told me it came from an expense account and for me not to worry. So she brought me a BBQ beef sandwich and a Pepsi. *Good Lord*, they tasted good! There were all kinds of vending machines out there that I didn't even notice when I entered and I *walked right past them*! Patty and I talked about a lot of different subjects; she had me talking so much about myself I didn't get a chance to learn anything about *her*! But I *do* think I settled her fears about the book. While we were visiting she had me sit by the window after she saw me looking out it before she joined me in the booth. Had a *great* view of part of the bay. Couldn't see *THE Bridge*, but I could see the toll bridge that we travelled over when I arrived here. The windows of the visiting room face East, so I get a fairly decent view of the San Francisco skyline. All in all, it was a very nice visit.

I got my hands on a very good Thriller/Mystery novel. Clive Cussler's "Night Probe." Also got the catalog of available books in the SQ library and noticed several more of his books that are available. I'm going to look forward to reading his "Vixen 03" and "Raise the Titanic!" All three books are 'DIRK PITT' books, the central character that has the most exhilarating adventures. In "Night Probe" he comes up against a British Intelligence Agent named 'Brian Shaw'. From hints and other statements, you know that 'Shaw' is an alias given to this "Super" agent when he retired from Her Majesties Secret Service. But the book doesn't come right out and SAY that Brian Shaw is James Bond, even though the hints are rife throughout the book. Anyway, it is a real good read. I haven't read anything I liked this much since I last read the Anne McCaffrey's Dragonrider of Pern series, 10 books strong!

My TV Guide subscription has finally been transferred to this new address. Now if I only had a TV to use it with. Still waiting for my crossword puzzle subscription to catch up with me. Going to be strange working crossword puzzles in ink again. I used to do my

crosswords in ink all the time. Bonnie would get frustrated working them in *pencil* and have so many erasures, she sometimes erased
through the puzzles. Cheryl hated crossword puzzles, just as she
hated *any* word game. Cheryl's speed was 'SORRY' and 'LIFE'! Any
game that required her to *think*, she stayed away from. Aw, but the
sad times in my life are depressing. I'd rather keep my mind occupied with the happier times. And that said—I think I'll end this
letter so I can get it out tonight. Take care and I'll talk to you on
the phone soon.

Best to you,
Bill S

....

25 December 1995

Brian—
    Just a quick note to let you know that the accompanying letter
from the memorabilia collector is the one I told you about on the
phone. If you *really* want a response written by me for the book, let
me know. Otherwise, I'll not be wasting my time on his letter.
    I hope today was a lot better for you than it was for me. One of
the c/o's finally got me a pair of shoes (that I was supposed to have
gotten when I first arrived here). Of course, they *were* a little late
as I already got a nice pair of Tennis Shoes on my own (going to
cost me 2 books of postage stamps when I get them). I stayed in all
day. Had a nice Christmas Dinner. Those were the *good* points.
The bad?! I had to put up with ear-shattering yelling from downstairs. And my allergies erupted with a vengence . . . Sneezing and
a nose-running marathon.
    While it was quiet this morning (people sleeping and out to the
yard), I re-wrote page 13 of "Whisper From the Dark". Changed
a few things, added a whole new aspect to the 'Cloaked Figure'!
That character is now an "outcast Ancient" by the name of
"ZERNEBOCK". By the way, the name *did not* come from
ZELLERBACH. According to the New York Times Crossword

Puzzle Dictionary, "Zernebock" is the name of the "God of Evil, incarnate"! *When* did the Ancients roam both the Land *and* the Earth? That will be answered in the story. But it coincides with a *minor* belief of mine about a missing part of the Bible in the book of Genesis. And it happened long, long before the Dinosaurs were roaming the Earth.

Now that I've piqued your interest, I'll close this short note here. Talk more on this later.

Merry Christmas and
Happy New Year
Bill S

---

15 January 1996
Sunday

Hello Brian,

Curiosity has finally gotten the better of me. What's going on? There were two weeks that went by when I was out of touch because the phone was out of order. When we got the phone back, I tried and tried to call you, Don, and Bobby. All without success. And now, there's a collect call block on your phone. I can't get ahold of anyone who knows what's happening. Florence and Dave, Roberta and Patty have not heard from you, either. Roberta hasn't even heard from Don, other than regarding my van. So, would you please let me know something? I'd really like to go on with our book. Please let me know.

As you can see, I got my typewriter. I also got my TV and head-phones. And I got a watch from Florence and Dave in a Quarterly Package. I actually got to watch the two championship games between the AFC and NFC teams today. The Steelers and the Cowboys won and are going to the Super Bowl like I was hoping. I will even get to <u>watch</u> the Super Bowl game. (Barring electrical and cable failures, of course.) Living under the current circumstances has finally become a little bit easier to live with.

The TV is a Panasonic with a few special features: Sleep timer, program timer, channel block, captioning, on-screen menu and channel programming. This typewriter is even better, with a bunch of special features. It's a Smith-Corona 450DLD. One of the features is a Spell-Right Dictionary of 79,000 words (I think). It also has **bold printing** and <u>underlining</u> capabilities. Left and right justification, search, insert, sub- and super-script features, special characters and much, much more. It will be a very big help with typing up my stories and other things.

By the way, you asked me to let you know if I came across any good books . . . I found a great series in the library here that I've gotten into: Piers Anthony's "XANTH" series. It's fantasy fiction, but the writing is fantastic! It's comparable to Ann McCaffrey's "PERN" series.

Well, I guess I'd better close here and get this into the mail. Please write back soon and let me know what's up.

> Sincerely,
> (signed)
> Bill L. Suff

....

27 February 1996

Hello Brian,

Long time no hear. Hope you are well and prospering. I am feeling better. The flu has been making the rounds here. I was down for two weeks with it. Just started feeling better this past Thursday (the 22nd).

Got your letter this evening (Tuesday) and was very happy to hear from you. I was beginning to think you had gone the same route as everyone else who knew me. I only get letters from 3 people regularly. Once in awhile, one comes from my Mother and Florence. So your letter was *very* welcome.

I had been given your phone number by Mom back last (1/29) month and your address from Mom on Wednesday (the 21st). I've tried to call you on the past dates: 1/30, 2/1, 2/2, 2/5, 2/7, 2/9, 2/10, 2/13, 2/16, 2/19, 2/21, 2/26. Whether you are aware of it or not, but your phone *does* have a collect charge block on it. I've heard that dog-gone message a dozen times so far. More if you count the number of times I heard it on your old number. Anyway, I haven't been able to call you for that reason. I *have* tried.

In order to come up for a visit you have to call ahead of time. The Visitor's Information number is (800) 374-8474. That number should answer all of your questions. If they aren't, try calling Patty or her secretary: Kathy. I, myself, haven't been able to find out much so far.

Sorry, you'll have to dig out your magnifying glass again. My typewriter ribbon finally ran out. I'm trying to make a deal to get another one. It's going to cost me stamps, but it's the only way to get a new ribbon when I'm broke. Don hasn't followed through on *any* of his promises about making sure I was taken care of. I talked to him, at Mom's, on the 16th of this month. He was astonished that I didn't have any money left over. I asked him what he thought the money was for. He said that I was supposed to buy an inexpensive T.V. and typewriter, not the most expensive ones I could find. I guess he doesn't understand that we are limited as to style, brand, and where we can purchase anything. He also wanted to know why I bought a set of headphones. Why I couldn't listen to the T.V. speaker like everyone else. He said I could have used the money I spent on the headphones to buy canteen. I almost hung up on him at that point. But I carefully tried to explain to him that regulations here dictate that the T.V. speaker has to be disconnected or removed. We *have* to order some kind of earphones and that I ordered the least expensive pair I could find that still gave good sound. I got the feeling that he didn't believe me about that or about the $10.00 charge for disconnecting the speaker or the 10% charge taken out for the welfare fund. You know, I'm beginning to get severely disappointed in Don. I'm not about to make any more deals with him and doubt that I'll even ask him to do anything for me again. He's too unreliable. All my life

I've tried to weed unreliable people out of my life. That's why I wouldn't have any dealings with Ken or Bob. But somehow I let Don slip by. Guess I was blinded by marrying Cheryl and then run into this mess and find myself convicted of crimes I had nothing to do with. Now I've had time to reflect on various events of the recent past and I'm not going to let it continue.

The next time I talk to Florence, I'll let her know that she needs to get in touch with both you and Randy. Yes, I *do* still want to have "that matter" handled the way we discussed. Remember, Joan Altman is willing to help out. By the way, Joan wants to come up here for a visit with me. I'll let you know when it, if it, happens.

Glad to hear that the book deadline has been extended. In case you still want it, I've rewritten 'Tranquility Garden' so that there are no syntax or other errors in it. I've let three people here (a neighbor, Unit Teacher, and an officer) read it. All three loved it, saying that it is extremely well written. The officer said that he could actually picture in his head the scenes as he read the story. He now wants to read anything else I've written or will write. This is the same officer that has treated me with open hostility since I got here. Insults, curses, etc. He heard my neighbor and I talking about it and asked if he could read it. I decided I had nothing to lose, so I let him. Since then, he's been treating me with respect; calling me Bill, instead of William or Suff; passing items from others to me and giving me extra food at suppertime. It's surprising how something like 10 pages of fiction can change a person's opinion of you. He now sees me as a person who is literate, rather than an ignorant animal.

Talking about the serial killing trials you've been researching: Have you heard about a black man convicted of serial killing in San Diego in '91 or '92? I saw a program about Serial Killers and this guy was mentioned. It was discovered that he killed several women in San Diego County. I don't remember his name or whether he killed prostitutes or just women in general. But from what I *can* remember of the program, he used a long, fixed-blade knife and there were several similarities between his crimes and those of which I was charged with and those I was convicted of. He is here at S.Q., also, but on a different yard and the other side of the building. Yes, he has a death sentence, also.

And, talking about the death penalty: As you probably know, Bill Bonin (the Freeway Killer), was executed at 12:13 A.M. last Friday (2/23). As you also know, he was on the same exercise yard as me. We wound up talking about death, reincarnation, space abductions, UFO's, Aliens and the supernatural. I understand why he wasn't afraid of death, especially after I got to talking to him about life after death. I do know that he became less ill-at-ease at the prospect of being executed. You might find some of these discussions he and I had interesting. I'll relate some of them to you later.

Well, I've missed mail pick-up tonight. So, I'll be sure to get this into tomorrow night's mail. I sure hope the rest of this year *is* healthy for me. The past two weeks were decidedly bad. For awhile there, I was wishing I was dead. That's how bad I felt because of the flu.

It's just after 1:00 A.M. and I need to get some sleep . . . I plan on going out tomorrow for some yard exercise. It'll be raining, but I can put up with that easily. Take care. Hope to see you soon.

> Best Wishes,
> (signed)
> Bill S

17 May 1996

Hello Brian,

I haven't been able to get hold of you for awhile now, so I thought I'd try it this way. I hope you get this letter before you come up here, if you're still planning on it. Things have been rather quiet here. It got *really* quiet for a couple days when the latest execution took place. In the early morning hours of May 3rd, Keith Danny Williams was executed. This was the guy whom the relatives of his victims pleaded that he not be executed and who was determined to have been mentally incompetent at the time of his crime. There were a lot of people here that were unhappy about that execution—both inmates *and* officers. A lot of people in here thought his death sentence should have been commuted to life without parole. But, the state had to get their pound of flesh in retaliation for his crimes. Ridiculous!

Brian—about that $50.00 I asked you to send to Jan Kolmetz for me, so he could order me some ribbons? Things have changed slightly. Instead of sending the money to Jan, would you send it to his sister, Margery.

She sent Jan some money and Jan used some of that money to place the ribbon order, so we both could get the ribbons now. Margery is also getting together a quarterly package and Jan wants the money you were going to send to him to go to his sister instead. That way she can use it to help pay for the contents of the package. If you can do that, I'd really appreciate it.

By the way, what do you think of my new typing font? It's costing me $10.00 (when I get some money, that is). As it stands now, I owe roughly $30.00 for this and that. I got a pair of good tennis shoes to wear, this type-wheel, the ribbon I'm now using and a few other necessities. Luckily, I can take my time paying off my debts because it's standard belief that no one's going anywhere for awhile.

Guess who I got a letter from? Tricia Barnaby. She has quit her private business and is now back with the Riverside Public Defender's Office. She says she's much happier there and, in the long run, will make more money. She runs into Peasley and Driggs all the time and she says they keep asking if I'm all right. She now works with Floyd Zagorsky a lot and he's constantly checking to see if she's heard from me. Of course, she hadn't. I sent her a card last Christmas and then a letter in answer to hers just last week. She asked a lot of questions about this place and my daily routine. I gave her a glossed over description of what life is like here, but not any great detail. I told her how you made it possible for me to get a tv, headphones and typewriter and that Driggs and Peasley haven't done a thing for me since I was sentenced. Something that bothers me, is that she says she feels responsible for my whole situation and wishes that she had more control over the outcome. She feels that my defense team, in toto, let me down. She wants the opportunity to help in any way she can to turn things around for me. She also says that while she turned her whole duplicate case file over to Peasley, she's retained all of her own personal work. She says she looks at it every day and is constantly on the lookout for material and information which can somehow be of aid to me. Since executions have started up again, she's more concerned than ever about my welfare. She also gave me her direct line at the PD's office and wants me to call her whenever I can. I haven't done so as yet. She wants to talk to me about conditions here and if there is anything I need or that she can arrange for me. I'm at a loss at what to do about her. For about the last several months I was in the county jail, I had a hard time talking to her and couldn't even look her in the eyes. I came to the realization that I had fallen in love with her and couldn't do anything about it. I can't even admit my feelings to her. I know that I have to be very careful as to what I say to her both on the phone and in my letters to her. That's the main reason why I haven't as yet called her. I *did* admit, though, that I always catch the sit-com "Home Improvement" because I like the character Jill (Patricia Richardson), and that she reminds me of her. We'll see how that admission goes across.

Since you haven't been able to make it up here yet, I decided to send you my answers to that death penalty questionnaire I filled out. You said that you were interested in reading them and possibly might want to include them in the book. Which raises that old question again: What's the latest news regarding it? I am rather concerned since the deadline has passed again. My mother has voiced her concerns regarding the book, also. So, the question remains: What's happening?

For your general information, I finally got a steady day and time scheduled for me to use the phone now. Every Sunday at 11:00 am I get to use the phone for one hour. So, plan on my calling every Sunday at 11:00, and 11:30 if you don't answer the first call.

I was watching a movie today that I found *very* interesting.

Especially the ending monologue by the actress. The name of the movie is "Listen to Me", starring Kirk Cameron, Jamie Gertz and Roy Scheider. It's a movie about a debating contest (West coast college vs Harvard) and the events leading up to the debate. Debate topic? Pro and con on the subject of abortion; Roe vs Wade. Rent the movie (I think it's on cassette) and pay close attention to the closing argument of the debate. The point that grabbed me so hard was Jamie Gertz's argument on life and death. She points out how important it is to *not* kill, regardless of the reasons or rationalizations. I think you might find it eye-opening and it would make a great argument for an appeal. If I could get a copy of that closing speech, I could turn it into what I think would be a powerful statement for a call to end the practice of administering a death sentence for any crime, especially one given to wrongly convicted people.

Well, I guess that's about all for now. Take care and I hope to hear from you soon, either when I call or when you get the chance to come up here for a visit. Until later . . .

Respectfully,
(signed)
Bill L. Suff

23 June 1996

Hello Brian,

How are you doing? I'm well enough now, but things are getting a bit tough here for me. I finally got over that respiratory flu that had me down and I'm still sleeping quite a lot, but I'm able to hold down all of my meals now. For awhile there, I felt like I was about to give up the ghost. Anyway, the sun out on the exercise yard helps a lot, too. I try to make it out there at least twice a week.

I guess you ran into some kind of difficulty again . . . the reason you still haven't been able to make it up here as yet for a visit. Sorry I haven't been trying to call you lately. Our phone lines on the fifth tier are temporarily out of order. The telephone people are rewiring the lines, adding some new features and some new hookups. They started working on the lines last week and the phones have been out since then. Trouble is, there's no definite date given when we are supposed to get to use the phone again. All of the other tiers still have their phones and can make calls. Their lines aren't being worked on yet. So, while others get to use the phone, those of us unfortunate enough to be up here on the fifth tier are stuck, unable to call our families or attorneys. Anyway, that's why I haven't called and am now resorting to this letter.

Got some interesting things to tell you about when I next get to talk to you or see you. There's someone new on the correspondence front for me. Someone new in Ireland. And the gentleman in Australia told me that there is a lady down under that is interested in writing to me and has asked if I want him to give her my address. I don't know about that. I haven't answered his letter as yet. I wouldn't mind writing to another lady, especially if there is a remote possibility of some kind of romance. I miss being allowed to say 'I love you' to someone and have them mean it when they say it to me. But I fear that most people want to correspond with me for the infamous prestige of saying they are writing to a death row prisoner, or specifically, to *the* Bill Suff! So I think I'll ask that guy to inquire further into her reasons for wanting to write to me. Oh yeah, he also wants to send me some nude photographs that he's latched on to. I'll have to tell him that I don't want them. Besides, they aren't allowed. I've found out that a few people on the bay side have subscriptions to Playboy. But that when the current subscriptions run out, they won't be allowed in again. Then the officers are supposed to begin shake-downs to take up all "pornographic materials." So if I don't have any of that stuff, they can't take it away from me. Right? Besides, that kind of material doesn't turn me on anyway. A fully dressed woman, wearing a nice blouse and skirt do more for me than nudity.

One of my next-door-neighbors got his hands on a couple "Writer's Digest" magazines and sent them over to me. I found some interesting articles in them: "Make Your Novel MOVE",

"How to Write Dialogue", "Find Your Novel's Missing Links", "Get Out And Write!", and "50 Best Short Story Markets". Very interesting reading. I kind of wish I had a subscription to this magazine.

When we last talked, you said that you were going to have an interview with Prosecutor Zellerbach. How did that interview go? Did he get upset for your asking pointed questions about some of the ambiguities in the evidence collected in my case? Did he stammer or hem and haw at answering them? Or did you get to ask those questions at all? Did he appear as bombastic as he did at my trial?

Now, on to another, more important matters. I'm in a little bit of a bind here. I relayed your words that you were going to immediately send that $50.00 to Jan's sister. Now Jan is rather unhappy with me because Margery told him the money never arrived. That's got Jan in a bind too, because Margery was going to use the money to purchase the things she was going to send in Jan's quarterly package. Now it's too late for Margery to send a 2nd quarter package. It seems those quarterly packages are something that people here get very upset about when they don't get theirs. Especially when they're used to getting them every quarter. My next door neighbor let me know that I can get a bad reputation among the other prisoners if I let things get out of hand. Making good on your word here is what keeps your reputation in good standing. If I tell someone that something is going to be taken care of and it isn't, my word isn't worth diddly-squat. To give you an example: a couple of weeks ago a guy on one of the other yards got sliced across his face and forearm. It seems he got something from one of the other guys on his yard and promised to pay for it with stamps. When he didn't pay for several weeks, he was approached about it. He said he was still trying to get them. A few more weeks went by without him paying his debt, so the second guy came out with a sharpened piece of hard acrylic and cut him. So anyway, if you're going to send that money to Margery (or Jan) please do so soon. If not, please let me know asap so I can try to find some other way of getting the money for Jan. Please, let me know something soon so I can get word to him. I don't want to get the reputation that I can't be trusted or one that is worse.

Well, all of that being said, I guess I'd better close here and get this into tonight's mail pick-up. Take care and write me soon . . . unless you're going to make it up here anytime soon. Take care and drive carefully.

Respectfully,
(signed)
Bill Suff

---

19 August 1996

Hello Brian,

Just a quick note to you before you come up (I hope). I'm enclosing a Visitor's Questionnaire Form for Lee (Lea, Leah, or Leigh, however she spells her name). She can fill it out and send it to the following address:

San Quentin State Prison
Visiting Room Office
San Quentin, Calif. 94974

This way she can come up whenever she wants to (Thursday through Sunday), to have me sign papers, or whatever, as need be. If she doesn't need it, save it for whomever might come along in the future (Bonnie?). Take care and I'll see you next Monday.

With best regards,
(signed)
Bill

PS: If you can locate any of this kind of plain paper in a stationery store, would you please send me a hundred sheets or so of varying colors? I can receive up to a hundred sheets per package. Also, from an office supplies store, could you locate a couple specific pens for me? They are the Papermate Flexgrip Roller • Fine point with a gray barrel. One black ink and one blue ink. The pens they have in the canteen here are worthless. They start skipping as soon as you begin using them. If you can do this, I'd really appreciate it. By the way, you cannot bring them up with you to give to me in our visit. Stationery, stamps and envelopes . . . yes. Pens . . . no. Thanks. Bill.

(signed)
BLS

4 September 1996

Brian,

As to those pens I wanted you to get me . . . I talked to the legal officer a little while ago and he confirmed that I cannot receive them in a legal supplies envelope. He talked to his boss and was told that. I'm only allowed to receive paper, envelopes and stamps that way. Like I told you today, I will have to get them in a quarterly package. So, what I will do is send you a 'Quarterly Package Form' for you to send them in to me. However, I think there is a specific limit as to how many I can receive in any one package. When you look over the rest of the list you will see some of the other items I'm allowed to receive and the limiting quantities of each item. If you want to include some of those other items, I'd appreciate it. However, there are some items listed on the form that I absolutely cannot stand, so there would be no sense in sending them to me. But, I'll point those items out when I send you the 'Q.P.F.' By the way, I forgot to ask when you were here today, but were you able to locate any of this type of paper? If so, you *are* allowed to send that to me via 'Legal Mail', as I've already explained.

I hope you were able to make it back to the airport without any trouble. I caught the 4:00 P.M. news a little while ago. They were reporting an auto accident on the Golden Gate Bridge that blocked traffic for awhile in both directions. It wasn't a bad one, the people involved only received minor cuts and bruises. I think the cars were even able to be driven away. There's been a big controversy going on these past few months regarding how dangerous it is to drive over it. There have been several rush-hour, head-on collisions and people are finally tired of it. Within the next six months, the traffic department in San Francisco is supposed to install a movable, cement barrier as a lane divider across the bridge. During the peak rush hours, there is only one lane open to the lesser amount of traffic. The major amount of commuting traffic gets the rest of the lanes. To date, they've been using those red and orange plastic posts as a direction divider. The new divider will be zipper-like cement barricades. Too many people have been driving head-on into oncoming traffic and getting killed in the accident. But it took the death of some assemblyman's teenage son or daughter recently before they began to consider serious methods of preventing these types of accidents.

Well, I guess that's about all there is to say to you for right now. Until later, take care and I'll talk to you as soon as we get our telephone back.

Best wishes,
Bill

BILL L. SUFF
J-83402 — 1EB65
SAN QUENTIN STATE PRISON
SAN QUENTIN, CA 94974

16 September 1996

Hello Brian,

FINALLY! I just got hold of the property officer today and got the enclosed Quarterly Package Form (QPF) from him. All you need do is sign your name and write your relationship as either 'Attorney' or 'friend' in the respective places at the bottom of the form. Then clip along the dotted line and make sure that it's securely attached to the *outside* of the package where it will be readily visible to the property officer when it arrives here. Be sure to follow the "General

Instructions" shown above the dotted line. If there is even a hint of an infraction to those rules, it will be refused here. You can send the package out by either U.P.S. or regular mail, certified. But, U.P.S. is preferred. As you can see under the heading of "Miscellaneous Items", #8 states that I can only receive (4) writing implements. So if you want to send me more, let me know and I'll get another QPF and send that one to you also.

The reason I circled #6 was to let you know that if you can find the type of paper this letter is typed on, you can put one or two reams of it in the package, also. Or the paper can come in under a separate cover as Legal Supplies. I cleared that one with the legal mail officer. The legal mail office considers envelopes, stamps and paper as legal supplies. For some strange reason, though, they don't consider a pen or pencil as legal supplies!!? The legal mail officer couldn't give me an answer on that one. San Quentin methodology!

If you decide you want to send some other items in the package, here's a list of what I would appreciate:

FOOD ITEMS

#1 - Any of the soft Granola Bars are good; M&M's, Lemon Drops, etc. Especially Tootsie Rolls (not the Pops - I guess they're afraid we'll make some kind of stabbing weapon out of the paper handle.)

#2 - Just about any kind of the cream filled cookies are good for me. No coconut types, though. Allergy.

#4 - Sunflower Seeds (shelled)! My great love. I used to stop on my way to work each morning and buy several bags of the Planter's type to last me throughout the day.

#6 - In particular, the Twinkies and chocolate cup cakes. None of those Puff Balls that Rosie O'Donnell loves so much, though . . . Coconut! Ugh!!

#7 - The only dried meat products I like are the beef, turkey, and ostrich jerkys.

#9 - Instant teas are great, especially with lemon and presweetened.

#10 - Any of the Kool-Aid powder drinks or Tang drinks.

#11 - Any of the large or twin size chips are okay. 'Tater chips are preferred over the Doritos brand. Doritos and Fritos are acceptable, though.

- and -

#12 - Any of the Hormel or Top Shelf type meals that only require boiling (my microwave oven blew a fuse and won't work now - ha, ha).

Any product that says "refrigeration recommended" on it is not allowed.

As to the Clothing and other Miscellaneous items listed goes, there are a few things I'd like, but not bad enough to trouble you with them.

Now, I'm not asking you to send any of the items I mentioned in this letter. But if you decide to make this dreary existence a little better and *want* to send some of those items, it would be appreciated more than words can describe. It's entirely up to you. You will notice, though, that I didn't list either tobacco or coffee. That's because I would have no use for them. Besides, all of the regular officers here know that I cannot deal with those items.

I got a visit today (Monday) from Patty Daniels. I hope you don't mind, but I gave her your new phone number and address. She wanted to talk to you about how you were going to set up our meeting in the conference room (that we didn't get). Seems the CAP attorneys have been told they cannot have any legal visits in that room. She was surprised when I told her that we were supposed to get that room. So don't be surprised if a phone call comes out of the blue from her for you. She was here to check up on me to see how I was doing. She almost blew a gasket when she saw that I still haven't received an order for modified cuffs. When she saw the marks on my wrists left by the single cuffs, she began to give the officer handcuffing me a tongue lashing. I calmed her down, though. But she's going to pull a run around the end play on the system to get me an order for modified cuffs. She was *very* interested in what

Don's up to now. She didn't know a lot about the stuff he's been pulling and she's got a little bit of temper directed at him. Anyway, all-in-all, it was a pretty good visit. She bought me a Pepsi and a chicken breast sandwich when she got here. Those were like manna from heaven. Only trouble is we only got to talk for one hour, instead of the two she had originally planned on. Seems, like our visit, someone else was booked into our visiting booth sooner than they were supposed to be. Oh well, mix-ups are still happening.

Well, I still have to write (type) up a couple things for Patty tonight, so I guess I'd better close here. Take care and write back when you get a chance.

All my best to you.
Respectfully,
(signed)
Bill L. Suff

CHAPTER 16

Piss-Poor Protoplasm

From the beginning, I assumed that if I dug hard enough I would find the "smoking gun" in Bill Suff's background that turned him into a serial killer.

And, once you've smoked out your killer, the profilers automatically assume that you will turn up a youth spent wetting the bed, starting fires, and vivisecting/dissecting small animals. This "unholy triad" of nasty behavior seems to be a constant. Once born, the serial killer "larva" does in fact behave in ways that give away the truth of his inner turmoil, if only we are wise enough to take heed. Of course, once he reaches the "pupal" state, he's killing people.

I asked Ann about Bill's activities as a kid.

"No, Billy was always a good boy," she said, then thought for a minute, and then added: "Now Donny, he wet the bed 'til he was six, and Bobby, well, he was the firestarter, and Kenny, well, we never could seem to keep pets very long. But Bill, no, he never did any of that stuff."

I believed her. But maybe Bill didn't have to dirty his hands because whatever release comes or whatever curiosity is fulfilled by such activity was his by osmosis, by vicarious living. Indeed, as the brightest, strongest, and oldest of the bunch, maybe Bill was the one who insidiously created the atmosphere where all these things could take place under the same roof. Maybe Bill sort of moved each of his brothers into doing the sick things he fantasized.

Bill hinted at it when he was recounting his heroic experiences as a volunteer firefighter, first with the forestry service while a senior in high school and then with the local Perris Fire Department immediately after graduation.

"Y'know, seems like every time I went out there to fight a fire, Bobby'd be there on his bike, cheering me on. He just always seemed to come riding up, like he knew I'd be there even before I did, before we got the call."

"You're saying he started the fires?"

"I'm saying he enjoyed watching his big brother be a hero."

And big brother enjoyed being a hero being watched and appreciated by everyone else.

But, if all this somehow represents Bill's expression of the "unholy triad", then the smoking gun had to have smoked long before.

And no one, from the prosecution to the defense to the reporters who mined this turf, none of them has ever come up with anything ghastly that Bill Suff endured while growing up.

The Suff home was not exactly the Cleavers'; there was definitely booze, adultery, and one-stop discipline, but not to an extent not prevalent in a great many American homes across all economic classes. The only rumor—and that's all it is—that there was something slightly more problematic was an indefinite allegation of incest between eldest sister Roberta and one or more of the brothers, but, sad to say, even that is not enough to make a serial killer, or else Miss America would be out there leaving bodies in her wake.

However, the Suff family does have a sort of paranoia that could prove more than a little disconcerting to a child, and, although the Suffs all talk to one another constantly, bicker at one another constantly, battle with each other constantly, move in and out of each other's homes constantly, depend on each other for everything, they make no bones about the fact that none of them trusts the other and that truth may be acceptably sacrificed for a perceived greater good or just to keep a momentary peace.

There probably never was any incest, but they all sure as heck do act inbred. Their world extends out over many siblings and marriages and friendships, across county and state lines, but some-how it's a very very small world indeed.

And, whenever you circumnavigate this world you always seem to find yourself coming back to Ann.

She's a subtle creature, that Ann. And remember, I like her. But, as direct and outspoken as she is, there are always layers of complex emotional meaning to her simple statements.

Remember the old joke about the two psychiatrists passing each other in the hall—one says to the other: "Good morning!" And the second psychiatrist replies: "Good morning to you, too!" And then, as they each walk away, they each say to themselves: "I wonder what he meant by that?"

Ann has that effect on you. She's like Chinese food. You order it with no MSG, you eat it and comment on how good it tastes without MSG, and then later you're sure it had MSG.

Both Ann and Bill tell the story of how one day she caught teenaged Bill naked in the bathroom in the presence of sister Roberta. Ann yanked Bill out of there by the ear, dragged him to his room, and grounded him for his impropriety, even though both she and he swear he had not touched Roberta in any way. Nonetheless, when Ann caught Bill, the first words out of her mouth were: "It's a damn good thing you didn't enter her!"

Now where in the hell did that idea come from? Either Bill was not merely naked but aroused, or he really did have Roberta cornered. Or perhaps Ann was flashing on some experience from the past, from Bill's or her own, but, no matter, her worry was infectious. And that desperate a worry can become a self-fulfilling prophecy. If you really are innocent but are consistently accused of a crime, then you might as well commit the crime. And, if your superego is thus far checking your baser instincts by making you feel guilty about having such impure thoughts, then those thoughts somehow become okay when your very own mom admits to them by accusing you. She didn't put the idea in your head, she just affirmed it.

And then, despite her ability to read your mind, all too often this mom couldn't find water if she fell out of a boat. Prescience turned to quackery, brilliance to folly, wisdom to naiveté.

She had no idea, for example, that William Sr. would abandon her that day after dropping her at work. And she never ever knew about the divorce suit and demand for custody of all the kids that he filed against her a few years earlier when the family lived in Fresno. Maybe he never served her, or maybe she's lying, or maybe she simply blocks out perceptions that would be too painful.

But, determined to protect her brood, Ann takes up her children's fights even as she won't allow them to defend themselves. Then she judges them. She loves them unconditionally but she pronounces their guilt. On *Leeza*, no less.

And Mama Ann never grants salvation.

She controls by threat of too much love. When second husband, Shorty, died, Ann devastated Bill by saying that she could not even read his will to the kids because in it Shorty admonished and chided them for not being caring towards him. He had served as the "real", I'll-stand-by-you father to them, yet they had not returned the favor and acted like his loving kids. Of course, Ann disagreed, knowing how caring and considerate Bill and the others had been to Shorty, but from his grave Shorty apparently had another opinion.

For Bill, once again, rejection. But rejection by whom? By Shorty, or by Ann? Because Ann would never show Bill the will, so maybe Ann was lying, maybe this was just her being cruel.

Interestingly, it is Bill who tells this story. Ann swears that she never told Bill any such thing, and that Shorty's will was not uncomplimentary to her children in any way.

At the time Shorty died, Bill was in the midst of his killing fury—hookers were dropping like flies—and so it may well be that his killing mind-set found fuel in rejection even where there was no rejection at all. He just needed to justify acts that he was powerless to control, to pretend that he was in control when he had no control.

Certainly, Bill sees rejection everywhere. He smiles and puffs himself up with positive thoughts, but he always expects to be whupped. In all things, he's never surprised when he finds himself surprised. He wears the martyr's robe well—just another of his uniforms.

The thing that amazes me is just how differently Bill and Ann remember past events. My sense is that Bill rewrites the practical truth to fit his emotional truth, so he's not being dishonest even though he's wrong.

In November of 1966, Ann went into labor. William Sr. drove her to the hospital, and the kids all stayed at home, with sixteen-year-old Big Brother Bill in charge.

Bill recalls being incredibly excited at the prospect of a new sibling, but, for two days, he heard nothing from his parents. Then Dad and Mom came home from the hospital without the baby.

Dad said the baby had died, and both he and Mom were not going to talk about it.

So they didn't.

The dead baby was named Glenda Marie.

And, according to Bill, there was never a funeral nor any explanation as to what happened. He was distraught, but he couldn't let on. He was also suspicious, but he couldn't prove anything. Years later, when he was in jail in Texas, he broached the subject of Glenda Marie to his mother. He insisted that he was saving money in order to buy the sister he never knew a headstone, and he wanted to know where she was buried. The answer was Lake Elsinore Cemetery.

Indeed, I checked—Glenda Marie Suff, born and died November 6, 1966, is buried in Lake Elsinore Cemetery. At the same time, the County has no live birth or death record.

Elsinore being Elsinore, you could pretty much get a cemetery to bury anything you wanted without any questions being asked. They'd probably dig stuff up for you, too. The cemeteries there need the business. It's tough to compete when sand dunes are free. And rattlesnakes do a dirge you don't forget.

Meanwhile, Ann tells me that Bill's story is all wrong anyway. Yes, Ann was an emotional wreck over the dead baby—Glenda Marie's lungs had collapsed just after birth, when the doctor clipped her umbilical cord—and Bill was also visibly upset when he heard the news, although he tried to maintain a stiff upper lip for the sake of his parents and siblings, but there was indeed a funeral several days later, special services attended by Bill and all the family in order to provide needed closure.

Ann has no idea why Bill can't remember the funeral other than the experience was too upsetting for him.

Not long thereafter, William Sr. fled.

Soon enough after that, Bill married Teryl even though she was pregnant with her stepfather's child.

After giving up that child, Bill and Teryl had children of their own—first Bill Jr. and then Dijianet. Teryl was always cheating on Bill, and during their fights she would tell him that his kids were not his kids and that blood-typing proved it, even though their resemblance to him was undeniable.

Bill Jr. was repeatedly and severely beaten until he suffered permanent brain damage. He was taken away from Bill and Teryl after they were arrested for killing Dijianet.

Had Bill's Riverside jury seen the autopsy photos of Dijianet, there would have been no need for a trial. There's a big tall tree out front of the courthouse and plenty of stout rope in Riverside, and Bill would have swung and everyone would have gone home and slept well that night.

In fact, I still don't know how Bill Suff, child killer, survived prison in Texas and ever swam back to Riverside—that's a Papillon-like feat. But that tells you just how truly innocent-seeming the captive Bill is.

During the two and a half months of her too-short life, Dijianet Suff had had virtually every bone in her body broken, all in various stages of healing and damage—she'd been beaten from the first day she came home from the hospital.

When she died, there were cigarette burns found on her feet, and bite marks on her arms. On her head was the hemorrhaged outline of a man's hand—even Chris Darden could've made that outline fit Bill Suff.

In Dijianet's stomach, the coroner found Kool-Aid and spaghetti.

But, what killed baby Dijianet was a ruptured liver. It had been exploded. Someone had squeezed her around the middle like Popeye bursting open a can of spinach.

Bill's next child, Bridgette, by second wife Cheryl, was mercifully but too late taken away by Riverside child welfare authorities after being hospitalized for a blood clot on the brain and all sorts of broken bones in late 1991. She was just three and a half months old. Like Bill Jr., she too suffers from permanent brain damage caused by the abuse.

Incredibly, Bill Suff was allowed to go on with his life and his murders even while under investigation for child abuse, even while on parole for child murder.

Bill said then and says now that both his wives were lousy mothers—"They'd always let me nurse," he smiles, "but never the babies."—and he blames a family friend and a photographer for Bridgette's injuries—the friend tossed the baby playfully and hurt her ribs; the baby fell on the floor and lifted up her head and hit the bedframe; her wrists were fractured when the photographer *posed her* with her sweet little head perched on her hands and looking at the camera.

At least the CIA wasn't involved this time.

But the question remains: How did all this horror come to pass?

And the answer seems to be: one horror at a time.

Building, building, building.

No smoking guns, no one to blame—no one, that is, except the monster himself. Nothing went wrong for Bill Suff until he went wrong, and that probably happened inside his head, happened to his worldview, long before he acted out in any way that would bespeak it.

Randy Driggs explains it thus: "Piss-poor protoplasm."

It was in the gene, man, maybe the same gene that makes Bill truly drunk on nonalcoholic grape juice or deathly ill from drinking just plain coffee or allergic to grass and pollen and life itself.

Because, growing up, nothing happened to Bill that hasn't happened to innumerable people, none of whom became serial killers. But, once Bill began to perceive horror and once he began to commit horror, there was no turning back. Once he was swelled with guilt, he was as good as dead, dead but alive, and fantasy took hold.

Could something have happened that would have saved Bill from the horror?

Maybe in a parallel universe, but not in ours. Bill's salvation is his creativity; his writing channels the monster within, holds it at bay, allows his humanity to come to the fore. Locked up in jail, there is no monster, there is only the writer, but ours is a universe where you don't get locked up until you prove you don't belong out there.

More's the pity, for him, for us, for his victims.

CHAPTER 17

The Death Sentence Equation

The air was chilly and the ground was moist and smelled like dirt. That fresh, crisp, thickening smell that tickles the insides of your nose and plumes its way into your head just up behind your eyes and somehow makes you feel really alive. Not like flowery smells, not all fake and syrupy and swallowed rather than inhaled. Dirt smells like, well, dirt, and not like anything else. It's got that clean, metallic bite. It's what our ancestors crawled out of, and it's where we all wind up—we've got a primal connection to it, and the smell awakens those connections and stirs our sense of belonging.

If only she could fire up that dirt and pump it into her veins, thought Carol Lynn Miller, maybe then she wouldn't need the heroin anymore. The heroin was so warm—a flood of warmth and passion and comfort that made her body feel dully right, that floated her up on gentle hands, passing her out of harm's way—but the cool, rusty dirt, that was a reminder that, if she cared, she could have a future again.

Carol was thirty-five years old. She'd had one marriage and it had been really bad. Actually, it wasn't the marriage that was so bad, it was her husband—he was a bad one, all right. He liked to rob people, liked to assault them, liked to take what he wanted when he wanted it. And he'd wanted Carol to join in. He was the one who'd introduced her to heroin. He'd shown her how to do it, how to tie off her arm just so, how to melt the drug over the flame, how to swill it into the hypodermic, how to blow out the air without losing even a drop of that precious liquid, that liquid heaven. And he'd told her quite correctly just how it was gonna be: you'll feel the prick and it'll hurt—hell, you knot the tourniquet *intentionally so it hurts, so it pinches your skin—you want to feel a little pain, because then you'll be amazed at how the drug takes it all away, the superficial pain and the deep-down heartaches, everything that bothers you just won't bother you anymore.*

At least, that is, not 'til the drug starts to wear off and then you find yourself facing a whole new fear.

But that fear you don't need to fear, because that fear is easily fixed . . . with a fix. And your whole life suddenly becomes so simple: You do what you have to do to get your drug. It's not that nothing else matters, it's that there is nothing else.

Interestingly, the heroin had saved Carol from her ex, had saved her life. Without the drug, she'd never have left him, and he'd probably have gotten her killed in one of his crime sprees, or else killed her himself in one of his rages.

But she'd needed her fix, and he was no provider, and so she'd lit out on her own.

She settled in Riverside, in a place called Rubidoux, by Lake Elsinore, and she took up prostitution.

Carol Miller had a home, a house she rented there, but she didn't like staying in it. Sometimes she was afraid her ex would show up, other times she was afraid no one would ever come knock on her door and she'd just die there, alone, unnoticed, undiscovered, with Publishers' Clearinghouse Sweepstakes entries piling up in her mailbox.

So, some nights—too many nights—Carol crashed at the homes of friends or regular johns. She'd put in her work hours, get a fix, and then knock on the door of someone she knew. If they let her in, she'd go to sleep, and then wake up in the dead of night and steal whatever cash she could find so she could buy her next fix. She expected her friends to put up with that, promising to pay them back, and the johns she'd repay with blow jobs issued on the spot. After a while her friends stopped letting her in, and even the johns insisted that, if she stayed, she had to sleep outside. But even that cost her blow jobs.

The week of February 8, 1990, Carol Miller ripped off one friend for fifteen bucks, fixed, and made her way to a john who'd actually sort of been a boyfriend for a few months the year before, before he'd gotten tired of her waking up, not knowing where she was, and then fleeing from him once she got her bearings. In fact, he appreciated and took it as a sign of caring that she got embarrassed when she sobered, but he'd suddenly realized one morning that he liked her better high, and that made him rethink what he thought about himself. So he called off their "relationship", bought himself two pairs of Dockers in the same olive drab, and actually joined a bowling league. Nonetheless, when Carol showed up early in the week of February 8, 1990, this john unzipped, sat back in his rocking chair, unloaded himself down her throat, and then told her it was okay with him if she wanted to sleep outside under his porch. Not on the porch where she could be seen by the neighbors, under the porch where it would be like she wasn't really there at all.

Gratefully, Carol Miller got down on her hands and knees, rolled under the porch, and curled up in the dirt.

And, when that tangy dirt smell permeated her brain, she just knew she was finally going to be purged. She was going to get off the drug, she was going to quit hooking, she was going to let Mother Earth herself show her the way.

Carol Miller sneezed. Then she smiled to no one but herself. What was it her grandma had told her when she was a little girl, what was that superstition? "If you tell yourself something and then you sneeze, you're sneezing to the truth of it—what you want will be."

Lying there in the dirt under that porch, it was the safest and most secure that Carol Miller had felt in a long time.

A stone's throw away, in Elsinore, Bill Suff was wooing Cheryl Lewis. Actually, he'd already wooed her and won, and now he was trying to sleep.

And Cheryl wouldn't let him.

She wanted to make love.

She was seventeen years old, a senior in high school, and not the sort of girl that men pay much attention to. A little too square, a little too squat, with teeth that came at you from all directions and red hair of a dark shade that always looked dirty even when it was clean.

But, Cheryl liked sex and she was free with it, and that attribute of personality made up for whatever she lacked in appearance. Sex was also a great way for her to connect with someone without having to talk, and mostly all she had to talk about was her life and how much she didn't like it. Cheryl was a born complainer, and she was shrill about it, as most complainers are. "Whine" is not merely a concept, it's a sound, the noise of a worldview gone small and sour, multilingual, multicultural, hell, multispecies. There is no animal that can't whine.

But Bill didn't seem to mind Cheryl's negativity. He seemed to want to fix her complaints and the main way he did that was by ordering her around.

Weirdly, it worked. It wasn't that she thought she was making him happy by doing what he asked, it was that he had her convinced that what he was telling her to do would make her happy. He really had her best interests at heart, and damn if they didn't coincide with his own! This was truly a match made in heaven.

The only problem was that Bill wouldn't make love to Cheryl. No sexual contact whatsoever. They'd known each other for a month now, and she'd moved in with him to get away from her parents, and she desperately wanted to show him just how warm and talented she could be, but he wouldn't touch her. He even tried to make her sleep on the couch, but she crept into his bed every night as soon as he started to snore. Then she cuddled him. If she went too far, he booted her back to the couch.

He'd told her they'd be married, and she believed him, so that only made it more incomprehensible that he wouldn't have sex with her. She just didn't quite believe it when he insisted that there'd be no sex until she graduated high school and turned eighteen. Since they were maybe going to get married in just a few weeks, in March, in Vegas, did that mean Bill didn't intend to make love to her on their wedding night? Was he really going to wait? Could he really resist? Could it be he wasn't attracted to her? What kind of marriage would they have if that were the case?

"We'll make love when it's right," he'd told her, "and then I'll show you how beautiful it can be."

He believed she was a virgin, and she let him believe it. She was not a good liar, but she lied when he put the question to her directly, lied in a way that she meant for him to see she was lying. It was okay to "pretend" things with Bill, that was the great and comforting thing about him: reality didn't matter, reality didn't exist for him—whatever he chose to believe, that became reality. Cheryl knew she wasn't too bright, wasn't too astute, but even she could see that Bill lived for his fantasies, and that meant that she could suddenly become everything she was not, everything she wanted to be. She might even find that, with Bill, she'd have nothing left to complain about. Wouldn't that be something! So, yeah, Cheryl became a virgin again, and someday Bill would teach her all about love.

Meanwhile, she was more determined than ever to seduce him. She even thought that might be part of his game. He wanted her to play the virgin but he also wanted her to be a whore. No matter what she did, it was what he wanted. She was completely in his thrall, completely in his control, everything she did was right. And so there would come a moment, she was sure of it, a moment when his guard would be down and she would do something irresistible, something fetching and winsome—Bill's first wife had been sixteen, Cheryl was seventeen, he obviously liked 'em young, so Cheryl would do something childish, something devilish, something to make him take her over his knee, and that would excite him—she knew it and the thought of it actually kind of excited her, too.

But one thing was for certain, when Bill and Cheryl first made love, she'd have to bleed. Instinctively, she knew he'd look, knew he'd want proof. He'd probably even want it to hurt a little, so he could be responsible both for the pain and for the pleasure that would take it away. Reality would momentarily intersect with fantasy, as it does now and again, and everything would have to be in its right place.

Cheryl had a friend at work, at the Circle K—she could talk to her about how to fake the blood. How hard could it be?

February 8, 1990.

Do you know where you were or what you were doing on that date?

I'd have to think a little to remember exactly where I was that particular year, but I know what I was doing that day without having to think at all. That's because I do the same thing every February 8, as the sun goes down wherever I am and the shadow fingers reach out for me.

February 8 is the anniversary of the deaths of my mother, brother, and best friend. I light candles to them every February 8, and, as I touch match to wicks, I close my eyes and I open my mind and I see the dead as they were in life. I make a new memory of an old one, of the last time I saw each of them, as I looked around at my mom and my friend in the backseat, as I turned and idly chatted with my brother in the passenger seat next to me. I think about their clothes, their eyeglasses, their posture, their skin tone, the expressions on their faces. Driving to Vegas that day was a time I actually took stock of them, actually listened to them, was actually concerned with how they were doing. For some years I'd been consumed with myself and my schoolwork and my creative projects, but this trip wasn't about me, it was about my mom and her new life, and I wanted to understand her fears and peer into her dreams. I wanted to return the favor of strength for once.

So, as I look back every February 8 and make that past present again, as I see my mother, brother, and friend, I remember them as innocent and I momentarily remember myself as innocent, too—I remember what it was like truly not to know that death was just a few yards and a blown tire ahead.

Yes, I remember how it felt to be in a state of grace; I remember life before the fall.

And I know now that, had I been less innocent, they'd all still be alive.

"Original sin" was a setup, a stacked deck, a sure thing—Adam and Eve never had a chance. As theologist, psychologist, and physiologist will tell you, the pursuit of pleasure is ingrained, the elements of survival are pleasurable, and babies are born to trust and count on the care and concern of others to feed that survival/pleasure drive; but pain is knowledge that has to be learned, and danger doesn't exist until you bite the apple and the serpent bites you back. You don't know about trouble until you get in some. And then it's too damn late.

Where our car slid off the road out in the middle of the desert, there just happened to be a flood control concrete culvert. That meant the grade dropped off sharply, and that meant the car would flip. Anywhere else—before or after—we come to a gentle stop, no harm done.

But, if we hadn't been speeding, maybe we don't slide off the road at all.

There's no safe speed for every eventuality, and going through life at a crawl is dangerous on its own terms and likely to get you run over; but speeding down the open road has always been a powerful seductress for me, not because I get someplace quicker, rather because the sensation of speed is an all-encompassing world where time, space, sight, and sound all merge, where I become that supercharged subatomic particle of no matter but infinite mass, in all the universe at once, not grounded at all, just blasting through the cosmos. I'd give anything to climb aboard the Space Shuttle—I can hardly wait for the "Jew in Space" program—but the next best thing is a fast car, a tank of gas, a fat cigar, rock and roll on the radio, and a long, paved spine up the middle of the night.

Risk isn't the issue. The rattle of a fast car gives way to eerie screaming white silence in a faster car, and the exhilaration is the rush itself, not being on the edge. The moment I feel on the edge—anytime anywhere—I ease off the accelerator pedal. I don't like taking chances, don't like feeling out of control. And that also means I don't like getting stopped by cops, don't like putting my life in the hands of "authorities" who could tell me to get down on my hands and knees and bark like a dog and respond to the name "Butt-boy". I steer clear of people with any kind of badge, express or implied. So, no matter that I used to speed like mad, I've never had a speeding ticket because I'm ever alert and always willing to slow. This isn't a game—I'm not out to prove I can break the law, not out to show that I'm cleverer than the highway patrol. Then again, at full speed on an open road, the only way you can possibly get caught is by not realizing that you just lapped the officer in question and sucked the ketchup off his fries with your tail-draft. Otherwise, if you're doing 110, 120, no cop's about to "routinely" prowl up on you at 130, 140, and give you the required quarter-mile pace before he hits the siren. As long as you always stay out of sight ahead of the cop on his beat, you don't exist for him. You're safe.

The key to life, the one true bit of grown-up wisdom true for everyone at every time, is that you must strive not to be noticed except when you want to be. And then, how and when you choose to be noticed tells us all what sort of person you are.

Back on the relevant February 8 on the highway to Vegas, I had no notion that I was taking a chance and no sense that I was even remotely out of control. Divorce was making my mother's and my brother's and my own future unclear but not uncertain. I didn't know what tomorrow would bring, but I had no idea at all that there might not even be a tomorrow.

So, as I had done on innumerable occasions, I sped. I had the car maxed out. We'd sonic boomed so many miles per hour and RPMs earlier, blasted clear of the turbulence, and now we were rocketing peacefully through the thin air at the top of the world. Beneath us, the rest of humanity moved at a slower pace, like their clocks were wound down. Yo, Einstein and your dog, Relativity! We've left you behind, man! Woof! We'd left our cares behind and our pasts behind, and the future was beautiful and limitless, and we were light.

Nothing and no one could touch us now.

Once we crashed, I learned different.

Danger is everywhere, it's there whether you recognize it or not. It's always been there from the moment you left the womb, from even before that. If I'd known, I wouldn't have sped. But no one had told me, and my mother and my father had gone out of their way to protect me from it. No serpents in the world they were bequeathing me. You can't conceive a child if you feel the hot breath of danger on your neck, if you see its yellow eyes burning through the mist, hear the sharp scrape of its scales as it climbs the next streetlamp. No, in order to parent, you delude yourself into thinking that your wisdom, your ability to recognize danger, will protect your child and help you steer him or her away from it.

Now I've learned. No more speeding. Not like before anyway. Not as fast. Not for long. Never with anyone in the car. Now when

I do speed it's not so much fun, it's not pure anymore. Now it truly is a sin.

So, on February 8 every year, I celebrate life by facing the death of innocence. It's a wrong equation, and someday I suspect I'll recompute it. I hang on to "the accident" as if, by forgetting it, I'll finally lose the people I love. I've learned a lesson, and I'm not ready to unlearn it. Meanwhile, I have a friend who was just sixteen when she lost her mother to cancer. She thinks of her mother by remembering how they'd do the bunny hop together, how they'd laugh and play. Someday I'd like to find those memories for myself. Someday I'd like to reclaim my innocence. I think I'm getting closer, sneaking up on it. Maybe this year I'll light candles on birthdays rather than deathdays.

As for Bill Suff, the week of February 8, 1990, he was avoiding sex with Cheryl because he'd learned his own lesson. No matter how he explained it to her, it really had nothing to do with any moral stand and even less to do with redemption. He knew that Cheryl's parents hated him, hated the very idea of him, this pompous, shiftless, grown man who'd seduced their childish child and borne her away.

Bill knew and Bill worried that if he screwed Cheryl, her parents could nail him for statutory rape, and that would be a parole violation that would send him back to jail in Texas for the rest of his life. That was Bill's equation.

So, he maintained the discipline to spurn Cheryl's hot advances, determined to stave off overdue punishment.

For anyone who believes that the threat of jail is a deterrent to crime, here's proof of it, but it doesn't work the way you'd think.

See, while Bill sighed relief and patted himself on the back for his show of inner strength and wisdom, it was a lot easier to avoid Cheryl on those nights when he'd come home after raping and murdering prostitutes. He was sated then, and he wanted to be alone with his fantasy memories and his totems. He wanted to make sure Cheryl didn't see the scratches that some of his victims gave him when they foolishly fought back. And, of course, Cheryl was his alibi, physically and psychologically. The times of the murders could never be re-created exactly by the cops, so Bill could always claim he was home with Cheryl. And why would a man go out and kill hookers when he was living with the woman he loved?

So much for deterrence. Somehow, even the threat of a death sentence was no deterrent at all to these new crimes. Deterrence only comes after you get caught, after danger becomes real, palpable. Now you know better for the next time. Once disaster came to pass for me, I didn't speed at all for years and years. I owned a Porsche and I never took it past fifty-five. My friends laughed at me, fellow motorists honked and cursed, and I just nodded inwardly: I knew something they didn't know, I was now right and they were all wrong. That's deterrence. It only works when you're not really a criminal.

As for Bill, he couldn't extrapolate that lesson from his learning. He was undeterred with respect to new crimes because he was only worried about doing the time for the crime he'd already been convicted of. That sentence hung over his head, but it did not exist for him until it was formally pronounced. I would trade my life to bring back my family—it's not a police matter, it's personal, it's internal; but Bill has never been concerned about bringing back Dijianet, he just doesn't want to be punished for her death, and he never once considered the possibility of punishment all the weeks he was killing her. To him, "law-abiding" means nothing more nor less than not getting caught, and, if you don't get caught or you don't get punished, then there was no crime at all. Criminality is to him a judgment imposed by others; he has no moral sense himself.

That's what makes Bill a criminal, and that's why he's undeterred when he contemplates the next horror he wants to inflict on the world.

So, being convicted of Dijianet's murder taught Bill one thing and one thing only: how to be a better murderer the next time around.

What he learned and learned well was how not to get caught.

And a whole lot of girls in Southern California proved his point.

Carol Miller was beat and cold and dirty and she had the shakes. Or maybe it was the mirror. Maybe she was rock steady and it was the mirror that was shaking. Just another California quake. Her friend—the john—had let her back inside his house so she could use the bathroom to pull herself together, and the fact that he didn't want a blow job told her that she probably needed more pulling together than she had the strength for. Sleeping in the dirt under the porch had seemed such a good idea—an inspired idea at the time—but now she couldn't quite remember why she'd done it. In fact, if someone told her she hadn't done it at all and that she was mistaken to recollect that she had, she would have been convinced to agree. But one thing was clear: She hadn't spent the night at the Waldorf, that much she could deduce by the reflection in the mirror.

It had been one long night, one of many.

Now what to do?

She stuck a hand up into her tremendous mass of matted black hair, shook her head and tried to ignore the stuff that fell out—best not to know if it was dandruff or leaves or wiggly things looking for warmth to stay alive—the less you know what's there the less you itch, she'd learned long ago—and she looked around and saw the john standing there and staring at her. He was by the chair where he'd carelessly thrown his Dockers before he went to bed. Now he was taking the wallet out of the pants pocket, yawning, crawling back under his shabby, big-flowered comforter, sliding the wallet beneath his pillow, still firmly in his grasp. He knew what she was thinking, and she hadn't even thought it yet. Next time she'd have to be quicker, next time she'd have to lift the wallet while he was still asleep.

"I need a loan," she said.

"Good-bye," said the john. "Lock the door on your way out."

"Can I have breakfast—some cereal?"

"Just leave me a little sugar this time, okay?"

She nodded. Last time she'd forgotten the cereal altogether and just ate a bowlful of milk and sugar. It had made her teeth ache but it stopped her twitching long enough to get her up the block to where a fake Rastafarian with a real gold ring in his nose and a cloisonne stud through his tongue sold drugs in the parking lot of a coffee shop. Somewhere on him he had a pager and a cell phone that always rang incessantly and he never answered, not in front of anyone anyway. "Step right over here into my office, mon," he would say to Carol with his fake Jamaican accent, the wooden beads in his hair clickety-clacking as he eased in behind a dumpster where there was just enough room to exchange cash for a condom filled with heroin cut by too much talc or flour or rat poison or whatever this "dude" happened to have had handy when his ship came in, "and mind my brother Lionel there—he's groovin'—this is some kind of potent shit, mon." Sure enough, squinched under the edge of the dumpster would be "Lionel", the fake Rastafarian's fake brother, eyes rolled up and white in his head and under his yellow and blue knit cap with the L.A. Rams logo patch removed, swaying to a reggae beat so distant as to be unheard by anyone but himself, shilling to the quality of this particular drug and this particular dealer. Lionel always had a gold shawl over his shoulders, the sun on one side, the moon on the other, stars in between, the skeleton of tarot card "death" stitched on the back, a prop-laden "fool" on the front. When he'd hear his name pronounced, Lionel would hold up a finger to his lips—"Shhhsh"—so as not to be diverted from his reverie. That's when you could see that his front bottom teeth were gold capped but the gold was going green/black, the color of algae.

Showmanship, mon, that's what it was.

Truth was, competition was fierce among the Riverside-area drug dealers. Demand was high, but so was supply, and the territorial lines of dealers were rather a blur, often bloody. The fake Rastafarian—who was actually a local kid named Al—decided early on that "exotic" implied mystery, knowledge, superior drug connections, and nonthreatening affability, at least that's what it seemed like to him when he watched reruns of Miami Vice on cable, so he got a whore-friend to knot the beads in his hair and he went singsong Jamaica mon ever been to the islands mon hey this is your space really that's cool no problem I can move on mon, even though he wouldn't know Haile Selassie from Santa Claus. The act was that the former Al smiled and emptied his empty pockets for anyone who asked; while it was Lionel who actually carried the piece and minded the stash.

And Carol was desperate to pull herself together and get down to the coffee shop parking lot, to the former Al's office, hoping that he'd still be in residence and he'd be willing to barter with her for a fix. She'd even lick the algae off Lionel's teeth if that's what it took. Their fantasy for hers—that would be the trade. Or so she hoped.

"Yeah, I'll be going," Carol said to the john. "Hey, you know what time it is?"

"Too early to be having this conversation, okay?" said the john irritably.

"Right. See ya."

"Preferably not," said the john.

Carol went out the door.

Fortunately or unfortunately, the former Al and the current Lionel were not in their "office" when Carol got there. She was prepared to wait them out, figuring that unless they were on their winter vacation practicing with the Jamaican bobsled team, they were bound to show up any minute and push their wares, mon, but then she saw the dried brown puddle of blood by the corner of the dumpster that Lionel used for support, and that gold shawl of his was peeking out from under some trash bags in the dumpster itself.

There appeared to be buckwheat pancakes and blueberry syrup soaking into the shawl from the trash, if that mattered.

Quickly, Carol decided that in fact very little mattered, that there was probably wisdom in not checking whether Lionel himself was still connected to his shawl, and there was certainly brilliance in hauling her ass out of there before anyone happened to notice her around. This was not a good time to admit to any real or imagined acquaintanceship with the former Al and the current Lionel, both of whom had more than likely run afoul of someone else's territorial imperative.

Yes, the heroin fix would have to wait and adrenaline would be the drug of choice for the next little while, although it remained to be seen how high its price might rise.

By the time Carol got home, on foot, well braced from the bracing walk in the crackling daybreak, she figured she was safe. No one had followed her, no one much cared that she might have had some tie to the drug-dealing fake Jamaicans who were probably pretty much now out of the business, dead for real and not faking much of anything anymore at all.

Carol gathered up all the mail that was piled in and around the mailbox—it had overflowed days ago apparently—and she went up the steps to her house. The key was in the flowerpot with the dead gerbera daisy by the front door.

She tossed the mail on the kitchen counter by the pizza carton, chanced a bite of the double-cheese double-pepperoni that was still left within, and reached into the bathroom to turn on the shower.

It got hot and steamy right away, proving to her that you really could ignore those pink-colored shut-off notices from the gas company for longer than they said, but, just the same, she stripped and hurried under the spray rather than push her luck.

Her skin got clean pretty quickly, her hair took some time, and her outlook took until the hot water started to get merely tepid. Then she decided that maybe things weren't so bad after all and maybe she was doing a hell of a lot better than a hell of a lot of other people no matter what. Despite the drug, she still had a full, glowing figure, good skin tone, good strength, if not exactly pretty then nonetheless attractive and sensuous. Her mind was clear and her life was her own—no pimp, no husband, no outside obligations. She still had options.

Carol Lynn Miller wrapped her body in one towel, her hair in another, and she padded into the kitchen. She chucked the pizza carton and the pile of mail into the trash. Then she stared at the phone. Today could be the first day of the rest of her life, or the last day of an obsolete way of life she might finally have the nerve to discard. It was a simple choice, and yet momentarily confusing—didn't she win either way? If so, then it was no choice at all. As long as she was determined to make the change, did it matter if it happened today, couldn't it just as well be tomorrow?

Sure. It would be tomorrow. Then she'd be ready for it and she wouldn't be headed off as she had in the past.

Carol dialed the phone, left a page. A few minutes later, the phone rang back. She'd been standing there, unmoving, waiting, counting the time. Nothing else mattered.

She answered the phone, gave several increasingly heated replies—"Yes" "Right" "I'll be there" "No, I'll have the cash" "Listen, when I say I'll have the cash, I'll have the cash" "See you tonight"—and she hung up. Then she took a nap 'til mid-afternoon.

When she woke up, Carol Miller had the shakes, but she was unperturbed.

Across town, at the Riverside County Materials Procurement Warehouse—the place where the county and city stockpile every damn thing they need from paper clips to bullets, air filter masks for sanitation workers to climbing belts and shoe spikes for power pole repair people— Bill Suff was putting in a ho-hum routine day. Accordingly, it would have come as something of a surprise (but not a horror) to his supervisor were he to learn that Bill planned on working overtime tonight. There just wasn't any overtime work that needed to be done, nothing that couldn't wait until tomorrow, and besides, workwise, Bill was always ahead of himself anyway no matter that he took off so much time for allergy shots, recuperation from phantom aches and pains loosely attributed to that motorcycle wreck or to just sleeping wrong, and innumerable hypochondriacal daytime visits to every doctor around.

There was no question that Bill liked to be sick, liked to get attention for being sick, liked to play the martyr who did his duty despite his ills, but the first lesson a supervisor learns is not to question the motivation and habits of an employee who's actually doing his job. As far as the supervisor was concerned, Bill could wear a dress, stand on his head, and fart "Nearer My God to Thee" if that's what inspired him. Live and let live, just don't make the supervisor look bad on the bottom line of the monthly inventory reports.

And the thing of it was, this Bill Suff was one smart cookie when it came to inventory management. He was no "stock boy". Bill could organize things in a way that bordered on genius, and he was methodical to the point of obsession. Dewey may have gained fame for his library decimal system, but Bill's tweaking of the county's computer program with respect to inventory—well, it was just plain inspired. The guy had a down-to-earth sense of how to file, pile, and place. It was a talent, a gift. Things didn't get lost with Bill around, you always knew exactly what you had and where it was so you never overbought and never shipped late, and so the supervisor relied on Bill more and more. With Bill around, no one had any idea that the supervisor was virtually computer illiterate. Bill had added years to the supervisor's own shelf life.

Of course, the supervisor wasn't stupid. He'd worked his way up from Bill's job, and he knew well that, at Bill's pay level, the temptation was simply too great and the opportunity even greater to pocket the occasional item out of inventory and take it home to the missus or girlfriend or shady parts-supply shop. A percentage of pilfering was just one of the perks of the profession. The key was not to get caught, and, on that score, the supervisor didn't have to worry about Bill at all. No doubt Bill simply deleted the computerized existence of anything he stole, and you can hardly accuse someone of stealing something of yours that you can't prove you ever even had.

Now this whole scenario might have given the supervisor pause for worried thought were it not for the fact that Bill Suff regularly gave gifts to his fellow workers, the supervisor included. Purses, clothing, cheap jewelry, personal knickknacks, stuff he said he'd picked up at swap meets—Bill Suff loved to be generous, with goods, with advice, with time and help. He even cooked pots of spicy chili and baked sweet desserts that he'd lay out on the lunch counter for everyone to feast on. Bill's idea of sociability was being the hero, he sincerely wanted to do you a favor, any favor.

To the supervisor, this magnanimity of Bill's reflected guilt, and that was good, because if the guy had a guilty conscience then he would never steal too much stuff. Everyone steals, everyone takes advantage, and then your conscience makes you stop before you go too far past the expected and allowable limits. That was the supervisor's equation for how things worked. And that was why the supervisor appreciated Bill Suff rather than fretted over him.

And that was why the supervisor only questioned Bill's putting in for overtime when the supervisor's own supervisor questioned the supervisor about it.

So, tonight, when Bill's supervisor waved good-bye and left at the dot of quitting time, he didn't bother with the fact that Bill was still busy at his computer and busy dipping into the footlocker he kept at his workstation. The supervisor didn't even consider the issue of whether Bill was going to put in for overtime—it never even occurred to the supervisor to think about it, the same way there are about a zillion billion things you don't think about and don't know you're not thinking about at any given point in time. The supervisor was thinking about stopping for a beer on his way home, and he was thinking he was pretty hungry and he hoped his wife had made a roast, and that was the sum total of his thoughts. So, by definition, he had not the slightest idea that, when Bill Suff woke up that morning, he'd planned his day so he could most definitely put in for overtime.

Not because he needed the extra couple of hours pay—in fact, it would have been fine with Bill if the supervisor later called him in and denied the overtime, that would have been better than fine, it would have actually been excellent—because the reason Bill needed to put in for overtime was to establish himself an alibi. It would indeed be excellent if the supervisor took special note of the requested overtime by denying it, because then the supervisor would remember the date, would remember that Bill worked late that date, and that recollection might well come in handy for Bill if anyone happened to inquire where he was that February night.

For tonight was to be a killing night.

It worked like this: All day long, in all outward appearance, Bill got calmer and calmer, more businesslike. At quitting time, everyone else would leave, but they'd see Bill still at his post. He'd make sure to stay until everyone else had gone. Then, when the coast was clear, he'd get some tools out of his footlocker.

When he'd been in jail in Texas, Bill had taken up engraving as part of the arts and crafts rehab training. Over the years he'd become a master at scoring and cutting and filleting, at working leather and metal and plastic. He'd made all sorts of wallets and purses and keycovers and wallhangings and belts and moccasins for his family and friends, and he'd embellished everything with etched artistic designs of birds and animals and whatever came to mind, all deftly painted in for full effect.

Over the years, he'd compiled a set of perfect paintbrushes and perfect paints and perfect tools, the best of the best, acrylic paints and lacquers that wouldn't chip, peel, or fade, diamond-tipped cutting tools that would make a surgeon proud.

All of this he kept in a tackle box, and the tackle box he kept in his footlocker at work, and, on killing nights, these became some of the killing tools. Added to that was a toolbox of more ordinary but terrific mechanics' tools which he'd stolen from his stepfather, Shorty. These tools had been items of special pride to Shorty, who paranoically worried that they might be stolen and so kept them well hidden, even going so far as to move them from hidey-hole to hidey-hole. Bill brought off the theft first by doing Shorty the favor of engraving Shorty's driver's license number on the tools as a means of identification in case of theft.

Of course, Shorty was grateful.

Then, once Bill finished the engraving job, now knowing exactly where the tools would be and when Shorty would be out, Bill snuck back in and snatched the tools away. Incredibly, no one ever suspected him. Occasionally Bill even contemplated returning Shorty's tools—he would say that they'd been recovered because of Bill's engraving—but heroism lost out to Bill's desire to have all manner of tool available to him for his killings.

Bill's initial plans for killing were essentially artistic—the corpse would have to be painted, manipulated, cut up in whatever way the muses tittered—he planned on treating the body as just another piece of leather—but reality and the threat of capture changed all that immediately.

The fact is that it's not so easy to cart around dead weight the size of a human body. Then lividity fights against the artist's vision. And, rigor mortis sets in pretty quickly, making the body difficult if not impossible to work with. Finally, were he to be too distinctive with his cuts and were he to use his distinctive tools and his distinctive paints, the forensic people could tie the killer and his killing tools to the murder as easily as if he signed his name "Bill Suff" to his deadly masterpiece.

As a result, in February 1990, with only a few murders under his belt, Bill was still experimenting with how artistic he could be and still not get caught. So, he still schlepped along all the killing tools, all the possibilities for artistic expression. Tonight, he would get the tools out of his footlocker at work, put them in his van, and say he worked overtime.

That would explain why he didn't make it home for dinner, didn't see Cheryl before she went to work at the Circle K. So long as he was home once she got home later, he could say he'd come home any hour he chose, and she'd back him up. When he told Cheryl something, she didn't just believe him: it became reality for her, it was as if she knew it firsthand.

Then, tomorrow night, from home, Bill would phone a few friends during the evening. Local calls—no toll charges, no phone records. He'd *have simple conversations, nothing too memorable, but then he'd mention something specific about getting together the coming weekend, some reference that you could date. Then he wouldn't talk to those people the rest of the week. Later, months later, if anyone should be so inclined as to inquire, Bill would say he had those phone conversations on the night of the killing—he was home, on the phone, how could he be out killing anyone? The friends wouldn't remember for certain what night they had the conversations, but they'd gravitate toward the night Bill suggested. It even helps you to mix up day and date—you refer to Wednesday the seventh, then "realize" that Tuesday was the seventh, so you must have spoken on Tuesday rather than Wednesday, because you know you remember having the conversation that night you worked late and you've got the overtime record to prove when that was, right? "Remember that conversation we had on February seventh, the night I worked late, that Tuesday?"— you'd be amazed how easy it is to talk someone into a memory of something mundane. Mundane for them, that is; life and death for you.*

So now, with his alibi preset that night in February 1990, Bill could go out and enjoy his killing.

On February 8, many years ago, the ambulance brought me, my mother, and my brother to the Loma Linda University Hospital Emergency Room. I'm still not sure whether Loma Linda is in San Bernardino or Riverside, but it's near where they border one another, and it's where Bill Suff plied his trade sometime later.

It was getting dark, and the darkness was swirling. My mother was DOA but they tried to revive her, I begged them to. Every available doctor and every available nurse went with her into some operating room I never saw. My brother, his collapsed lung wheezing, his condition comatose but stable, was taken up an elevator for a CT scan. A doctor shined a penlight in my eyes, had me touch my nose a few times, popped his mallet against my knee, rolled some prickly metal thing hard against the arch of my foot, and then sat me on a table behind a curtain and told me to wait. I was deaf in my left ear, everything I looked at was red and fuzzy, my head was swelled up on the left side like another head was growing there, and my right hand was twisted and mangled, but caked-on dirt and sand had pretty much sopped up all the blood.

The doctor who examined me fled into the OR where my mother was—I got a brief glimpse of a flurry of activity and a flurry of people and someone looking back at me and making sure to close the door so I couldn't see anymore.

Suddenly, I was all alone. There was no one anywhere in all of the emergency room. I remember thinking how few lights were on, like the place had been closed and they'd just opened up for us, like they'd all been asleep or something when the ambulance had radioed we were on the way.

The obvious thought suggested itself: This can't be happening. But the essence of that realization was that I no longer mattered, I no longer existed. What was going to happen, was going to happen; this drama, this tragedy, was going to play itself out on its own terms, and nothing I said or did was going to make one whit of difference.

In fact, that was the tragedy.

From somewhere in the ER, a phone rang and kept on ringing. With my blown eardrum, it was difficult to place the unseen phone in time and space, and my brain was pretty much ringing continuously inside itself even without the phone, so all this noise began to hurt and then it got all knotted up and seemed to float away and I saw the floor rushing up at me from the end of a dark tunnel, and I knew that I was passing out.

I found myself on the cold linoleum and I was angry. I needed to stay alert and focused. I climbed up onto the examining table and stretched out, fighting the waves of wooziness. The ringing had stopped, but now I heard soft rubber footsteps approach.

A nurse peered in at me—she was holding a telephone. "There's a call for you," she said.

I took the phone and the nurse disappeared.

"Hello," I said into the receiver.

"This is Officer Tucker of the California Highway Patrol," said the stern voice on the other end of the line. "I need to ask you a few questions."

The words hit me square in the gut and I lost all ability to breathe. Cops scare me. The legal system terrifies me. Cops have absolute power to invade your privacy, to take away your property, your liberty, your life. Judges are paid to judge you. Lawyers in the American adversarial system seek victory rather than truth—it's lawyer versus lawyer, with the clients as the pawns. And the first thing that cops and judges and lawyers are taught in school is never ask a question you don't already know or suspect that you know the answer to. If you're truly open-minded, you can be fooled. You must start with what you believe to be true, and then see if the evidence fits. Without a theory, you don't even know where inquiry begins.

The only thing that had been on my mind was the health of my mother and brother. That was the last thing on this cop's mind. What was to me an accident was to him a crime. And I was the chief suspect. You don't call and question someone who's being treated in an emergency room, someone who's been knocked unconscious, who's in shock, who's been horribly damaged physically and psychologically, you don't call and interrogate someone who's in *extremis* if you want legitimate information. In my state, nothing I said or remembered would be reliable, and the cop knew that. The only purpose for this call was to see if I'd say something inculpatory because my defenses were down. On the one hand, if I admitted to some guilt it would justify some theory this cop was operating under, and that admission would be admissible in court. On the other hand, if I said I was innocent it would be discounted because nothing I could say would talk this cop out of some hard evidence he thought he'd culled at the scene of the crash. Finally, on that "third hand", always the most damning hand, if I refused to answer his questions the cop would take that as a sure sign that I was covering up.

I knew all this in a split second, and I knew that all I wanted to do was tell the truth—that's the rule I've always lived by—but the truth was that I didn't know the truth. I didn't know then what had caused the crash, and I didn't know how fast I'd been driving at the moment of the crash. I only knew that I'd been driving safely and usually. I usually sped. My father, mother, and brother usually sped. My friends sped. Everyone sped in those days, and not just because the speed limits were higher. Cars were advertised for engine size and speed. A great car was a fast car, and a greater car was a faster car. Luxury cars were fast and powerful—enjoy the drive because this car's smoother than that one at high speed. My mother always referred to my father as "Barney Old-field", the former Indy driver, and my mother herself drove a striped, finned, spoilered Cougar Eliminator which we kids had prompted her to buy. My friend's father owned a Mercedes because it was then the quickest accelerating car in the world, between twenty and eighty miles per hour, and, supposedly, at a hundred and thirty you felt like you were doing sixty. Status was how high the numbers went on your speedometer, whether you ever drove that fast or not.

At the time of the crash, I know I wasn't going as fast as fast I'd gone during the many hours of our drive that day. I slowed when I was around traffic—you could never trust what other drivers would do, whether they'd pop into your lane or not; I slowed when I was near civilization where traffic might appear or cops might be hiding; I slowed whenever I saw a reflection in the rearview mirror and couldn't identify it as either friend or foe. I drove at whatever speed felt safe, and I drove so as not to ever get a speeding ticket.

But I could hardly explain all that to this cop. He was going to judge whether I had done something wrong, and the basis of his judgment would have nothing to do with how my family and I had lived or how good and innocent were my intentions. His morality was about to be imposed completely and utterly and with great authority in place of my morality. Even if I told the truth, my life was about to become a lie—thanks to this cop.

"You there?" said the officer.

"Yeah," I said.

"What happened on the road?" he asked.

"I don't know," I said, "I heard a bang, and then I couldn't keep the car on the road. I kept us from skidding, but we still went off the road. It must've been a blown tire—but I don't know."

"Yeah—looks like a tire went. Have anything to drink before you drove? Take any drugs or prescription medications?"

"Orange juice and iced tea—that's all I had—this morning for breakfast."

"Yeah, the doc there at the hospital said you were clean."

"Sir, officer, I'm in an emergency room, I'm pretty banged up and my mother and my brother are dying—I can't talk anymore."

Officer Tucker was undeterred. "When you were driving, you remember seeing a Pantera?"

There it was, the question I'd figured was coming.

While we were cruising along the road, a bright yellow Pantera had raced past us, weaving in and out of traffic, vanishing into the heat-wave distance. My brother and I had looked at one another, and he—car expert that he was—proceeded to rattle off the engine, suspension, and speed specifics of a Pantera, a foreign sports car just then being imported by Ford. It was sort of the poor man's Porsche or Ferrari, and my brother was none too impressed. In fact, he suggested rather strenuously that the Mercedes sedan we were driving—rented for this drive to Vegas—was a damn sight faster and certainly more comfortable and safe than that stupid-looking Pantera with its stupid-looking driver who clearly but wrongly and stupidly thought he was tough shit.

I had pursed my lips in thought and then wondered aloud what my brother and I ought to do to set this egomaniac Pantera driver straight.

According to my brother, our top speed would be sufficiently more than the Pantera's, and, even though the Pantera was way out of sight, we ought to be able to catch him and smoke him within ten miles.

In fact, it took only six.

We reeled in the Pantera, laughed and gave the high sign to its stunned driver, and then blew on down the road. He was just a little yellow speck in our exhaust. He was a limp dick.

Later, I'd slowed down near a truck stop, and the Pantera flashed by us. Later again, I'd gone by the Pantera again and lost him completely. He knew we were just toying with him, that he was ours whenever the mood struck us. Next time maybe he'd get a real car.

We continued down the road for quite some time, speeding, slowing, speeding, slowing, and I never saw the Pantera again, except that, after we crashed, when I was being helped up into the ambulance and we were spitting dust and sand and smoke and tearing away, the disjointed, moving horizon revealed a yellow glare, possibly the Pantera parked amongst some other cars at the crash scene.

"There was a Pantera—a yellow one—on the road," I said to the officer on the phone, "we passed him once or twice, I'm not sure."

"He says you were racing."

So that was it—this Pantera driver who'd felt his manhood violated when we'd kicked his ass, he was now claiming that we'd been racing, and that he'd slowed down to be safe while I'd raced on and crashed. *He'd let us win*. He'd turned a non-race into a race and his loser lemon-colored lemon car into a trophy winner. He'd rewritten history. According to him, he was not only innocent of any wrongdoing, he was humble, he didn't have anything to prove by going fast. That had to be his story—it was the only story that justified the cop's questions.

"We'd passed the Pantera—he was nowhere around when we crashed," I said.

"Know how fast you were going?"

I didn't know, not for sure, but I certainly knew that the officer knew—all he had to do was measure the skid marks, which I was sure he'd done. He was asking me a question he knew the answer to, solely to hear if I'd incriminate myself. He was also lancing my guilty conscience—regardless of the fact that I always sped, that my family always sped, that my dead and dying friend and family had encouraged or at least ratified my speeding, the more this officer asked me questions, the more I felt I'd done something wrong and that this disaster was all my fault after all.

"The speed limit," I said. "Or maybe a little faster."

In those days, pre-radar, cops gave you a little grace over the speed limit so you couldn't argue a ticket if their speedometers were slightly off calibration. So, you could admit to traveling within that grace index. That was how I explained my answer to myself. In fact, I was foolishly red-flagging the fact that I felt guilty about something.

"A lot faster," said the officer, hoping to prompt a numeric declaration from me.

"At the time of the accident, there was traffic and we were slowing down," I said, which was true so far as I remembered or told myself I remembered.

"But you were racing the Pantera?" he asked again.

I sighed relief at the repeat question—now I could accurately divine the complete theory from which the officer was working. In fact, we must have been going comparatively slower at the time of the accident, or else the officer would have flat-out accused me of a high speed. So, the only way he could make me out to be a criminal would be by "proving" that, regardless of speed, we were in a reckless race with the Pantera. If we were racing, then I could be damned for prior speed even if I weren't speeding at the time of the accident itself. The crash would be deemed the product of the race, and I would be deemed a manslaughterer who'd endangered everyone on the road and killed his friend and family.

Of course, the truth was that I was not racing. We'd long before passed the Pantera and been cruising along, minding our own business, with my friend and my mom falling asleep from the sweet monotony, the cradle-rocking throb of the road. So as not to wake our passengers, my brother and I had been whispering about the song on the radio just before the crash, and he was leaning against the doorjamb and thinking about snoozing himself.

"I'd passed the Pantera a long time before the accident," I said with finality to the officer. My own sense of guilt was back to being my own business—clearly I was guilty of no crime under law.

"Okay," said the officer; and then he sneered, making sure I knew that he didn't believe me: "Whatever you say." And he hung up. Not a word of condolence or a hope for the best, no concern for my mother or my brother. This cop had gotten a statement for his report, he'd make his recommendation for or against prosecution, and that would be that.

And I promised myself quite sincerely that, if I was charged with any crime for the crash, I would kill myself—it was obviously a mistake that I had survived anyway.

As it turned out, Officer Tucker had a policy: If someone died on his beat, then he pushed for prosecution. Let the court sort it out, was his thinking. Luckily, the local prosecutor felt otherwise and filed no charges, but not before my father and I hired a local lawyer to keep track of things and make sure the prosecutor knew the whole story while he was considering the matter. An L.A. judge who knew me on a personal basis also chimed in to vouch for my character. I think everyone knew but didn't want to tell me they knew what I planned on doing were I to be charged. People kept telling me how strong I was, but it was blind strength and certain to crumble if reality opened my eyes.

As for Officer Tucker's report, I was certain it damned me, and even more sure I'd been misquoted. My lawyer told me that it had been a mistake to take that phone call, that you should never talk to the cops, that everything you say *will* be used against you. Count on it.

Nonetheless, if you're innocent, you think you can clear yourself just by telling the truth as you know it. Innocent instinct says say more, not less. Meanwhile, if you're guilty, you tend to think you can admit to a little something, that you can throw the cops a bone without having to feed 'em the whole steak. When I interned as a lawyer at the L.A. City Attorney's, prosecuting drunk drivers, there was not one case where the detained driver didn't confess to drinking "two beers", like that was an okay amount and not enough to constitute DUI. Of course, "two beers" was really two six-packs, and the cops knew it.

In fairness to cops, they always get lied to—"two beers" is the least of it—so it's no wonder they can't recognize truth when it crosses their paths. But doesn't that tell us that there's something wrong with our system, that cops are sent out on the street with wrong marching orders and wrong attitudes?

Convicts like Bill Suff learn—or at least they're supposed to learn—to shut the fuck up when anyone asks them anything about anything. Nonetheless, guilty or innocent, that's a tough row to hoe. When someone's accusing you of something, you want to respond. And, when you're the lead detective in the biggest murder case your county's ever had, you're determined to interrogate and keep on interrogating until you decide your work is done.

As typed by the Riverside Police Department, here is the transcript from the last minutes of Bill Suff's interrogation the night of his arrest in January 1992. He'd been in custody for the better part of a full day by this point, held incommunicado, interrogated repeatedly, overridden by his inquisitors whenever he raised the subject of being given legal counsel; he'd been caught in lie after lie, bluff after blown bluff. Now lead homicide Detective Keers moved in for her own "kill". None of this has been made public before, and none of it was admissible at trial. The primary murder referred to is Eleanor Casares, the last of the spree, December 1991.

RIVERSIDE POLICE DEPARTMENT INTERROGATION
CONTINUATION SHEET
(Transcribed from audiotape)

		File No. P3-91-357-142	
1/10/92	187 P.C.	C. KEERS 488	cd

DATE   01-10-92

TAPE 3, SIDE 1   4:50 p.m. - 01-10-92
_____ SIDE 2   5:40 p.m. - End of Tape

KEERS = Detective C. KEERS   (RPD)
DAVIS = Detective John DAVIS (RSO)
SUFF = Bill Lee SUFF   (SUSPECT)

KEERS: Okay. And and this is the time when you listen and we talk. Okay? One other thing I wanna tell you is this. In listening to you, we can tell you certain things. You have given us some truths.

SUFF: Yes.

KEERS: But you have told us some lies. I wanna point those lies out to you. This is going to be your opportunity to straighten them out now. 'Cause you don't get another chance, do you understand this? You understand the difference between a truth and a lie? All we ask for you to give us the truth and nothing more. You understand that?

SUFF: Ahm.

KEERS: Okay. One of the main issues that I would like to talk to you about is your time in prison. Now you want to discuss that with us?

SUFF: No. I was, I was, at the time that I was working for the prison industry I was

KEERS: You were in prison.

SUFF: Yes.

KEERS: You were not working there; you were an inmate. Is that correct?

SUFF: Yes.

KEERS: So you're telling the truth here.

SUFF: I know.

KEERS: And we know that, and we appreciate the truth. We're not asking you to tell us anything that's a lie but we know what the truth is and that's what we're asking you to do, to tell the truth. Do you understand that?

SUFF: Yes, I do.

KEERS: Now, what did you go to prison for?

SUFF: It was Murder without Malice.

KEERS: And who was murdered?

SUFF: My daughter was. Belongs Teryl and wasn't mine, the the daughter that she gave birth to.

KEERS: Did Teryl go to prison with you?

SUFF: Yes.

KEERS: Now, why would you tell me that you worked there?

SUFF: I don't know.

KEERS: I want you to understand something, okay?

SUFF: Ahm.

KEERS: We're not here because we wanna entertain you

SUFF: I know.

KEERS: and we're not here for you to entertain us.

SUFF: I know.

KEERS: We're here because we have some hard, solid evidence. Do you understand that?

SUFF: Yes.

KEERS: Now, I have let you go on and on and on about stories that you told. Okay? Now we're gonna get down to the truth. You understand that?

SUFF: Yes.

KEERS: We're gonna talk the truth. Okay?

DAVIS: Bill, everything comes out in the wash.

KEERS: Everything.

DAVIS: Everything comes out in the wash when it co, when everything is over, this is a done deal, everything's out.

KEERS: Including the clothing, the clothing that you said you found in your hamper.

SUFF: Ahm.

KEERS: You didn't find it, did you?

SUFF: Yes.

KEERS: No, you didn't.

SUFF: Yes, Ma'am.

KEERS: Ye, let me tell you where that clothing came from

SUFF: Okay.

KEERS: 'cause I know the girl that was wearing them. You understand that? Now we just got through talking about truth and lies.

SUFF: Yes.

KEERS: And you started off real good. You started off real good. We talked about you going to prison and you came up and you told us the truth. Okay?

SUFF: Right.

KEERS: Now, we wanna talk about your vehicle on Victoria Avenue.

SUFF: Okay.

KEERS: We wanna talk about it. On December the 23rd, does that vehicle belong to you?

SUFF: Yeah it is.

KEERS: Okay.

SUFF: Yes.

KEERS: Well, wait a minute, before you say another word, okay?

DAVIS: Listen to what she has to say.

KEERS: Every time you start to lie to me I'm gonna stop you.

SUFF: Okay.

KEERS: We're here to tell the truth. You're not gonna tell any lies.

SUFF: Okay.

KEERS: Okay? Now, your vehicle, on December the 23rd, was in the orange grove and you know how I know that?

SUFF: No.

KEERS: Why don't you take a chance?

SUFF: I don't know.

KEERS: Well, let me tell you why. Because your tire tracks are there. You wanna know what else is there?

SUFF: What?

KEERS: You know what's there, don't you?

SUFF:　　What?

KEERS:　You know what's there, don't you, Bill?

SUFF:　　Tell me.

KEERS:　I will. But you know what's there, don't you?

SUFF:　　Tell me.

KEERS:　You know what's there, don't you?

SUFF:　　No.

KEERS:　Yes, you do. Now see every time that you start to tell a lie to me I'm gonna stop you. Now you know we've got your tire prints there, don't you? And you know we've got something else there, don't you?

SUFF:　　I don't know.

KEERS:　Don't you?

SUFF:　　Yes.

KEERS:　Now, what do we have there, Bill?

SUFF:　　There was a dead body there.

KEERS:　That's right.

DAVIS:　And who put that dead body there, Bill?

SUFF:　　I don't know.

KEERS:　No.

SUFF:　　No that I don't

KEERS:　We,

SUFF:　　Know.

KEERS:　we, we're gonna stop right here.

DAVIS: Don't raise your voice.

KEERS: We're gonna stop right here

DAVIS: Don't raise your voice at us, mister.

KEERS: because we talked about this evidence that we have, okay?

SUFF: Yes.

KEERS: The truth. We know the truth and we're only asking you to give us the truth.

SUFF: Okay.

KEERS: Now, you started off right. There was a dead body there, wasn't there?

SUFF: Yes, but I

KEERS: Now, wait a minute,

SUFF: didn't

KEERS: no, I'm not gonna let you tell a lie. There

DAVIS: You put the body there.

KEERS: was something else there, right? There was something else there, wasn't there?

SUFF: A dead body.

KEERS: Yes, and something else that belonged to you. Did you leave your shoe prints there, Bill?

SUFF: Yes.

KEERS: Yes, you did. Now, the truth, you see? You're coming out with the truth. Do you think we didn't know this?

SUFF: Yes.

KEERS: I gave you the opportunity to tell the truth and you told some lies. This is your opportunity to clean it up now, Bill. Do you understand that?

SUFF: Yes.

KEERS: Now tell me about the body you left there.

SUFF: I didn't do it.

KEERS: Tell me about the

SUFF: I better get a lawyer now. I better get a lawyer 'cause you think that I did it and I didn't.

KEERS: Who did it?

SUFF: I don't know but I didn't do it. I swear to God I didn't do it.

KEERS: Are you telling me that you don't want to talk to me right now, Bill?

SUFF: I'm telling you the truth.

KEERS: I've given you the

SUFF: Trying to

KEERS: opportunity.

SUFF: I know.

KEERS: Okay, I'm giving you the opportunity to talk to me.

SUFF: I know.

KEERS: Do you wanna do that?

SUFF: Yes, I do, because

KEERS: If you want, okay.

SUFF: I do.

KEERS: Great. Do you want to tell the truth or do you wanna lie?

SUFF: I do not want to lie.

KEERS: Okay, now, we'll start slow. Okay?

SUFF: Yes.

KEERS: I'll take you through this alright?

SUFF: Okay.

KEERS: Will you feel better if I take you through that?

SUFF: Please.

KEERS: Okay. Well, I'll take you through that, okay? I understand.

SUFF: OO. Okay.

KEERS: You drove your van in there, didn't you?

SUFF: Yes, I did.

KEERS: Tell me how you drove your van in there.

SUFF: I drove in backwards.

KEERS: Okay. What did you do when you drove in backwards?

SUFF: I went to look for some oranges.

KEERS: Okay. Tell me what you did. Tell me where you're coming from in your van. What direction were you coming from?

SUFF: What do you mean what direction I

KEERS: Okay,

SUFF: was coming from?

KEERS: where were you driving on? What street?

SUFF: Victoria.

KEERS: Okay. Which way were you going on Victoria?

SUFF: I was going towards, uh, Riverside from Tyler.

KEERS: Okay. So you were going eastbound on Victoria,

          (Knock on Door)

KEERS: is that correct?

SUFF: Yes.

KEERS: Fine, just a minute.

          (You have an emergency outside.)

KEERS: Hold on, please.

          (Door Closes)

SUFF: I didn't kill her. Honest I didn't. I swear to God I
          did not kill her. I found her body there. I did.

DAVIS: Bill, you wanna talk to us?

SUFF: Yes. I do.

DAVIS: Couple minutes ago

SUFF: Yes.

DAVIS: you said you wanted a lawyer, now you wanna
          talk to us about this?

SUFF: I think I'm, need a lawyer over here.

DAVIS: Did you want to talk to us?

SUFF: I wanna try to clear this up. I wanna make sure you
          end up knowing I didn't kill her. I took the clothes
          because they were lying near by her and that's it.

(Door Opens)

SUFF: Like I told you.

KEERS: Yes.

KEERS: Do you want to talk to me, Bill? I wanna make this perfectly clear to you, okay?

SUFF: I know.

KEERS: You know yourself that you don't have to talk to us, you know that, don't you?

SUFF: I know.

KEERS: I have asked you if you wanna talk to us, if you wanna tell us the truth. Do you understand that?

SUFF: Yes.

KEERS: Do you wanna tell us the truth, Bill?

SUFF: Yes.

KEERS: Do you wanna talk to us and tell us the truth?

SUFF: Yes.

KEERS: Okay. Would you like me to help you get through this?

SUFF: Anyway you're talking to me about the truth.

KEERS: Alright we'll get you the truth. Is that what you wanna do here is just tell the truth?

SUFF: Yes.

KEERS: Okay. That's all you wanna do is tell the truth?

SUFF: Yes.

KEERS: So you wanna talk to us?

SUFF: Yes.

KEERS: Okay.

SUFF: To clear up this stuff.

KEERS: Alright.

SUFF: Whole thing.

KEERS: Tell me what you were doing now. You were driving eastbound at Victoria. Is that correct?

SUFF: Yes.

KEERS: Okay, what did you do then?

SUFF: I saw an opening that I could park the van in so I could see if I could find some oranges.

KEERS: Okay, so what did you do?

SUFF: I backed in because I had already gone past it, backed up, and backed into it. Got out and started to walk around the van to hunt, hunt for oranges and I saw something lying on the ground. I walked over to it and it was a girl there. There was some clothing strung around her, I picked up the clothing and then I decided I'd better get out of there and I got out.

KEERS: And so what did you do with the clothing, Bill?

SUFF: I took the clothing home with me.

KEERS: You did?

SUFF: And I, I threw it in the van.

KEERS: Okay. Now.

          (Throat Clearing)

KEERS: Okay, you took the clothing home with you, Bill.

SUFF: Because I picked it up and

KEERS: Okay.

SUFF: I thought I'd do something with it.

KEERS: Okay. What did you do with the clothing when you got it home?

SUFF: Uuuhhh.

KEERS: Tell me, what did you do with the clothing when you got it home?

SUFF: The sweater went into the clothes, into the dirty laundry.

KEERS: Did you wash it?

SUFF: Yes. Yes.

KEERS: Okay. Why did you wash it? Please tell me the truth.

STUFF: Because I was washing a bunch of dark clothes and I just grabbed it, too.

KEERS: Ahm. What else besides the sweater, Bill?

SUFF: There were some pants.

KEERS: What color pants?

SUFF: I don't remember for sure.

KEERS: Okay. Well, take a guess and I'll tell you if you're right or wrong.

SUFF: Blue jeans, I think.

KEERS: Okay. What did you do with those blue jeans?

KEERS: I think I washed them and folded up and set it in the other, our bedroom.

KEERS: Okay.

SUFF: Second bedroom.

KEERS: What else?

SUFF: That's all.

KEERS: Okay. Were there any shoes out there?

SUFF: I don't know. I don't remember.

KEERS: Okay. Let's let's stop for just a minute. Take a break. We just talked about the truth, okay?

SUFF: Yes.

KEERS: What did you do with the shoes?

SUFF: I don't know.

KEERS: The truth. What did you do with the shoes?

SUFF: I don't recall seeing any shoes.

KEERS: Okay.

SUFF: I don't.

KEERS: You picked up the shoes, now, did you throw 'em away somewhere?

SUFF: No.

KEERS: Tell me what you did with the shoes.

SUFF: I didn't have the shoes.

KEERS: Okay, what did you do with the shoes, did you leave 'em out there?

SUFF: They weren't there.

KEERS: Okay. What else did you see out there, Bill?

SUFF: Saw a body sitting there, laying down.

KEERS: What the body looked like?

SUFF: Uuuhh, it had a tit removed.

KEERS: It had a tit removed?

SUFF: Yes, it was this part, the ti, tit was gone on this part of her body. It was gone.

KEERS: What time did you go the grove, Bill? The truth. The honest truth because that's all we're after here is the truth.

(Throat Clearing)

KEERS: What time did you go to the groves?

SUFF: It was about nine o'clock.

KEERS: Nine o'clock.

SUFF: Ten o'clock.

KEERS: When?

SUFF: On the 23rd.

KEERS: In the morning?

SUFF: No.

KEERS: In the evening?

SUFF: At night.

KEERS: That's not true. Now I will give you a chance to think about what you, wait a minute

SUFF: Yes.

KEERS: let me finish

SUFF: Yes.

KEERS: what I have

SUFF: Okay.

KEERS: to say.

SUFF: Okay.

KEERS: I'm gonna give you a chance to think about it, okay? Now. Think about it. On the 23rd of December

SUFF: Ahm.

KEERS: that's the day before Christmas Eve.

SUFF: Right.

KEERS: You drove to the grove area. Is that correct?

SUFF: Yes.

KEERS: You backed into the dirt portion of Victoria Avenue.

SUFF: Yes, wait.

KEERS: Let me finish.

SUFF: Okay.

KEERS: Okay. Did you do that?

SUFF: I got the date wrong.

KEERS: Okay. What was the date?

SUFF: The 22nd when I drove in there. And it was about nine or ten o'clock at night.

KEERS: Okay.

SUFF: On the 22nd.

KEERS: Okay.

SUFF: I wasn't in there on the 23rd.

KEERS: Well, Bill, now we just went through this, okay?

SUFF: Okay.

KEERS: We went through all of this. We went through every stinking bit of it, okay?

SUFF: Right.

KEERS: And we talked about the truth and we talked about lies, didn't we?

SUFF: Yes we did.

KEERS: Now. I'm gonna give you the opportunity the thing you that just said, 'cause that's a lie. I want you to think about what you did. What did you do on Monday? You were off work that week. Think about it, what did you do on Monday?

(Door Opens and Closes)

SUFF: I know I was at Cheryl's work for awhile.

KEERS: You were where?

SUFF: At Cheryl's work.

KEERS: And what time was that?

(Sound of Paper Shuffling)

SUFF: It was late at night because I was there to take her home.

KEERS: Okay. What did you do in the morning?

SUFF: We were

KEERS: No.

SUFF: asleep.

KEERS: No. We're talking about the truth. Okay, you tell me

SUFF: Aha.

KEERS: what time you drove into the orange grove. Now I don't wanna hear that you drove in there at nine o'clock at night becau

SUFF: ....

KEERS: wait a minute. I wanna hear the truth.

SUFF: Yes.

KEERS: We discussed this, we talked about the truth, what the evidence is that we have.

SUFF: Okay.

KEERS: Now I am giving you the opportunity to tell the truth now. Putting all this out.

SUFF: I know.

KEERS: Okay. So I'm gonna shut up and I'm gonna let you tell me the truth. And if you need my help, you say, "I need you to help me through this."

SUFF: Okay. With, I need your help. The afternoon she was found, what day was that on?

KEERS: Do you know

SUFF: Was it

KEERS: She was found in the afternoon?

SUFF: According to the newspaper she was found in about one-thirty in the afternoon, somethin' like that. Uh according to, no it was according to the news, I heard it on the radio.

KEERS: Okay. I'm gonna listen.

SUFF: She was, she was found uh by a worker or somethin', somebody.

KEERS: I'm listening.

SUFF: Okay, what day was that? I was there the night before.

KEERS: The night before what?

SUFF: The night before she was found by this migrant worker or the uh grove worker. I was there the night before.

KEERS: Okay. You were there the night before. We'll we'll go this route, tell

SUFF: You said.

KEERS: me what you were doing there the night before.

SUFF: Exactly what I told you. I pulled in to look for some oranges.

KEERS: Ahm.

SUFF: I got out of the van and walked around, opened up the back sliding, put the oranges in a box that I had back there and then I started into the orange grove and that's when I saw the body. I did exactly what I told you, uh, she was missing a breast and I picked up the clothes, uh I don't know why I picked up the clothes, looked around and then I thought I'd better get out here before I

KEERS: Okay.

          (Throat Clearing)

KEERS: Okay. Okay we're gonna stop right now.

SUFF: Okay.

KEERS: Because now I'm gonna give you a little more. You were told to tell the truth, okay.

SUFF: Okay.

KEERS: Is that what you wanna do is tell the truth?

SUFF: Please.

KEERS: And you have not told it all have you? Bill,

SUFF: I did.

KEERS: you haven't told all the truth, have you?

SUFF: Go ahead.

KEERS: When you admit to me the truth. Have you told me all the truth?

SUFF: As far as I could remember, yes.

KEERS: Okay, I'm gonna help you, Bill. But I need you to tell me, you have not told me all the truth have you?

SUFF: Uuuhh, as far as I can remember, yes, I have been.

KEERS: You have a knife, Bill?

SUFF: Yes, I do.

KEERS: Okay, does that help you along a little bit, Bill?

SUFF: No. I didn't stab her.

KEERS: Listen to me. You didn't stab her?

SUFF: No. I didn't cut her in any way at all. I swear to God I didn't.

KEERS: Now Bill, we were just talking about the truth, okay?

SUFF: I didn't do it.

KEERS: If you need me to help you get through this, I'll do that because all I'm after here is the truth, okay? I'm here for the truth and the truth only and you know the truth. Okay?

SUFF: But I've been telling you the truth now.

KEERS: You haven't. No, no you haven't. Now I've give, I've given you, here's what I've given you. I've given you the tire prints, I've given you the shoe prints, and now I'm gonna talk about your knife.

SUFF: I haven't

KEERS: First of all, I'll let you explain the knife. I'll let you tell the truth now. I will let you do that. I want you to tell the truth.

SUFF: The knife was there.

KEERS: The knife was there.

SUFF: When I was there.

KEERS: The knife was

SUFF: It wasn't my knife.

KEERS: It wasn't?

SUFF: No. It was, the knife was sitting there.

KEERS: So what did you do with the knife?

SUFF: I picked that up also,

KEERS: In the orange

SUFF: with the clothes.

KEERS: groves. And where'd you, the knife?

SUFF: In the car.

KEERS: In the car.

SUFF: Yes.

KEERS: Now, where did you put it in the car?

SUFF: Uuuhhhh, it was in the box first. When I got home I took the clothes out and I stuck the knife up front.

KEERS: Ahm.

SUFF: In front of the tire.

KEERS: Aha.

SUFF: I found it there last night before I got stopped and I was thinkin' I gotta get rid of this

KEERS: Ahm.

SUFF: and then the policeman was there. So I took it, slipped it up underneath the seat.

KEERS: You put the knife under in, what seat?

SUFF: The driver's seat.

KEERS: Of your van.

SUFF: Yes.

KEERS: Okay. Was there anything on the knife?

SUFF: I don't know if there was or not. Uh, it looked like there was some blood on it, but I didn't know if it was blood or rust.

KEERS: Did you wipe it off?

SUFF: No. I didn't think to do that.

KEERS: You didn't. Now, okay, now why didn't you tell the truth? I can tell you are, I really can tell you are. You've given some truth, you've given some lies.

SUFF: I am telling you the truth.

KEERS: Bill, Bill, I know you're not giving me all the truth and you know you're not giving me all the truth and I'm gonna give you some more information to help you get there.

SUFF: I don't know.

KEERS: Okay? Do you wanna tell the truth?

SUFF: Yes.

KEERS: You wanna get this all done?

SUFF: Yes.

KEERS: Then you can't lie.

SUFF: I don't want to lie.

KEERS: Oh, I know you don't.

SUFF: I want the truth out.

KEERS: I know you want to the truth out but you're havin' a hard time in telling the truth, Bill.

SUFF: I'm having a hard time remembering it all.

KEERS: Okay. Okay. Now let's talk about the knife.

SUFF: Okay.

KEERS: Where'd you find the knife at Bill?

SUFF: The knife was stick, sticking out of her chest.

KEERS: Okay. Where in her chest?

SUFF: In the middle of her chest.

KEERS: Okay. And what did you do?

SUFF: I pulled it out.

KEERS: Okay. Then what did you do, Bill?

SUFF: I gathered the clothes up, so I thought I'd pick up the clothes. I put the knife with the clothes, then I put it in the car and I left.

KEERS: Are you right-handed or left-handed, Bill?

SUFF: I'm right-handed.

KEERS: You are?

SUFF: Yes.

KEERS: I heard you. I did. I told you that we have evidence. We have lots of evidence, okay? Now. You did something else with the knife, okay? Now I'm gonna give you the opportunity to tell me the truth, Bill. I don't have to give the opportunity. You have to

SUFF: Yes.

KEERS: listen to me.

SUFF: I don't remember.

KEERS: Okay. Let me finish. You have to give now of yourself the truth. I can't give you everything. You have to give the truth. It's right there. That was your knife that was in that girl.

SUFF: No, it wasn't my knife.

KEERS: Okay. Okay. You found the knife in her chest.

SUFF: Yes.

KEERS: What did you do with it?

SUFF: I pulled the knife out.

KEERS: And?

SUFF: That's it, Ma'am.

KEERS: You don't

SUFF: I don't.

KEERS: remember what we just got through talking about the truth?

SUFF: Yes.

KEERS: I'm giving you the opportunity to tell the truth.

SUFF: I don't remember anything else. Honest.

KEERS: You're lying. You're trying to tell the truth. You really are. Now all you gotta do is tell it, Bill. Okay? Because I'm not gonna let you lie to me. What did the girl look like that was laying there? Describe her to us.

SUFF: She was, she was a Mexican, dark haired, and she was naked.

KEERS: She was naked?

SUFF: Ahm.

KEERS: Anything else unusual about her?

SUFF: She was missing a breast.

KEERS: Which breast?

SUFF: Uuh I was thinkin' the left one. I don't, she was missing one of her breasts.

KEERS: Okay. Consider yourself standing over the body, which one of her breasts was missing? Picture yourself, sleeping, face down beside the body. Which one of her breasts was missing?

SUFF: I think it was at her head, and it was her right breast.

KEERS: It was her right breast.

SUFF: I think so.

           (Throat Clearing)

SUFF: That looks a little bit like her.

KEERS: That looks like her?

SUFF: Ahm.

KEERS: What looks like her in the picture?

SUFF: The facial features.

KEERS: Facial features.

SUFF: Aha.

KEERS: Okay, Bill. Something else happened. It happened maybe in your van. Let me think. Now. We're talking about the truth, okay now? And you, you know as well as I do that you wanna tell us the truth.

SUFF: Yes.

KEERS: And you're tired of these lies that you've been telling us.

SUFF: Yes, but I did tell the truth.

KEERS: Fine. Okay, what do you need me to help you do, Bill?

SUFF: I don't remember.

KEERS: Well,

SUFF: Okay.

KEERS: close your eyes, close your eyes.

SUFF: Okay.

KEERS: Okay. Where are you, Bill?

SUFF: I'm standing over her body.

KEERS: No. No. Keep your eyes closed. You're driving in your van.

SUFF: Yes.

KEERS: Okay? Where you driving at?

SUFF: On Victoria.

KEERS: Before you got to Victoria you were driving somewhere else, weren't you, Bill? Weren't you, Bill?

SUFF: Yes.

KEERS: Where were you driving at Bill?

SUFF: Over by Kaiser Hospital.

KEERS: Okay. And before that Bill, you were driving somewhere else, weren't you, Bill?

SUFF: On the freeway.

KEERS: And before that?

SUFF: Home Club on the freeway to La Sierra at Kaiser.

KEERS: Okay. Close your eyes. Okay, you're gonna tell the truth now. You want to tell the truth. You told me that, but you're telling me you need me to help you.

SUFF: Yeah.

          (Throat Clearing)

KEERS: Maybe if you close your eyes you'll remember where you were. Do you remember where you saw that girl?

SUFF: Yes.

KEERS: Where is that?

SUFF: Up on University.

KEERS: Do, do you see yourself driving on University Avenue?

SUFF: Not that day I don't.

KEERS: Did you see yourself driving on 14th Street?

SUFF: Not that day I didn't.

KEERS: Where do you see this girl at? She's out on the street. Where do you see her up on the street? Close your eyes. She's walking or standing somewhere. Where do you see her?

SUFF: First time I saw

KEERS: Think about it,

SUFF: her was in the

KEERS: think about it,

SUFF: orange groves.

KEERS: no. Think about it. Think about it.

SUFF: I am thinking about it.

KEERS: Okay. Remember. All you have to do is remember. That's how I'm helping you at this point, you to remember. Because I will tell you when you have told the truth. You know what the truth is and that's all we're here to do is to get the truth. Where do you see her?

SUFF: In the orange grove.

KEERS: What, what is she doing in the orange grove?

SUFF: She's lying on the ground.

KEERS: No, she's not.

SUFF: Yes, she is. She's lying on the ground.

KEERS: Okay. We'll go over there first. She's lying on the ground. What happened? What are you doing? Think about it. What are you doing, Bill?

SUFF: I walked up to her, picked up her clothing. I walked around the head of her and I saw the knife then and I pulled it out of her chest.

KEERS: Okay. And what did you do then?

SUFF: I folded the clothing and I left.

KEERS: Beautiful. Now before the knife got in her chest.

SUFF: I didn't stab her.

KEERS: The knife was in your hand.

SUFF: No.

KEERS: See

SUFF: No.

KEERS: you you

SUFF: No.

KEERS: Listen to me. You tell me that you want to tell the truth.

SUFF: I'm telling the truth now.

KEERS: No you're not.

SUFF: Honest I am.

KEERS: Listen to me, okay? You've given us a lot of what we knew.

SUFF: Okay.

KEERS: We've got a lot more but you give it to us. I'm not gonna give it to you. Listen to me.

SUFF: I gave you

KEERS: One hint.

SUFF: Because I did not know anything else.

KEERS: Yes, you do, Bill.

SUFF: No I don't.

KEERS: Yes, you do. Yes, you do. Uh we are not going to set here and let you tell a lie. You told me you want to tell the truth.

SUFF: Yes, I do.

KEERS: You said to me, "Help me tell the truth".

SUFF: I did that.

KEERS: Haven't you?

SUFF: Yes.

KEERS: I am helping you to tell the truth.

SUFF: The truth is I found her body.

KEERS: You did.

SUFF: Yes. But I did not put her there.

KEERS: Okay.

SUFF: No.

KEERS: How about the ride, when you gave her a ride?

SUFF: I didn't give her a ride.

KEERS: Bill, we're talking about the truth.

SUFF: I did not

KEERS: Yes.

SUFF: give her

KEERS: You did.

SUFF: No.

KEERS: Yes, you did.

SUFF: I did not.

KEERS: We have evidence here that clearly shows who did this. That's why we're talking to you.

SUFF: You do?

KEERS: Listen to me. We are giving you the opportunity to tell the truth. I have not asked you to lie, I have not asked you to give us anything that we do not already know.

SUFF: You're gonna have to tell me it, this because I do not know anymore. Honest.

KEERS: Well, when you closed your eyes you could see things.

SUFF: Yeah, I do. I saw her body lying there. She was never in my van.

KEERS: Did you see yourself putting the knife in her chest?

SUFF: No.

KEERS: Well, it sounds like you didn't because you're not ready to tell the truth yet.

SUFF: I'm

KEERS: When you are ready to tell the truth, you will tell me what you did.

SUFF: I have.

KEERS: Because, as I told you,

SUFF: I didn't do it.

KEERS: we have evidence that shows that you are clearly the one who did this.

SUFF: No, your

KEERS: Now.

SUFF: evidence is wrong.

KEERS: No, it is not.

SUFF: It's got to be wrong.

KEERS: It's not wrong. I'll tell you, I told you that we have your tire prints and what do you tell me? "Yes I was there." I tell you that we have your foot- prints and you say, "Yes, I got out and I walked up the body. I pulled the knife out of her chest, I collected her clothes and I left." You're leaving out some very important parts, aren't you?

SUFF: No.

KEERS: Yes, you are.

SUFF: No, I'm not.

KEERS: Yes, you are.

SUFF: No, I'm not.

DAVIS: Bill, what did you do with the breast?

SUFF: I didn't do anything with the breast. I did not. It was already gone when I got there. Yes, it was.

DAVIS: Was it next to her?

SUFF: I didn't see it. I didn't see it there. I don't know.

DAVIS: Bill, everything comes out in the wash.

SUFF: I know it is. I did not do that.

DAVIS: You said that you wanna talk to us. You wanna clear this up. But you're not saying how.

SUFF: Yes, I did.

KEERS: Did you want to tell the truth?

SUFF: Yes, I did.

         (Throat Clearing)

SUFF: I have told you the truth.

KEERS: Some of it.

SUFF: No, ma'am, I've told you it all.

DAVIS: Are you, are you tellin' us

SUFF: Yes.

DAVIS: the whole truth, Bill, or are you just tellin' us things that you want to remember?

SUFF: No.

DAVIS: So, if you don't want to remember the whole truth

SUFF: I'm telling you exactly what I do remember.

KEERS: well, how about if I tell you what you don't remember?

SUFF: Tell me what you've got. Because I don't, I don't remember doing anything else. Honest, I did not pick her up, I did not take her there. I found her there.

KEERS: Okay. Okay. Let's go and let's think about who else you found, okay?

SUFF: I

KEERS: Maybe that will help you.

SUFF: I didn't.

KEERS: Maybe that would help you, because obviously you have been, you're unlucky, you to find these girls? Now who else have you found for us? Okay.

DAVIS: How

KEERS: Yes.

DAVIS: about in September, Bill? When we were talking about those County Hills, up in Lake Elsinore?

SUFF: I haven't been there.

DAVIS: You were there.

SUFF: No, I wasn't there.

DAVIS: Bill, you're lying to us again.

SUFF: No, I'm not lying.

DAVIS: Bill, you're lying to us again.

SUFF: No, I'm not.

DAVIS: Bill, you're not telling us the truth. You were up in Cook County Hills.

SUFF: I'm not.

DAVIS: I've got evidence to show you up there.

SUFF: You you'd never show any evidence because I was not up there.

DAVIS: Okay. You weren't there.

SUFF: No, I was not.

DAVIS: We've got your tire prints up there. Your tire tracks are there, Bill.

SUFF: They're not mine.

DAVIS: The tire tracks are there.

SUFF: They're not my tire tracks.

DAVIS: They're your tire tracks.

SUFF: No.

DAVIS: Know what else we got up there, Bill?

SUFF: No, I don't.

DAVIS: What do you think we have up there?

SUFF: I don't know.

DAVIS: Think about it, Bill.

SUFF: I do not know.

DAVIS: Think about it.

SUFF: No.

DAVIS: Think about going up to those County Hills.

SUFF: I haven't been up in Cook County

DAVIS: You know

SUFF: Hills.

DAVIS: when I talk about those County Hills, you know where I'm talking about?

SUFF: That new housing development that's going on up there.

DAVIS: Up where?

SUFF: Off, off the hill above um above new houses.

DAVIS: Big development, isn't it?

SUFF: I don't know how big it is, I haven't been up there.

DAVIS: Bill, why are you

SUFF: All I

DAVIS: lying?

SUFF: Another dead body?

DAVIS: I don't know. You tell me. Did you find

SUFF: I

DAVIS: one up there?

SUFF: No, I didn't. I didn't go up there.

DAVIS: Yes, you did.

SUFF: No, I did not.

DAVIS: You went up there in your van.

SUFF: No, I did not.

DAVIS: Your tire tracks are there. You know what else is there?

SUFF: No, I don't.

DAVIS: Guess.

SUFF: I don't know.

DAVIS: Guess what you left there.

SUFF: I don't know.

DAVIS: Think about it, Bill.

SUFF: I don't know.

DAVIS: You ought, you oughta know. You were there.

SUFF: I do not know. I was never

KEERS: Bill,

SUFF: there.

KEERS: we're not gonna let you lie. As I told you, every time that you start to tell a lie we're gonna stop you. Do you understand that?

SUFF: I didn't lie.

KEERS: You told us that you wanna tell the truth. Now do you wanna

DAVIS: She look familiar

KEERS: tell the truth?

DAVIS: to you, Bill?

SUFF: No, she doesn't.

DAVIS: No, she doesn't. Look at it. Look hard at that picture.

SUFF: She does not look familiar.

DAVIS: Yes, she does.

SUFF: No, she does not.

DAVIS: You saw her.

SUFF: No, I

DAVIS: Your saw her

SUFF: did not.

DAVIS: up in those County Hills on the dirt road.

SUFF: No, I didn't.

DAVIS: Your shoe prints are up there, Bill.

SUFF: No.

DAVIS: Along with the tire tracks.

SUFF: No.

DAVIS: Yes.

SUFF: No, not mine.

DAVIS: Yes, yours.

SUFF: Not me.

DAVIS: Yes.

SUFF: It was not me.

KEERS: Bill. Yes.

DAVIS: We found her up there.

KEERS: We're not gonna let you lie.

SUFF: I did not

KEERS: We're not gonna

SUFF: up there.

KEERS: let you lie.

SUFF: I did not

KEERS: That's a lie.

SUFF: find her. I have not seen her before.

DAVIS: Tell us about the way you found her.

SUFF: I didn't find her.

DAVIS: Yeah you did.

SUFF: No I didn't. I have not.

DAVIS: Look hard at the picture. Does she look familiar to you?

SUFF: I don't

DAVIS: So look

SUFF: No.

DAVIS: real hard. Well, well, let's put your glasses on and look at her.

SUFF: I can't see with my glasses up

DAVIS: ....

SUFF: in the hills.

DAVIS: Well, look at this picture.

SUFF: I don't know her.

DAVIS: Tell us about her, Bill.

SUFF: I don't know her.

DAVIS: You know we're talking the truth and everything comes out in the wash. This is just one more thing in the wash that's coming out.

SUFF: No, it isn't.

DAVIS: Yes, it is.

SUFF: Not in my wash. No, it isn't.

DAVIS: Yes, it is.

KEERS: Bill?

SUFF: What?

KEERS: We already told you. I'm not gonna let you lie. We're gonna give you the opportunity to tell us the truth, okay?

SUFF: Okay.

KEERS: You, you wanna tell the truth,

SUFF: Yes.

KEERS: I know you do. I can tell you have sat here and you have told us that you want to tell the truth, have you not?

SUFF: I have.

KEERS: Do you wanna tell the truth? Or do you wanna go on with these lies?

SUFF: I don't wanna tell any lies.

KEERS: Okay. Okay. You said, "I do not wanna tell any lies."

SUFF: Right.

KEERS: Okay. 'Cause John Davis here is trying to tell you what we know. What we know. Not what we're guessing, not what we think. What we have evidence to and what we know. You under-stand that?

SUFF: Yes.

KEERS: Now, it's you, time, stuff that you know.

SUFF: I did not

KEERS: Now, listen to

SUFF: Okay.

KEERS: me. Okay? You say you don't recognize her?

SUFF: No, I don't.

KEERS: You say you don't but we know that you were up there. Now this is your opportunity to tell the truth.

SUFF: I'm telling the truth. I did not go up there.

KEERS: I told you that every time you start to

SUFF: ....over

KEERS: tell a lie,

SUFF: over and over again.

KEERS: I will

SUFF: I do.

KEERS: because you

SUFF: Yes.

KEERS: we have evidence that clearly shows that you were the one that did this.

SUFF: No.

KEERS: And we are not gonna let you sit here and lie to us.

SUFF: We can't

KEERS: Okay?

SUFF: talk anymore then. We can't talk anymore then. Because you think I'm lyin' and I'm not.

KEERS: You can't talk any more

SUFF: I'm trying to.

KEERS: about what? Are you saying you don't want to talk to us any more?

SUFF: I can't talk any more about any of it any more because you're saying I'm lying and I'm not.

KEERS: Okay, Bill, we're gonna terminate this interview because you don't want to talk to us anymore.

SUFF: I want a lawyer.

KEERS: Okay.

SUFF: I want a lawyer.

KEERS: Okay. Um I'm going to just wait one second, to the left, I'm going to look here at your scratch marks and we're going to take photographs, okay? Okay, Bill, so we have to do this.

SUFF: Okay.

KEERS: I'll be back.

SUFF: Okay.

           (Door Opens and Closes)

(Inaudible Voices)

(Door Opens)

KEERS: Bill, would you take off your jacket? I want to take some photographs of you.

SUFF: Let's wait

KEERS: We need them.

SUFF: until my lawyer gets here.

KEERS: Well, um we're gonna do this okay? 'Cause then you're gonna be taken and and be booked. You're gonna be booked on your parole. ....Okay? So why don't you go and stand there. We're not gonna ask you any questions. You've already told us you didn't want to talk to us, so we'll go ahead and let you do that. Unzip your jacket please and take it off. We want you to remember that we cannot contact you, but at any time during the week, Bill, if you would want contacting us leave a message over here, you know where we're at. You've got my card in your pocket. Go ahead and take, your shirt open please. You still have it, is that correct?

SUFF: What?

KEERS: My card.

SUFF: Yes.

KEERS: I need you to take your shirt off, please.

(Inaudible Voices)

KEERS: Okay. They're rolling the film again, it just takes a second. Okay. Then we'll get you out of here, this place here, and take you to the jail.

DAVIS: Okay, go to the first one 32. Okay, can we get you to do that? Thank you. Can you look right at me with your eyes please open? Thank you. That's it. These marks here?

KEERS: Ahm. Aaaand let me see you hands please. You know, hold them out this

DAVIS: The mark on the wrist, is that a scar?

KEERS: It's a scar.

DAVIS: Okay.

KEERS: These here.

DAVIS: Here, I'll hold

KEERS: These here. Are these new marks?

KEERS: What were these? Take some of these please.

DAVIS: Okay. Just look up (camera clicking) and just look to the wall over here, okay. (camera clicking) Okay, can you just ....here. Is there something you think?

KEERS: Yeah, up on the nose.

DAVIS: Up here.

KEERS: Yeah.

RSO TECH: Okay. (camera clicking) Okay one more. Okay ....keep looking to your left over here. Thank you. Okay .... okay. (camera clicking) .... back?

SUFF: I don't know ....

RSO TECH: Okay, be patient. We're gonna take 'em all over again. We double shoot .... (camera clicking) Okay. Look to the wall ....

.... just a little bit turn your ....
(camera clicking) Okay, thanks. (camera clicking)
...................................now.............................
okay (camera clicking) Okay, hold your thumbs
down, thank you. (camera clicking) ....
..........(camera clicking)..................okay now ....
(camera clicking) ....
(camera clicking) okay.....................(camera
clicking) one of your hands (camera clicking) .....
okay...
....................Is that your cigarette?...................

SUFF: Okay.

....

SUFF: I tried it didn't uh, ...

RSO TECH: Oh yeah sure. Well, you should put your two shirts and then we've gotta get one with, are these your glasses?

SUFF: Yes.

RSO TECH: Okay, I wanna get one with your uh glasses on. Okay. Let's let's get them an' put them on.

SUFF: Okay.

RSO TECH: Hold on, let me just get a shot at that.

....(camera clicking)

....

Ahm. (camera clicking).....................................

SUFF: ....

Inaudible Voices

(camera clicking) Okay. (camera clicking)

KEERS: ....You guys..............................

Is there anything in these two pockets?

SUFF: I don't know.

KEERS: Okay. That's enough of the hands, you can come on.

(Inaudible Voices)

By this point in our story, you know Bill Suff almost as well as I do, so I'm going to let you come up with your own answers as to why he answered as he did during his interrogation, but notice how his lies built and twisted and folded in on themselves.

Here are some questions to ask yourself:

Why did he lie about his prison term in Texas when he knew darn well that the Riverside cops would find out all about it any minute?

When Bill admitted to "finding" Casares' body, to taking her clothes, to removing the knife from her chest, did he really think they'd believe him? Does he think any of us believe him now, as he still maintains this preposterous story?

The central core to Bill's defense is that he had hidden the fact that he was an ex-con, hidden it from friends, family, employer, lest they desert him, so he panicked when he "found" the body. He knew that evil cops try to frame ex-cons just because ex-cons are ex-cons and therefore disposable, and desperate cops become evil cops out of desperation, and these Riverside cops were long desperate and now turning evil.

However, the essence of what I see in all Bill's answers is that, despite Detective Keers' misguided "Murder, She Wrote" belief that Bill wanted to get caught and confess and unburden himself, *in fact Bill never ever thought he would be singled out and accused. He knew he was innocent under the law.* He was dead solid certain he'd gotten away with murder—he'd left no clues—and so he was stunned when they hauled his ass down to the station and turned on the spotlight. If he could just give them a few glib answers, then they'd have to let him go. Better to say something than nothing, because dummying up would look like covering up. The cops were all bluff and bluster—give them their due and maybe they'd cease their inquiries. Worse come to worst, there was still no hard evidence, there was only gut-level suspicion.

On this basis, even including his lies about his Texas past, don't you have to conclude that all Bill's responses are consistent with the attitude of someone who believes in his own innocence? Like the cops, we read guilt into Bill's responses because we've already judged him guilty, but, is his approach to his defense, his take on the truth, really any different than was my own when I was fingered by Officer Tucker? Guilty or innocent, doesn't the instinct for survival cause absolutely everyone to hesitate and fudge and try to find a way out of the hot seat? And, when personal morality and legal morality diverge, is there any way to get at objective truth through a directive interrogation? When you tell someone you know he did something even though you can't prove it, how does he change your mind? You can't prove and he can't disprove—it's a stalemate, but it's actually a loss for personal freedom.

Some years ago I went to Europe on lawful legal business, depositing money in a Swiss bank account for an actor-client. When I returned I went through Customs at LAX, stepping into the "Nothing to Declare" queue. The Customs Agent eyed my "Nothing to Declare" card and immediately waved me off to the side where three armed agents escorted me to a windowless cinderblock room. There I was ordered to strip down to my underwear.

I had nothing to hide but I nonetheless knew I was in trouble and I had no idea why. I couldn't keep *Midnight Express* out of my mind.

Suddenly the lead agent pointed to the gold neck chain and gold hockey puck medallion I wear under my clothes for luck. "Why didn't you declare that?" he demanded.

"Because I've had it for ten years and I bought it here in L.A.," I replied.

"Prove it," he said.

"It's listed on my insurance policy from before I went on this trip to Europe. And the jeweler that made the puck is in Beverly Hills and can verify whatever you need to know," I said.

"I don't believe you," said the customs agent. "I believe you bought this in Europe just now and you were trying to sneak it in without paying duty."

"This is crazy—look at it—the puck's dirty and worn down, the chain's old and worn and welded—look right here." I illustrated my points.

"I'm going to have to confiscate that," said the agent. "It's your legal obligation to have paperwork proof of origin on your person at the time you pass through Customs."

"I'm supposed to carry around insurance policies and old purchase receipts for everything I take on a trip with me?"

"That's the law," he said. "I'll need to confiscate that now. If you really do have the appropriate paperwork you can come back with it tomorrow and go to our main office."

"And I'll get my jewelry back?"

"Probably," he said. "But not for certain. It will be up to the agent there to decide."

"And my recourse?"

"You can go to court. But we resell confiscated items fairly quickly, and once they're in the system they're hard to track down."

"And I have no other option?" I suspected there was an ulterior motive here, and I was right.

"You can pay duty right now and be on your way with your jewelry," said the agent.

In other words, this clown was working some sort of quota—he needed to collect a certain amount of money each month or his boss would think he wasn't doing his job. Or maybe he and his pals just pocketed this as a "bonus".

"How much?" I asked.

"First you need to sign this new declaration," he said.

It wasn't so much a declaration as a false confession.

I signed. And then I paid $1,200 as duty and penalty. And I got to keep my nondutiable stuff. And somehow I felt relieved, relieved just to get out of there without a body cavity search or an arrest. Innocence was not the issue. Escape was everything. Survival put pucks and business trips all in perspective.

Later a law school chum of mine went to work for Customs. He learned that LAX Customs targets that particular London-LAX flight for middle- to upper-class travelers who routinely "smuggle" in costly goods without paying duty. Every eighth person in line gets dragged to the cinder-block room. You don't need to fit any profile, you just need to be number eight in line. Then they make a big show of taking you away, so the seven people who escape will think twice the next time about what they do or do not declare. Random terror replaces real investigative deduction, extortion is accepted in lieu of legitimate legal enforcement, and revenues beget pay raises for the agents involved.

Your government at work, ladies and gentlemen.

Proving that authority obscures rather than encourages truth. I now have a false confession on file with the U.S. Customs Service. I've admitted to smuggling that I didn't do. And I would have demanded credit for kidnapping the Lindbergh baby or admitted that I was O.J.'s accomplice if that would have gotten me out of that cinder-block room. When an animal gets caught in the head-lights, it doesn't run, it freezes.

When Bill Suff was arrested, he froze, stunned, and with good reason—he knew the cops had nothing on him. His arrest was unlawful, and his subsequent interrogation became a travesty. It ended, as you read, with Keers screaming "You did it!" and Bill shouting "I did not!" back and forth at one another, his vast arrogance incredibly one-upped by hers. In between, exhausted though he was, Bill kept asking for a lawyer, to no avail.

Desperate cops. Desperate situation. The cops were determined to stop the killing and they believed Bill was their man. But they broke the rules just as much as he and then justified it by insisting that what they did was okay because they were the good guys. Might made right and right made might.

But what if they were wrong about Bill? The crimes were awfully close to perfect—in the end, only the tire tracks gave Bill away. Keers knew she needed a confession to make the case—hell, she needed a confession even to justify a search—but Bill wouldn't confess. None of his admissions ever amounted to an "Okay, you got me, I did it". In the face of insistent accusation, he always maintained his innocence and always explained away the evidence and the theories against him.

Perhaps that was the most guilty-seeming thing he did. Maybe innocent people break down and confess just to get out of the cinder-block room. Maybe, whether you're guilty or innocent, you just can't win once the police decide to come after you. Certainly, that was Kafka's take, and he believed it so strongly he wouldn't even publish the stories he wrote about it. He even willed that the unpublished stories were to be burned upon his death. He was afraid the authorities could still get at him once he was in the grave.

In fact, it was only after the police decided that Bill was their man that new "evidence" magically appeared to seal the case. Initial searches yielded nothing, but later searches came up with items that had been "missed".

Once again, the police really missed the opportunity to close this case for good, to shut Bill up for all time. All the cops had to do was do their job according to the rules. They had no lawful reason to stop and question Bill, let alone to arrest him. But, once they had him in their sights, they were afraid to let him go. Despite all their profiles and researches to the contrary, the cops were afraid that this killer would suddenly stop killing and would destroy all possible evidence.

To this day the Riverside cops and prosecutor just don't understand what a serial killer is all about. They don't get that, once they suspected Bill, all they had to do was give him enough rope, watch from a distance, and he would try to kill again. Then they'd have him with his hand in the cookie jar.

That is, if he's really the killer.

Cheryl was giggling so hard, she was on the verge of peeing her pants. Her friend Judy, the store manager, was laughing so loudly, customers in the Circle K at that late hour were sure the two girls were on drugs. It just couldn't be legal for any two people to be having that much fun.

Down behind the front counter by the cash register, Cheryl had a one-gallon plastic bucket full of water. In the water she was soaking a tampon that she'd dipped in blood from a package of hamburger meat. The instant the tampon had hit the water it mushroomed and started to disintegrate. Now Judy was plucking the tampon from the water and dangling it, holding it out of Cheryl's reach as the younger girl jumped at it. Reddish water was flying everywhere, and, when Judy swung the tampon, it went flying too, out of her grasp—KERPLOP!—landing on the window top of the ice cream freezer.

Judy and Cheryl laughed all the harder.

The experiment was a bust. Cheryl had been hoping she could save a used tampon from her next period, moisten it, and briefly reinsert it to kind of wring out some of the blood back inside her before she had sex with Bill, and have him think that he'd drawn the blood in the process of tearing her hymen.

But, clearly, a tampon was not going to work.

Now she was left with the possibility of squirting a basterful of chicken or beef blood into her, or ketchup even, but what if Bill tasted her like she hoped he would?

"How about—while he's in you, you reach down there and scratch yourself and bleed for real?" suggested Judy.

"Youch!" replied Cheryl. "Besides, at some point he'll see the scratch and know that's what bled."

"Okay, okay, then I've got it—prick your finger with a tack, and then rub it on him when you're getting him all worked up."

"A prick, for a prick's prick?" Cheryl laughed.

"Bill is not a prick," said Judy, "he's one terrific guy."

"Except for this virgin business. What is the big deal anyway? A girl who's doing it for the first time is lousy at it."

"And a girl who's too good at it is a whore."

"Why are men so fucked up, huh?"

"Who cares—just be glad you got one."

"You're so hot for him, you take him."

"Maybe I will."

Cheryl dagger-eyed Judy. "Don't you dare," said Cheryl.

It was late—Cheryl had overstayed her shift to play around with the tampon. Bill would be home and Bill would be worried about why she was late. He liked to keep tabs on her, liked to know for certain where she'd be when and when she'd be where. Right now he'd be reading in bed, and, as soon as he heard her key in the lock, he'd shut off his reading light and pretend to be asleep. Cheryl could see the light go off from under the front door of their apartment. It was just one of his little games.

Later, as soon as Cheryl shut off her light and tucked herself in to the sofa, Bill would masturbate. She was certain he wanted her to hear it, but if she surprised him by creeping into his room during his self-abuse, he would roll over and make a snoring sound. Sometimes she waited until she heard him come, and then she'd go to his door and smell it in the air. That got her excited. Then she'd return to her sofa and diddle herself.

More games.

Cheryl longed for a normal sex life with this man, but she was intrigued by what they had. Older men definitely had more complex sexuality than the teenagers she knew—all her peers wanted to do was fuck.

"I better get home," Cheryl said to Judy.

"If he calls I'll tell him you left a while ago but you were gonna stop for gas."

"No, he checks the gas gauge."

"Really?"

"G'night."

Cheryl headed out.

It was odd—some nights Bill insisted on dropping Cheryl off at work and picking her up after, and sometimes he'd call at the last minute and ask if Cheryl could hitch a ride with Judy—but he never seemed to have any real rhyme or reason for it either way. He was always possessed by some premonition of an earthquake or robbery or some disaster that would befall Cheryl without his protection, and he liked to terrify her and make her take his advice by warning her of his worry, but it really seemed like even he knew he was making it all up just to divert everyone's attention from some secret agenda he had going.

Tonight Cheryl hadn't heard from Bill at all, and that was definitely odd. If she didn't know better, Cheryl would have believed that Bill was cheating on her.

In fact, at that very moment, high in the not-so-high Ortega Mountains behind Lake Elsinore, in a kind of canyon within a canyon, hidden from sight above and below, at a place that would always be for him "Tranquility Garden", Bill Suff was alone with Carol Lynn Miller and Cheryl was most definitely not on his mind.

Earlier in the evening, Carol had missed her drug connection. Actually, she'd been at the rendezvous point on time and ready to score, but her dealer hadn't shown, no doubt wisely aware that Carol wouldn't have the cash to consummate the transaction.

Carol was angry at first, angry at the no-show, but then she decided it was some sort of a sign, that all the forces of nature and even the drug dealers of the world were unifying to tell her she couldn't afford her addiction anymore. She was financially and emotionally bankrupt, bereft. She needed to get whole, she needed to get clean.

In response, she decided she'd go cold turkey—after all, she was already more than a few hours into it, and it wasn't really so bad.

Unfortunately, per usual, resolve turned to challenge.

Who was that motherfucking dealer to decide for her when she would kick or not?

She'd show him, she'd show them all. Carol would take her life back her way, in her own damn time. If she wanted to hook and she wanted to fix, that was her business, her life.

She headed down to the local "business district" where she and her kind earned their keep. No welfare for Carol Miller—she was no charity case—she had something to sell, and there were plenty willing to pay.

Tonight, Bill Suff picked her up.

To Carol, Bill seemed just the kind of guy you could weasel more and more loot out of as the evening progressed. He was embarrassed but he was excited. She could tell that this was a fantasy for him, and you just can't put a price on fantasy—once committed, price would be no object. Carol would quote Bill twenty for a straight lay, then tease him with a little head and tell him that'd cost him a little extra or else she'd stop. Maybe then a prostate massage or a few different lovin' positions— Carol was plenty flexible and plenty strong, her body was soft and curvy all over, and she'd charge for each angle of attack. She'd let him have any part of her he wanted, even parts he would never have asked for on his own. She could make enough off this guy, she could call it a night.

So she gladly climbed into Bill's rig and agreed it was a terrific idea he had about heading up into the hills where they could be alone. "I'm kind of choosy," Carol told Bill, "and when I meet a man I like, I like to give him my undivided attention. Turn up that music, okay?"

She reached over to unzip Bill's fly, and he reached to turn up the volume on the radio. It was an easy listenin' station—not rock, barely pop. "Careful how you drive now, sugar—keep your concentration on the road," she said, and then put her head in his lap. After a lick or two, she looked up at him for a moment: "Tonight's your lucky night, big guy. Big guy, big tipper, right?"

He looked down at her as she went back at him with relish.

And then he smiled.

"Wrong," he said.

And so now Bill and Carol were in Tranquility Garden and the only reason it was tranquil was because she was tied up with sisal rope, her black cotton undershirt stuffed in her mouth.

Carol was naked, lying on her back on a plastic tarpaulin, and she didn't notice the cold. All around her, Bill had his toolboxes, his paint, his killing kit. Light came from one of those blue-glowing liquid light tubes, the kind you bend and crack so the chemicals mix and light up for a while—eerie but gentle.

Bill had really really really wanted to cut up and paint up Carol, but he just knew it would come back to haunt him, forensically speaking, so now he thought he'd etch and paint an image of her lying there like that—he had a leather belt he meant to use as a canvas—but, once again, he was finding that the artistic and the practical didn't go together: it was gonna take way too long and he was gonna feel way too pressured to etch and paint while tucked into that dark hillside on this cold desert night. You just shouldn't force art, that's the whole point.

So, while Carol lay there, Bill closed up his toolboxes, put away his paints, stowed it all back in his rig. He didn't let himself rush, instead he savored each moment. Behind the driver's seat he saw his tape recorder still taping—now he shut it off. This wouldn't be a tape much worth listening to. This woman had been different from all the rest: she hadn't screamed, hadn't fought, hadn't tried to talk her way out. As soon as he'd had her by the throat, she'd gone limp on him, gone unconscious. He knew he'd been getting better at just blacking someone out with his first assault rather than squeezing all the life out of her, but this one—it was like his touch hypnotized her or something.

Even now, now that Carol'd come to, with her eyes wide open and her breathing raspy loud, she just lay there impassively. The other girls, they'd resist to a point and then resign themselves to their fates, but it was active resignation—he could see their lips move as they prayed, tears on their cheeks, and he hated them for that, hated them for praying to a false God who would grant them no salvation. Bill was their God and they should have recognized it—he alone could and would deliver them from evil. Through death, he would save them from himself. That's what aroused him. He was God and man to them. He would kill them and then he would fuck them.

Then again, what he'd always fantasized, what he really wanted, was the sacrificial virgin, the woman whose whole life had been lived for the moment Bill would deflower her, and whose whole existence would be justified by death immediately following. A flower buds, grows, gains secret and wondrous beauty, and then, from the moment it opens it is dying. That's a fact. From the moment the flower opens, it is a burden to the plant, pulling moisture and nutrients away from the needy buds. Once opened, the flower's only true purpose is to crumble, to give off its pollen, its seed, and the sooner it swoons and snaps from its stem, petals falling from its heart, the sooner its legacy is secured and its life given meaning only in retrospect.

And this woman, this hooker, Carol Miller, she was the first who seemed to know that. She seemed not so much to be accepting her destiny as welcoming it. Yes, she knew about the flowers, she knew about sacrifice, and she was honored that she, of all people, had been chosen.

Bill was certain of it.

He reached under a floor mat and pulled out a dagger, grasped it tight. It was really just a kitchen knife, and it would go back to being a kitchen knife by light of day—in fact it would go back into Bill and Cheryl's kitchen—but right now it was a mythical dagger transformed for extraordinary purpose. It had the blood of the ancients on its blade, the hand sweat of the holiest of holy men on its grip, the symbols of all knowledge and all power erupting into Bill's palm, there to be felt but never seen.

Carol Miller watched her killer approach. He'd opened his jumpsuit, and his penis was engorged, leading him toward her. She was beyond hope, beyond fear. Somehow, everything that was happening was everything that she'd always expected. This was why she'd long sought the numbness of the drug, but now she was numb even without it.

Bill Suff knelt down between Carol's legs. "I'm going to take the gag out of your mouth so long as you promise not to scream," he said, "otherwise I'll have to hurt you."

Carol knew she was dead, but she didn't want any more pain—she nodded agreement with her eyes, and Bill removed the shirt from her mouth. She was too dry to swallow, but she gave a dry cough. Bill looked down, reached down and positioned himself to enter her, the head of his penis against her folds.

"Never before and never again," he intoned the heavens, and, in one thrust, forced himself inside her as his hand came up holding the dagger, plunging it down square into her chest where it hit bone and bounced angrily away.

She would have screamed in agony but he didn't give her the chance—before she could inhale to scream, his one hand grabbed her throat and closed like a vise while the other drove the knife down four more times through her ribs, her sternum, until he felt the comforting tension, stretch, and pop as the blade pierced Carol Miller's heart and killed her, leaving her eyes wide open. Now the killer bent forward, careful not to let his chest rub against the rivulets of blood which were pouring in all directions from Carol's chest, and he licked her lips, kissed her. Then he sat back, pulled the knife out of her chest, pulled himself out of her, stood up, looked down at her, and decided to wrap her undershirt over her face.

For the next several minutes, Bill cleaned up the scene and packed everything away, walking around Carol like she was just another rock in the garden. Finally, he pulled up the plastic tarp around her and hefted her into the back of his rig. The blue liquid light was just about faded out, *and the stars winked from their canopy. Down below, there were just a few lights still on in Elsinore. Bill checked the time—it was late, later than he planned. Cheryl would be home by now and his alibi might be iffy.*

Suddenly, he had an idea that flushed him with excitement: He wouldn't dump the body tonight. He'd keep it in the rig—take it home with him, take it to work tomorrow, and then get rid of it tomorrow night. That would really be something—to go through the day acting normal when you knew you had the corpse of a dead girl in your rig. He'd have a hard-on all day long. And the police would get all screwed up trying to figure out time of death. Bill would create a perfect alibi for himself for tomorrow and make it look like the girl died then, when Bill couldn't've done it.

That would be the final equation for Carol Miller.

When Bill got home, Cheryl was asleep on the sofa. This was the first time after a killing that he really wanted to fuck the girl he was living with, but he stopped himself. So long as Cheryl was underage, he had to maintain his discipline.

Bill went into his bedroom and jerked off. At one point he thought he saw Cheryl's shadow standing by the door, but he wasn't sure. Afterwards, he found he couldn't sleep. He crept out to his rig half a dozen times or more between then and morning, making sure that Carol's body was hidden from view. Cheryl woke up at Bill's peregrinations, asked him what was going on, what was the rumpus, and he told her his allergies were acting up and he was going outside to sneeze. He actually thought she believed him, but the truth was she just didn't mind his lies.

Early on the morning of February 8, 1990, a migrant worker found the body of Carol Lynn Miller in a grapefruit grove in Rubidoux by Lake Elsinore. She was naked, lying on her back, laid out evenly, legs spread, her black cotton undershirt draped at an angle across her face, a sort of exotic harem veil, with one eye covered and the other open and exposed. She'd been dead at least all night and maybe another full day, too. Her lower lip was crunched and folded down and there was some lividity in her face, so she'd spent her first hours after death in a different position than she was found, maybe with her head bent under or curled up.

Some paint chips were found on her skin—just a few, blue and white and clear layers of lacquer, just like chips found on Darla Ferguson, the most recent victim of the Riverside Prostitute Killer prior to Carol. These were the only two victims ever found with paint chips.

There were conflicting stories as to when Carol had last been seen alive. The john said she'd slept under his porch on Monday the 5th, but in fact Monday was the 6th. A dealer said he'd seen Carol on the street the night of Tuesday the 6th, but of course Tuesday was really the 7th.

Nobody keeps dates straight anymore.

Bill claimed to have worked late one night and gone to the hospital for an allergy shot on another night, and records bore him out. Cheryl said she was home with Bill both nights after work.

When bodies are left outside, you can determine time of death by maggots if you have to. Literally the moment you die, carrion flies land on you, feed on your cells as the dead cell walls burst and ooze their juices, and then the flies lay eggs. And the eggs hatch maggots after only a few hours, a set number of hours varying only between the different types of flies. Then the maggots turn into adult flies over the course of the next few hours, and these flies have a nosh and lay eggs and start the process all over again. Along the way, other flies land and lay eggs, so your corpse is pretty quickly a multigenerational breeding ground, and you can accurately backdate to time of death just by counting up the generations buzzing around.

Unfortunately, no one bothered to run a maggot-check on Carol Miller, so there was no way to prove when she died. Had Bill Suff been charged with only her murder, he would have walked. No evidence placed him anywhere near her, not then, not ever.

Nonetheless, Carol Miller helped Bill earn the death penalty.

Next to Carol's leg, on the ground, a peeled grapefruit had been found. The press, the police, and the prosecutor all asserted that this cold-blooded killer had stood by the corpse and calmly eaten the grapefruit. Surely you have to execute a man who snacks over the bloody body of his victim, right?

This was the death sentence equation. As noted, it was raised exponentially by Dijianet, but Carol was the only victim found near "food evidence" like this.

The problem is, the killer didn't eat the grapefruit at all, didn't even attempt to. This killer would never have taken a bite out of an object and then left it for police to take dental impressions and recover pristine DNA saliva residue. And this killer didn't leave any fingerprints on the peelings either.

What you should be struck with when you examine the photo of the grapefruit is that it has been peeled and then placed whole on the ground near Carol Miller's leg. And the pieces of peel have been dropped in a pattern inconsistent with the notion of a callous guy just standing around peeling and eating a grapefruit. The peels are mostly lumped in one area, but too many are scattered all around, including between Carol's legs. Also, aerodynamics says that if the peels were just dropped or even tossed, they should have landed outside down—that is, the curving, yellow side down . . . yet, most of the pieces were found yellow side up.

You may have your own theories as to the meaning of the grapefruit and its peels—like clouds and constellations, you can see all sorts of imagery from a bird to a man to whatever if you squint from different angles and let your mind go free.

But I think the grapefruit was an offering symbolic of Carol's virginal sacrifice. Bill was in a grapefruit grove, so he peeled—deflowered—a grapefruit; had he been in a rose garden I believe he would have pulled the petals from a rose.

The peelings were clearly accumulated in his hand, all together, and then hurled down all at once, scattering in a spray pattern, hurled with enough force to override aerodynamics. This was an *I Ching* throw of the markers—fate would determine the meaning of the spray/landing pattern. Bill believes in tea leaves and every other prescient symbol, even though he tends to read them pursuant to his own rules, and the meanings tend to be pre-determined in his own mind.

Accordingly, after raining down the peelings, Bill knew to place the grapefruit itself at the head of the spray. Now he had a pattern creepily similar to the "maps" of McCaffrey's Pern solar system from which Bill's own fictional universe was derived in his story "Crash Landing". The pattern mimics the actual crash of the spaceship—an impact crater and a spray of material from ship and ground.

The grapefruit and its peelings therefore comprise a map, a hieroglyph, directing us to the other world where Bill really lives, the world where Carol Miller's soul has now gone. It is the parallel world of both "Crash Landing" and "A Whisper From the Dark".

Carol's body may be here in this earthly "graveyard" (an orchard to us, a graveyard to Bill), but her spirit, her real self, is alive and well and now embodied on another world, worlds away.

A world where Bill Suff is loving, kind, generous, and heroic. A world where Bill Suff is for all time an innocent man. It is the world of good intentions, the world of a child.

As for Carol, she was uniquely special to Bill and his fantasies, in the pantheon of his victims she mattered in a positive way. Unlike other victims, he didn't mutilate her, and he killed her twice—both the strangling and the stabbing were fatal—not as overkill, but to be quick, certain, and painless about it. He also did not demean her in final repose—in death she was left laid out as in life, with her face discreetly covered. Interestingly, Eleanor Casares was also left in an orchard, and her face was covered, too.

Finally, Bill's attitude toward his victims—how he perceived them—was no doubt more a function of his "outside" life than any actual reality respecting the victim. When Bill killed Carol, he was in love with Cheryl and believed in her and her virginity. Despite her best intentions, Bill later found out that Cheryl was no virgin, and, as bad as that betrayal was for him, the only thing worse was when she got pregnant. Once again he decided that he was with a woman who lied to him, cheated on him, and might be bearing another man's child. Teryl's betrayals became ascribed to Cheryl, even though there's no evidence at all that Cheryl ever betrayed Bill.

But, once Bill turned on Cheryl—once he'd concluded that she'd turned on him—the violence of his killings escalated. The first killings—including several in Elsinore attributed to him but for which he has yet to be charged—involved sacrificial stabbing of the heart. Clearly, he then began stabbing the vaginas of his later victims because the wombs of the women in his life had cuck-olded him in the most emotionally profound and painful way, and drawing blood from the vaginas of his victims was his way of finally getting the virginal blood that both Teryl and Cheryl had promised and then denied him.

Does all this fantastic fantasy make sense?

Sure.

Isn't it just plain nuts?

Definitely.

So what do we do with these people, with the Bill Suffs of the world?

That's the question.

And the answer is that, all this horror aside, I am still anti–death penalty and particularly anti–death penalty for Bill Suff.

Murder is wrong, and, as a society, we have to find a way to stop it. But the death penalty has no deterrent effect. It also dehumanizes us, it turns us—the innocent—into murderers. More, the system is all-too-often fallible, and one too many innocent men have been executed for my taste.

Giving the State a mechanism of legalized homicide is an open invitation to abuse and disaster. It scares me. The cinder-block room is bad enough.

Nonetheless, I feel for the families of crime victims, and I know that if someone murdered someone I loved, I'd be the first out there with my nine-millimeter Beretta looking to get even.

I don't find that hypocritical. My suggestion is that we re-write the laws and go back to our English common law tradition. It used to be that, if you saw a guy killing your daughter, you could chase him down the street and blow him away, and, at worst, you were guilty of manslaughter but probably you were guilty of no crime at all.

So, I say if we insist on having a death penalty, then work it as a writ of execution issued to a family member of the victim. If Dad wants to see his daughter's killer killed, let Dad himself throw the switch on Old Sparky.

Murder is personal—let's keep it that way.

As for Bill, it's easy for me to push for reversal of his death sentence because, no matter what, he's going to spend the rest of his life in jail. Nonetheless, he's proved he's no danger to anyone while in jail, and he's always protested his innocence to these crimes where the evidence was hardly beyond a reasonable doubt and where the investigation, arrest, and trial were anything but fair.

People will say that, by his convictions, Bill has forfeited his right to be heard any longer, but his is a unique and powerful voice that will go a long way toward helping us save ourselves from future Bill Suffs. We really have to decide whether we want to prevent murder or merely be content with mopping up the blood afterward.

Finally, to be noted is that Bill has his share of supporters who fully believe in his innocence. To them and to Bill, I say that the simple test of the truth would be to let Bill out of jail and watch what he does. As smart as he is, as clever as he is, as creative as he is, if he is what we think he is, then, loose in the world, he will attempt to kill again.

A serial killer can't stop himself.

That's the whole point.

And, to me, that's insane.

And we don't execute people for insanity.

The final chapter has yet to be written on the Bill Suff case, but this book is now done.

With this book, Bill will think that I have betrayed him, but the truth is that I consider him a friend. Regardless of what pain he may or may not have inflicted on others, his relationship with me has made my life better, has caused me to look into myself, to resolve issues that were long troubling and self-destructive.

I wish the same personal growth for him.

And I will fight alongside him to get his death sentence overturned.

CHAPTER 18

"A Disaster in Justice"

written by
Bill Suff

A Disaster in Justice

He was unbelievably shocked. He hadn't committed the crimes he had been convicted of but it looked like he was the one who was going to suffer the punishment. Only a few people believed he was innocent. But there were others who knew he was innocent: the real killers, some of the police investigators, and, to a more limited degree, some of the other members of the district attorney's office. Even the prosecuting attorney knew he was wrongly accusing this man on several accounts. But he sure wasn't about to admit it. Unfortunately, the people who knew him best (his wife, old girlfriend, co-workers, family), believed the lies and innuendoes told to them by the police investigators. The alibis that the witnesses had testified to were not believed. Evidence that proved innocence wasn't presented in a convincing manner so it would overcome the lies and supposed facts presented by the prosecution. Statements pointing out that DNA evidence directly opposed the teachings of the Bible were ignored. Of course, if not for the news media, the trial might have been a fair one. The news media had assumed the worst, accepted the "leaks" at face value, and convinced the public that he had done every horrible crime the prosecution was claiming. Long before the jury was chosen, the news media had brainwashed everyone into believing in his guilt. It was the opinion of many that the jury came in predisposed to a guilty verdict, despite their claims of being able to wait for the evidence before making a decision. That opinion was based upon the questionnaires the jury panel answered before being subjected to the voir dire. There were many responses like "He's guilty!" and "If he wasn't guilty, he wouldn't be in jail!" One respondent went so far as to say "If he's guilty, give him death! If he's not, give him life without parole!" He had read the questionnaires and knew what they said. More than 90% were negatively oriented toward him. So the topic of fairness still nagged at him.

After receiving the death sentence, Lee was consoled by several members of the jail staff that had gotten to know him. They couldn't believe he had been found guilty, let alone sentenced to death. Talking to these people that believed in his innocence only brought on tears for all concerned. Just about everyone else who knew him had turned their collective backs on him. His own family thought he was guilty after listening to the lies and exaggerated evidence the investigators told them. And that really hurt him, because in his experience most families stuck together through thick and thin. Blood didn't turn their backs on blood. He couldn't believe his own family was not standing up in his defense, backing him regardless of the consequences.

The investigator that had spent so many hours alone with him in a small, locked room, that had stood beside him in court and had helped to build a case for his defense, no longer came to see him. The feelings for her that had grown within his heart, began to change into the pain of being forsaken. Phone calls to her were now refused. That he could no longer even talk to her, hurt much more than his being found guilty of crimes he hadn't done. But then, she wasn't aware that he had started to fall in love with her, either. He was at loss for words because of the pain he felt. He had trouble concentrating on things now. He only stared at the television, the programs going unseen. When he did pay attention to the movies and such, his emotions exaggerated the feelings produced by the programs. Tears often came unbidden. He just couldn't believe what was happening to him.

He was awakened early on the morning of November 1st by two of the jail deputies.

"All right, Lee, roll it up," one of them said. "It's time for you to leave our accommodations."

They stood in the door of his cell, watching him gather his meager belongings together. He was aware of what they were really doing. They were making sure that he made no phone calls to alert anyone that he was going to be on the road that morning, heading for San Quentin State Prison. The thing was, people would already know. He had talked to friends on the phone the night before, letting them know that if he didn't call them right after breakfast, for them to be aware that he was no longer in town. It wasn't for nefarious reasons, though. He didn't want his friends or attorneys to travel all the way for a visit and be turned around without seeing him.

He was dressed in an orange jumpsuit, shackled with waistchains and leg-irons. Two sheriff's deputies transported him in a black and white squad car, leaving the county jail at 6:00 in the morning. Driving north on Interstate 5, they kept their speed hovering between 75 and 90 mph. They only made three stops along the way: a gas refill, a restroom break, and to pick up food and drink. During the entire trip, the two officers never spoke to their prisoner, never offered him a restroom break, food or drink. As far as they were concerned, he was a non-person. It was a six-hour trip and they arrived in San Rafael, at San Quentin, right about 12:00 noon. The two deputies turned over their weapons at the gate and then drove onto the prison grounds. Arriving at the reception and processing center, they got out of the squad car and entered the building. After awhile they returned to the squad car to let their prisoner out. They removed his waistchains and leg-irons, told him to enter the building and had nothing more to do with him.

Inside the building, Lee was told to strip completely and was then given a new orange jumpsuit and slide-on shoes. An hour later, he was processed into the prison system and given a sack lunch to eat. Soon, two escort officers handcuffed him and began the long walk to the Adjustment Center.

They hadn't taken more than two dozen steps out of the reception center, when Lee heard his name called out. He glanced over his shoulder, toward the general population exercise yards. Inmates dressed in blue were all over the place. But there were three inmates standing off by themselves, looking right at him.

"Hey, Lee," they hollered. "Welcome to the place you're gonna die! We're gonna getcha before you're executed!"

He glanced at the two escort officers to see if they gave any reaction to the death threat. Neither officer gave any sign that they had heard anything. They had to have heard it, he thought. But neither glanced in his direction. They just kept walking along on either side of him, not speaking and all but ignoring him.

Soon, they arrived outside the Adjustment Center and the first thing he noticed was a sign: "NOTICE: NO WARNING SHOTS ARE FIRED IN THIS BUILDING!" That sign frightened him more than he cared to admit. That meant if something happened, it would be stopped by the firing of weapons. He'd heard stories of prison guards shooting inmates at the slightest provocation. He'd also heard about guards who retaliated against one prisoner for wrongs committed by another prisoner. He hoped that they weren't true here. Just the same, he made a mental note to pay close attention to what was going on around him and if anything did happen, he was going to hit the ground.

After entering the Adjustment Center building, he was taken upstairs to the third floor where he would be assigned to a temporary housing cell. He had trouble climbing those four sets of stairs. A knee injury from the mid-'60s and an ankle injury from a motorcycle accident left him with an unstable center of balance. The strain of climbing that many stairs on his left leg caused pain to shoot through his entire leg and hip. The escort officers grabbed his arms and helped him climb the steps between the second and third floors. They didn't care, though. They just wanted to get him to his assigned place and then go on to other things. They locked him into a holding cell on the third floor and left. The officer that was working that floor made him strip once again. While standing there naked, he was told to go through what was to become a regular routine. He showed the backs and palms of his hands. He held up his arms to show his armpits. Opened his mouth and lifted his tongue to show it was empty. Had to turn around and show the bottoms of his feet. Had to bend over and cough to show he hadn't hidden anything in his rectum. That was a ritual he was now expected to go through every time he left his cell to go somewhere. He was then given a pair of bluejeans, socks, undershorts, a T-shirt and the slip-on shoes he had been given earlier. He quickly got dressed, not liking to be naked in front of anyone, male or female. Handcuffs were then put back on him, he was pulled out of the little holding cell and walked through another door, down a cell-lined row to one about three-quarters down the tier. The cell door was opened, Lee stepped inside, the door closed and then the 'cuffs were removed. Looking around his new home, he felt a pang of despair enter his heart. That lump grew to the point that it felt like his heart would burst.

This cell was only 4½ feet wide by 6 feet long. It was furnished with a sink (hot and cold water), a toilet bowl, and a metal bunk with a very thin mattress rolled up on it. He was soon brought two sheets, a pillow case, a towel, soap and a toothbrush that had been broken in half.

He was in the process of making his bed up, when he heard his cell number called out by another inmate. He didn't answer right away, for he had been previously warned by a friend that other inmates would attempt to find out who he was and from which county he had come. He had also been warned that he should make a strong attempt at keeping anyone from finding out what he had been convicted of so they wouldn't hold his convictions against him and possibly take vengeful action on him. So he kept quiet and continued making his bed. When he was done, he laid down and tried to take a nap. By taking a nap he knew he could block out the heartbreak that was tearing him apart.

A couple of hours later, he awakened to a loud, reverberating shout that echoed up and down the row and into his cell.

"Chow time. All lights on or you don't get fed!"

He quickly arose, slipped his shoes on and stood at his cell door, waiting for whatever would happen next. He didn't know if he would be pulled out and taken to a chow hall or if he would eat in his cell like he did in the county jail. After a couple of minutes went by, two officers pushed food carts past his cell to the end of the row. Several minutes after that, they returned, stopping at each cell to feed that particular inmate. When they reached his cell, his food port was unlocked and opened, then a tray of food and a drink was passed in to him. The food was plentiful and palatable, even tasty. The drink, though, was coffee. Lee couldn't drink coffee. He was allergic to an acid that was in the coffee-bean. One cup of coffee would cause him to start bleeding internally from every inch of tissue which the coffee came into contact with.

When he had been found guilty of the charges filed against him, he almost decided to end everything right then. He was not going to give the state of California the satisfaction of executing him for a crime he hadn't committed. If he had to die, he was going to rob the state, and everyone else, of their pleasure in executing him. He would drink a cup of coffee, and that would be that—he would die on his own terms.

But, suicide was morally and spiritually repugnant to him. In his mind, committing suicide was almost as bad as taking another's life! So instead, he promised himself that he'd give his attorneys and the good Lord a chance to prove his innocence. He could always kill himself—there was no need to be hasty. Maybe there was still a chance to get out of this mess, for the truth to be revealed and set him free.

After he finished eating and the trash was picked up, Lee laid back down. He had nothing to read, no writing supplies to write letters with, nothing at all to occupy his time. Lee decided to go back to sleep. Time would pass much faster that way. But it wasn't easy to go to sleep here. The noise coming from the other cells was deafening. One inmate was hollering to another as loud as he could in Spanish. Others were yelling back and forth to each other in

English and Spanish. Further down the row, it sounded like another inmate was yelling at the top of his lungs for his mother. Those cries for his mother were heart-rending and interspersed with heart-felt sobs. They made Lee feel like crying himself. But not for his mother. He felt like it was for too many other reasons to list. Among those reasons, however, was the loss of his daughter, wife and friends, not to mention the loss of his freedom.

Over the following three weeks, with the exception of two days, his routine didn't change. Those two days, he was taken out of his cell and brought before the Inmate Classification Committee. His assigned counselor told him that he should only be in the Adjustment Center for about a week. It actually proved to be over two weeks before he left that building for good. He was asked a series of questions: Did he use drugs, alcohol, smoke? Was he ever under psychiatric care or prescribed mood altering medication? The counselor actually seemed disappointed when all of his questions were answered in the negative.

"You don't seem to fit any of the normal profiles of a condemned prisoner," he said.

"Maybe," Lee responded rather sarcastically, "it's because I'm *not* one of your normal condemned prisoners. *Maybe* I was actually wrongly convicted!"

The counselor scoffed and answered "Yeah! Sure, and so is everyone else in here." He spoke as if the judicial system would never make a mistake.

When he was seen by the Classification Committee, he was told that none of the paperwork pertaining to his case or time in the county jail had been received. The only reason the prison had accepted him was because the court paperwork committing him to prison had come up with him in the transportation car. Because of the lack of paperwork, he could count on staying in the Adjustment Center for another two weeks. He told them about all of the death threats he had received and requested protective custody status. He was refused and assigned to an integrated exercise yard. They told him that he would have to identify the persons that were threatening him before they could act on it. Lee thought to himself 'Guess I'll have to have a knife in my gut before they believe me!'

During his second week in the A/C, he began to hear his name spoken by some of the other inmates on the floor. They were speaking Spanish and he was able to pick up the word "muerte". He had taken a year of Spanish in high school. He didn't know a lot of Spanish, but he knew that word! Requesting to see his counselor again, he related the new threats to his life and renewed his request for protective custody status.

"You know," his counselor said, "once you're assigned to the PC yard, no change in status will ever be allowed."

Lee looked directly into his eyes and spoke softly. "If it's a choice between spending the rest of my time here on a PC exercise yard or going to an integrated yard and having my throat cut, it's not a hard choice for me to make!"

The next day, he saw the committee again and his request for protective custody was finally granted. He was then told that his paperwork still hadn't arrived, but that it was no reason that *he* should be punished by being forced to remain in the A/C. He was told that he would be transferred to the condemned row building later that morning. At 11:30, he was told to pack up his gear . . . it was moving time.

Once again he was handcuffed, his arms behind his back, and escorted out of the building by two officers. As they exited the building, Lee saw several inmates wearing blue working on the surrounding grounds. As the escort officers and he walked out of the gated door, one of the officers yelled out "Escort!" Immediately, all of the nearby inmates arose from their tasks and walked a short distance in the opposite direction, away from the escorts. Lee was then led out of the building, around a security checkpoint, and along a paved walkway. After the walkway, they exited onto a large, paved yard. There were more inmates all over the yard dressed in orange jumpsuits. Walking around the circumference of the yard, Lee felt the scrutiny of many of the inmates around the area. Fingers were pointed at him and secretive nods made in his direction. These indications of identification only served to make him uneasy. The two escort officers seemed to take no notice of the other inmates. Their main function seemed to be only to walk him to the East Block Condemned Row, hollering out 'Escort!' every dozen strides or so. They passed the prison kitchen and chow hall. The smells of cooking food assailed his senses. Then the prison canteen (store) was passed. Two officers and an inmate stood nearby, talking. Their voices carried to him easily in the pre-noon air.

"Is that him?"

"Yeah, that's him."

"That's one son-of-a-bitch that needs his throat cut as soon as possible!"

Finally, they arrived at two huge doors. As one of the officers opened a small door set in the huge ones, he again yelled out "Escort!" Inside, Lee heard a bustle of quick movements. When he walked through the door, a blast of air hit him. He almost dropped to the floor, but then recognized it as an insect guard attached above the doorway. As his eyes adjusted to the darkness of the interior of the building, he noticed several inmates moving around huge laundry machines. They were moving away from him, but kept their eyes focused on him. He was then walked through a gate, another gate, and then placed in a small holding cage. There, he was once again told to go through the strip down routine, then told to get dressed again. He was brought several sheets of paper, told to sign some of them and then was once again handcuffed. Then he was escorted up the four flights of stairs to the fifth level tier and locked into a cell a little more than half way down the tier.

This new cell was even smaller than the one he had just left. This cell was 10 feet long by four and a half feet wide. Three solid walls, the fourth being a wall of bars and small-grade mesh wire. As he looked around this new home, the tears began to fall. Despair overwhelmed him and his body began to shake with the sobs that erupted from the very depths of his soul. The circumstances of what the prosecution and prosecution witnesses had done to him with their lies and innuendoes was completely overwhelming him.

Through the tears that were obstructing his vision, he made up his bed. When that was done, he put away the other items he had been given: a new toothbrush, tooth powder, a bar of soap, laundry soap, a comb, a mirror, extra sets of under- and outer-clothing, and a plastic spoon and fork. While doing this, the tier officer came by with a sack lunch. Lee didn't have an appetite, so he set the lunch aside and finished trying to straighten up his cell. After that, he laid down and immediately lapsed into the unconsciousness of sleep. He was now sleeping much more than he ever used to, but he didn't care. The losses he had suffered were just too great to bear. By escaping into the realm of sleep, he didn't have to face those losses.

That afternoon, he was awakened when the third shift tier officer came by.

"Listen up, you newcomers." His voice was shrill and nagging on the ear as he yelled at the new inmates. "Let me tell you right now, I ain't putting up with any of your bullshit! Don't give me any grief and you won't get any from me! And don't ask me for nothing 'cause I ain't gonna give it to you!"

He closely resembled one of Lee's brothers. He immediately thought of the officer as a short blowhard with an attitude, trying to make up for his lack of height by appearing a giant in voice and ill attitude. Just like Lee's brother! A few minutes later this officer came up to his cell.

"Lee. You know someone named Slim Blackman on the first tier of the other side of the building?"

"I know a *Jake* Blackman. He was my cell partner in the county jail." He replied. "He sometimes goes by the nickname of Slim, though."

"That's him. He said he's going to send you a kite a little later. You're also scheduled for the phone at 8:45 this evening. You want to call someone?"

Lee thought for a moment. He only knew one phone number: the husband and wife couple who had stood beside him throughout this whole terrible ordeal. He told the officer that he *would* like to use the phone and that he would appreciate it very much. The officer made a notation on a notepad, then left.

Dinner came about an hour later. The food was almost tasty and included one of his favorite foods: Chinese food and cottage cheese. When it came time for him to use the phone, he called his friends. They only had 15 minutes to talk, and it was a very sad conversation. Dave had turned the phone over to his wife so she could talk to Lee. She knew him better than Dave anyway. When she got on the phone with Lee, her voice started to crack badly. She sounded very sad, which made him feel even worse than he felt before he had placed the call. She missed him terribly and told him so. Dave and Flo had come to the county jail to visit with him often during his stay there. In the background, Lee could hear Flo's children calling out to speak to him. They were unhappy at not being allowed to talk with him because of the small amount of time available. And that time went all too quickly. He could tell she was crying openly by the time they had to hang up. As he hung up, he noticed that he was crying pretty profusely, himself. It took him a couple of minutes to regain his composure. When the officer returned to take the phone away, Lee thanked him for the use of it.

"What are you thanking me for? No one else in here ever thanks me for anything."

"Because I always thank a person when they do something for me," Lee said, "whether it's of their own free will or because it's part of their job. It's the way I was raised and I believe people should be treated with respect, regardless of their position in life or their individual situation."

The officer cocked his head to the side slightly and said, "Lee, you're one strange puppy!" With that said, the officer walked away, pushing the phone in front of him to the next person scheduled for its use.

When he laid down on his bunk, he just stared at the ceiling. He couldn't think any coherent thoughts, nor could he immediately go to sleep. His mind was too active with the terrible visions that were passing before his mind's eye. They weren't the visions of expectant death. They were the visions of being in a situation he had no control over, for something he had not been responsible for. Those visions once again caused the tears to start running out of his eyes and only stopped when he finally lapsed into unconsciousness for the night. He no longer called it sleep. It was the lack of consciousness to the mental horrors he expected to be piled upon him. He had not yet been in the prison long enough to find out if the prisoners were subjected to the same mental cruelty that was heaped upon him in the county jail. He'd heard that mental games were played by most prison guards. So far, though, he'd not come across any of the guards that were into playing those mental games. He hoped he'd be spared that indignity.

About two weeks after arriving in the East Block condemned row, he received a letter from his mother. That letter was very discouraging. The majority of his family had left California and were fighting over his property. Two brothers, his mother and a sister were all fighting over who should get the van he owned. One of the brothers wanted to sell it to the highest bidder at a "crime afficionado" auction, so he could use the money for his own purposes. His sister, mother and another brother all wanted the van for their own use. Lee had been an amateur photographer and had raised saltwater fish before he was arrested. But now, his various cameras and marine aquarium had just plain disappeared. Everything Lee considered important to him, physically and emotionally, had been taken away from him or had disappeared. If the truth ever did come out and he was released from prison, he had no hope of ever getting any of his property back. In essence, he had effectively lost his own blood family. He believed this was a fact because he felt that all his family wanted from him was everything they could get their hands on. No matter what it would cost him, they were going to take advantage of it.

One brother was telling everyone he knew, that he was writing a book about what had happened to the family because of Lee. None of which was true, of course. This brother of Lee's also heaped the blame for all of the other bad things that had befallen him personally, at Lee's feet. Lee was really beginning to resent the things this brother was saying.

He was rather concerned about his safety, also. He had now gone out to his assigned exercise yard several times. Although he was very nervous at first, Lee's old cell partner, Jake, had told him not to worry about anyone on their yard, that there were people on the yard with worse crimes than those of which he had been convicted. He was told that if anything was going to happen, it would have already happened to someone else first. That didn't make a lot of sense to him, but he was finally able to relax to a limited degree. He had made several friendly acquaintances on the yard that promised to watch his back, as long as he would do the same for them. But that didn't really make him feel any better. With all of the death threats he had received, he was aware that a killing blow could come from anywhere, at the hands of anyone, at anytime! He knew of incidences when friends turned against each other and one or the other was killed. It had even happened between brothers and other family members.

As the days merged into weeks, Lee began to feel like he was going mad. He had nothing to truly occupy his time. He liked to write, but had almost nobody to write to. When he finally got some lined paper, he began to write some more on a fantasy novel he had started in the county jail. He was also finally able to get books from the prison library. That helped a great deal, because he loved to read extensively, mainly science fiction and fantasy novels. He also came across an address for an overseas group that dedicated themselves to writing to condemned prisoners to give them a touch of compassion they could receive nowhere else. Lee began to receive letters from Australia, Ireland, and England, not to mention the few he got from Southern California, and Florida. Those letters were a welcome source of relief from the boredom he was experiencing. Lee couldn't even get that from his own family.

One benevolent person went so far as to send him enough money so he could place an order for a television and a few other items. On January 12, 1996, Christmas-time came to Lee's world. The television he had been awaiting so patiently for, had finally arrived. So did a wristwatch that was sent to him in a quarterly care package that his friends, Dave and Flo, had bought for him. Between his pen-friends and Dave and Flo, these caring people were a great assistance in maintaining Lee's sanity, or what little was left of it. Lee was the type of person who needed to know exactly what was going on in the world as much as was humanly possible. Being so deeply in the dark, knowing absolutely nothing as to what was happening in the world and what time it was, began to be almost as maddening as having nothing to do. Now, at least, with the television and a watch, he could feed that need, the hunger that was a constant, tangible presence in his mind. Then came a day that almost destroyed Lee emotionally.

One of the people he had met since coming to prison, was a man who was measuring his life in days, hours and minutes. His name was Bob and he had been convicted more than a decade before of killing several young men and boys, then leaving their bodies along the side of one of Southern California's major highways. On the yard, Bob was a polite conversationalist, aware of other people's feelings and the need for courtesy and respect. Bob and Lee would have long, intense discussions on several subjects. They often slowly walked around the yard, talking about their similar religious beliefs, supernatural subjects, the uselessness of the death penalty, and why death should not be feared. That last subject was becoming increasingly important to Bob as each day passed. The reason became apparent when the second week of February arrived. The last day Lee saw him, Bob immediately called him to the side of the yard. He was very agitated and began asking question after question, querying once again about Lee's beliefs in life after death. Lee had experienced two separate Near-Death Episodes and had talked to another person who had witnessed one herself. He disliked talking about them, though. Not because he was afraid of what he had seen, but because he knew the ridicule and criticism he had received in the past, and would more than likely receive in the future. However, Bob didn't ridicule him. He was very interested in finding out every aspect of those three episodes which Lee could recall from his memory. They sat in one corner of the yard and spoke quietly to each other, Lee going over and over every point which Bob was unsure about. When their yard time was over for the day, they shook hands and Bob whispered quietly to Lee . . .

"I don't have much time left. I'll see you on the other side when the time comes."

Lee didn't quite know what to say, but just then it was his turn to leave the yard.

Just over a week later, on February 22, 1996, thirteen minutes past midnight, television stations broadcast that Bob had been executed in the San Quentin death chamber. Lee had heard several of the broadcasts following Bob's death and was very upset. Once more, tears began to fill his eyes; they didn't, however, fall this time. There were people who were attempting to describe what type of person Bob was. Those people didn't know him the way Lee did. Lee knew that they were wrong and felt they were only beating their chests like some gorilla in a forest, trying to gain status in the eyes of others. Lee had very strong feelings about the death penalty and the execution death of anyone. It was wrong, regardless of any rationalizations. Lee found that many of the prisoners tried to rationalize their reasons for killing someone. Those reasons and rationalizations were still called murder by society. But an execution of a prisoner was nothing more than a different kind of rationalization for killing someone. Murder, by society's own definition. That, among other reasons, was why Lee felt that society was inhumane, sick, morally decadent, and decling very rapidly. He had met a couple of prisoners who believed there was nothing wrong with the death of the person or persons they killed during the commission of their crimes, because society saw nothing wrong with executing prisoners.

Lee also had some strong opinions as to why there was so much crime these days, as opposed to when he was growing up. He felt that if certain steps could be set into motion, then most of the crimes could be stopped before they were even thought of by the perpetrators. But then, who was *he?* Who would possibly take *his* ideas seriously. As far as society was concerned, Lee was nothing more than an evil, cruel and indifferent man, an illiterate monster, intent only on causing pain to others. Little did society know how wrong they were. He had attended college under the most difficult of circumstances and gotten both his associate degree and a bachelor's degree in the combined fields of Sociology and Psychology.

Just under three months after Bob's passing, another prisoner was put to death in the execution chamber, the second person to die of lethal injection in California. Lee didn't personally know Danny Williams, but that didn't lessen his disbelief in the practice of executing prisoners. He still felt pain at the death of a living being, any living being, whether human or animal. Life was precious to Lee. That society could toss these lives away so callously, just reinforced his feelings about the decline of today's society.

After those two deaths, Lee began to feel even lonelier. Sure, he had a television, books, writing supplies, pen-friends in Southern California, Florida, Australia, England, and Ireland; he even knew several people that under different circumstances he would call friends—both among fellow prisoners and some of the guards. Still, he was feeling lonely. But he knew that coping with that loneliness was a sign of strength. He turned that loneliness into productive thinking, creative writing. If nothing else, being in prison gave him an opportunity to think and create. But with the thinking, came the memories. Memories of his ex-girlfriend, his wife and daughter, his co-workers, his work, his neighbors and friends; going to Zion National Park, the Grand Canyon, Sequoia National Park, and to beaches along the southern coast of California. Memories of raising chickens, ducks, and quail from their eggs in an incubator. Memories of traveling to many beautiful places, taking photographs and displaying them proudly. All of which were now just memories that brought him happiness in his dreams and tears when he was awake.

He often had trouble sleeping at night. He never went to sleep before midnight, usually staying awake until two or three in the morning, writing or reading, listening to music on one of the prison television channels. On the days that he did not go out to the exercise yard, he slept late, just like he did on his days off before being arrested. He'd wake up for breakfast, then would lay back down and sleep. Wake up to take a shower and shave, receive a sack lunch, then go back to sleep again. He'd finally awaken for the day around three in the afternoon, staying awake until those early morning hours. For the most part, he kept his silence, speaking only when someone else spoke to him first. He kept his eyes open and his mouth closed, did what he was told to do, and wouldn't let anyone talk him into doing anything he could get into trouble for.

Finally, Lee obtained the phone numbers for several family members: two of his three brothers, the eldest of his three sisters, and his mother and youngest sister. He placed calls to each of them, hoping to re-establish some kind of familial relationship with them. He had made the same request of both brothers, only one: would they please send him a couple dollars worth of stamps so he could continue writing letters? Both brothers promised him that they would send stamps. But neither followed through on their promises. He made the same request of his sister and got the same result. His mother and youngest sister were more receptive. They sent what they could. Some stamps, a quarterly care package. It wasn't much, of course. His mother was on a fixed income. But she wanted him to keep calling her to let her know how he was and what was happening with his case. She always accepted the collect charges when he called. But he wouldn't call her more than once a week, unless it was an emergency, because he didn't want her phone bill to get too high.

That phone, however, was in the name of a third brother, the brother that had been circulating lies about Lee and attempting to build his own reputation up on other lies; the opportunist. For one reason or another, that brother put a collect-call block on their mother's phone so Lee was no longer able to call her. This was

Edward, the brother who made promise after promise to make sure Lee would be taken care of and would want for nothing in prison. Promises that he broke as soon as he made them. Promises that Lee now believed Edward had never even intended on keeping. Edward claimed that his own marriage ended because Lee was found guilty of the crimes filed against him. In actuality, Edward's marriage ended because he molested his wife's baby sister, going to jail and being put on probation because of it. Edward also claimed he was a partner in a non-alcoholic, teenage night club that was shut down because of Lee's troubles. In actuality, he was not a partner in the business and it folded because it was in the wrong location. All Edward was doing was trying to divert the blame from himself and build himself up in the eyes of others at the expense of everyone else. Something he had been doing all his life.

This story is by no means finished. Lee's having been sent to prison with a death sentence is a sad tale of a travesty of justice, a disaster in his life and in our legal system. Guilt declared on an innocent man who respects people, a man who befriends everyone no matter what their station in life. A man who accepts each person he meets at face value. He often ignores wrongs done to him and never retaliates against those people. He feels no anger at anyone for the situation that has befallen him. Not even the prosecutor or the judge in charge of his case. During the final moment's of Lee's trial, the prosecutor said that Lee must not like him very much, and then he'd chuckled. But the prosecutor was wrong. Lee felt no dislike for the prosecutor. He felt afraid of the power that the prosecutor has at his command. That he could prosecute an innocent man, convince the public that someone had committed such heinous crimes with as little true evidence as he had presented at the trial. That kind of power should not be in anyone's hands. So Lee now sits in his solitude, feeling the pain and loneliness that has come with his current circumstances. Yet he silently laughs at the people who think they have hurt him by sentencing him to death.

Little do they realize just how much they have helped him. He *knows* the truth! He *knows* that he is innocent. He isn't afraid of death. He has been to the other side and come back. He is aware of things that others don't even suspect. Lee *knows* what is coming next and he welcomes it!

CHAPTER 19

Last Words

On Death Row, Bill Suff has a color television and a memory typewriter. The TV comes with its speaker disconnected internally—you have to use headphones to hear. Inmates can buy TVs and typewriters and radios and computers and all manner of goods and appliances from a catalogue supply service managed by the warden's wife. In fact, inmates cannot get major goods or supplies any other way, not even as gifts.

Books are not allowed in under any circumstance.

Even lawyers cannot bring books to their inmate clients.

Accordingly, Bill Suff will not see this book in print, and so I had to read it to him over the phone once it was done. I had always pledged to him that his response to the book would be printed herein.

When I finished reading to Bill, there was silence on the other end of the line.

"Bill? You still there?"

"Yeah. I'm here."

"Not what you expected, right?"

"No, not what I expected—parts of it anyway."

"And?"

"You make me sound guilty."

"And, for the record?"

"I'm innocent."

"Of everything?"

"Everything they charged me with."

"I truly believe this book will help your case, help your cause,"

I said. "Now you're a human being rather than just a headline."

"Except you make me out to be a monster."

"You've never treated me monstrously. And you've treated a whole lot of people well. You've done good for many, and, if any writer's view of the world is worth reading, then yours is—you have a lot to say."

"Yes. That's true," he said. "But I'm concerned about what *you* had to say."

"What I have to say is nothing more than what *I* say. It's what *I* believe to be true. You don't have to agree."

"Believe me, I don't. Everything you say about me being guilty is fiction. I don't know where you heard it, but it didn't come from me."

"Have I betrayed you?"

He hesitated; then: "I don't know."

"At various points in your life, you've felt that both friends and family betrayed you, but they nonetheless remained your friends and family."

"That's true."

"I remain your friend. I believe this book may well save your life."

"Do you really believe I'm a killer?"

"Yes," I said.

He thought for a moment, and: "It's possible to be friends with people who've done bad things—I'm friends with many people here in prison . . . but I don't know that it's possible to be friends with someone you think did something he didn't do. That means you don't really know the person, and how can you be friends with someone you don't really know?"

"Maybe I know you better than you think," I said.

"Maybe."

"Friends?" I asked.

"I'm torn," he said.

"Fair enough," I said.

"When are you going to come up and visit me?" he asked.

"Later this month," I said.

"Great!" said Bill Suff.